Love in Focus volume 2 is a work of fiction. Names, characters, places, and incidents are the products of the author's imagination or are used fictitiously. Any resemblance to actual events, locales, or persons, living or dead, is entirely coincidental.

A Kodansha Comics Trade Paperback Original

Published in the United States by Kodansha Comics, an imprint of Kodansha USA Publishing, LLC, New York.

Publication rights for this English edition arranged through Kodansha Ltd, Tokyo.

ISBN 978-1-63236-769-3

Printed in the United States of America.

www.kodanshacomics.com

9 8 7 6 5 4 3 2 1
Translation: Alethea and Athena Nibley
Lettering: Sara Linsley
Editing: Haruko Hashimoto
Kodansha Comics edition cover design by Phil Balsman

EDENS ZERO
エデンズゼロ

HIRO MASHIMA IS BACK! JOIN THE CREATOR OF *FAIRY TAIL* AS HE TAKES TO THE STARS FOR ANOTHER THRILLING SAGA!

A high-flying space adventure! All the steadfast friendship and wild fighting you've been waiting for...IN SPACE!

At Granbell Kingdom, an abandoned amusement park, Shiki has lived his entire life among machines. But one day, Rebecca and her cat companion Happy appear at the park's front gates. Little do these newcomers know that this is the first human contact Granbell has had in a hundred years! As Shiki stumbles his way into making new friends, his former neighbors stir at an opportunity for a robo-rebellion... And when his old homeland becomes too dangerous, Shiki must join Rebecca and Happy on their spaceship and escape into the boundless cosmos.

KC
KODANSHA
COMICS

LOVE IN FOCUS

2

Yoko Nogiri

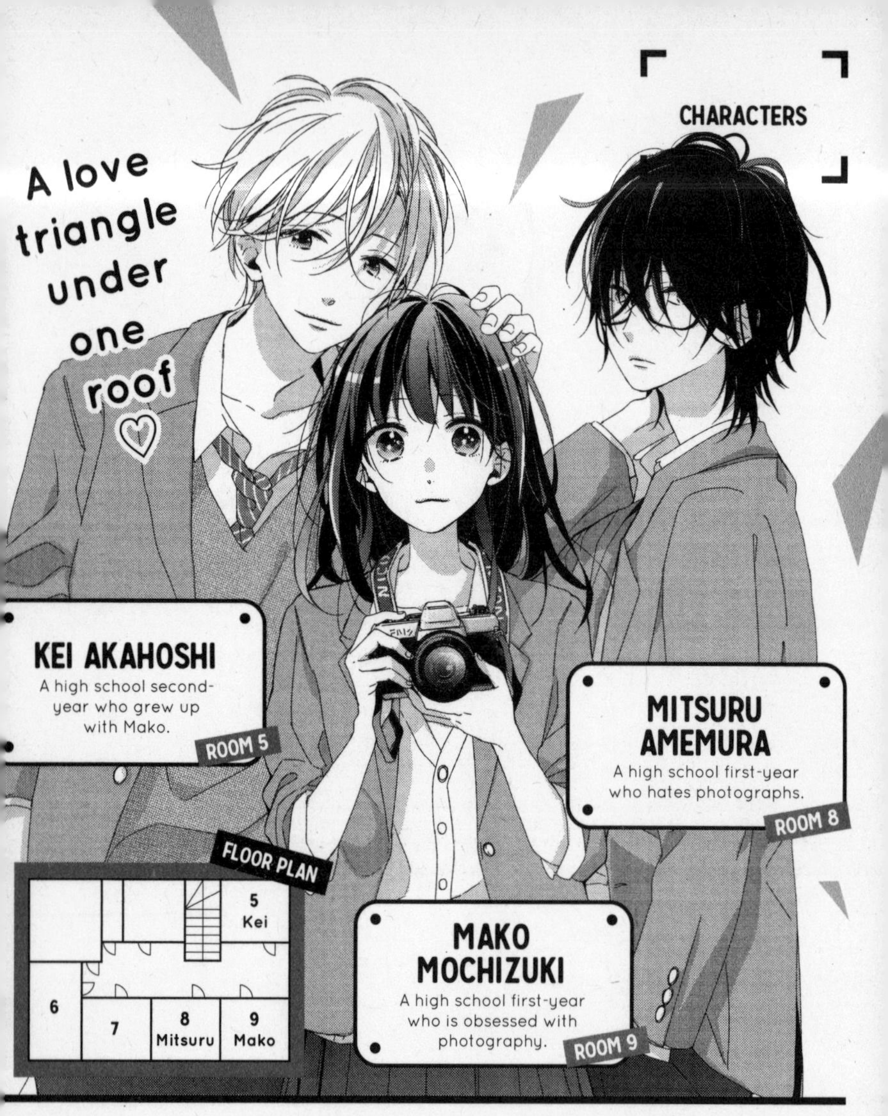
CHARACTERS
A love triangle under one roof ♡
KEI AKAHOSHI
A high school second-year who grew up with Mako.
ROOM 5
MITSURU AMEMURA
A high school first-year who hates photographs.
ROOM 8
FLOOR PLAN
5 Kei
6
7
8 Mitsuru
9 Mako
MAKO MOCHIZUKI
A high school first-year who is obsessed with photography.
ROOM 9

STORY

Mako is a high school girl who is obsessed with photography. At the invitation of her childhood friend Kei, she enrolls in a school that is famous for its photography club. Then, she starts her new life in a boarding house with a triangle roof.

There she meets Mitsuru, who hides his face and insists, "I don't like pictures." When Mako asks Mitsuru to let her take his picture, he flatly refuses!

She manages to convince him to be her model anyway, and through their first photo shoot, Mako and Mitsuru gradually grow closer.

Kei notices the change in their attitudes toward each other and warns Mitsuru, "You can't have Mako."

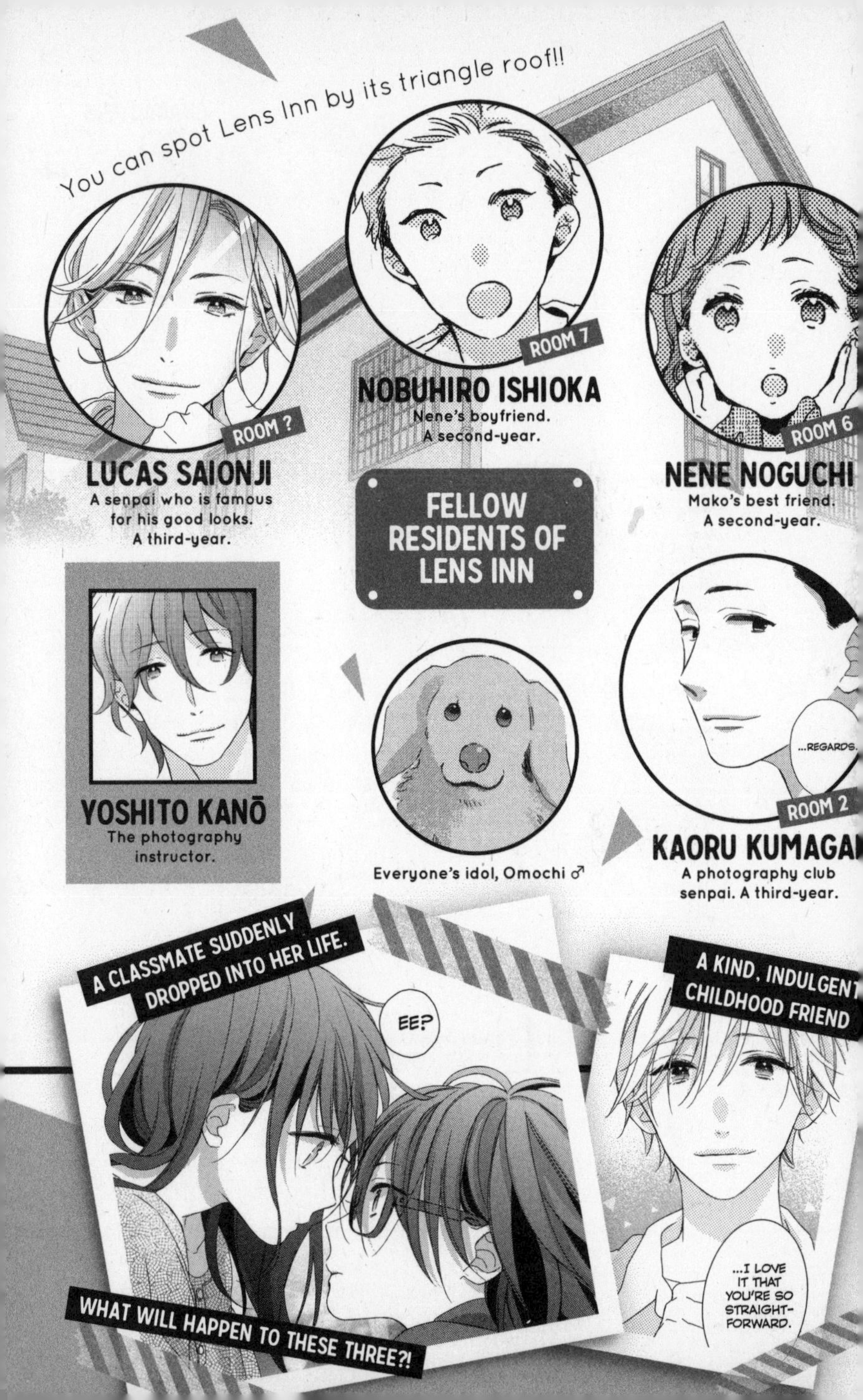
You can spot Lens Inn by its triangle roof!!
FELLOW RESIDENTS OF LENS INN
ROOM 6
NENE NOGUCHI
Mako's best friend. A second-year.
ROOM 7
NOBUHIRO ISHIOKA
Nene's boyfriend. A second-year.
ROOM ?
LUCAS SAIONJI
A senpai who is famous for his good looks. A third-year.
...REGARDS.
ROOM 2
KAORU KUMAGAI
A photography club senpai. A third-year.
Everyone's idol, Omochi ♂
YOSHITO KANŌ
The photography instructor.
A KIND, INDULGENT CHILDHOOD FRIEND
...I LOVE IT THAT YOU'RE SO STRAIGHT-FORWARD.
A CLASSMATE SUDDENLY DROPPED INTO HER LIFE.
EE?
WHAT WILL HAPPEN TO THESE THREE?!

CONTENTS

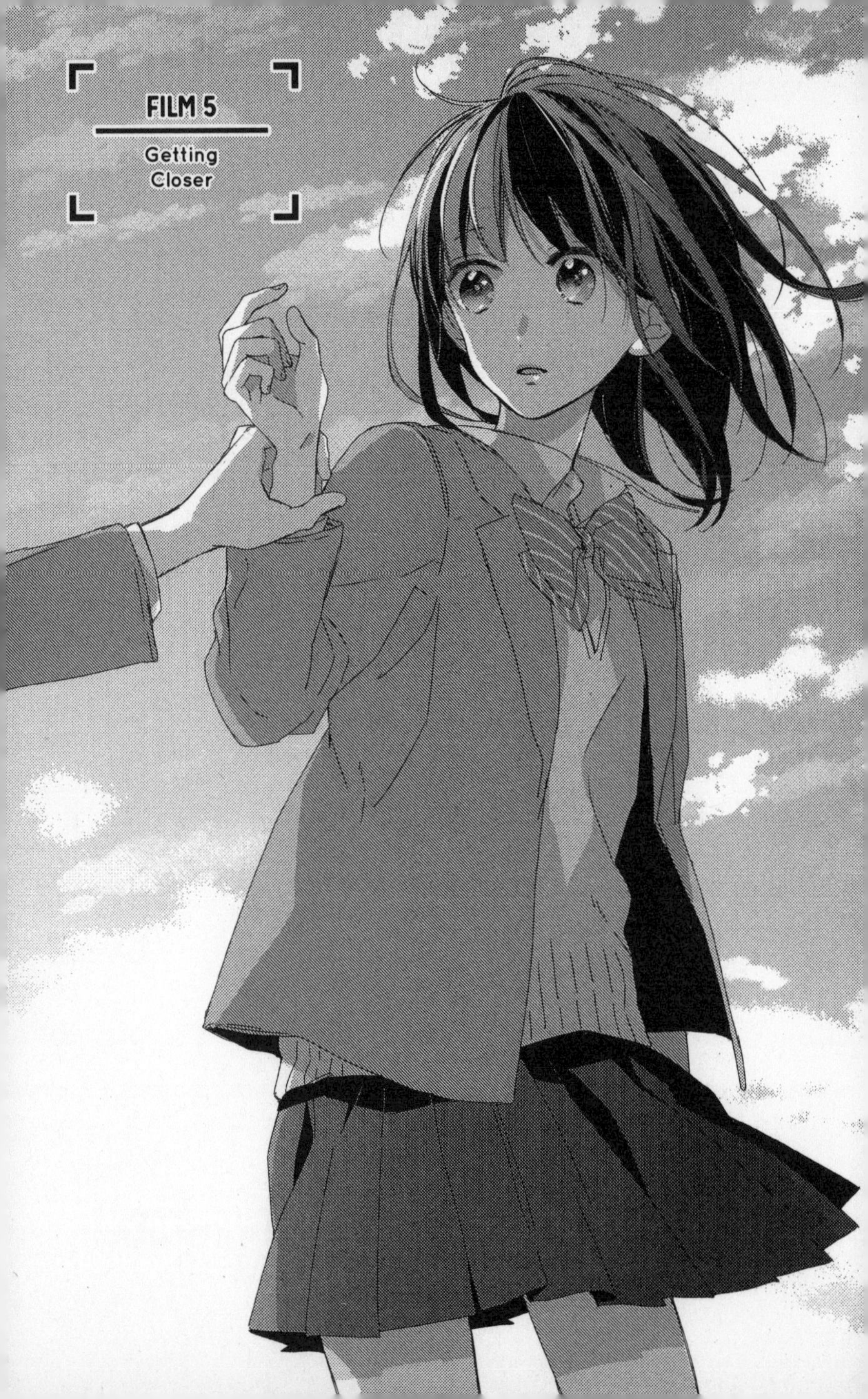
FILM 5
Getting Closer

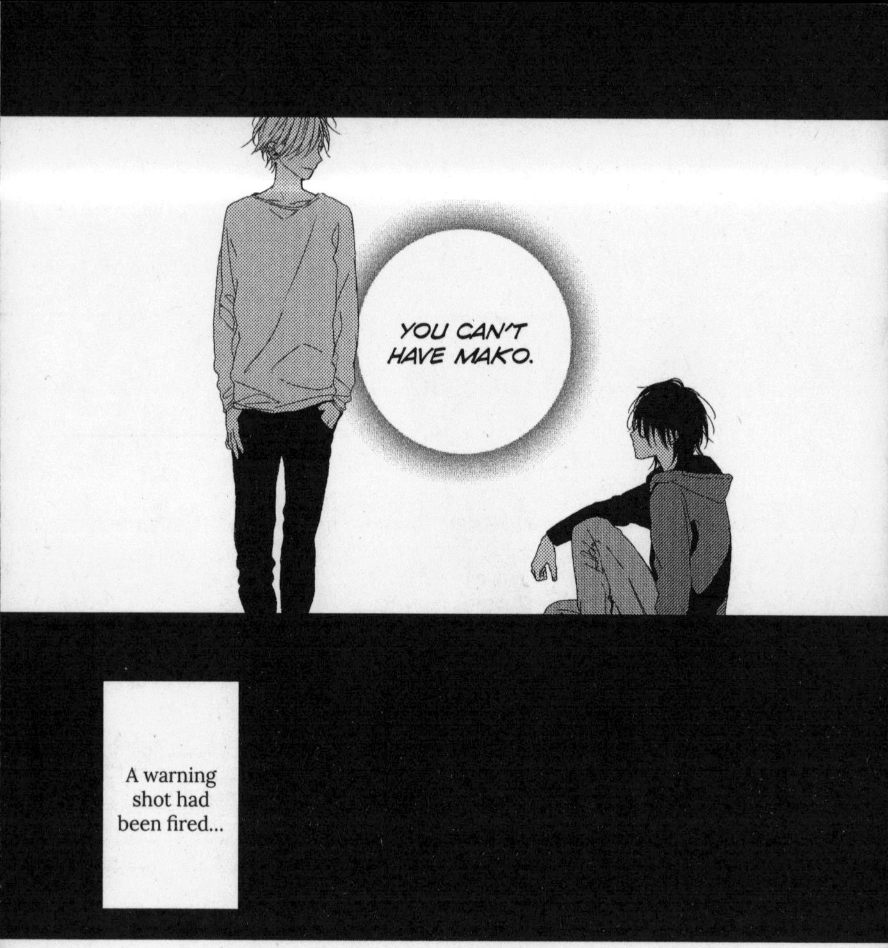
YOU CAN'T HAVE MAKO.
A warning shot had been fired...

LOVE IN FOCUS

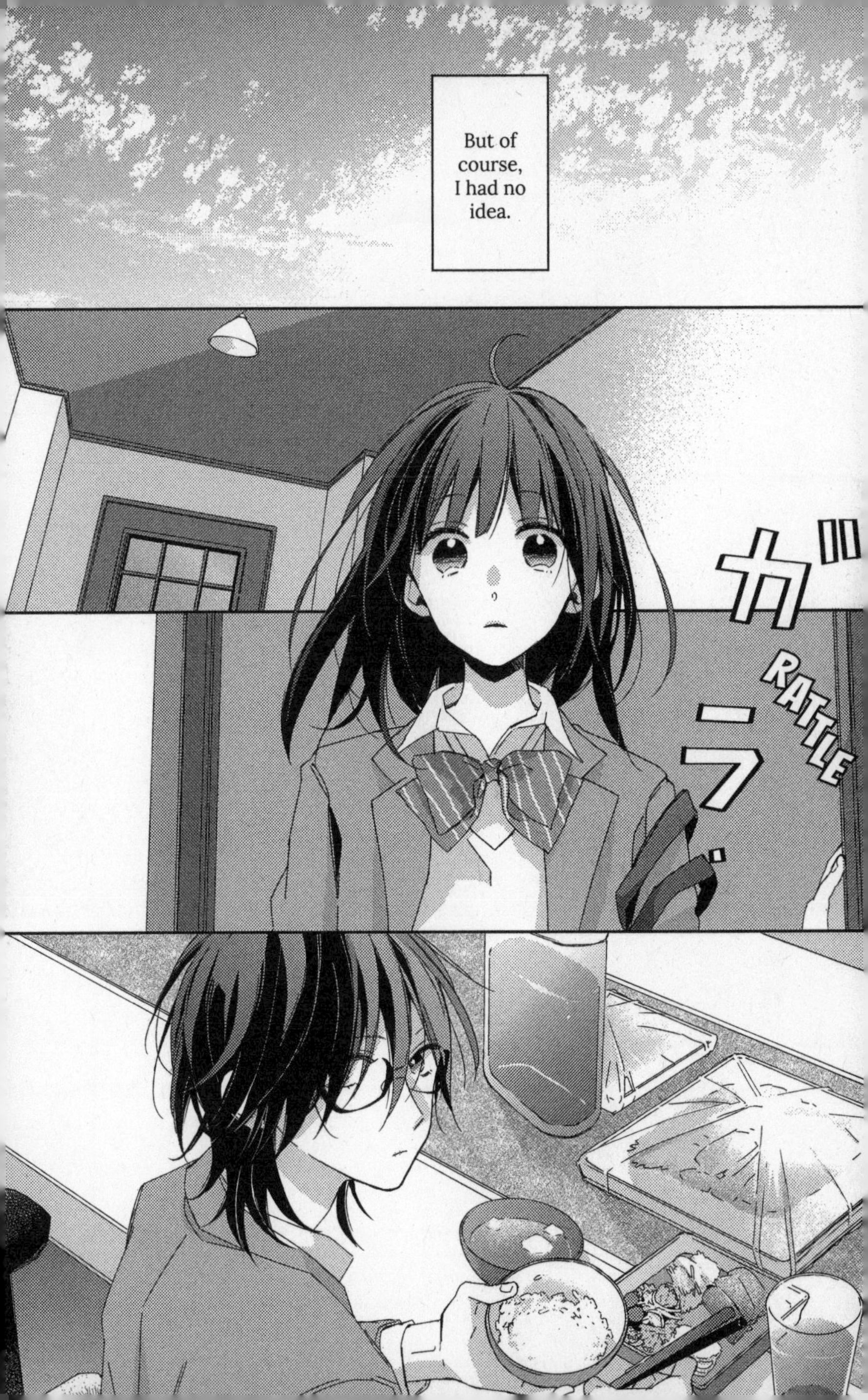
But of course, I had no idea.
ガラッ
RATTLE

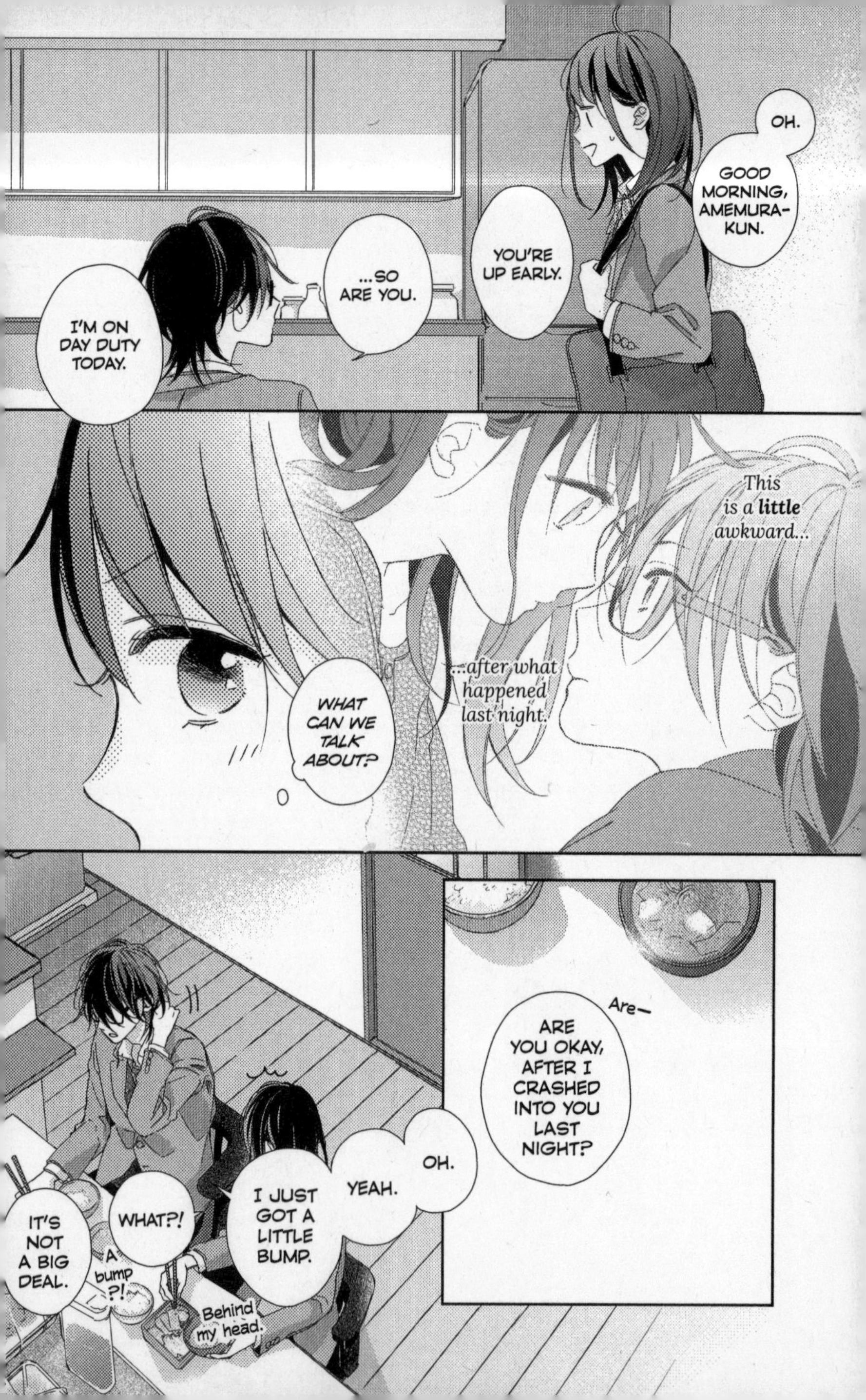
OH.
GOOD MORNING, AMEMURA-KUN.
YOU'RE UP EARLY.
...SO ARE YOU.
I'M ON DAY DUTY TODAY.
This is a **little** awkward...
...after what happened last night.
WHAT CAN WE TALK ABOUT?
Are—
ARE YOU OKAY, AFTER I CRASHED INTO YOU LAST NIGHT?
OH.
YEAH.
I JUST GOT A LITTLE BUMP.
Behind my head.
WHAT?!
A bump?!
IT'S NOT A BIG DEAL.

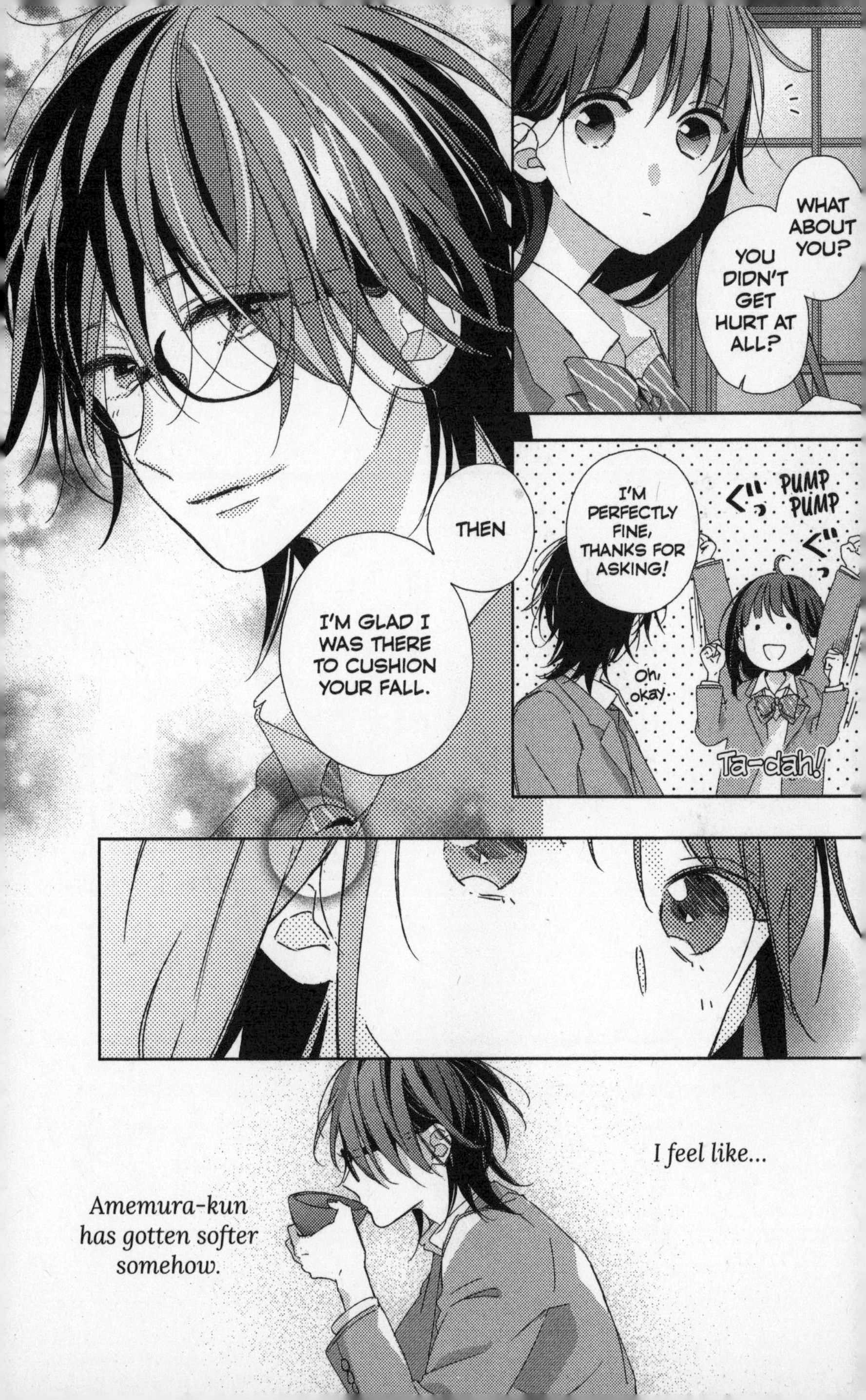
WHAT ABOUT YOU?
YOU DIDN'T GET HURT AT ALL?
I'M PERFECTLY FINE, THANKS FOR ASKING!
PUMP PUMP
Oh, okay
Ta-dah!
THEN
I'M GLAD I WAS THERE TO CUSHION YOUR FALL.
I feel like...
Amemura-kun has gotten softer somehow.

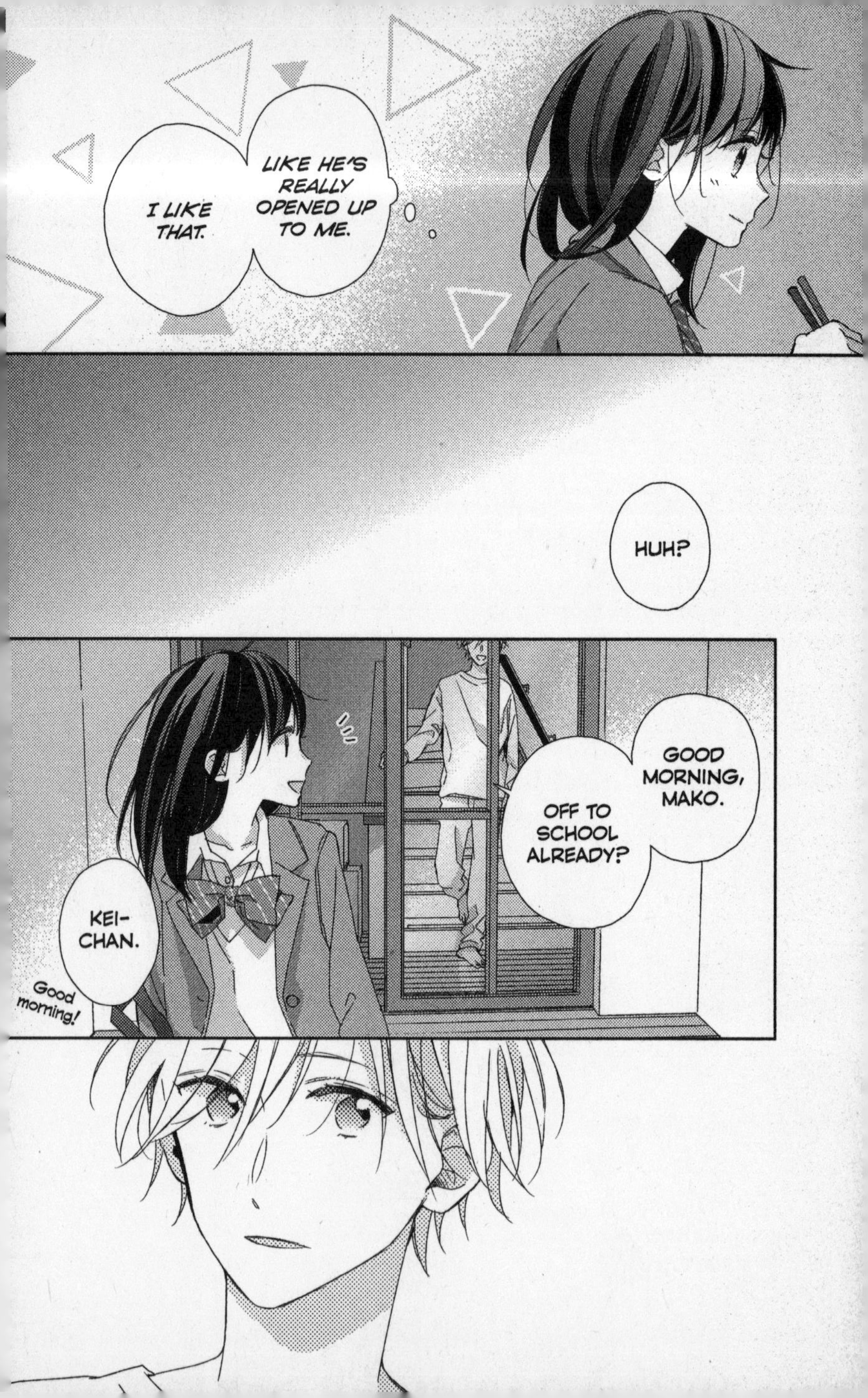
LIKE HE'S REALLY OPENED UP TO ME.
I LIKE THAT.
HUH?
GOOD MORNING, MAKO.
OFF TO SCHOOL ALREADY?
KEI-CHAN.
Good morning!

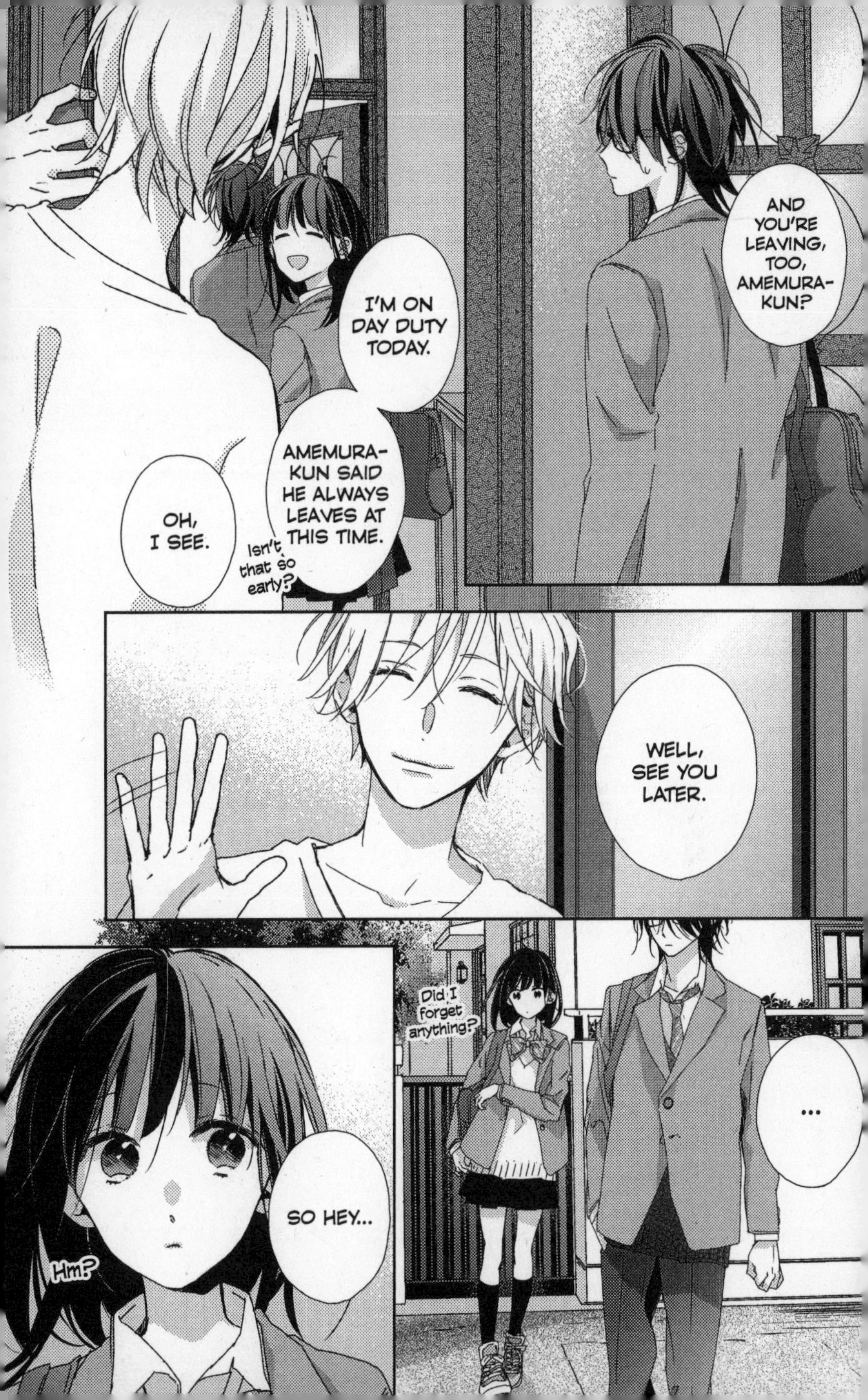
AND YOU'RE LEAVING, TOO, AMEMURA-KUN?
I'M ON DAY DUTY TODAY.
AMEMURA-KUN SAID HE ALWAYS LEAVES AT THIS TIME.
Isn't that so early?
OH, I SEE.
WELL, SEE YOU LATER.
...
Did I forget anything?
SO HEY...
Hm?

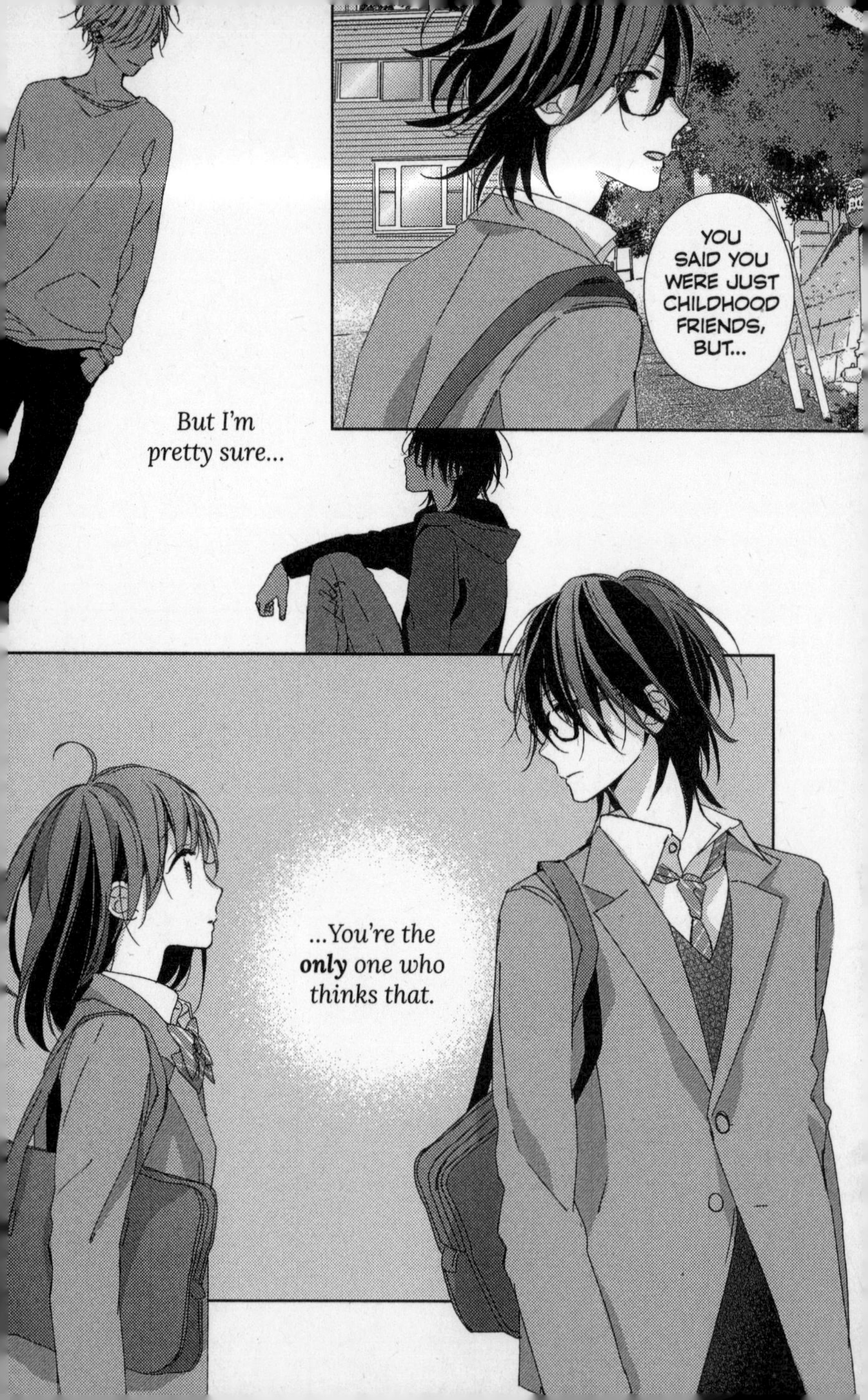
YOU SAID YOU WERE JUST CHILDHOOD FRIENDS, BUT...
But I'm pretty sure...
...You're the **only** one who thinks that.

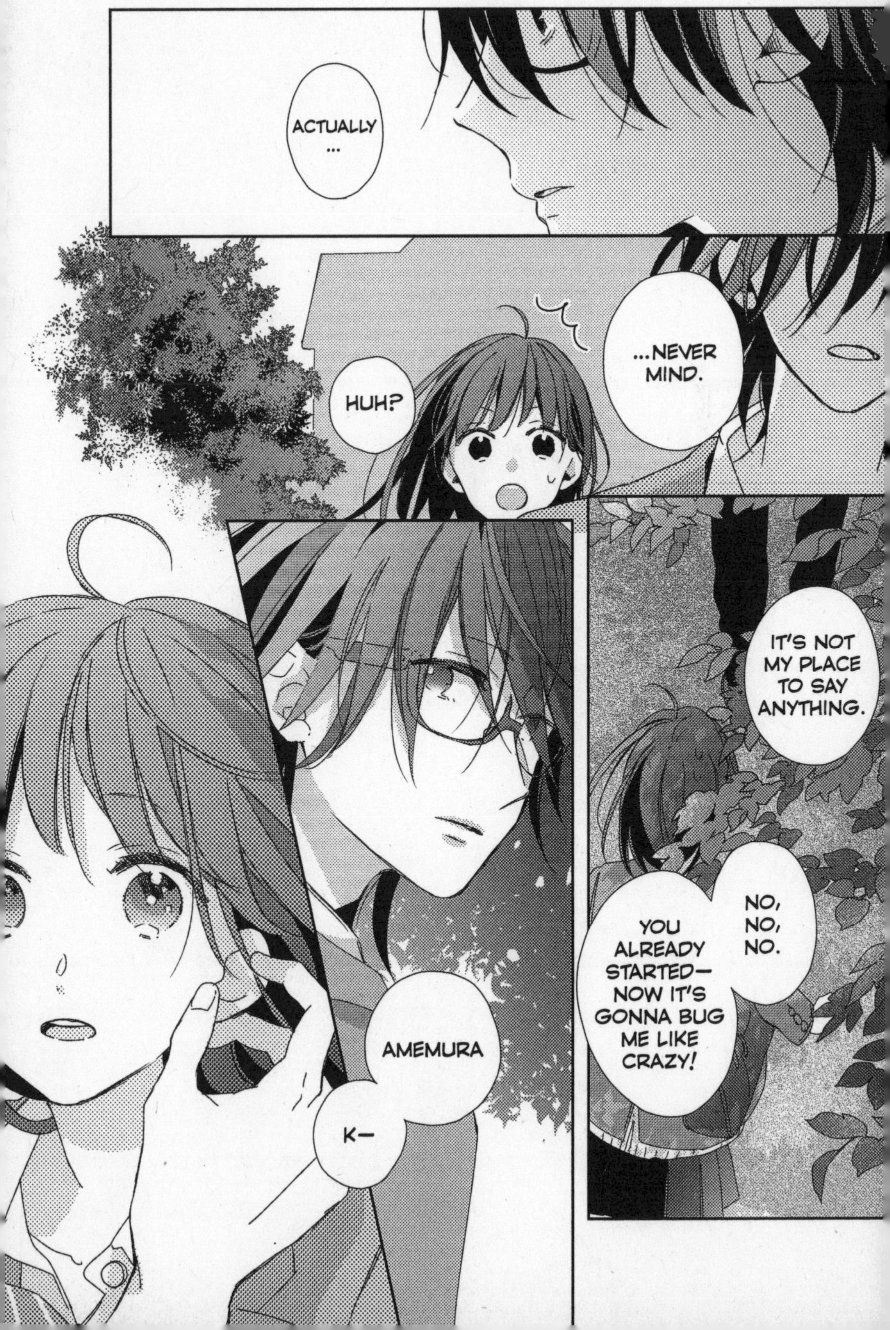
ACTUALLY ...
...NEVER MIND.
HUH?
IT'S NOT MY PLACE TO SAY ANYTHING.
NO, NO, NO.
YOU ALREADY STARTED— NOW IT'S GONNA BUG ME LIKE CRAZY!
AMEMURA
K—

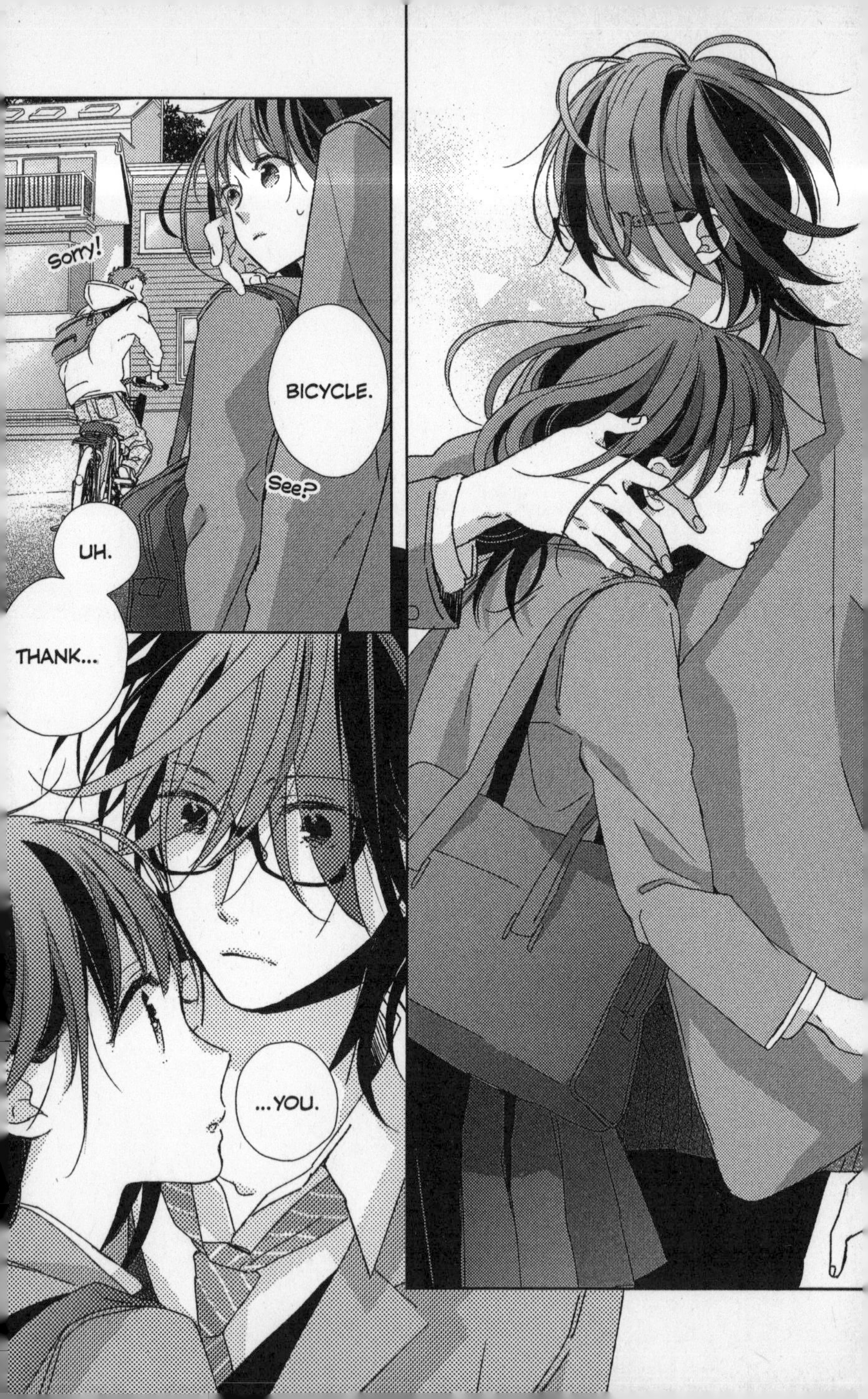
Sorry!
BICYCLE.
See?
UH.
THANK...
...YOU.

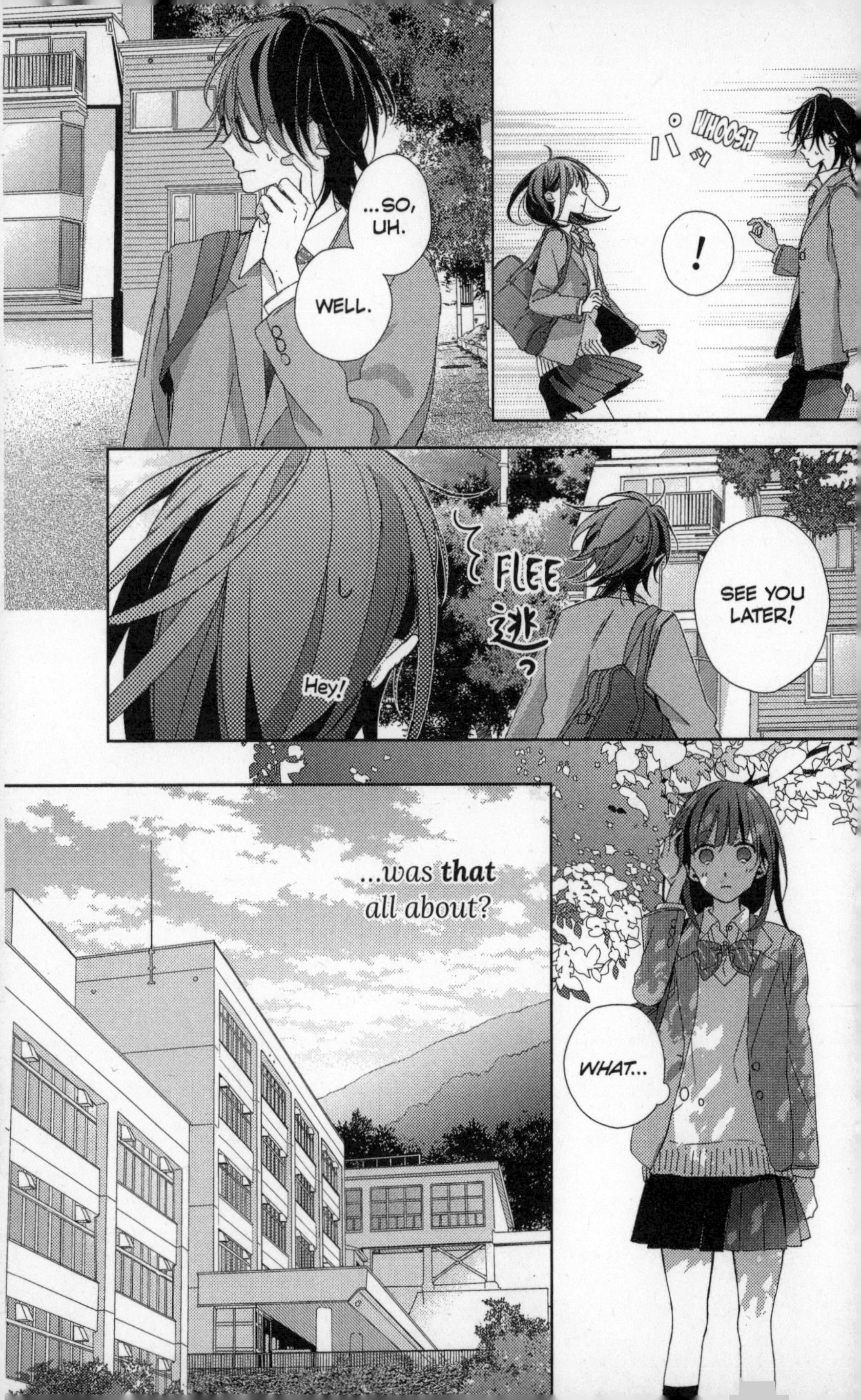

パッ
WHOOSH
!
...SO, UH.
WELL.
SEE YOU LATER!
FLEE
逃っ
Hey!
WHAT...
...was **that** all about?

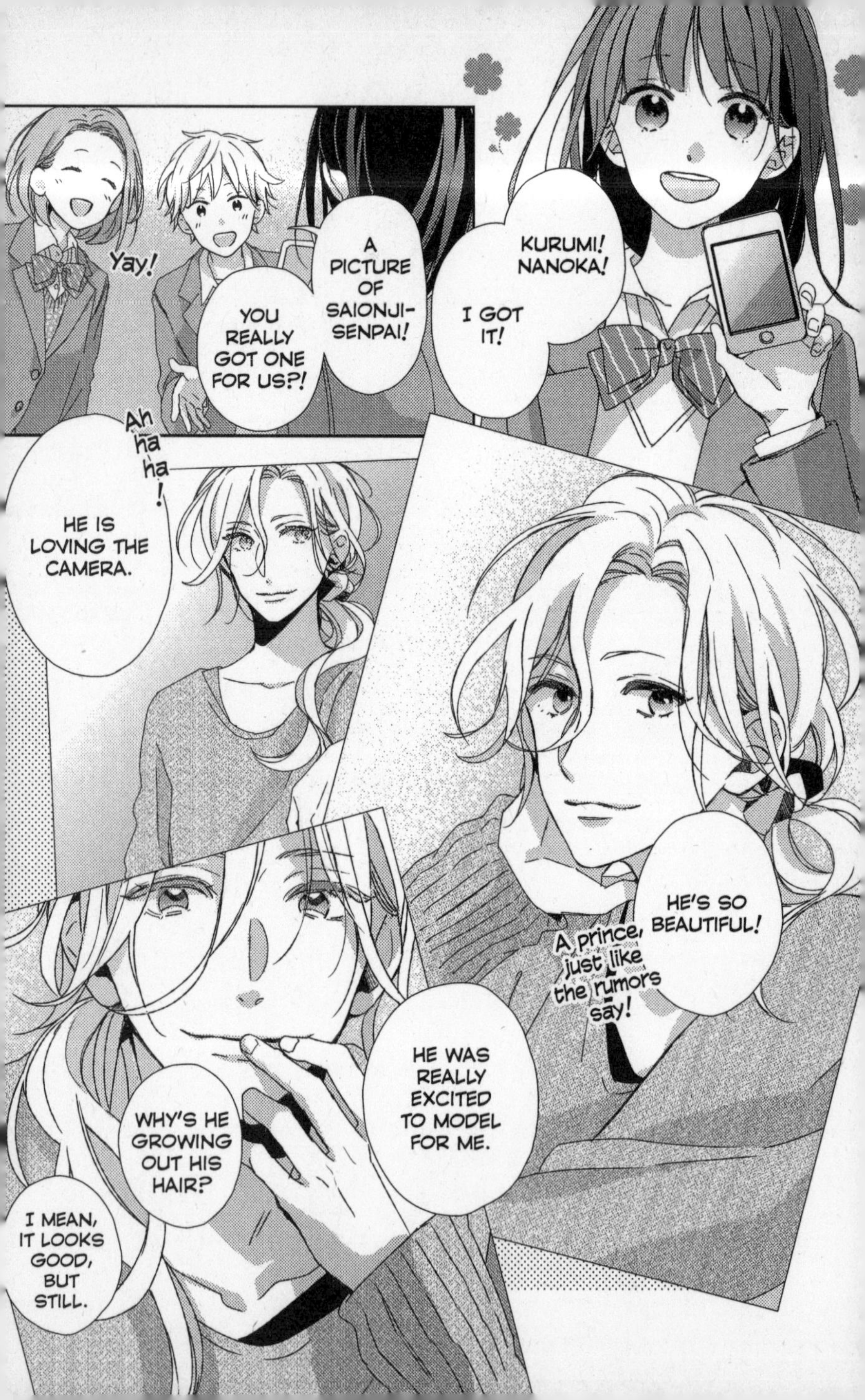

KURUMI! NANOKA!
I GOT IT!
A PICTURE OF SAIONJI-SENPAI!
YOU REALLY GOT ONE FOR US?!
Yay!
HE'S SO BEAUTIFUL!
A prince, just like the rumors say!
Ah ha ha!
HE IS LOVING THE CAMERA.
HE WAS REALLY EXCITED TO MODEL FOR ME.
WHY'S HE GROWING OUT HIS HAIR?
I MEAN, IT LOOKS GOOD, BUT STILL.

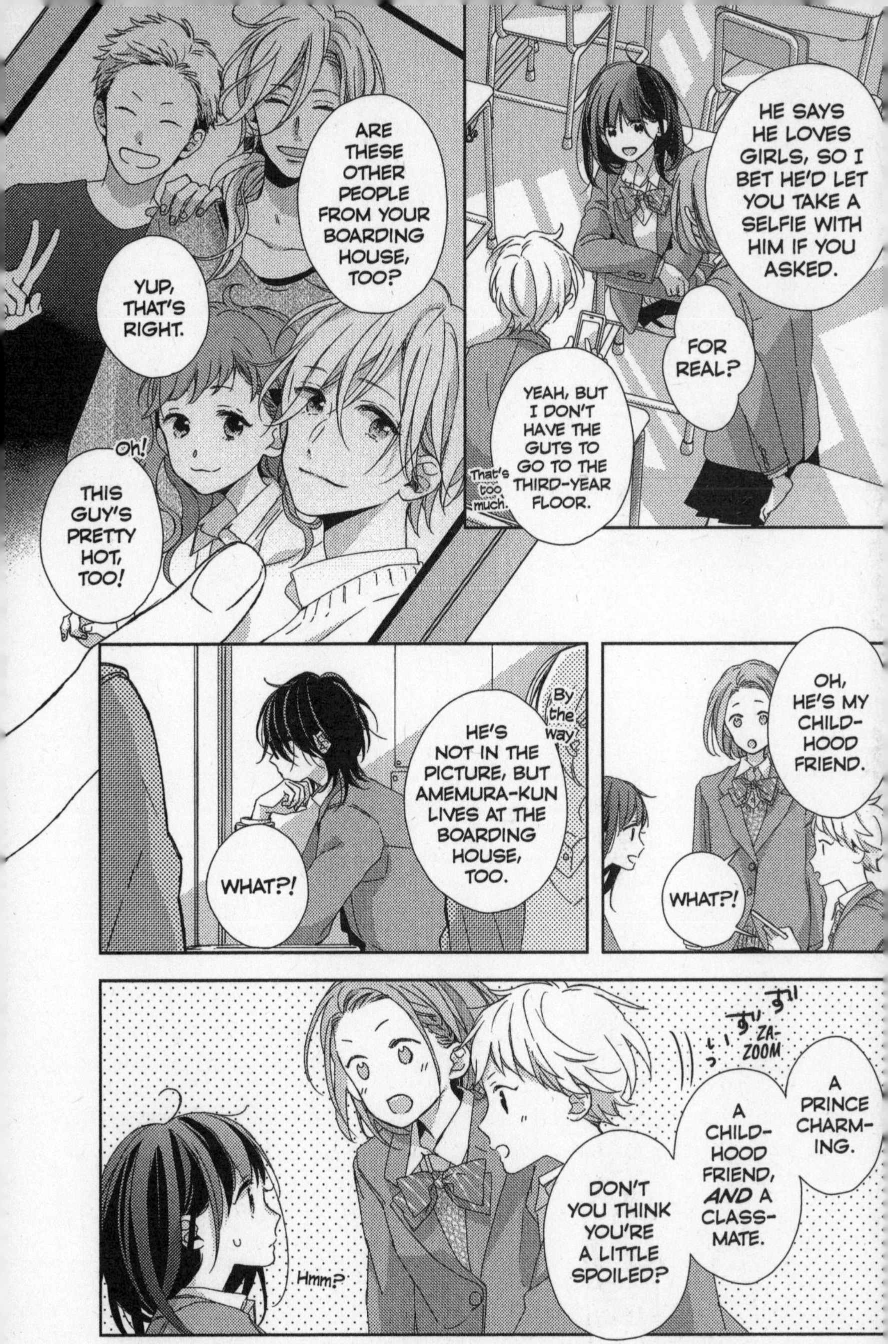
HE SAYS HE LOVES GIRLS, SO I BET HE'D LET YOU TAKE A SELFIE WITH HIM IF YOU ASKED.
FOR REAL?
YEAH, BUT I DON'T HAVE THE GUTS TO GO TO THE THIRD-YEAR FLOOR.
That's too much.
ARE THESE OTHER PEOPLE FROM YOUR BOARDING HOUSE, TOO?
YUP, THAT'S RIGHT.
Oh!
THIS GUY'S PRETTY HOT, TOO!
OH, HE'S MY CHILDHOOD FRIEND.
WHAT?!
By the way
HE'S NOT IN THE PICTURE, BUT AMEMURA-KUN LIVES AT THE BOARDING HOUSE, TOO.
WHAT?!
ZA-ZOOM
A PRINCE CHARMING.
A CHILDHOOD FRIEND, *AND* A CLASSMATE.
DON'T YOU THINK YOU'RE A LITTLE SPOILED?
Hmm?

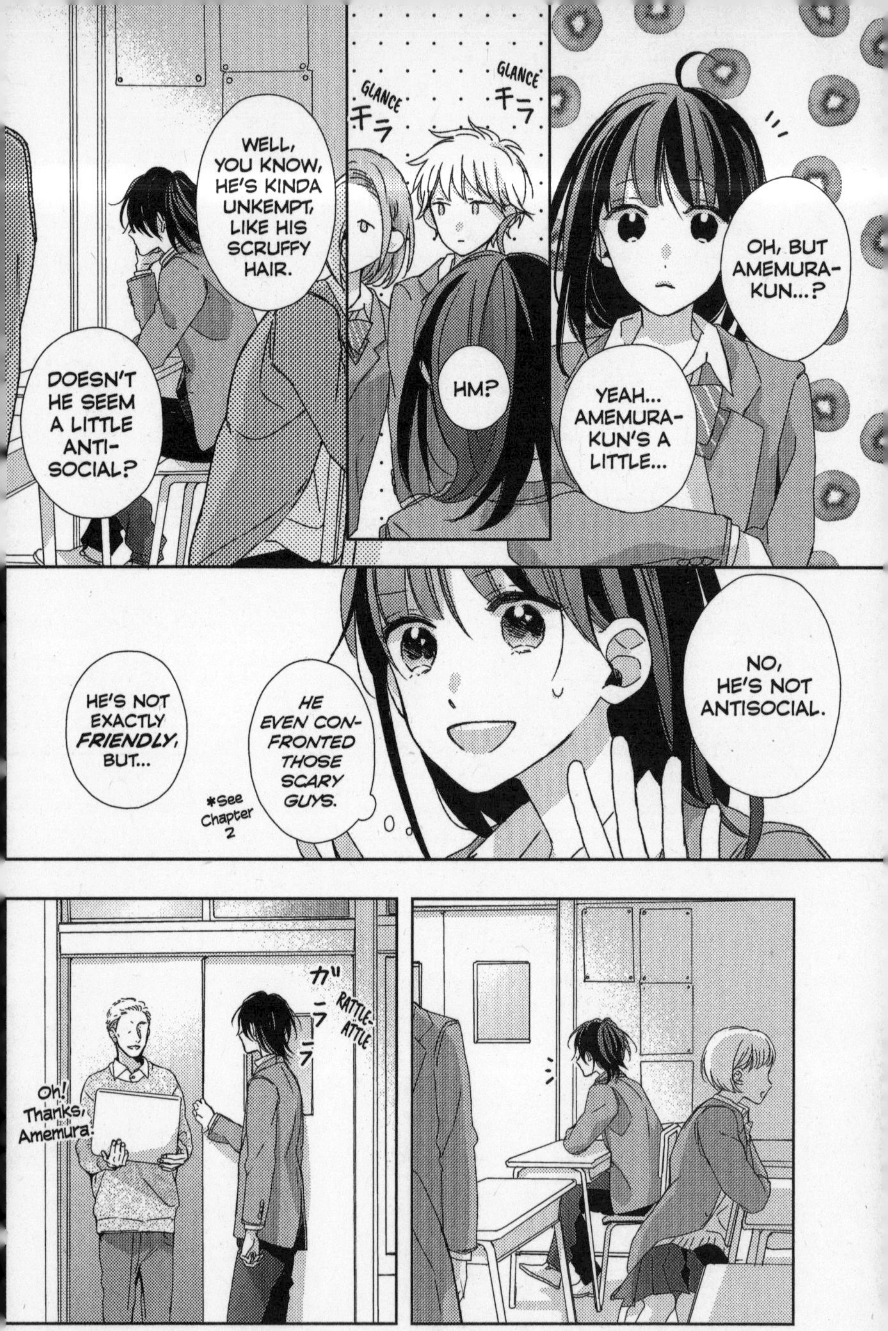
OH, BUT AMEMURA-KUN...?
YEAH... AMEMURA-KUN'S A LITTLE...
GLANCE キラ
GLANCE キラ
HM?
WELL, YOU KNOW, HE'S KINDA UNKEMPT, LIKE HIS SCRUFFY HAIR.
DOESN'T HE SEEM A LITTLE ANTI-SOCIAL?
NO, HE'S NOT ANTISOCIAL.
HE EVEN CONFRONTED THOSE SCARY GUYS.
*See Chapter 2
HE'S NOT EXACTLY FRIENDLY, BUT...
ガラ
RATTLE-ATTLE
Oh! Thanks, Amemura.

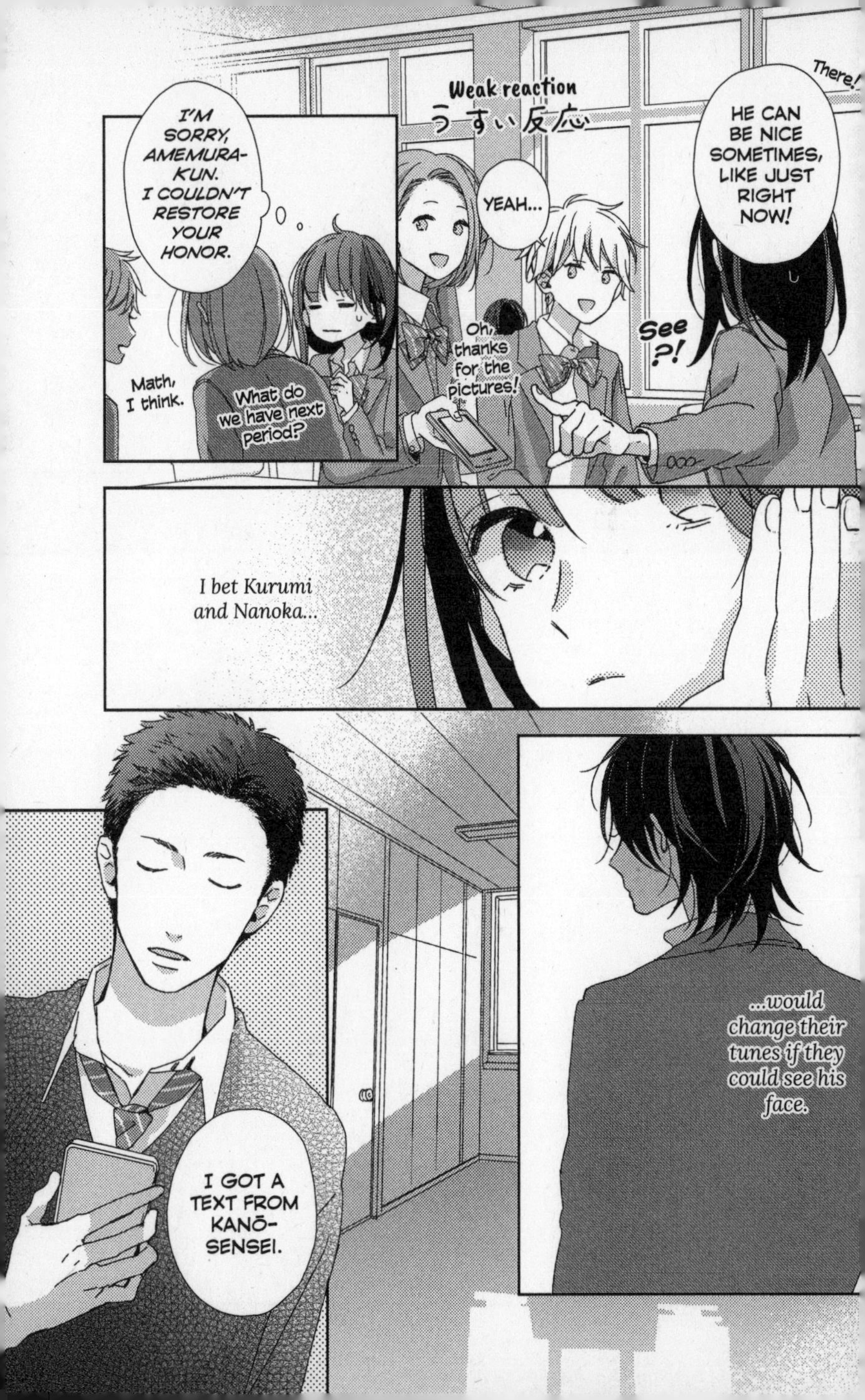
There!
HE CAN BE NICE SOMETIMES, LIKE JUST RIGHT NOW!
See?!
Oh, thanks for the pictures!
YEAH...
Weak reaction
うすい反応
I'M SORRY, AMEMURA-KUN. I COULDN'T RESTORE YOUR HONOR.
What do we have next period?
Math, I think.
I bet Kurumi and Nanoka...
...would change their tunes if they could see his face.
I GOT A TEXT FROM KANŌ-SENSEI.

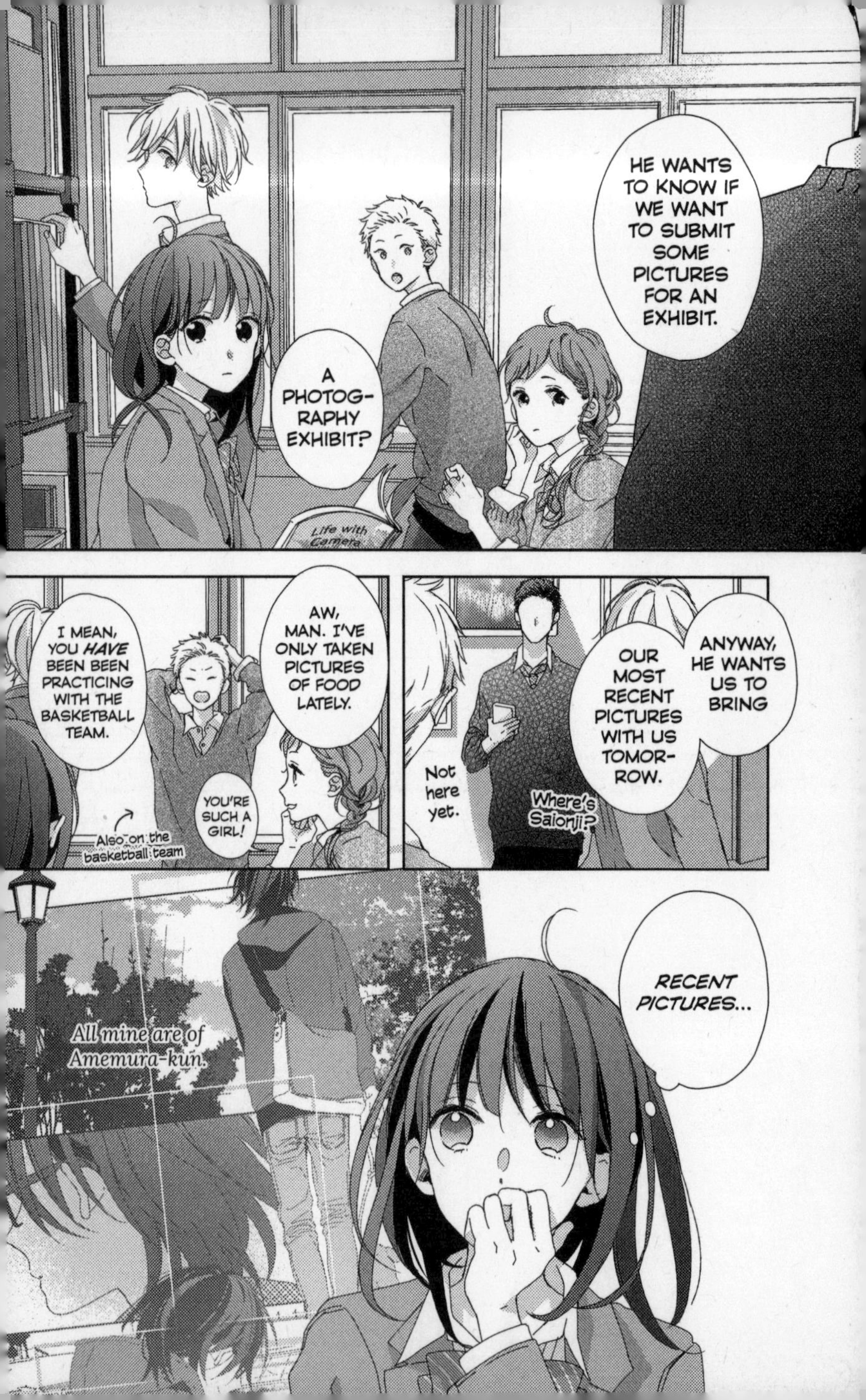
HE WANTS TO KNOW IF WE WANT TO SUBMIT SOME PICTURES FOR AN EXHIBIT.
A PHOTOGRAPHY EXHIBIT?
Life with Camera
ANYWAY, HE WANTS US TO BRING
OUR MOST RECENT PICTURES WITH US TOMORROW.
Where's Saionji?
Not here yet.
AW, MAN. I'VE ONLY TAKEN PICTURES OF FOOD LATELY.
I MEAN, YOU *HAVE* BEEN BEEN PRACTICING WITH THE BASKETBALL TEAM.
YOU'RE SUCH A GIRL!
Also on the basketball team
RECENT PICTURES...
All mine are of Amemura-kun.

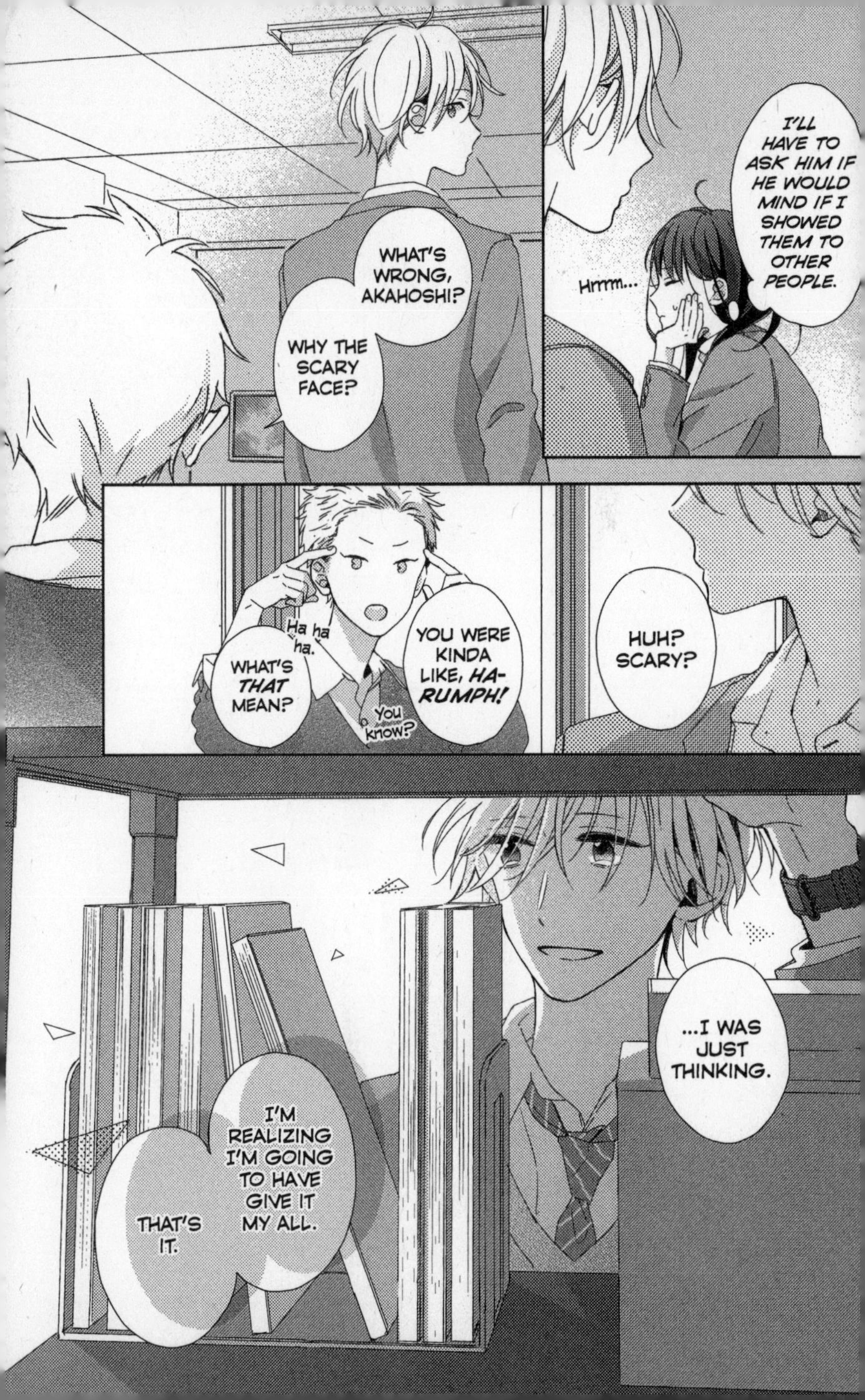
I'LL HAVE TO ASK HIM IF HE WOULD MIND IF I SHOWED THEM TO OTHER PEOPLE.
Hrrrm...
WHAT'S WRONG, AKAHOSHI?
WHY THE SCARY FACE?
HUH? SCARY?
YOU WERE KINDA LIKE, *HA-RUMPH!*
You know?
Ha ha ha.
WHAT'S *THAT* MEAN?
...I WAS JUST THINKING.
I'M REALIZING I'M GOING TO HAVE GIVE IT MY ALL.
THAT'S IT.

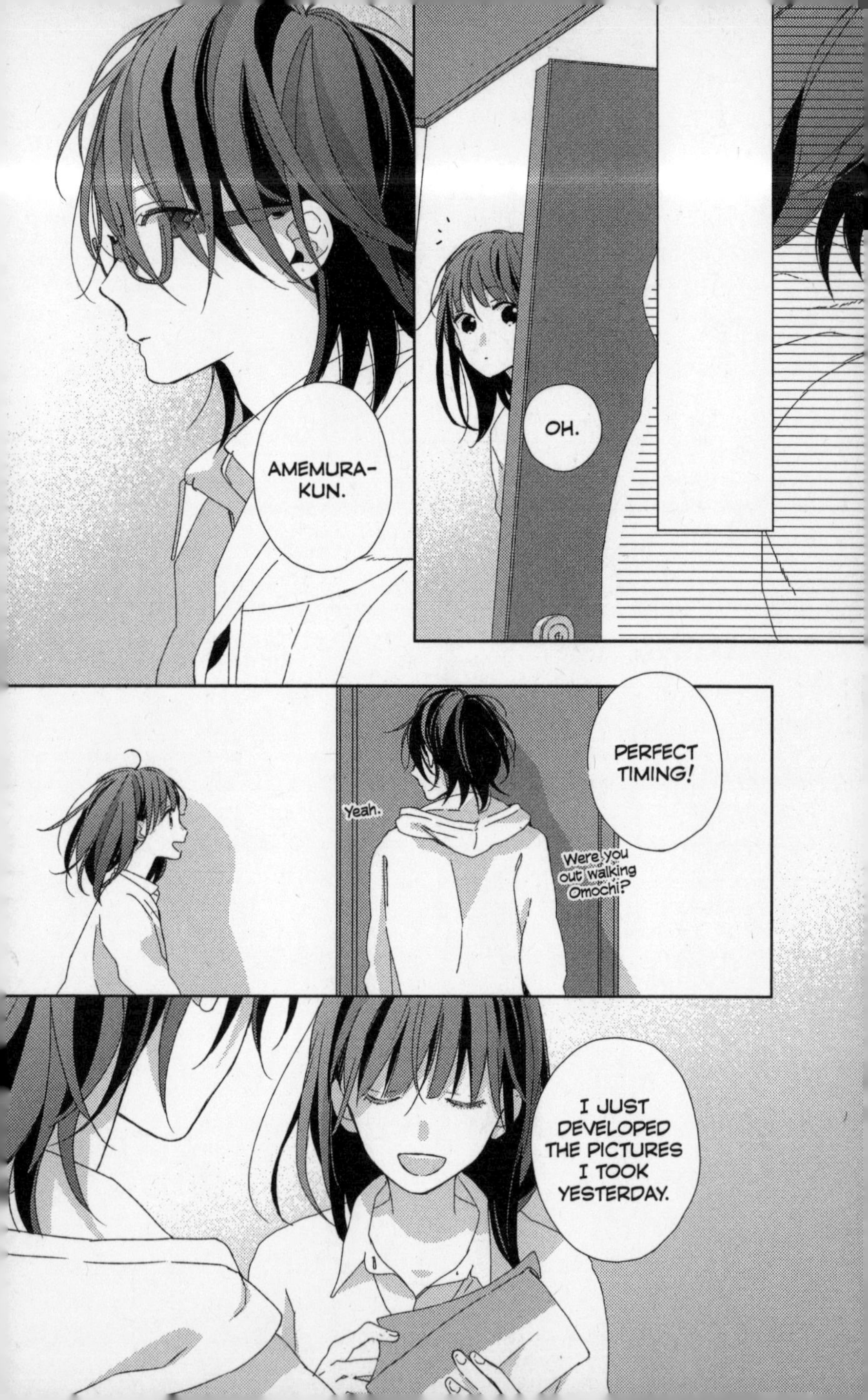
OH.
AMEMURA-KUN.
PERFECT TIMING!
Were you out walking Omochi?
Yeah.
I JUST DEVELOPED THE PICTURES I TOOK YESTERDAY.

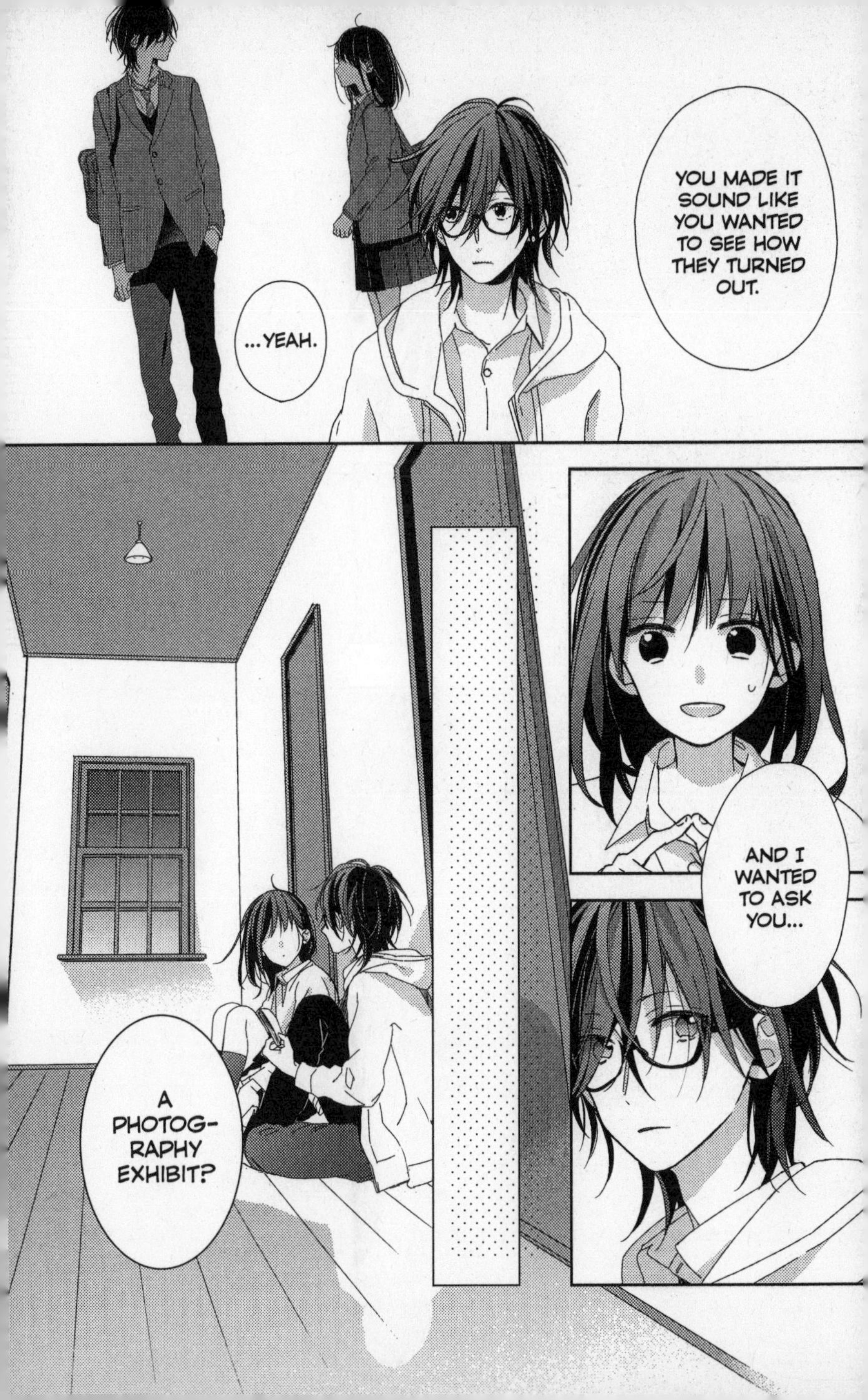
YOU MADE IT SOUND LIKE YOU WANTED TO SEE HOW THEY TURNED OUT.
...YEAH.
AND I WANTED TO ASK YOU...
A PHOTOG-RAPHY EXHIBIT?

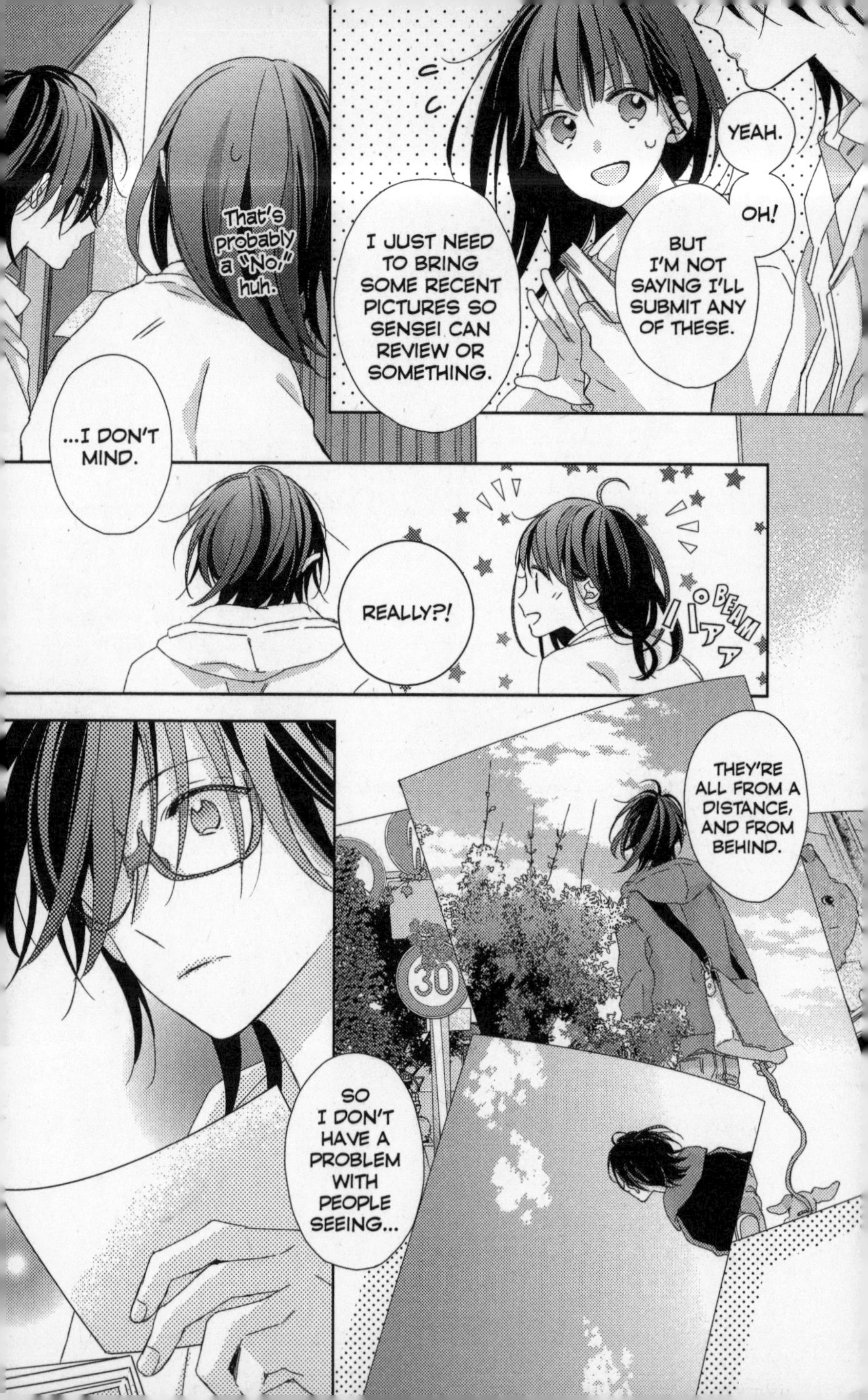
YEAH.
OH!
BUT I'M NOT SAYING I'LL SUBMIT ANY OF THESE.
I JUST NEED TO BRING SOME RECENT PICTURES SO SENSEI CAN REVIEW OR SOMETHING.
That's probably a "No," huh.
...I DON'T MIND.
BEAM
REALLY?!
THEY'RE ALL FROM A DISTANCE, AND FROM BEHIND.
SO I DON'T HAVE A PROBLEM WITH PEOPLE SEEING...

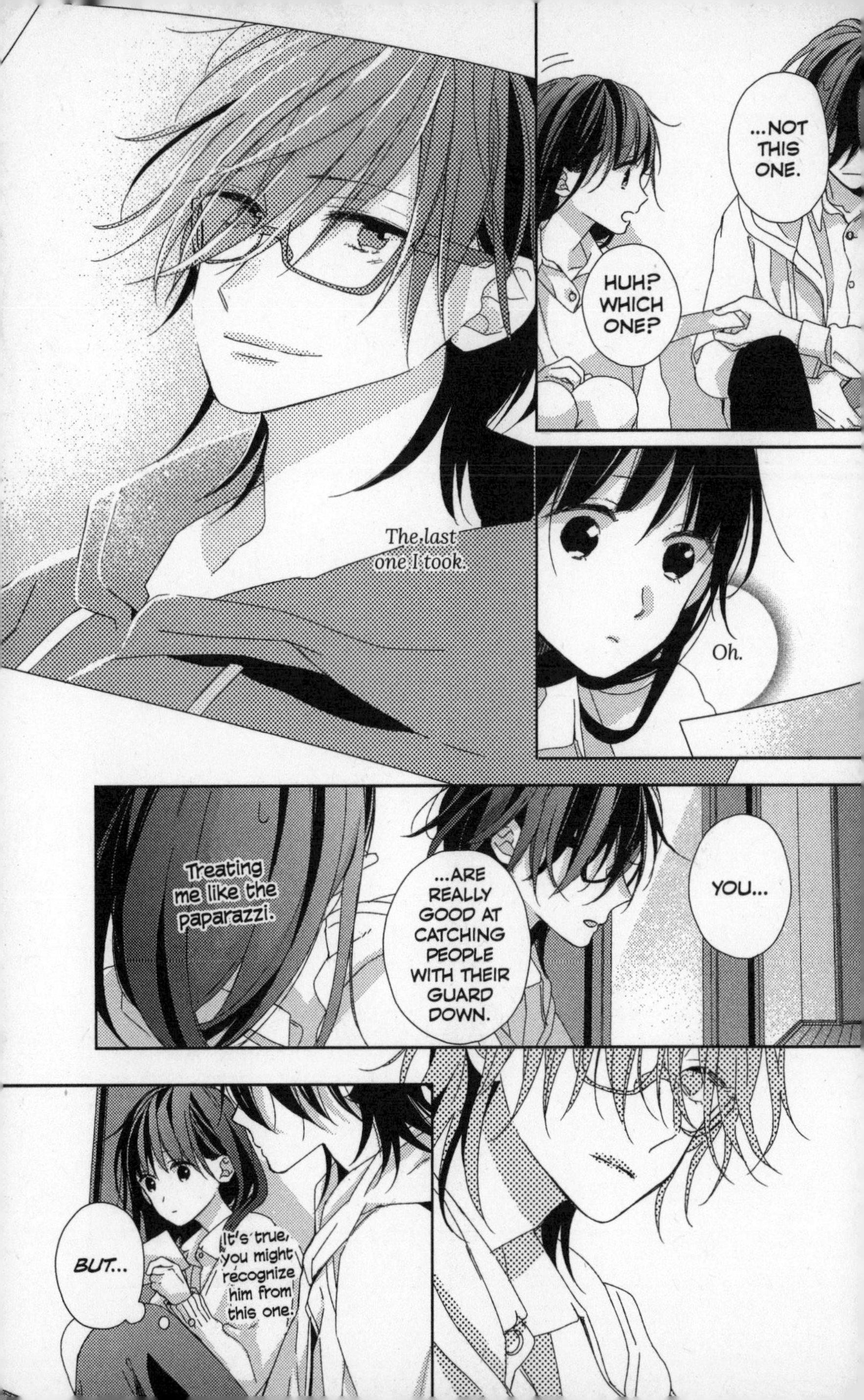
...NOT THIS ONE.
HUH? WHICH ONE?
Oh.
The last one I took.
YOU...
...ARE REALLY GOOD AT CATCHING PEOPLE WITH THEIR GUARD DOWN.
Treating me like the paparazzi.
It's true, you might recognize him from this one!
BUT...

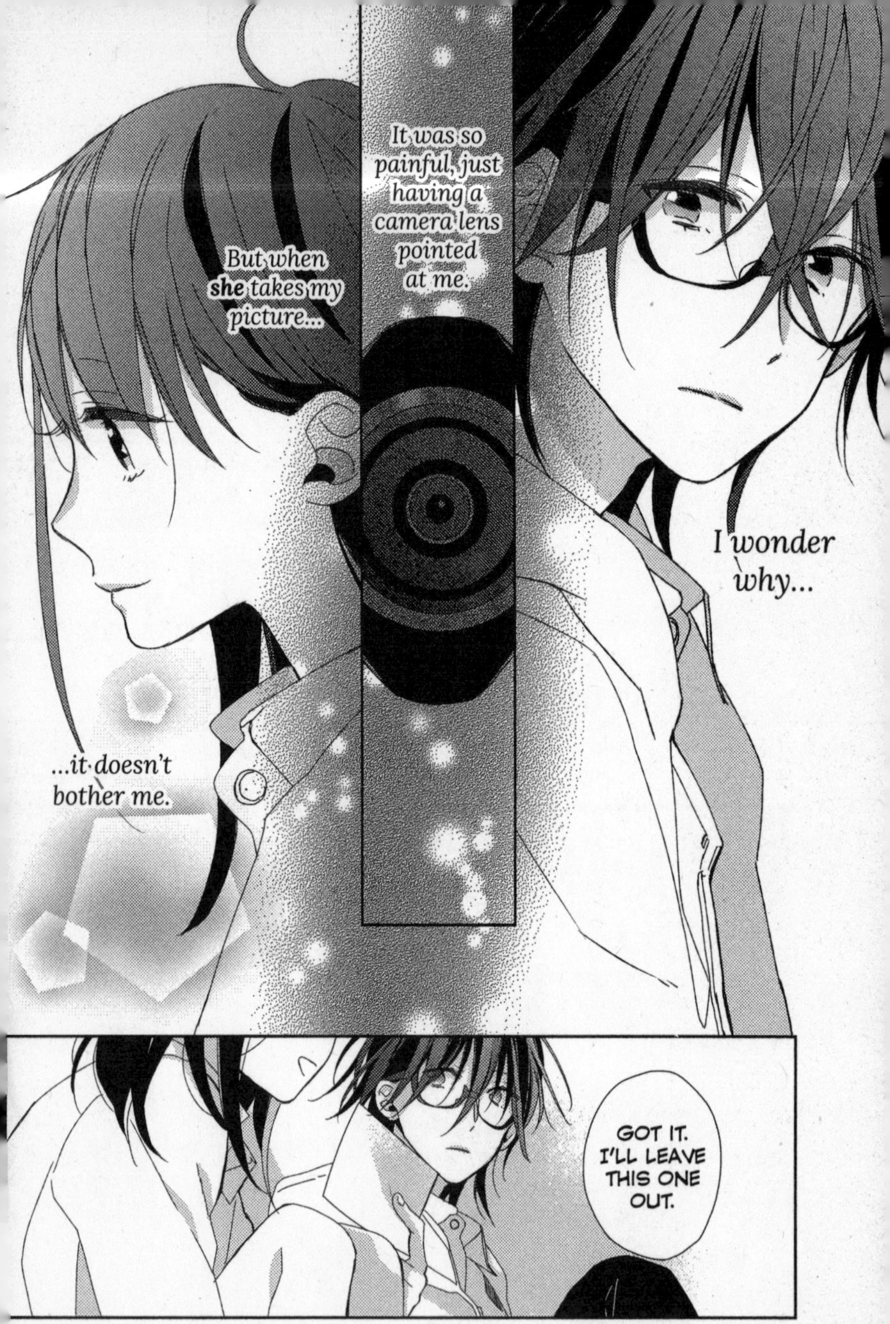
It was so painful, just having a camera lens pointed at me.
But when **she** takes my picture...
...it doesn't bother me.
I wonder why...
GOT IT. I'LL LEAVE THIS ONE OUT.

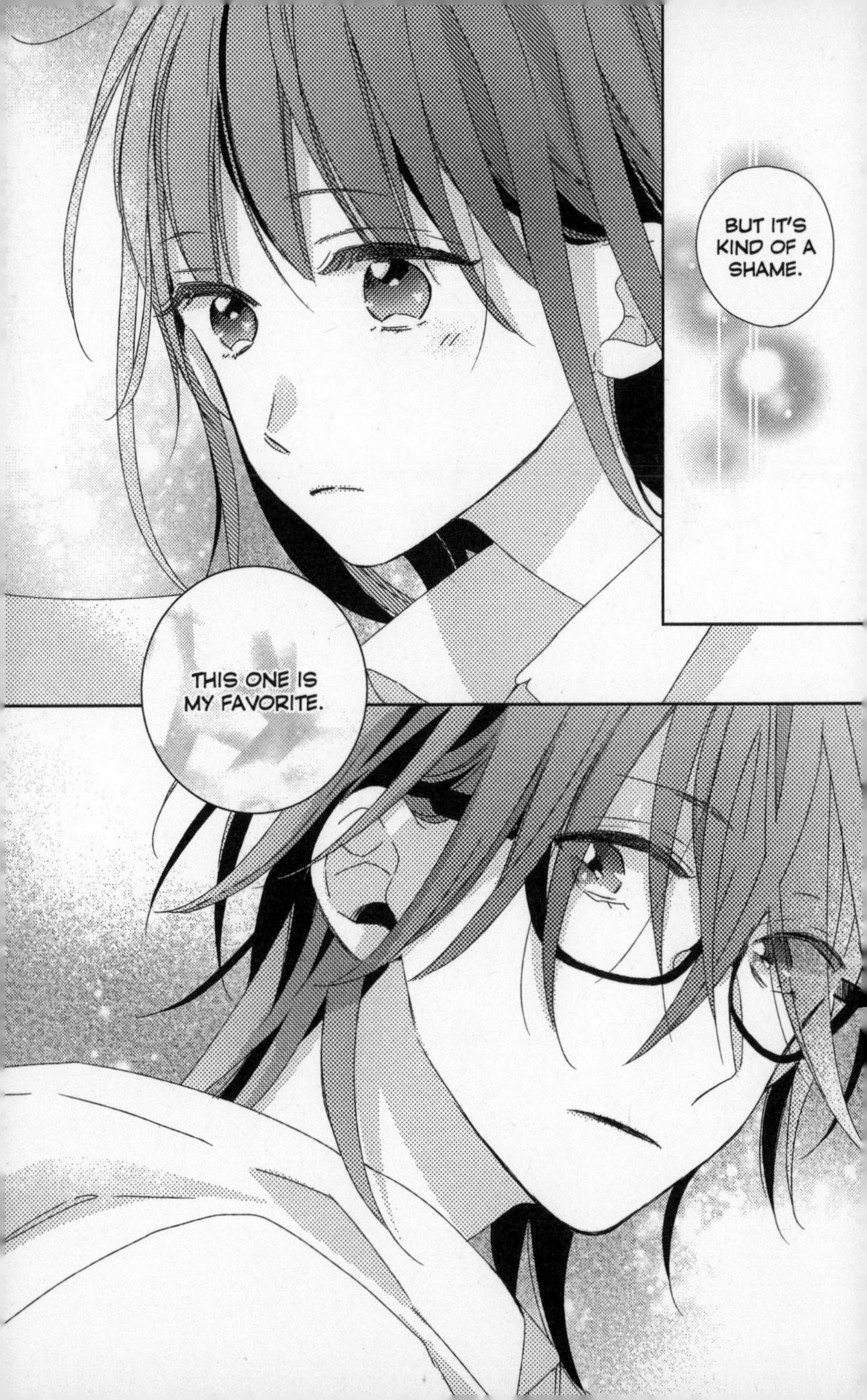
BUT IT'S KIND OF A SHAME.
THIS ONE IS MY FAVORITE.

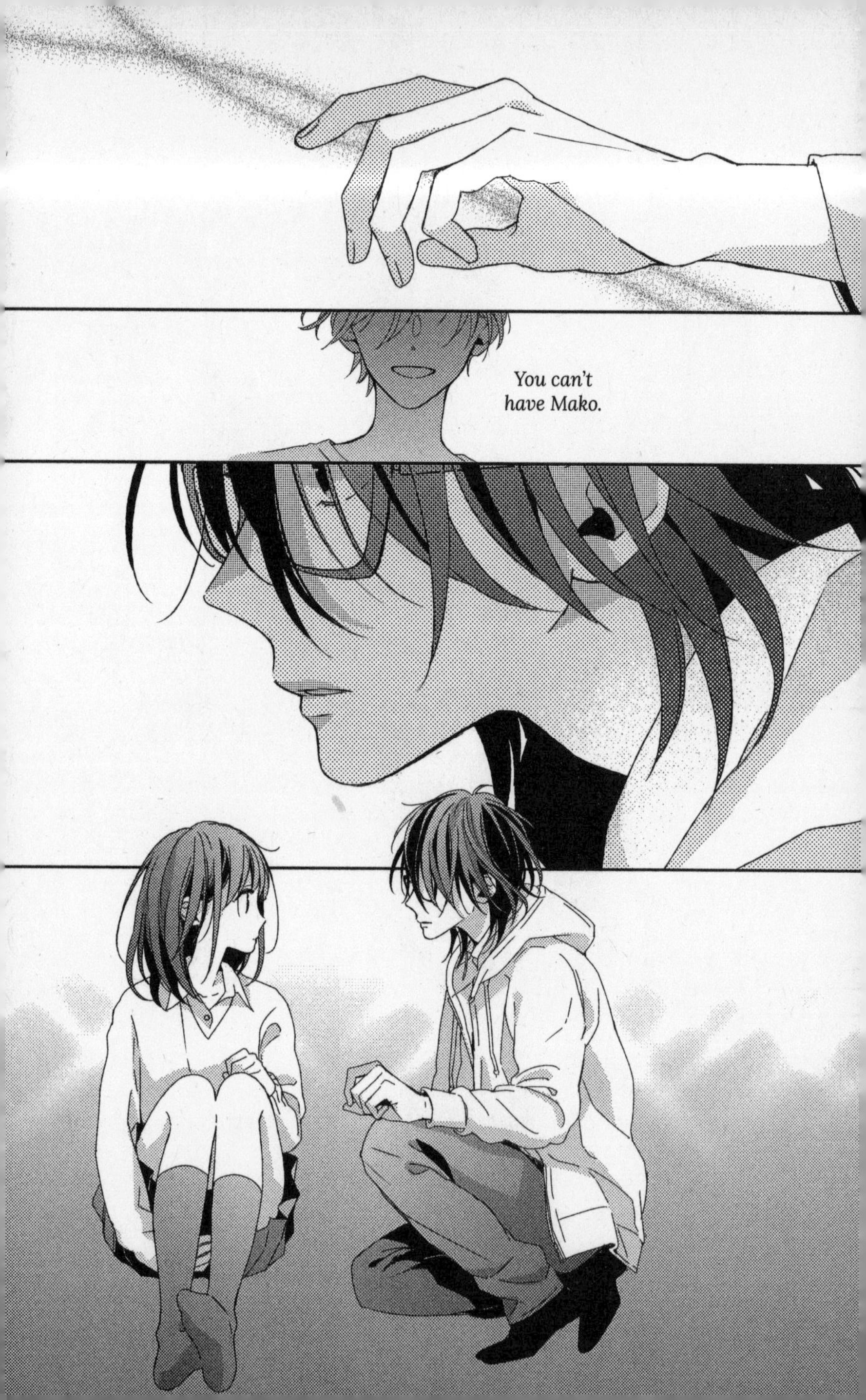
You can't
have Mako.

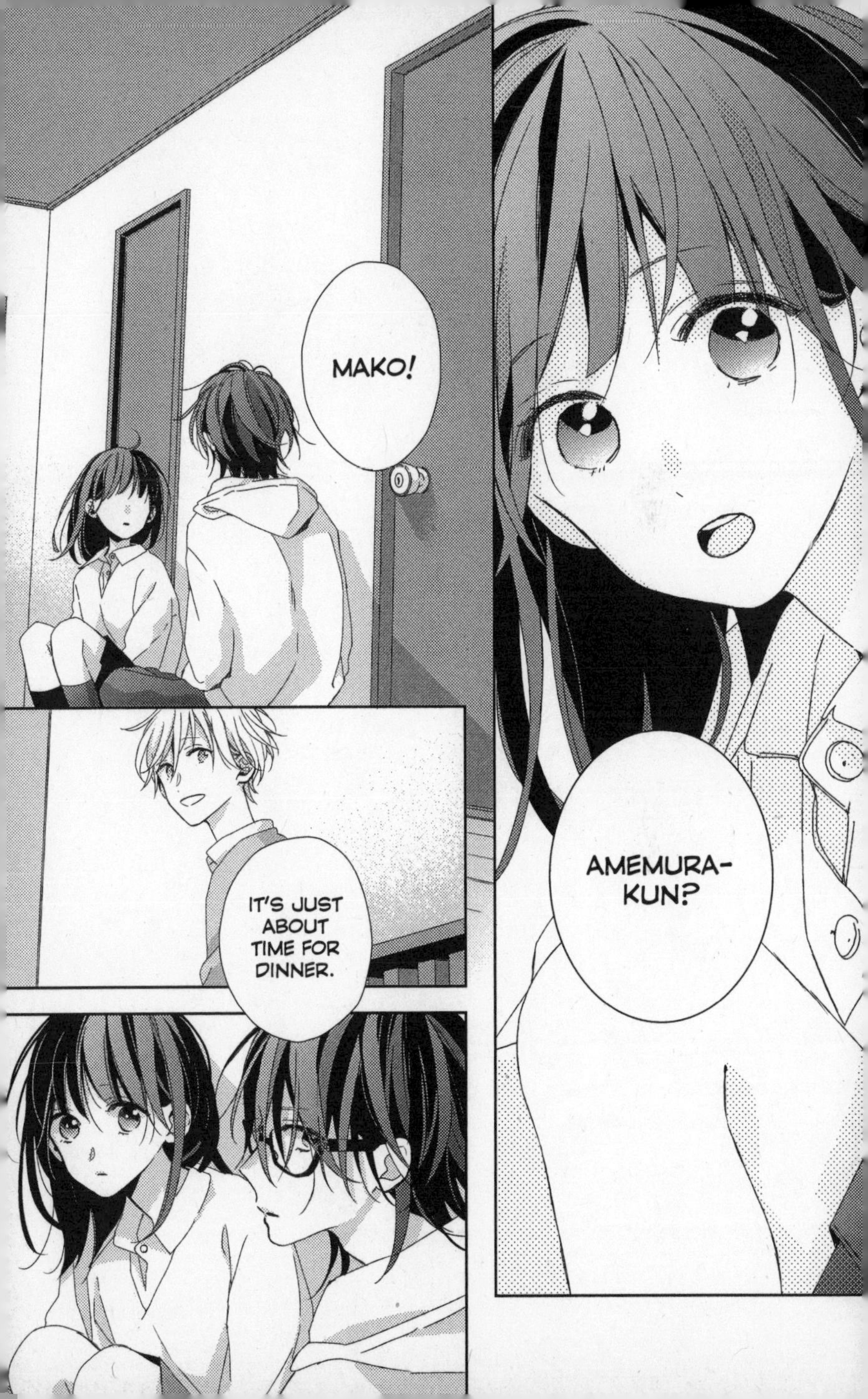
AMEMURA-KUN?
MAKO!
IT'S JUST ABOUT TIME FOR DINNER.

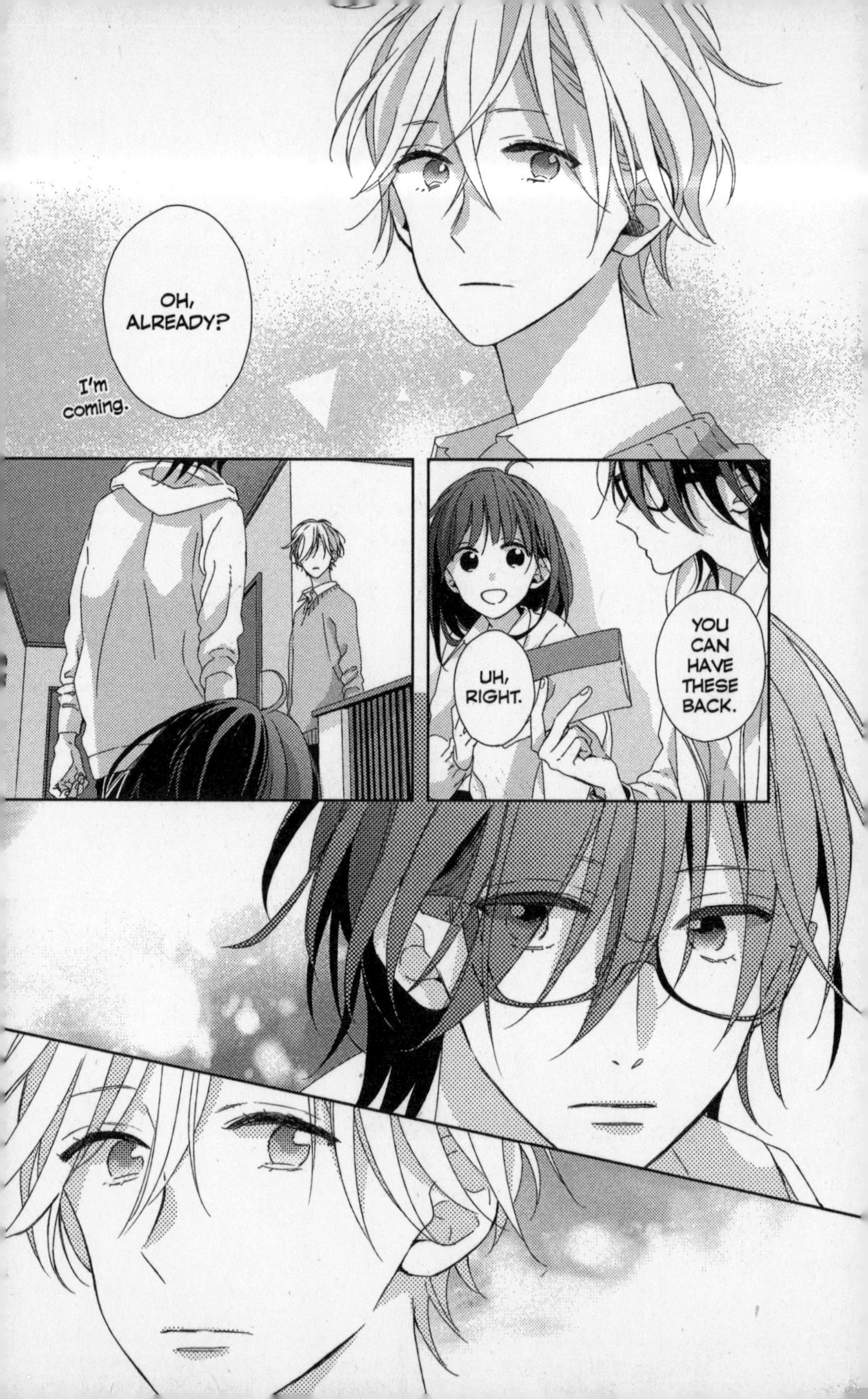
OH, ALREADY?
I'm coming.
YOU CAN HAVE THESE BACK.
UH, RIGHT.

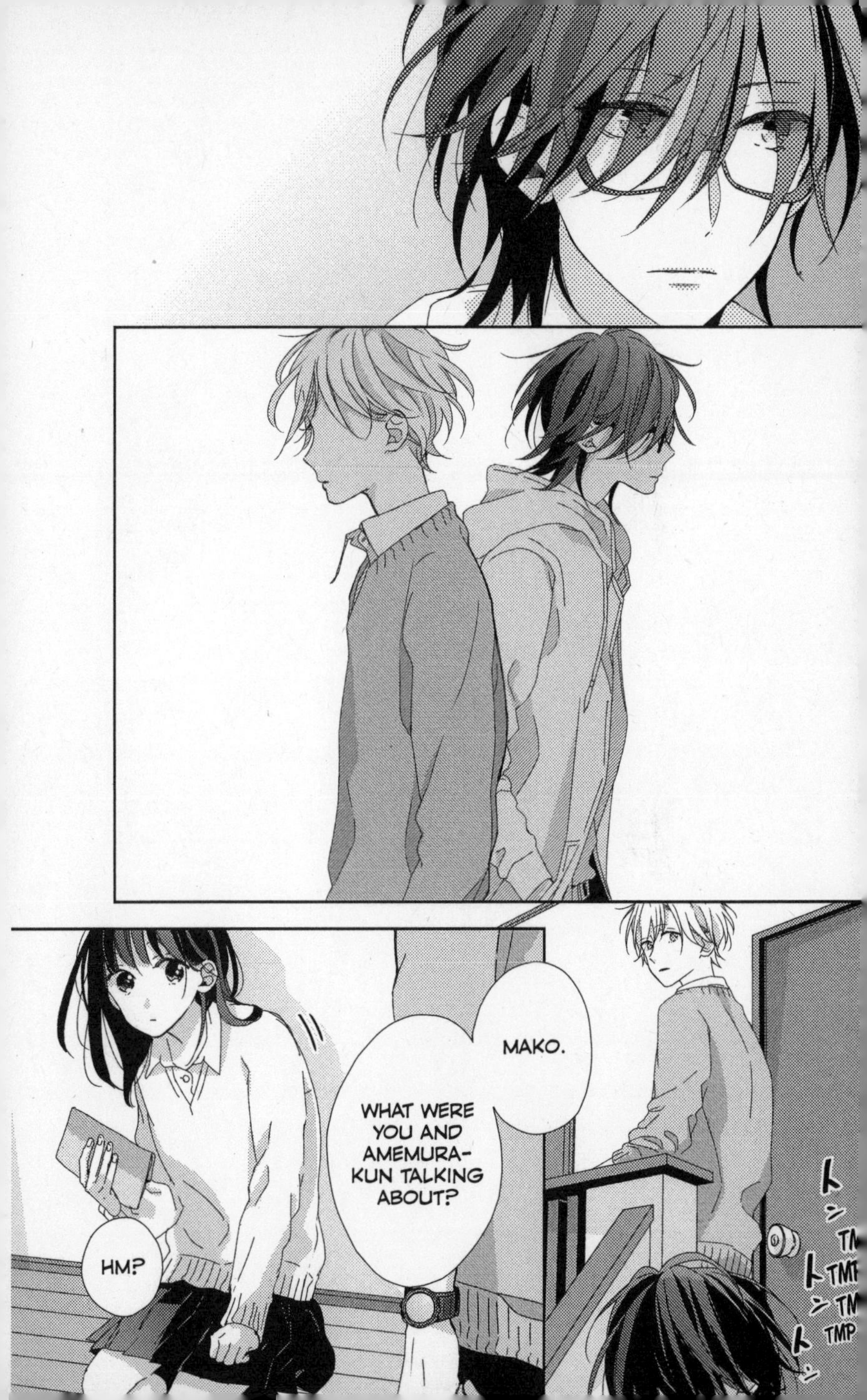
トントントン
TMP
MAKO.
WHAT WERE YOU AND AMEMURA-KUN TALKING ABOUT?
HM?

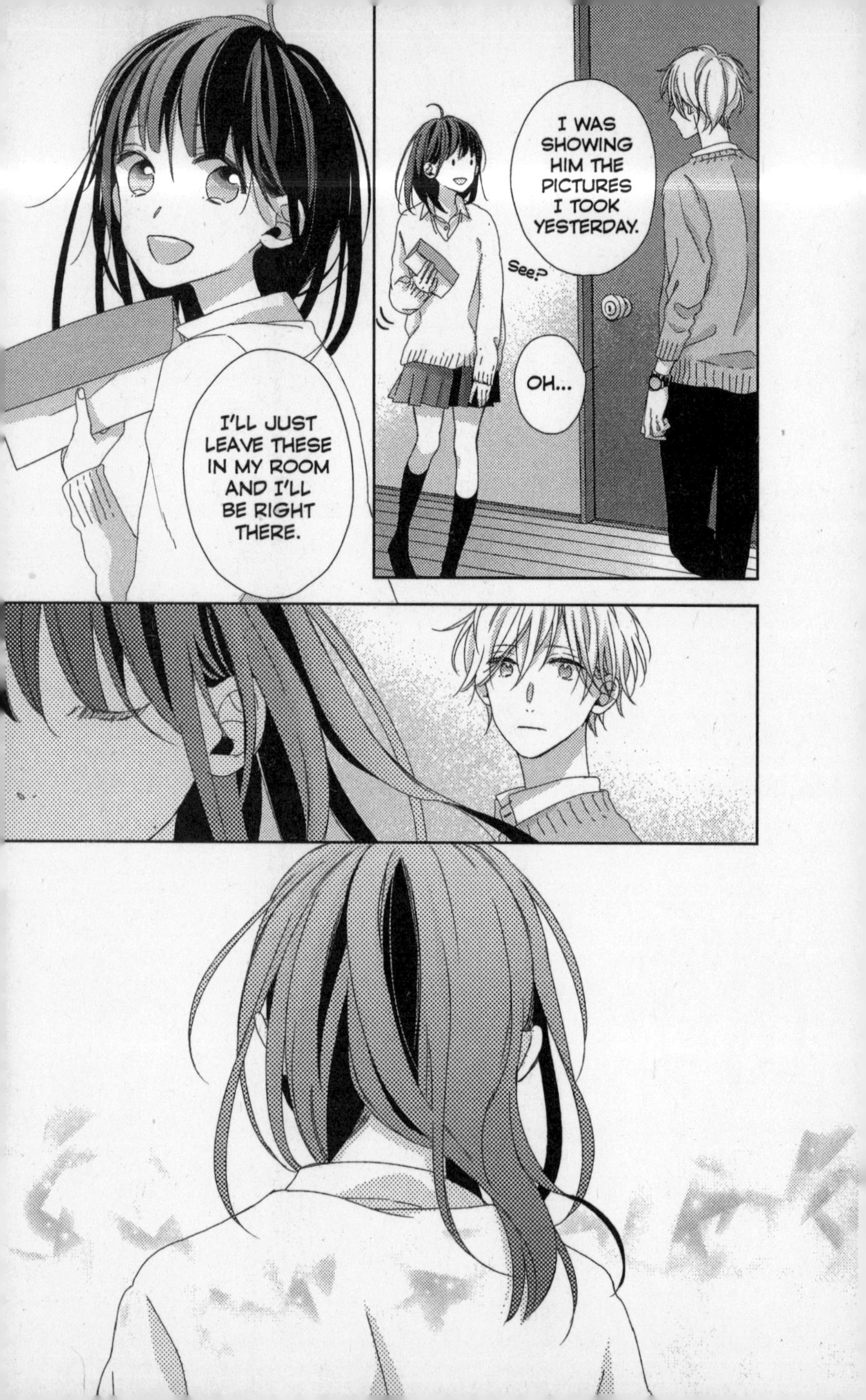
I WAS SHOWING HIM THE PICTURES I TOOK YESTERDAY.
See?
OH...
I'LL JUST LEAVE THESE IN MY ROOM AND I'LL BE RIGHT THERE.

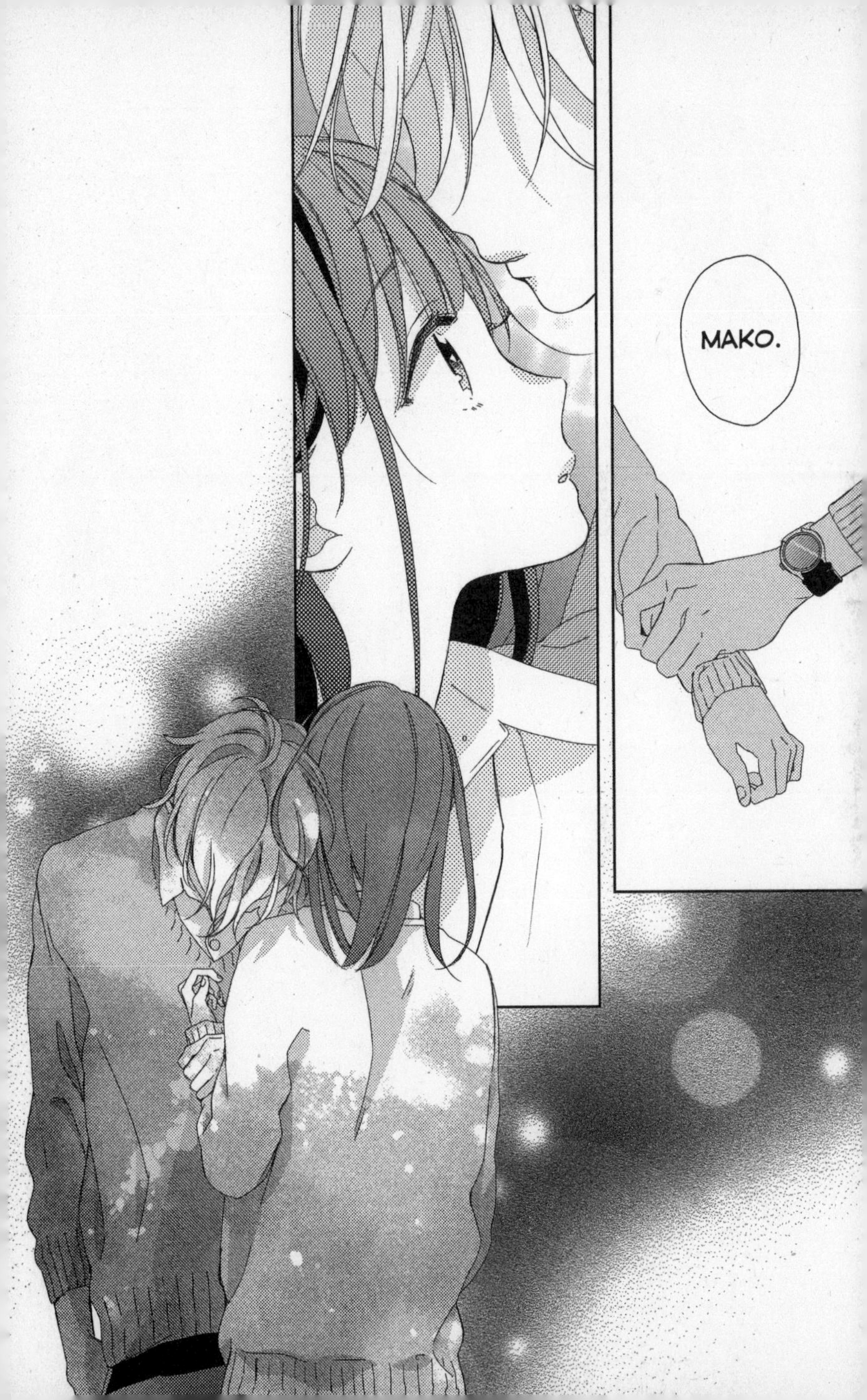
MAKO.

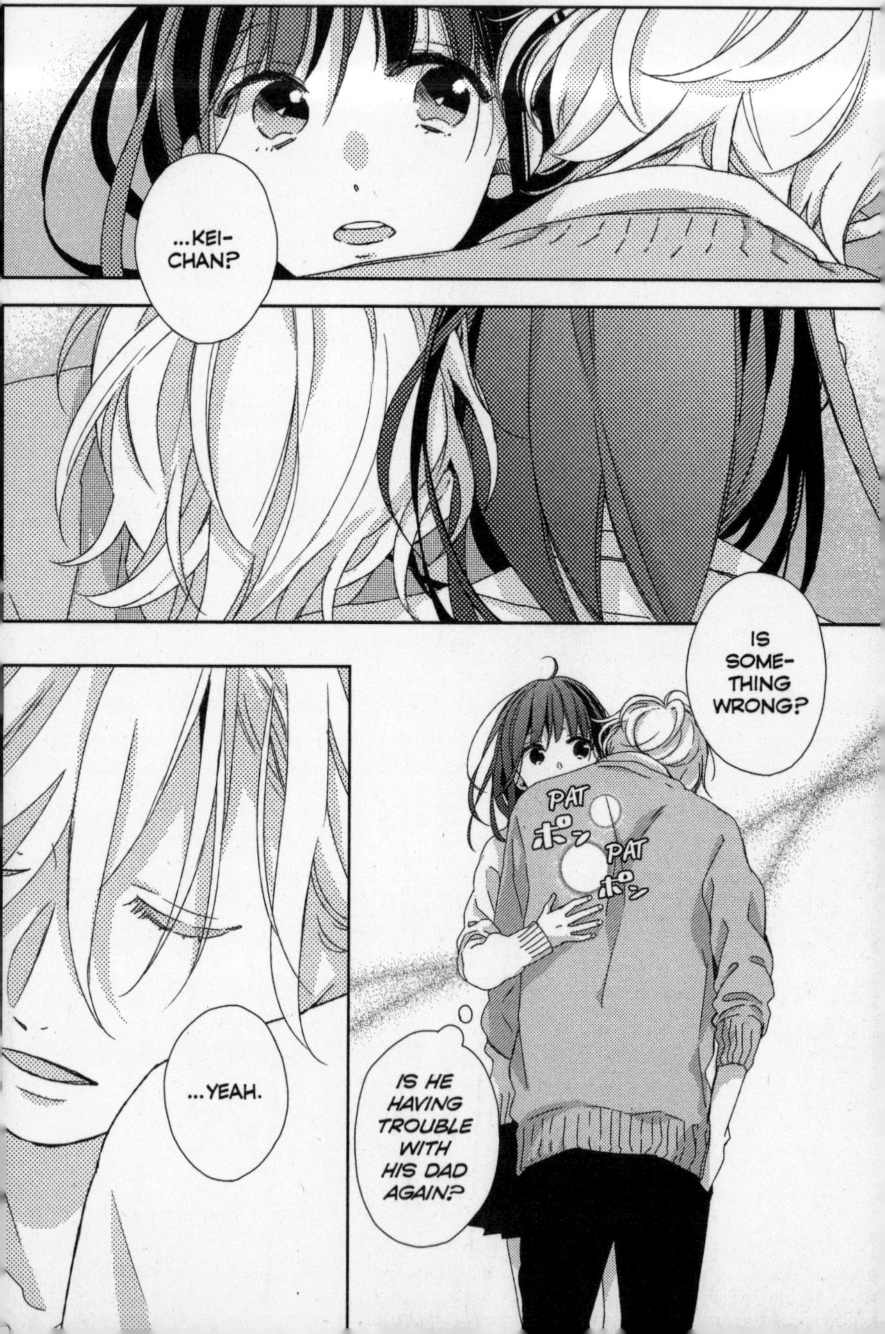
...KEI-CHAN?
IS SOME-THING WRONG?
PAT ポン
PAT ポン
IS HE HAVING TROUBLE WITH HIS DAD AGAIN?
...YEAH.

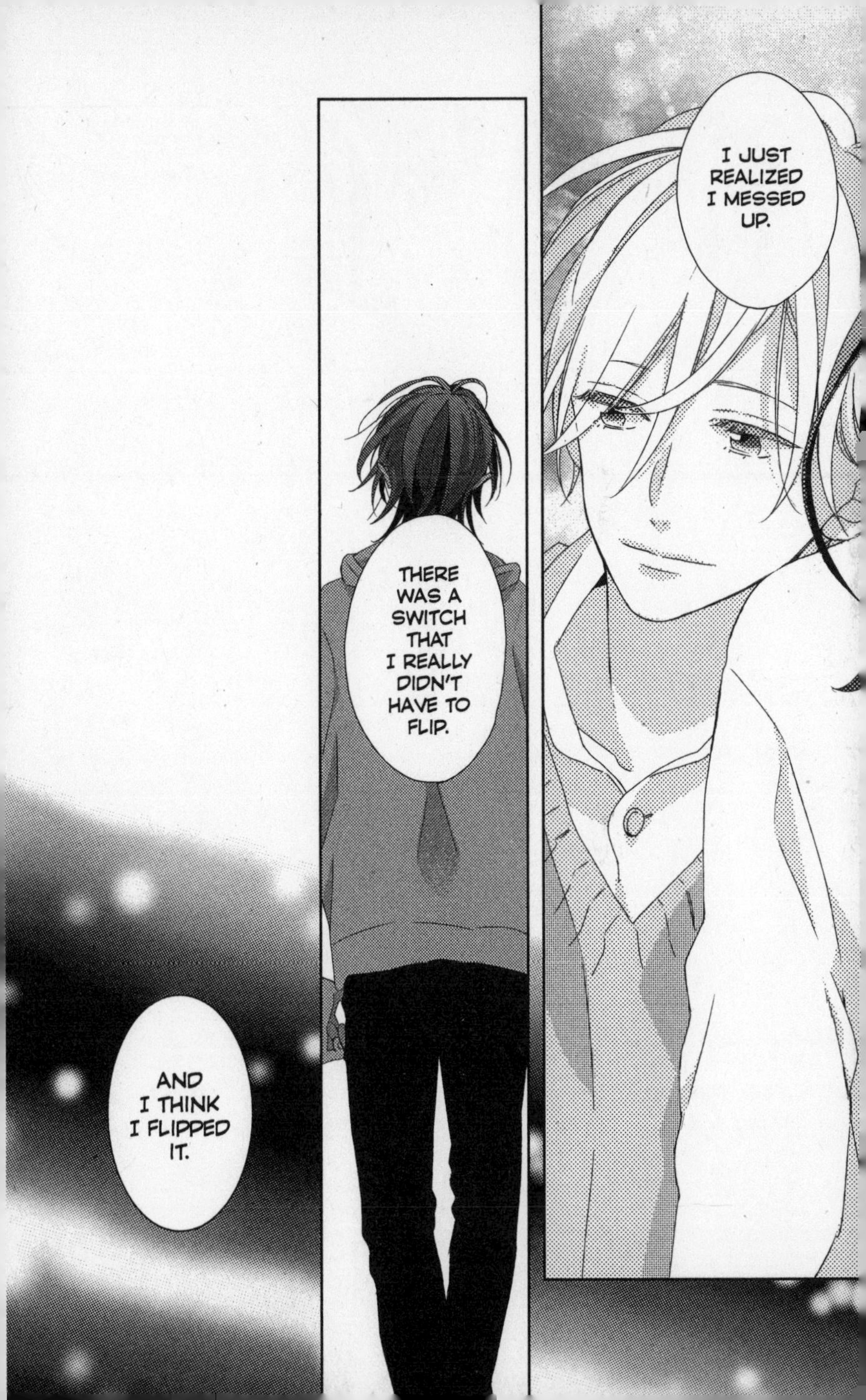
I JUST REALIZED I MESSED UP.
THERE WAS A SWITCH THAT I REALLY DIDN'T HAVE TO FLIP.
AND I THINK I FLIPPED IT.

LOVE IN FOCUS

FILM 6

My Only Salvation

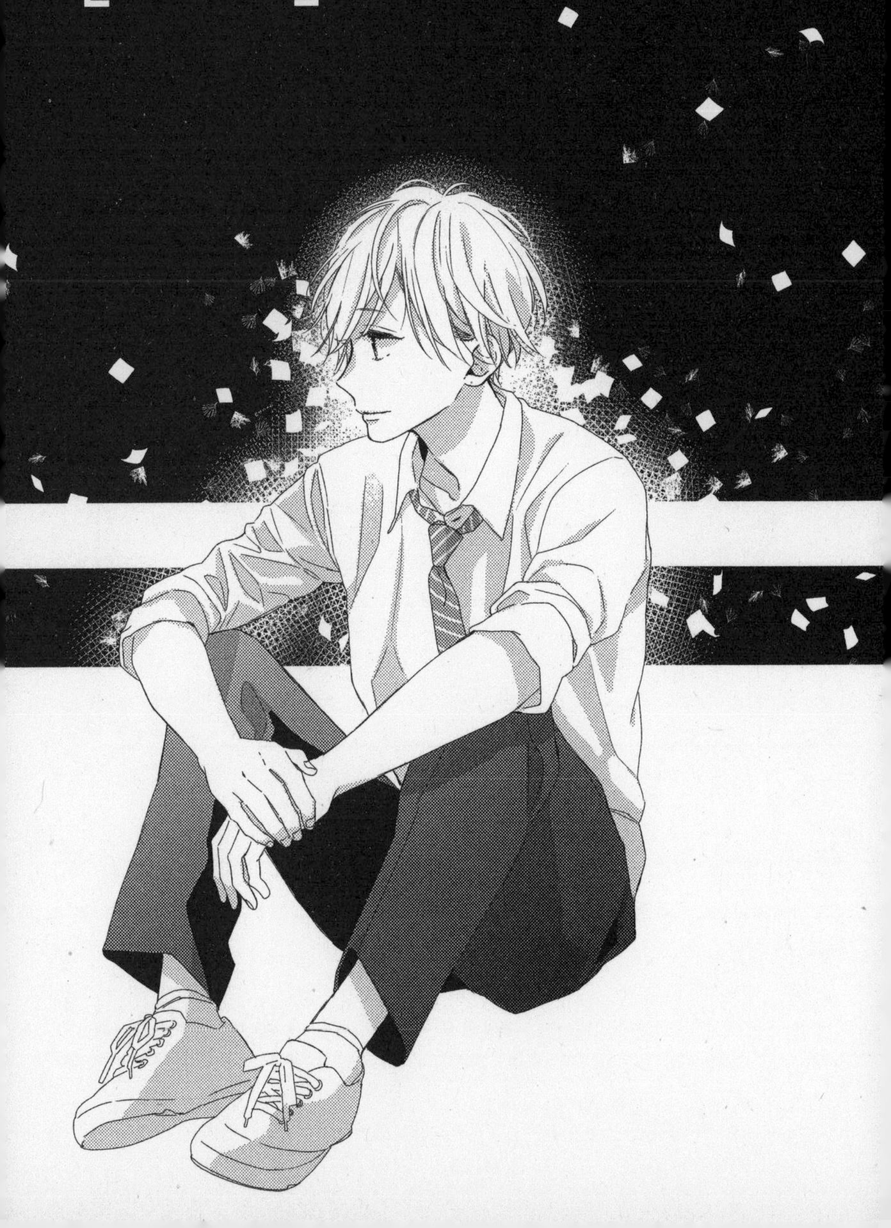

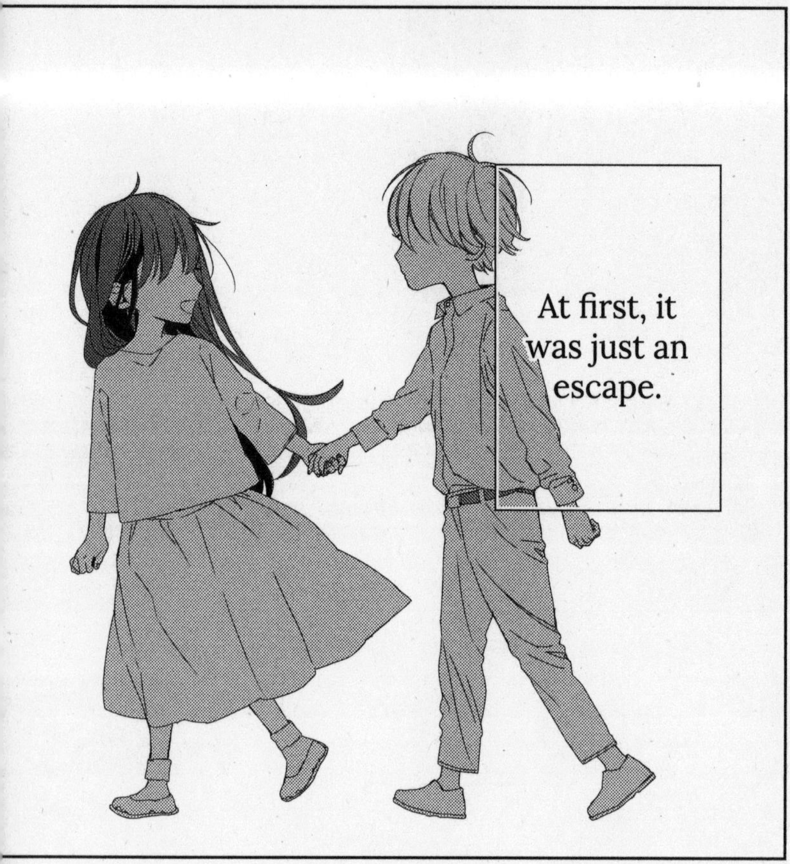
At first, it was just an escape.

LOVE IN FOCUS

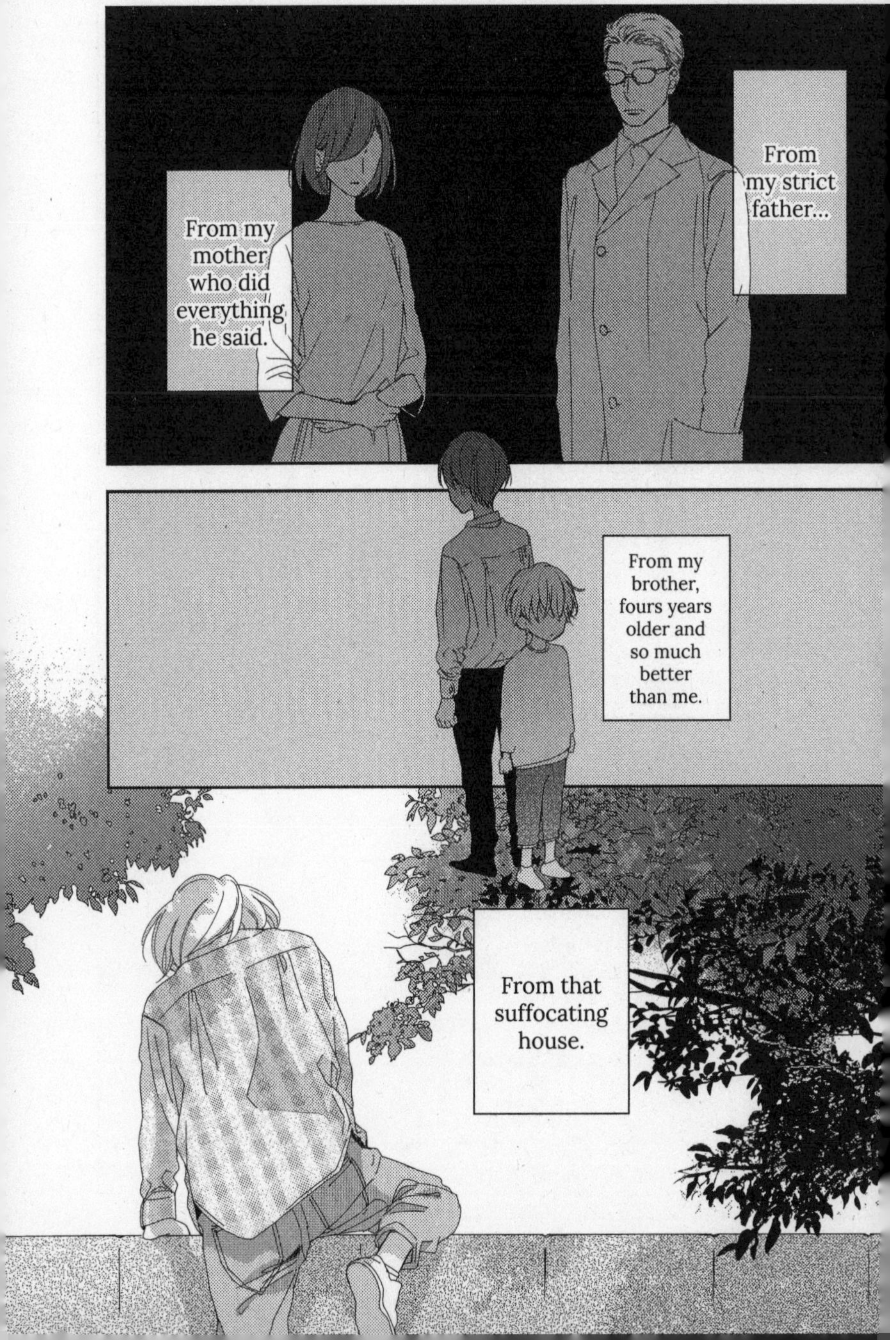
From my strict father...
From my mother who did everything he said.
From my brother, fours years older and so much better than me.
From that suffocating house.

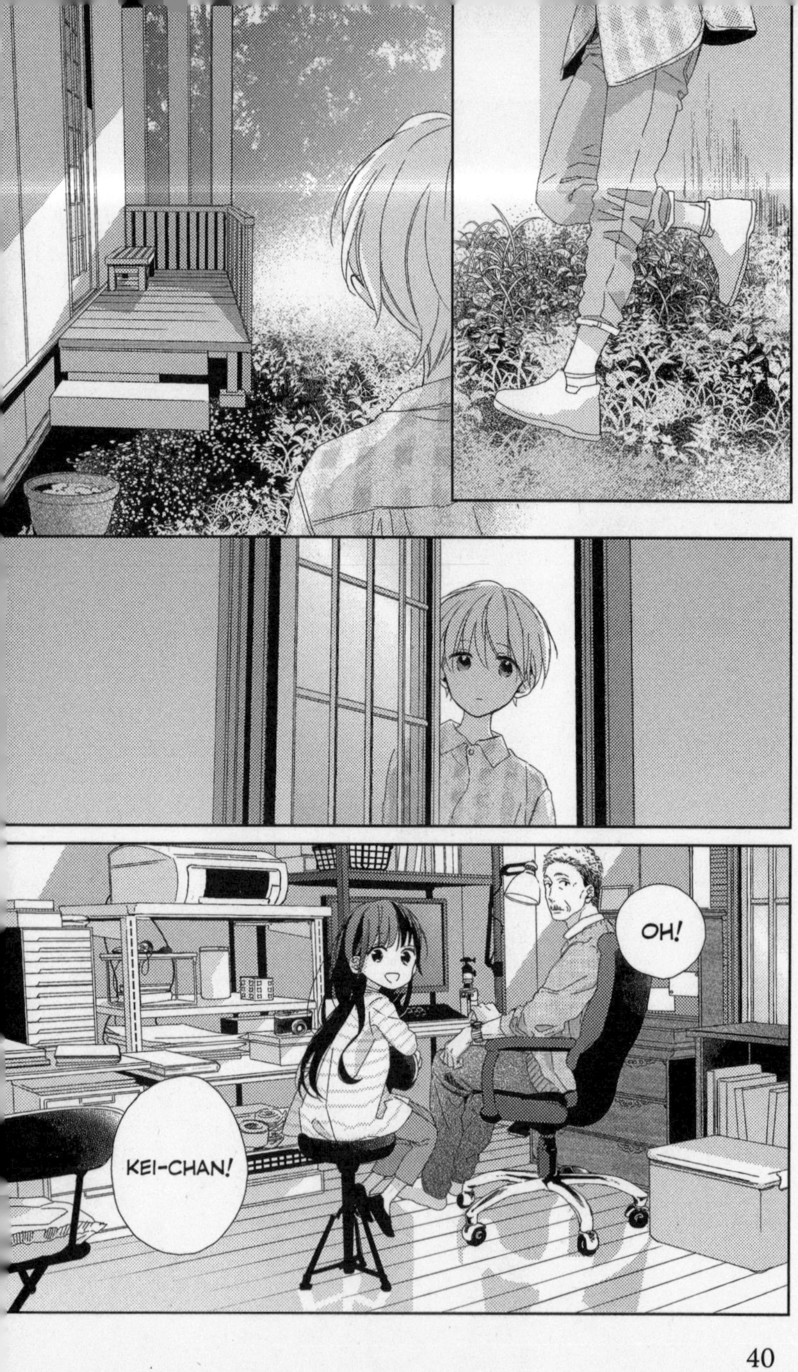
OH!
KEI-CHAN!

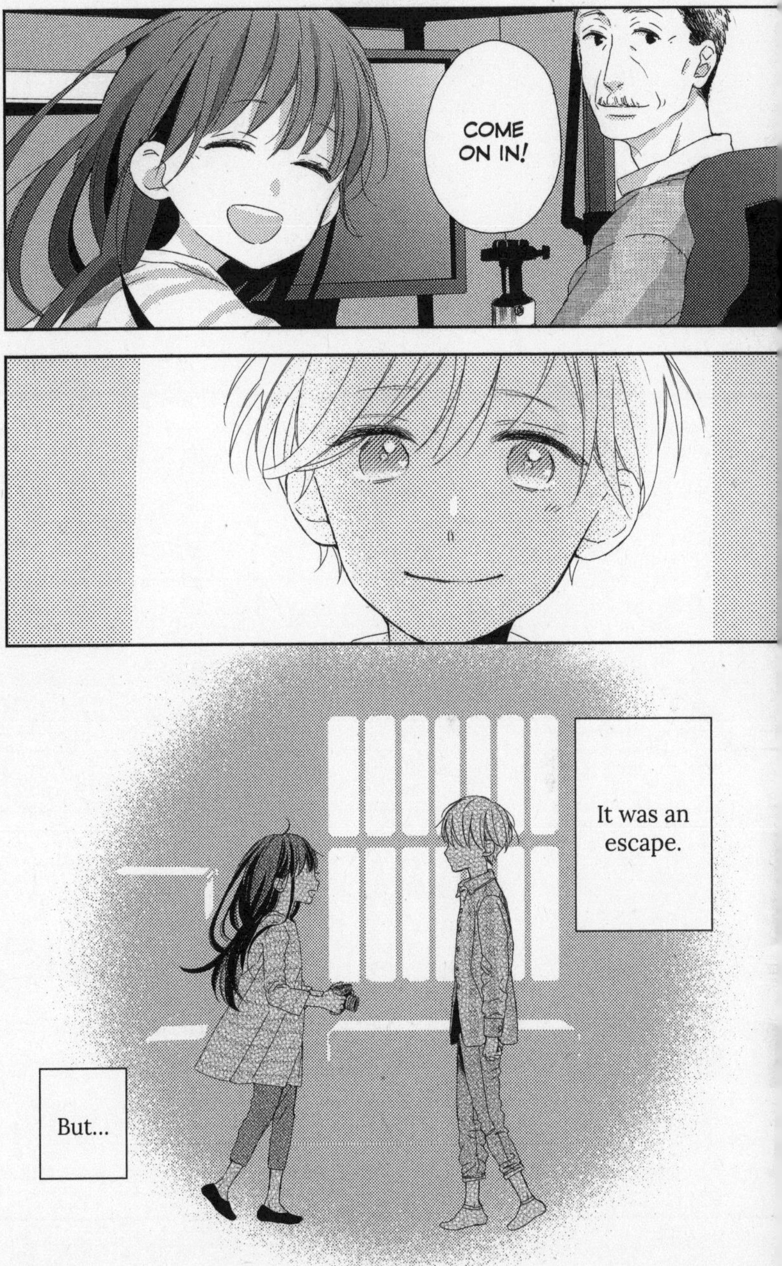
COME ON IN!
It was an escape.
But...

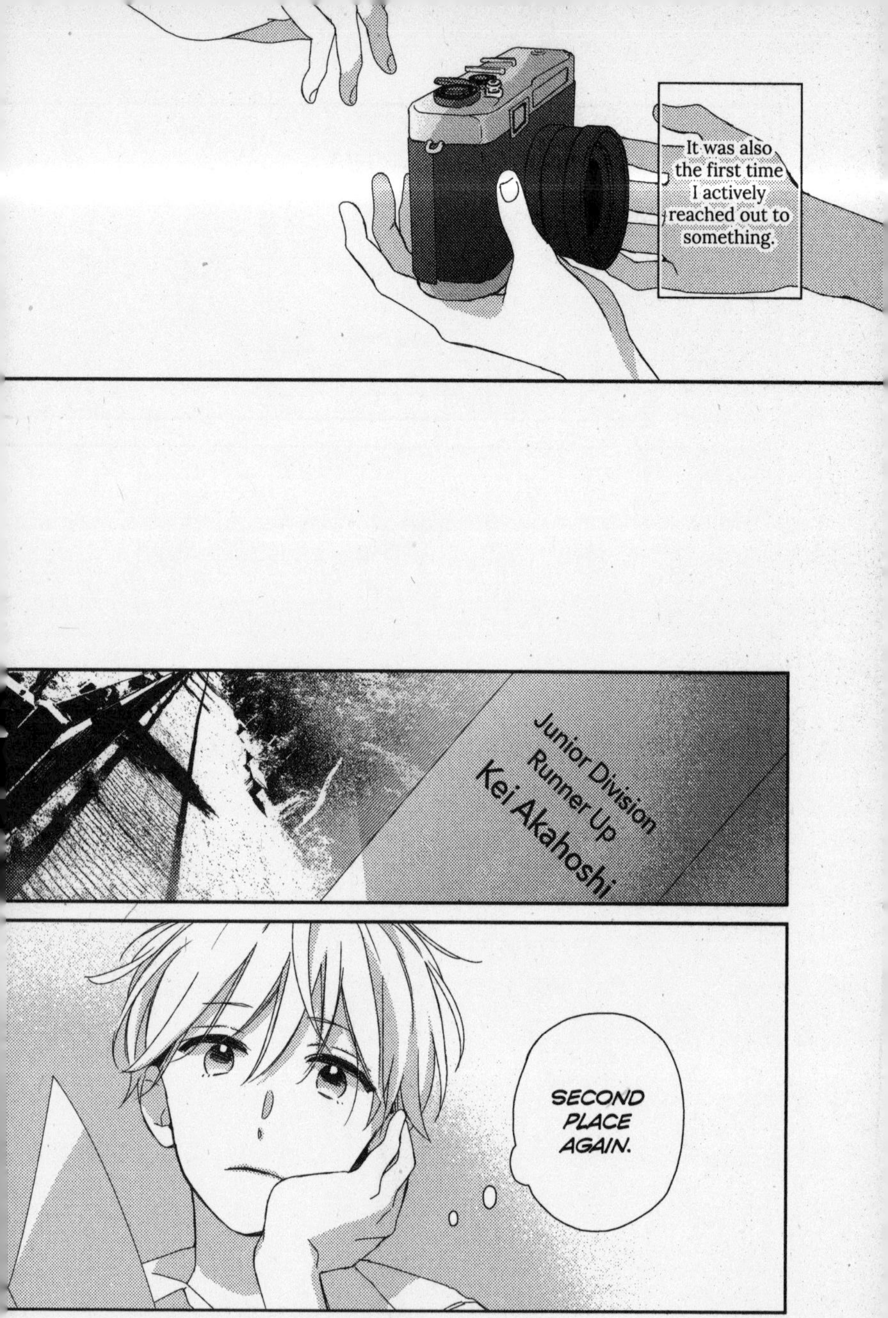
It was also the first time I actively reached out to something.
Junior Division Runner Up
Kei Akahoshi
SECOND PLACE AGAIN.

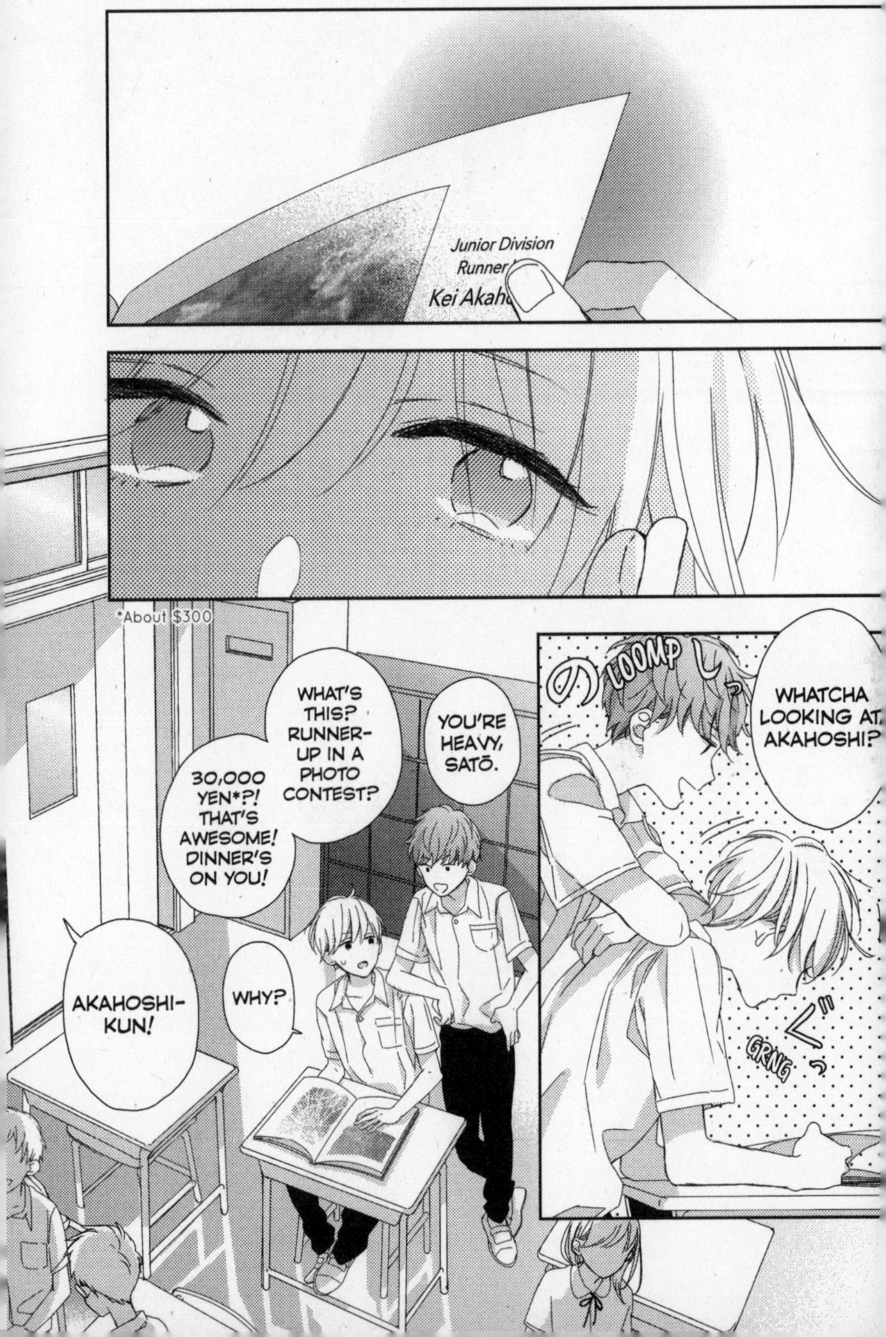
Junior Division
Runner
Kei Akaho
LOOMP
WHATCHA LOOKING AT, AKAHOSHI?
GRNG
YOU'RE HEAVY, SATŌ.
WHAT'S THIS? RUNNER-UP IN A PHOTO CONTEST?
30,000 YEN*?! THAT'S AWESOME! DINNER'S ON YOU!
WHY?
AKAHOSHI-KUN!
*About $300

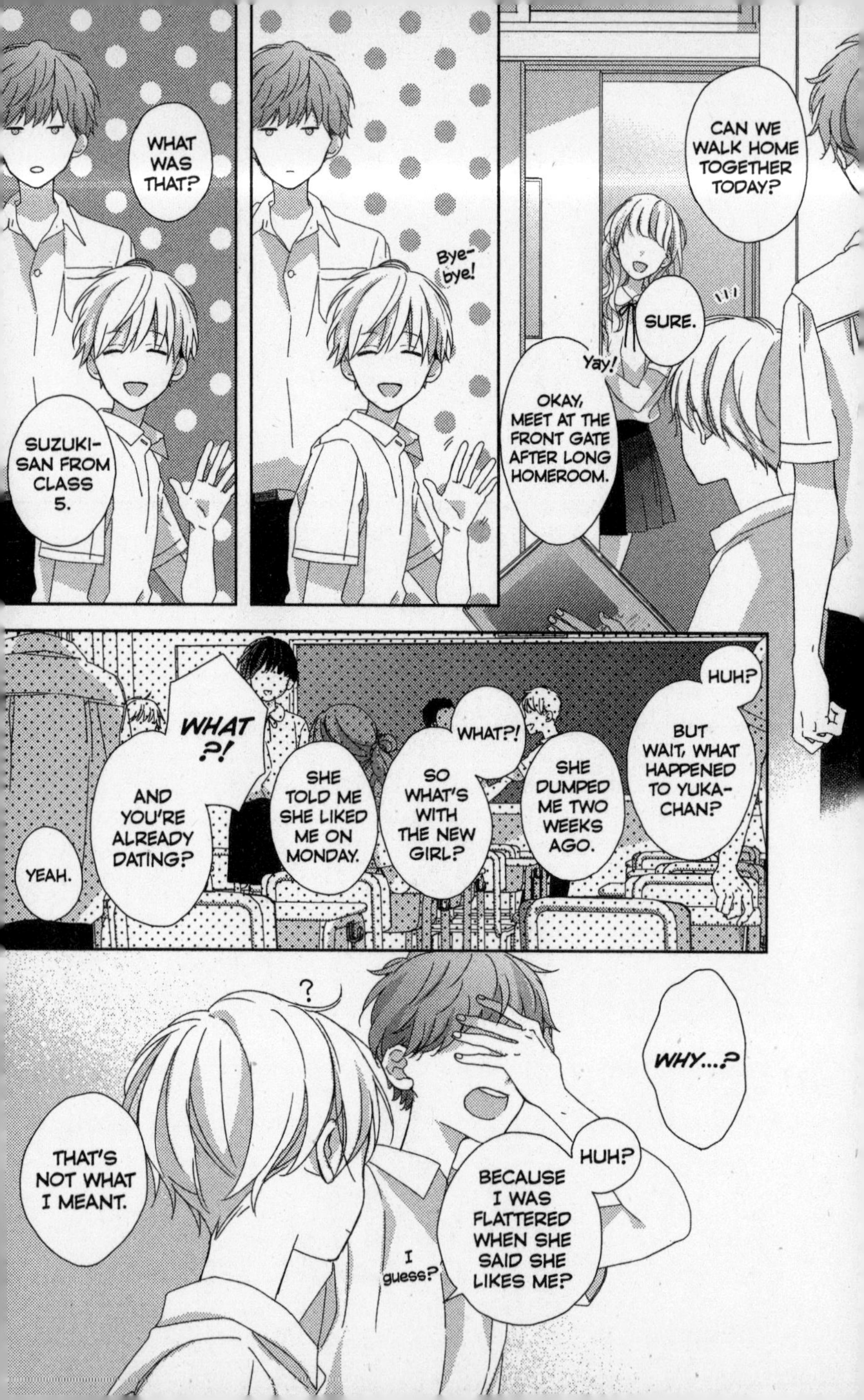
CAN WE WALK HOME TOGETHER TODAY?
SURE.
Yay!
OKAY, MEET AT THE FRONT GATE AFTER LONG HOMEROOM.
Bye-bye!
WHAT WAS THAT?
SUZUKI-SAN FROM CLASS 5.
HUH?
BUT WAIT, WHAT HAPPENED TO YUKA-CHAN?
SHE DUMPED ME TWO WEEKS AGO.
WHAT?!
SO WHAT'S WITH THE NEW GIRL?
SHE TOLD ME SHE LIKED ME ON MONDAY.
WHAT ?!
AND YOU'RE ALREADY DATING?
YEAH.
WHY...?
HUH?
BECAUSE I WAS FLATTERED WHEN SHE SAID SHE LIKES ME?
I guess?
THAT'S NOT WHAT I MEANT.

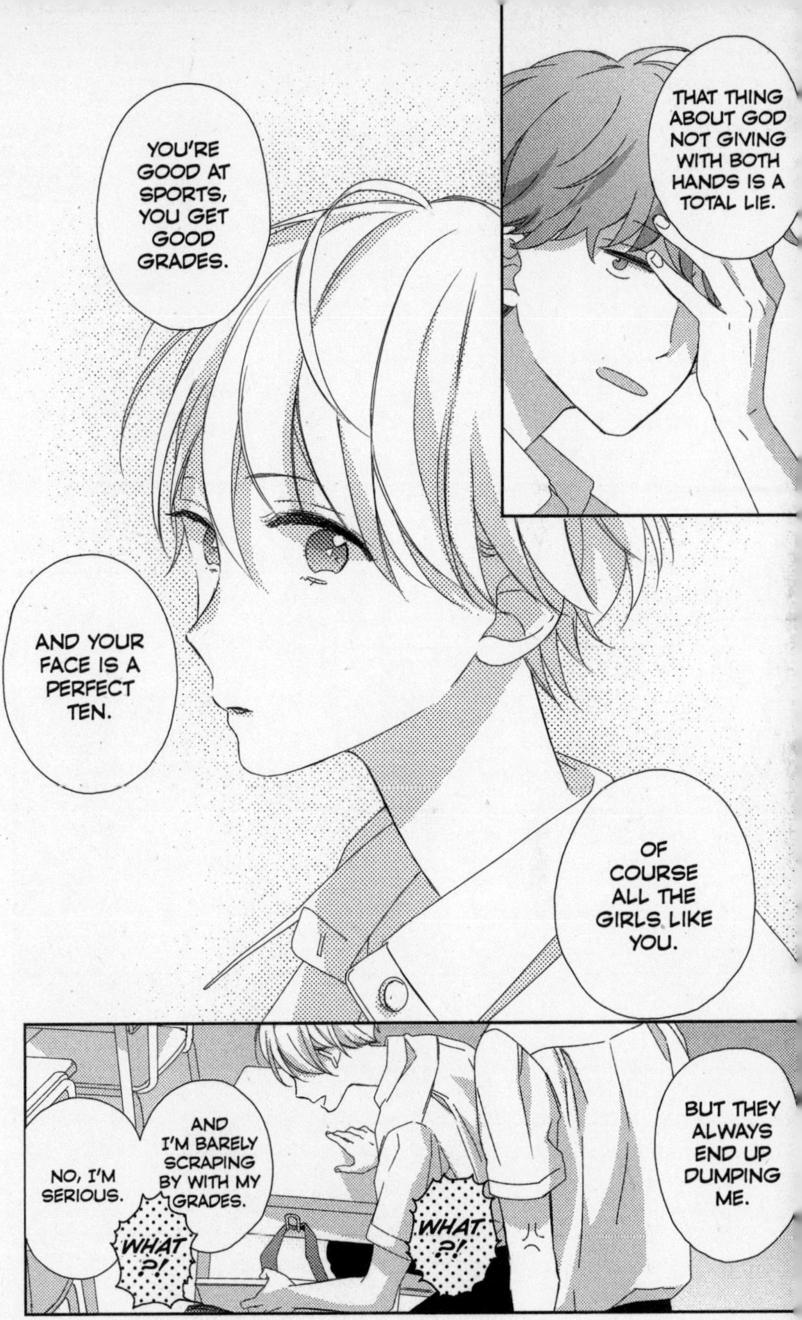
THAT THING ABOUT GOD NOT GIVING WITH BOTH HANDS IS A TOTAL LIE.
YOU'RE GOOD AT SPORTS, YOU GET GOOD GRADES.
AND YOUR FACE IS A PERFECT TEN.
OF COURSE ALL THE GIRLS LIKE YOU.
BUT THEY ALWAYS END UP DUMPING ME.
WHAT ?!
AND I'M BARELY SCRAPING BY WITH MY GRADES.
WHAT ?!
NO, I'M SERIOUS.

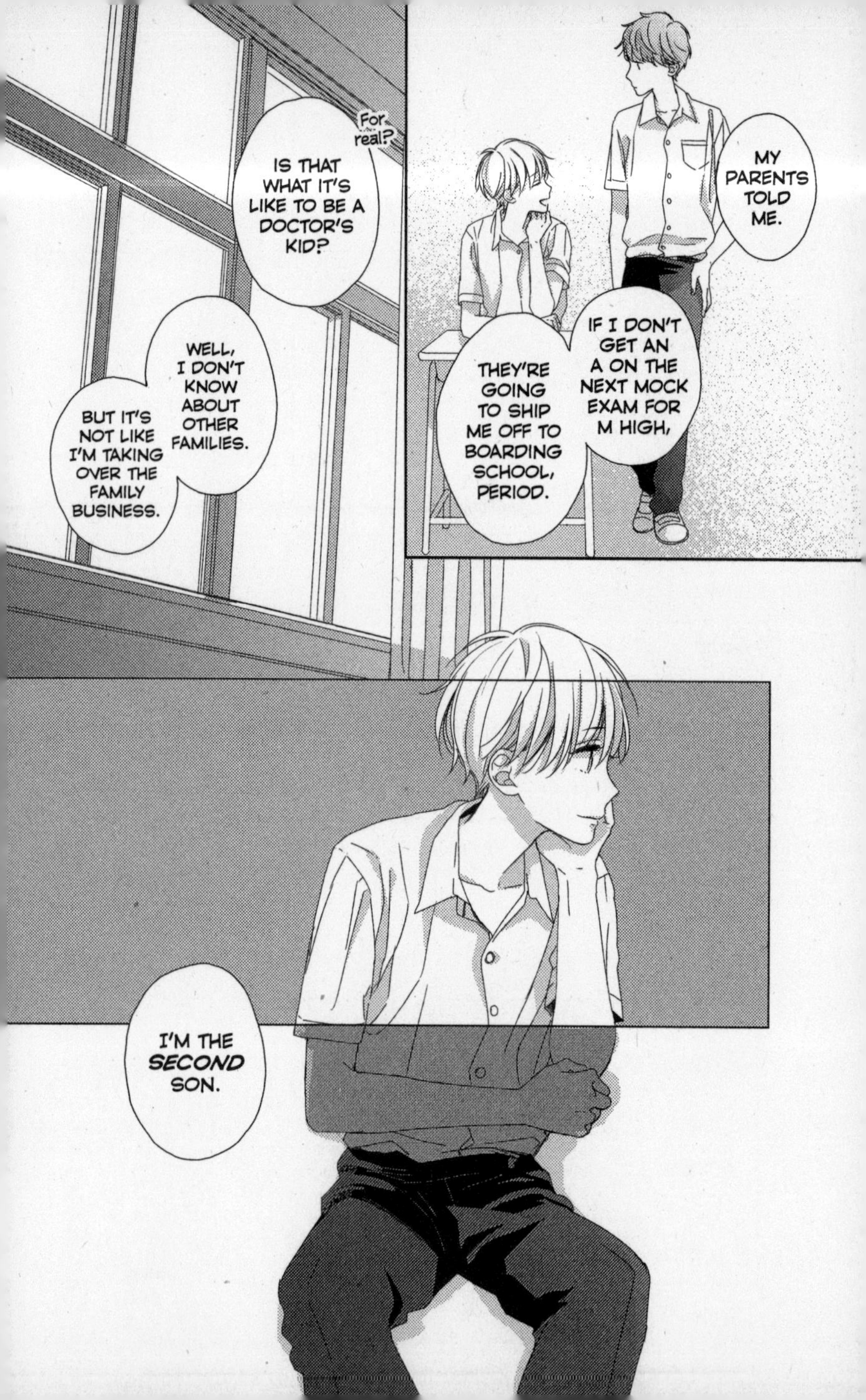
MY PARENTS TOLD ME.
IF I DON'T GET AN A ON THE NEXT MOCK EXAM FOR M HIGH,
THEY'RE GOING TO SHIP ME OFF TO BOARDING SCHOOL, PERIOD.
For real?
IS THAT WHAT IT'S LIKE TO BE A DOCTOR'S KID?
WELL, I DON'T KNOW ABOUT OTHER FAMILIES.
BUT IT'S NOT LIKE I'M TAKING OVER THE FAMILY BUSINESS.
I'M THE *SECOND* SON.

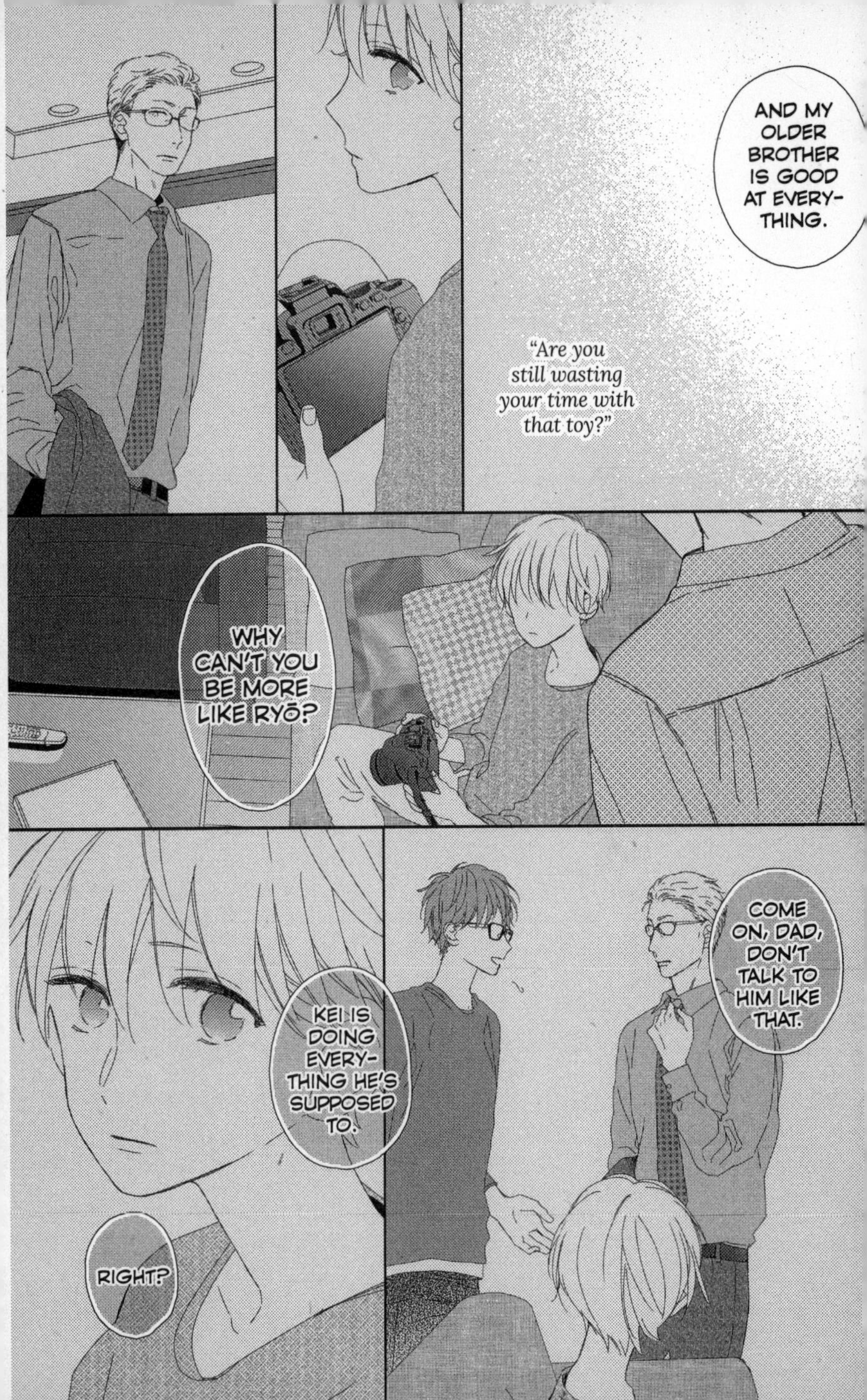
AND MY OLDER BROTHER IS GOOD AT EVERY-THING.
"Are you still wasting your time with that toy?"
WHY CAN'T YOU BE MORE LIKE RYŌ?
COME ON, DAD, DON'T TALK TO HIM LIKE THAT.
KEI IS DOING EVERY-THING HE'S SUPPOSED TO.
RIGHT?

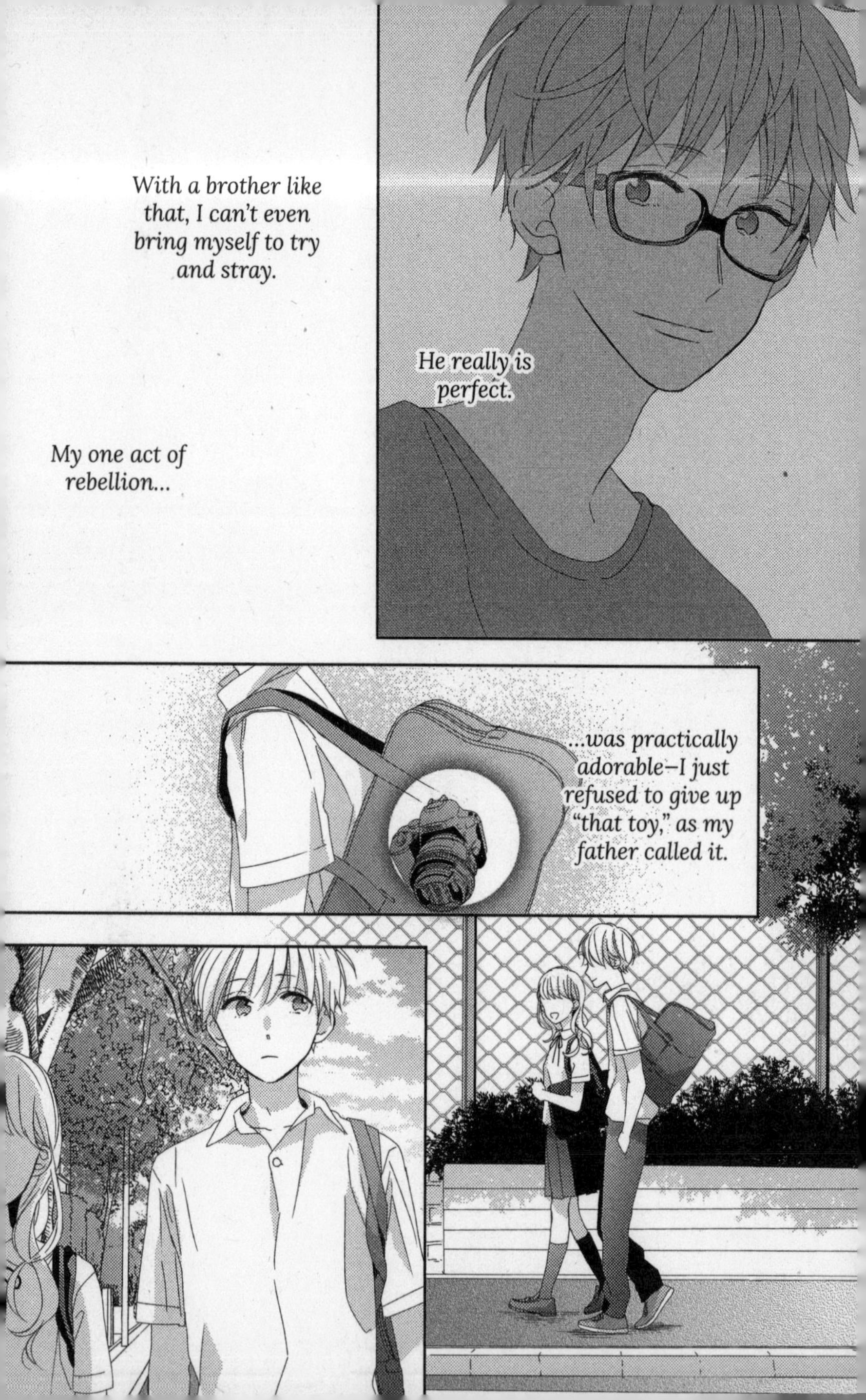
He really is perfect.
With a brother like that, I can't even bring myself to try and stray.
My one act of rebellion...
...was practically adorable—I just refused to give up "that toy," as my father called it.

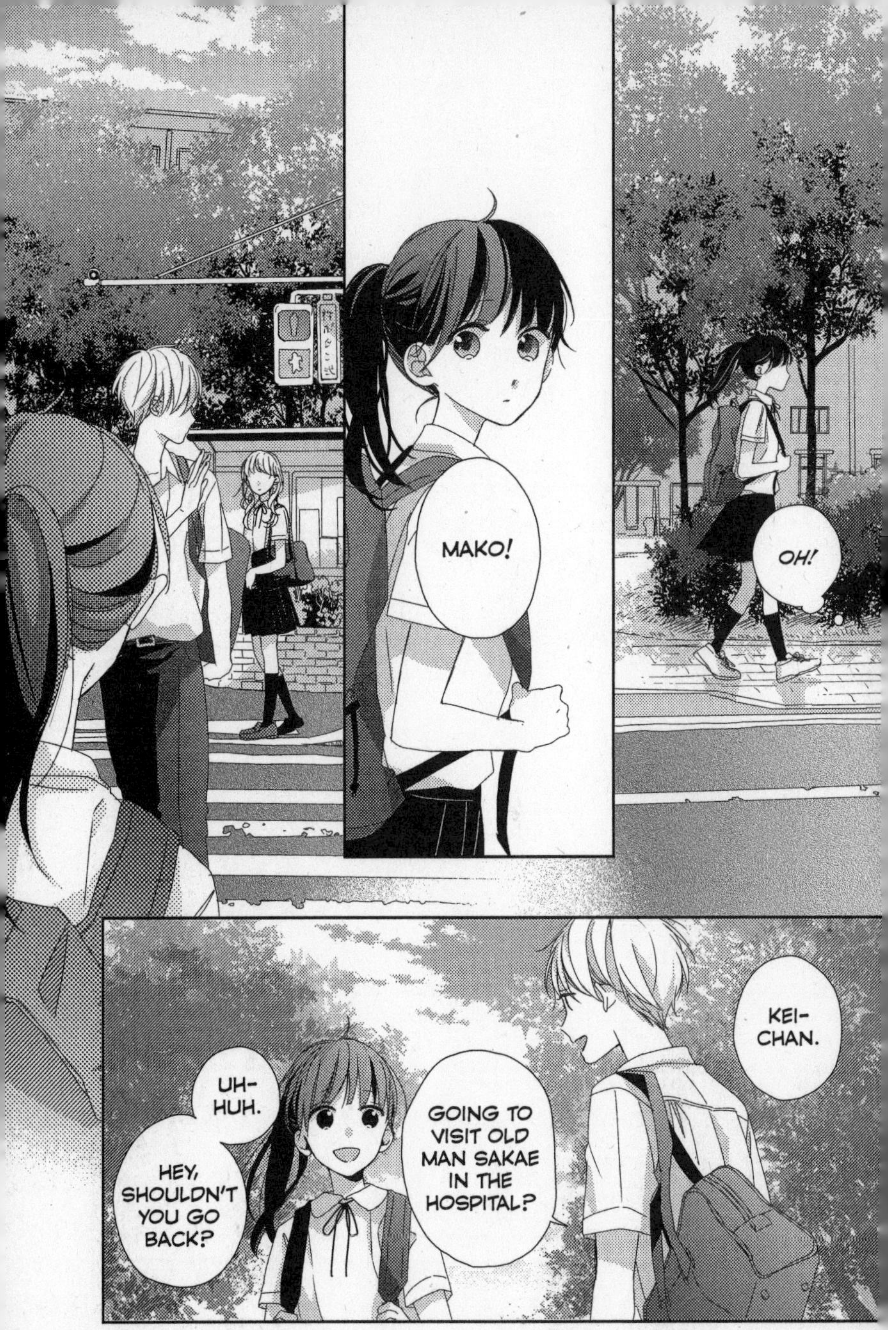
OH!
MAKO!
KEI-CHAN.
GOING TO VISIT OLD MAN SAKAE IN THE HOSPITAL?
UH-HUH.
HEY, SHOULDN'T YOU GO BACK?

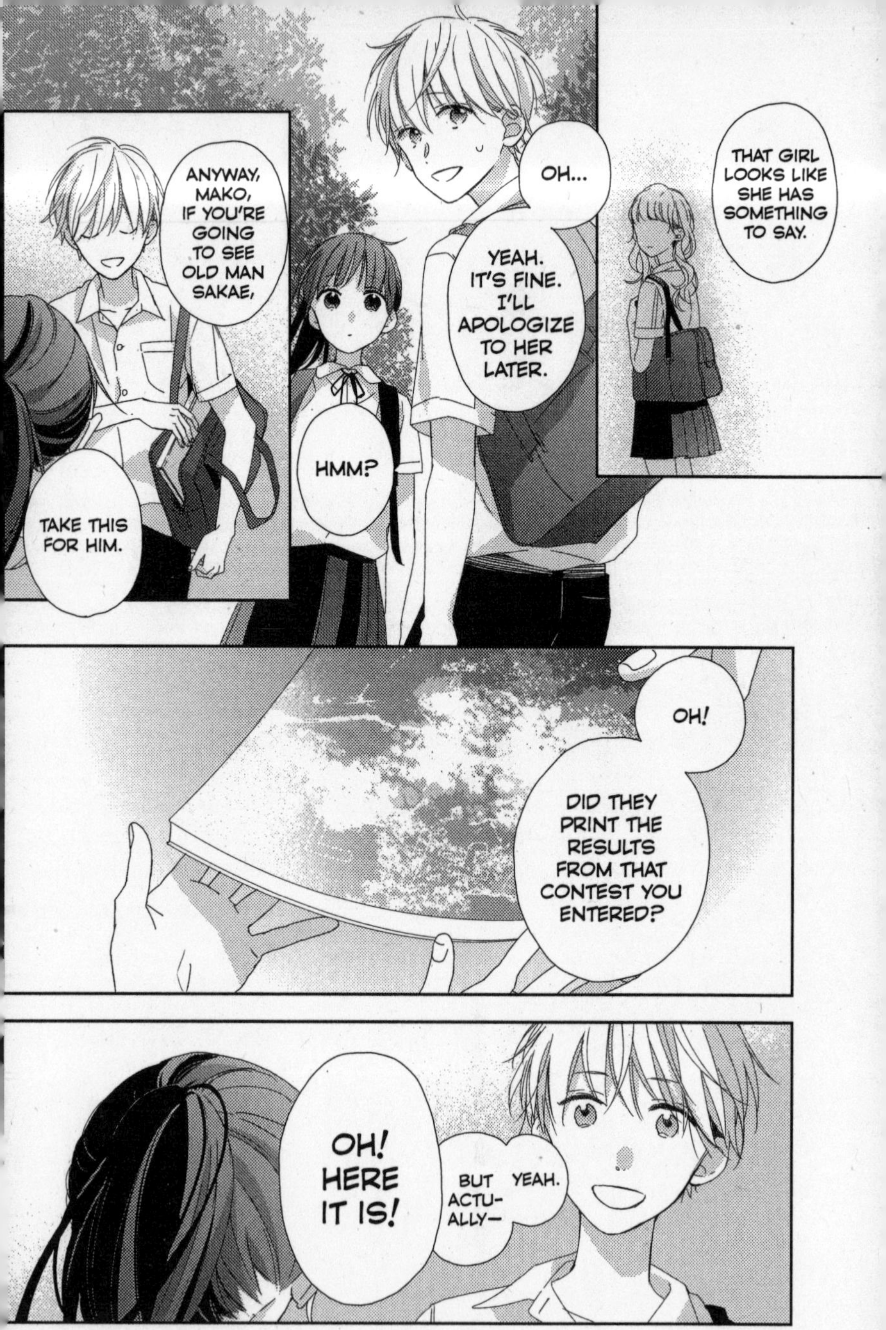
THAT GIRL LOOKS LIKE SHE HAS SOMETHING TO SAY.
OH...
YEAH. IT'S FINE. I'LL APOLOGIZE TO HER LATER.
HMM?
ANYWAY, MAKO, IF YOU'RE GOING TO SEE OLD MAN SAKAE,
TAKE THIS FOR HIM.
OH!
DID THEY PRINT THE RESULTS FROM THAT CONTEST YOU ENTERED?
YEAH.
BUT ACTUALLY—
OH! HERE IT IS!

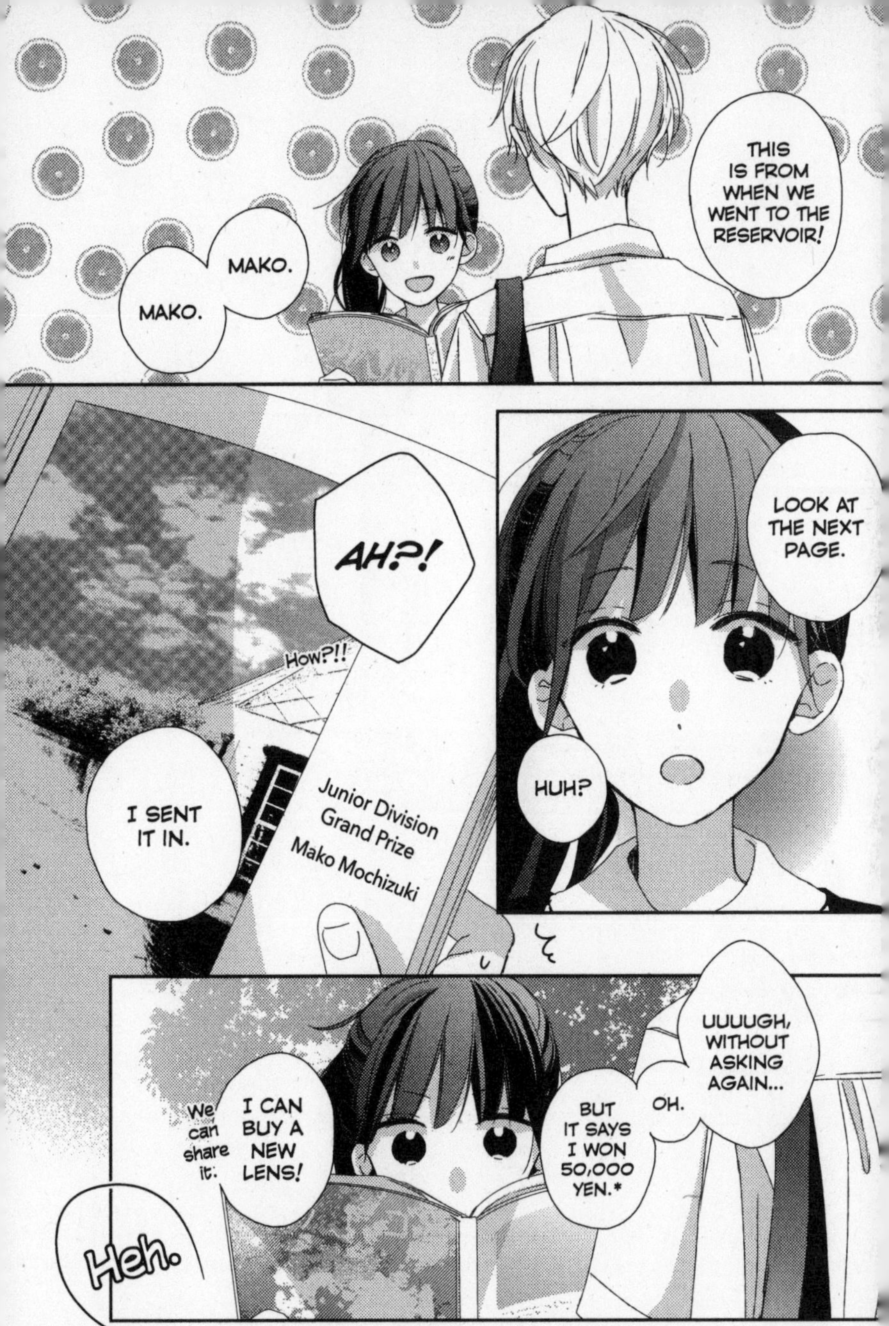
THIS IS FROM WHEN WE WENT TO THE RESERVOIR!
MAKO.
MAKO.
LOOK AT THE NEXT PAGE.
HUH?
AH?!
How?!!
Junior Division Grand Prize Mako Mochizuki
I SENT IT IN.
UUUUGH, WITHOUT ASKING AGAIN...
OH.
BUT IT SAYS I WON 50,000 YEN.*
I CAN BUY A NEW LENS!
We can share it.
Heh.

*About $500

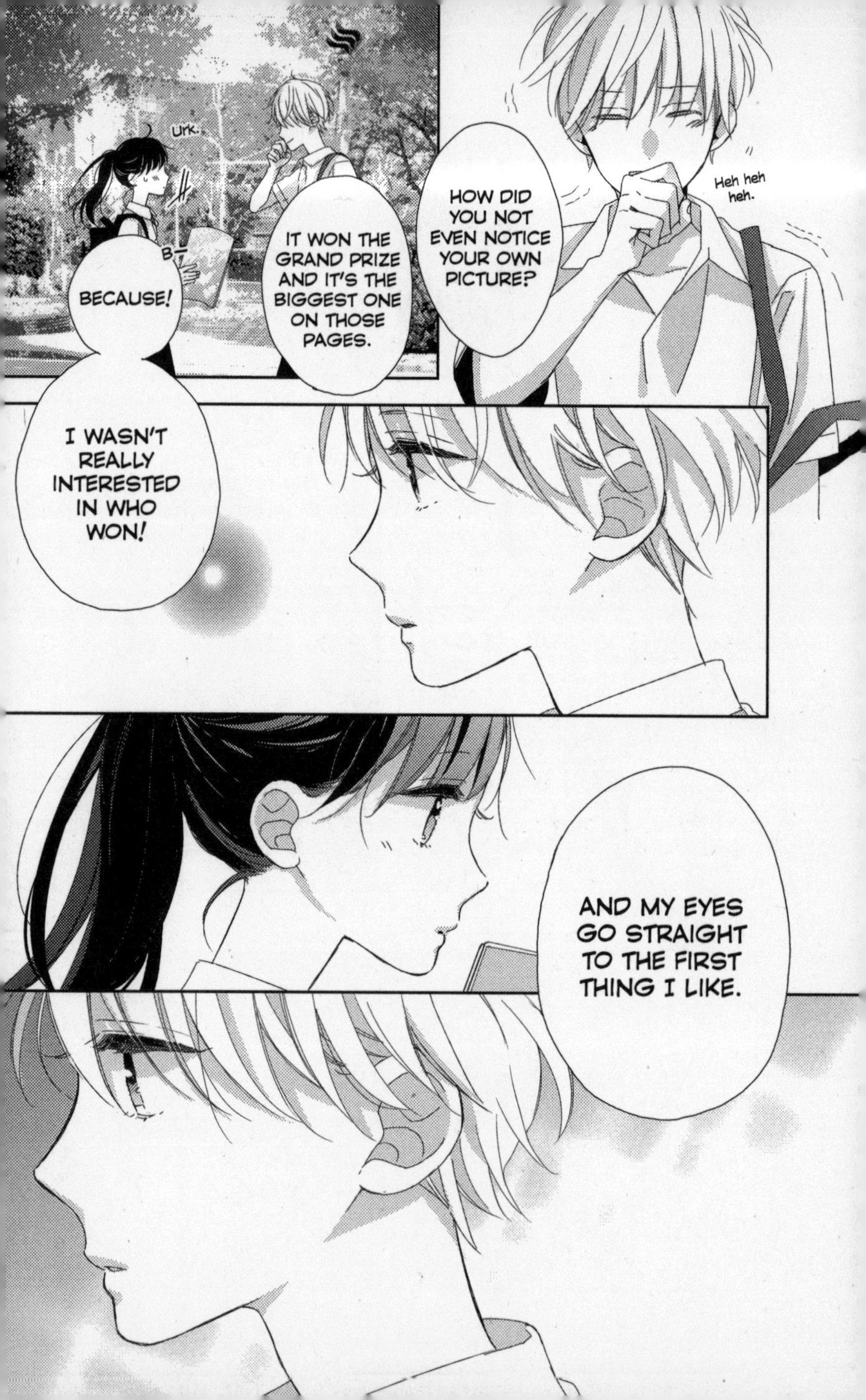
Heh heh heh.
HOW DID YOU NOT EVEN NOTICE YOUR OWN PICTURE?
IT WON THE GRAND PRIZE AND IT'S THE BIGGEST ONE ON THOSE PAGES.
Urk.
B—
BECAUSE!
I WASN'T REALLY INTERESTED IN WHO WON!
AND MY EYES GO STRAIGHT TO THE FIRST THING I LIKE.

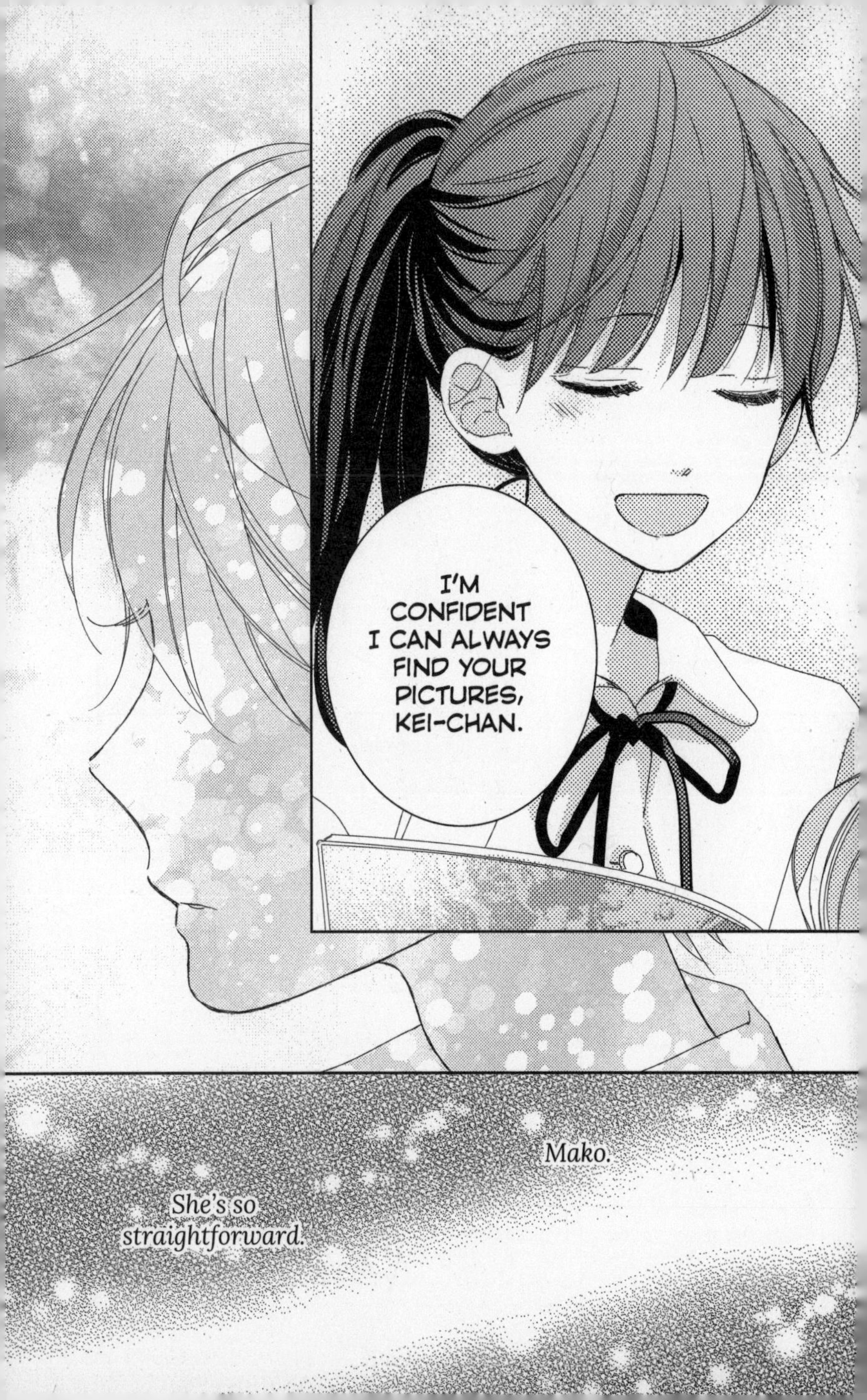
I'M CONFIDENT I CAN ALWAYS FIND YOUR PICTURES, KEI-CHAN.
Mako.
She's so straightforward.

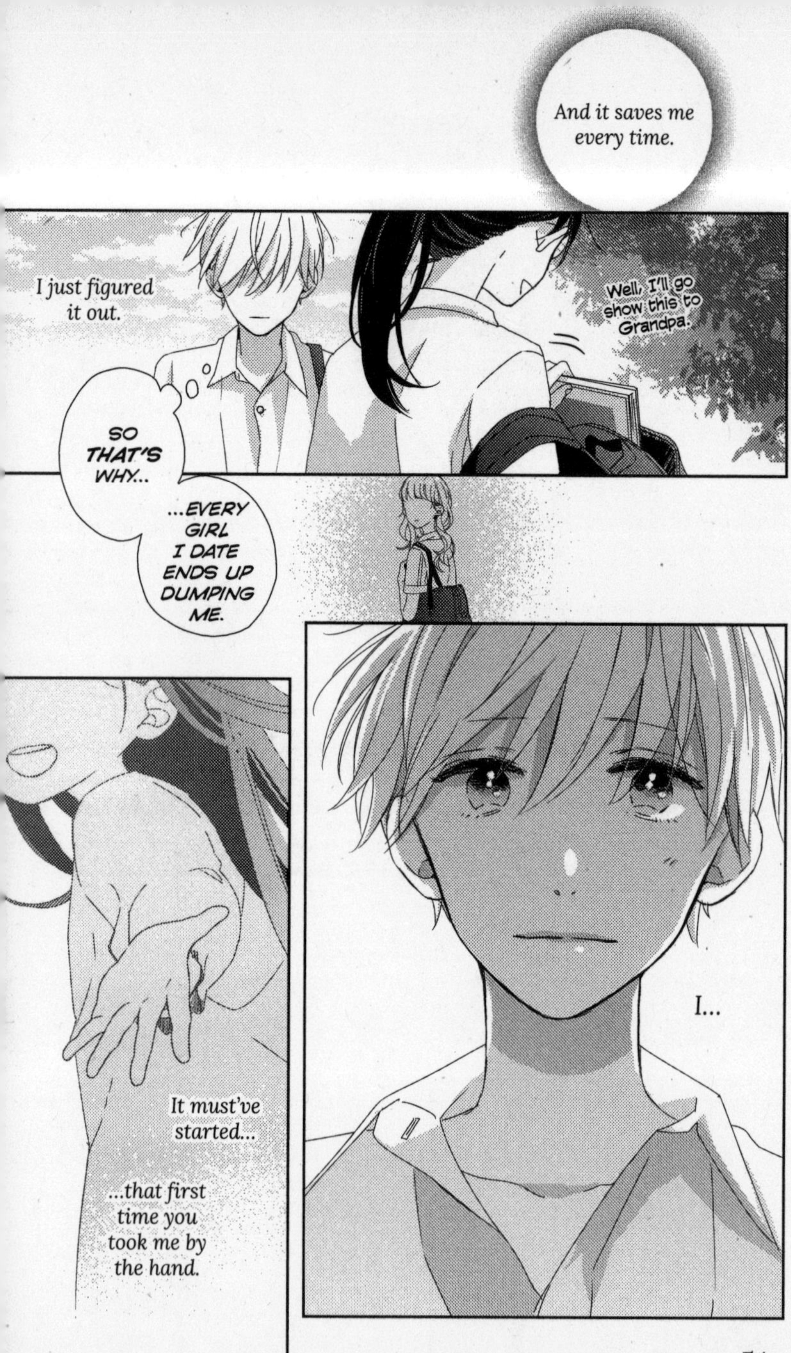
And it saves me every time.
Well, I'll go show this to Grandpa.
I just figured it out.
SO THAT'S WHY...
...EVERY GIRL I DATE ENDS UP DUMPING ME.
I...
It must've started...
...that first time you took me by the hand.

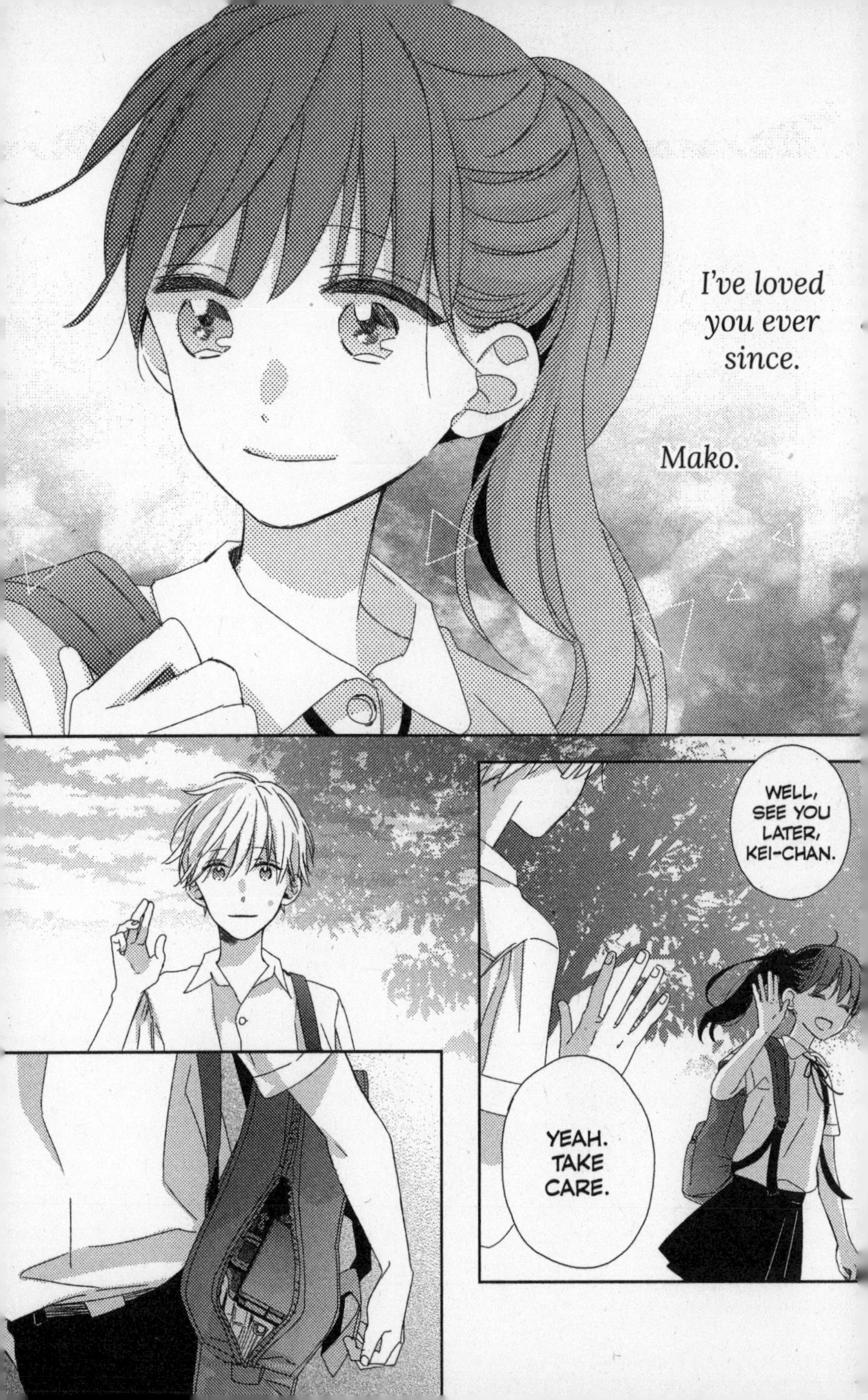
I've loved you ever since.
Mako.
WELL, SEE YOU LATER, KEI-CHAN.
YEAH. TAKE CARE.

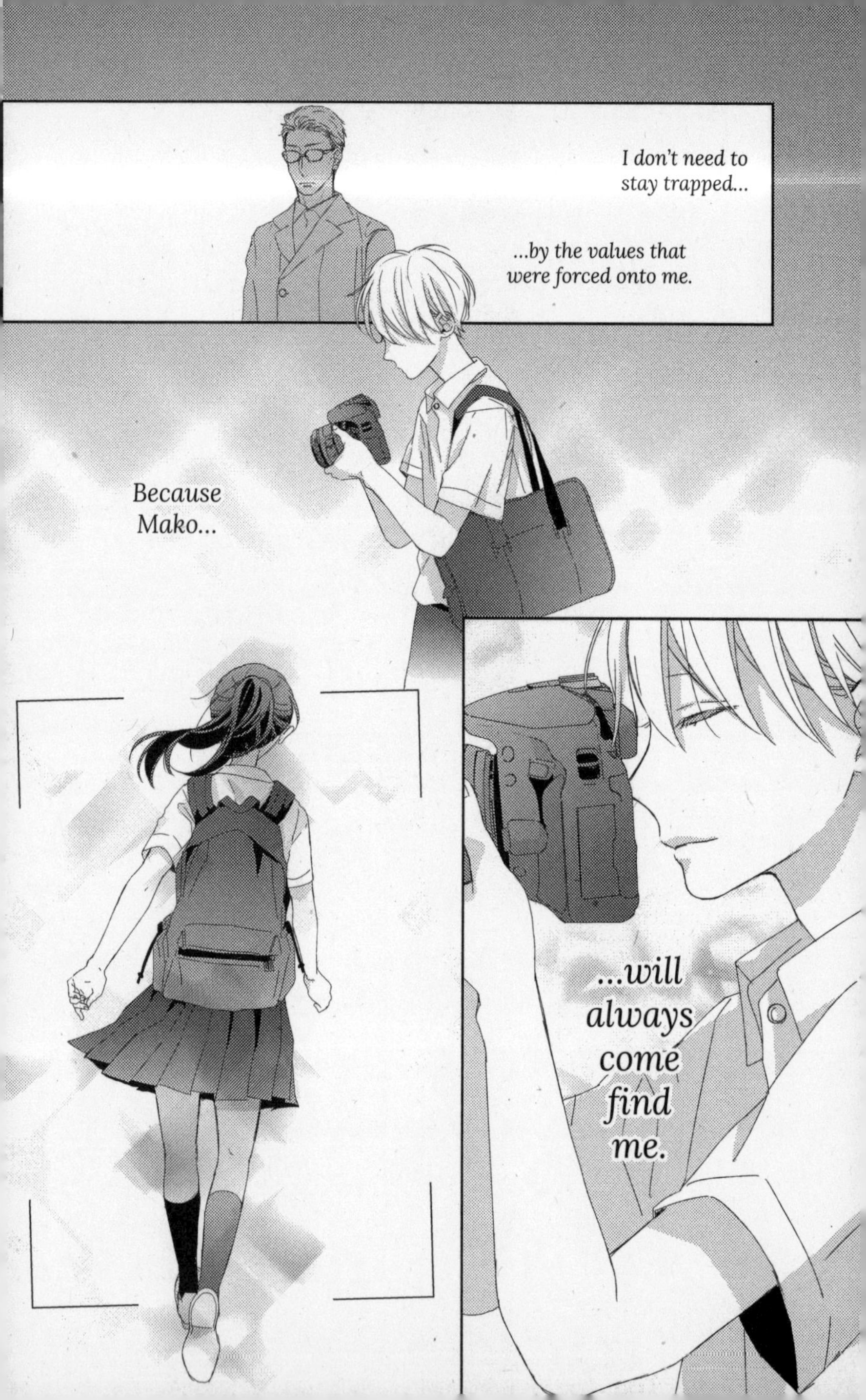
I don't need to stay trapped...
...by the values that were forced onto me.
Because Mako...
...will always come find me.

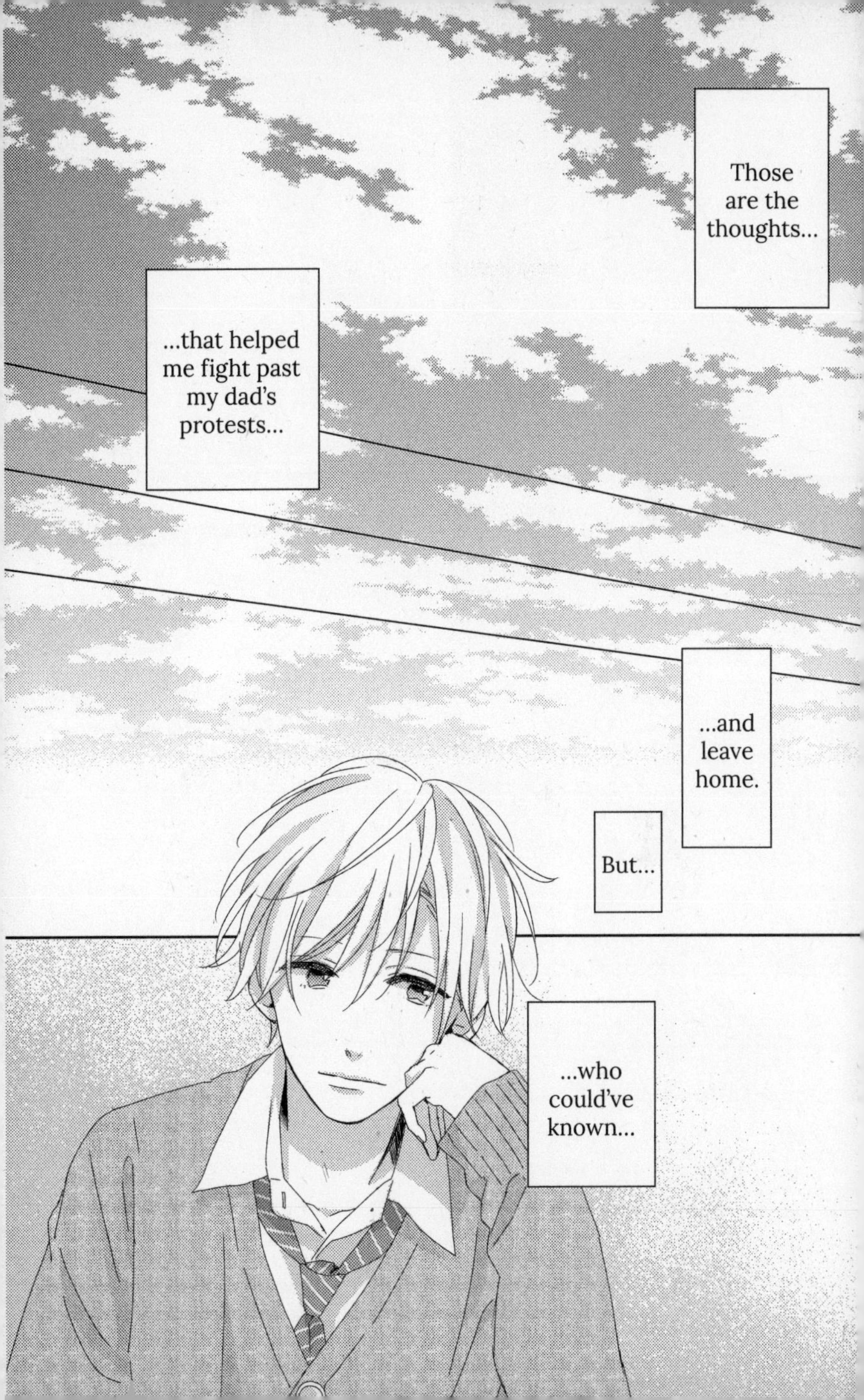
Those are the thoughts...
...that helped me fight past my dad's protests...
...and leave home.
But...
...who could've known...

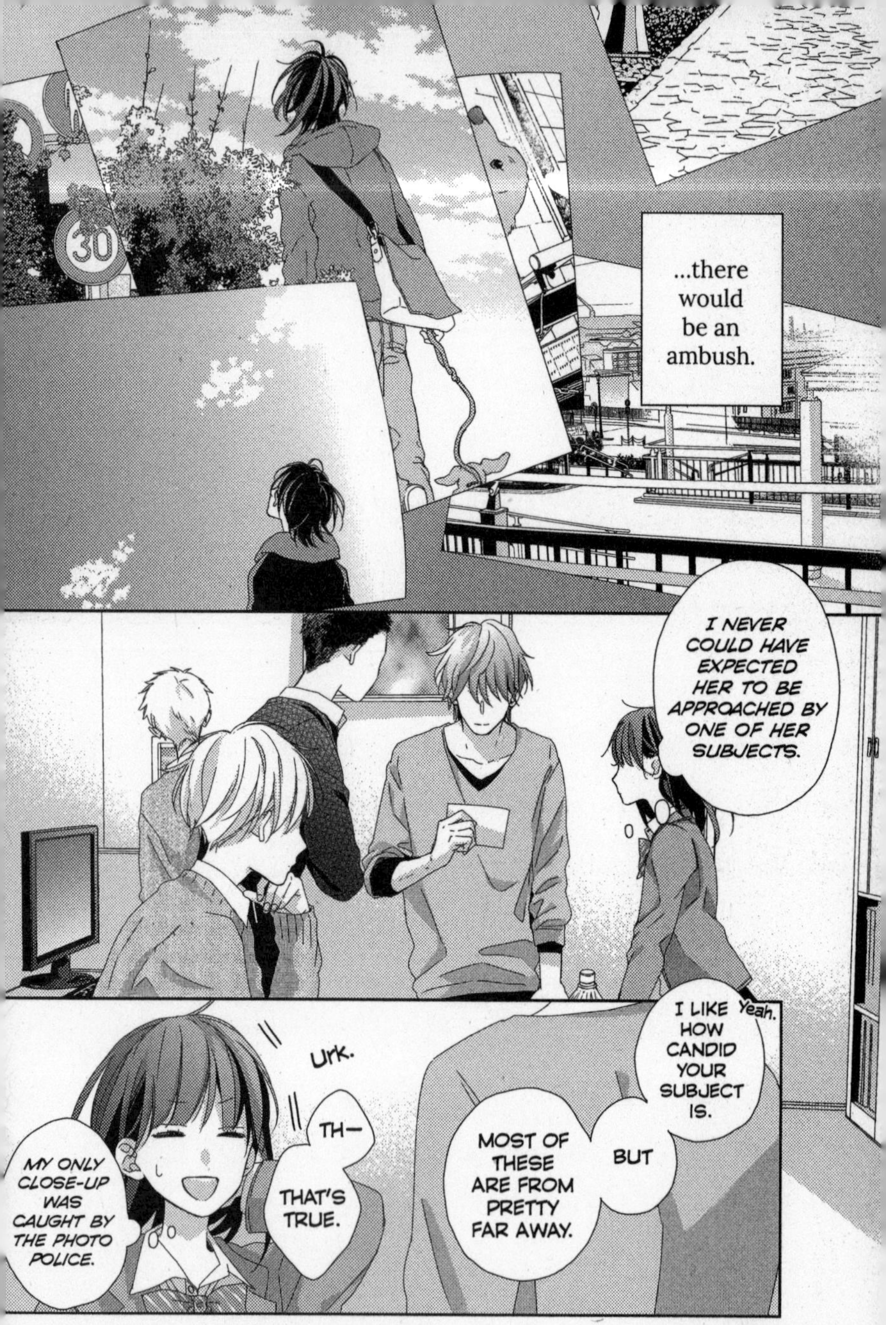
...there would be an ambush.
I NEVER COULD HAVE EXPECTED HER TO BE APPROACHED BY ONE OF HER SUBJECTS.
Yeah.
I LIKE HOW CANDID YOUR SUBJECT IS.
BUT
MOST OF THESE ARE FROM PRETTY FAR AWAY.
Urk.
TH—
THAT'S TRUE.
MY ONLY CLOSE-UP WAS CAUGHT BY THE PHOTO POLICE.

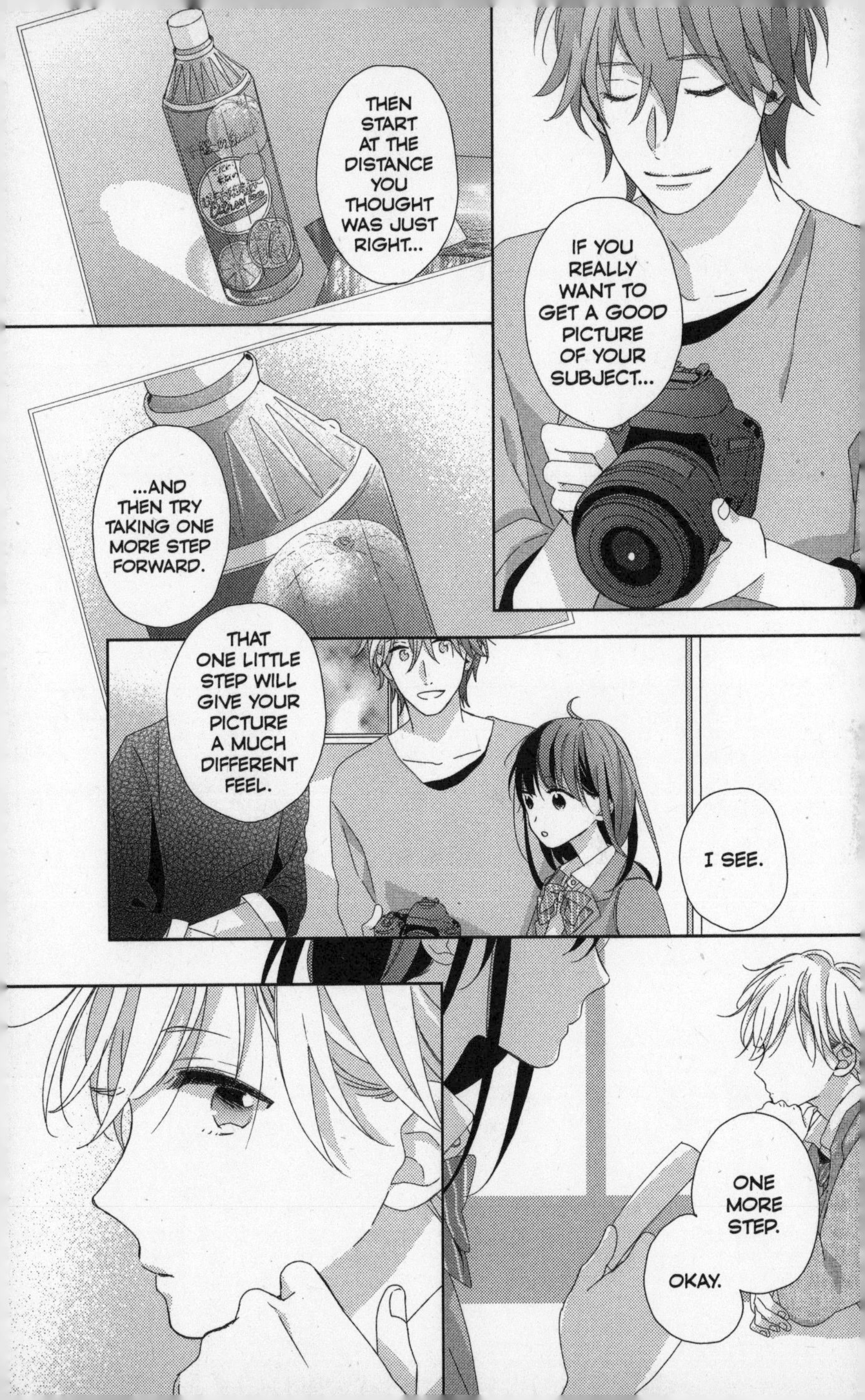
IF YOU REALLY WANT TO GET A GOOD PICTURE OF YOUR SUBJECT...
THEN START AT THE DISTANCE YOU THOUGHT WAS JUST RIGHT...
...AND THEN TRY TAKING ONE MORE STEP FORWARD.
THAT ONE LITTLE STEP WILL GIVE YOUR PICTURE A MUCH DIFFERENT FEEL.
I SEE.
ONE MORE STEP.
OKAY.

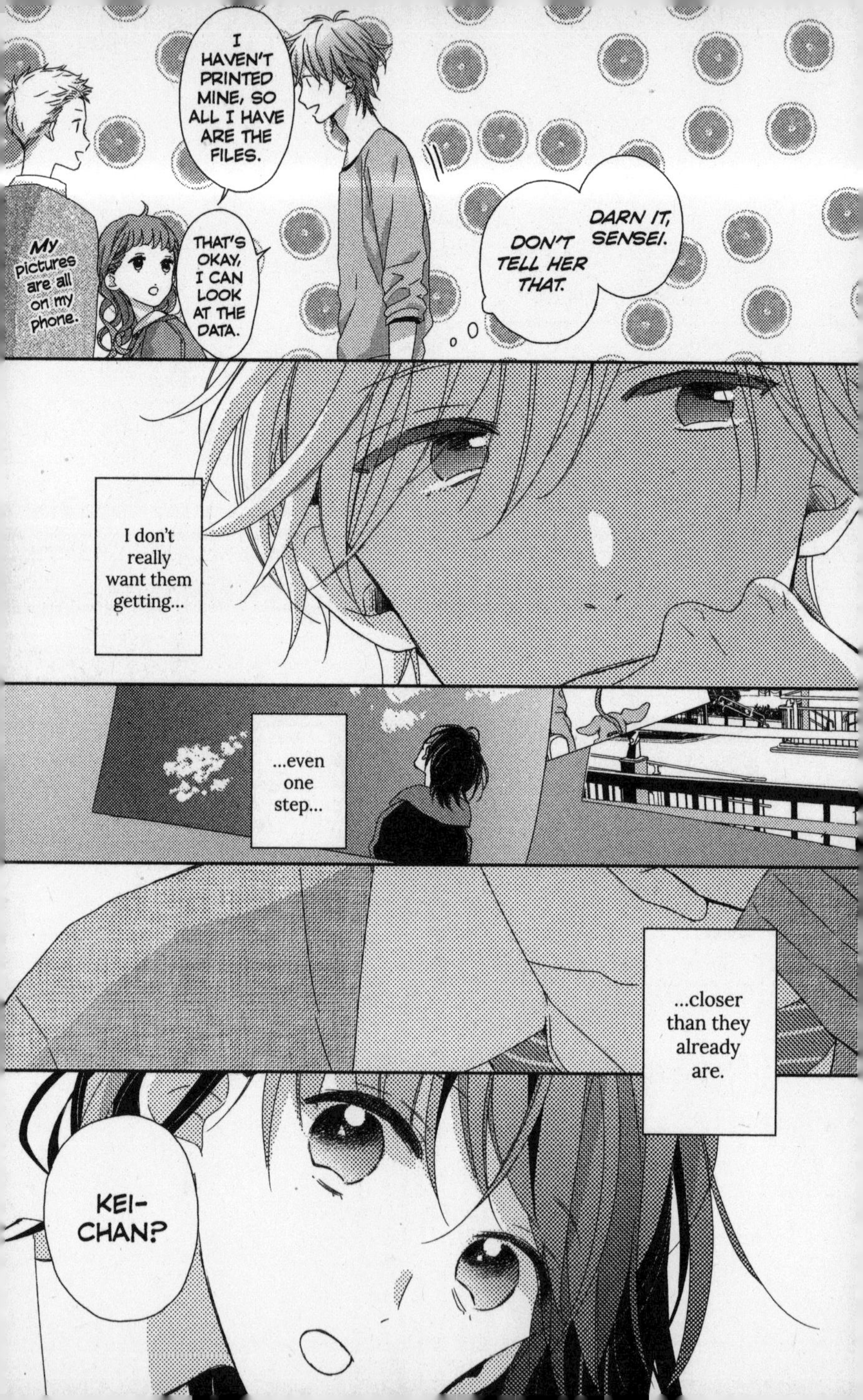
I HAVEN'T PRINTED MINE, SO ALL I HAVE ARE THE FILES.
THAT'S OKAY, I CAN LOOK AT THE DATA.
DARN IT, SENSEI. DON'T TELL HER THAT.
My pictures are all on my phone.
I don't really want them getting...
...even one step...
...closer than they already are.
KEI-CHAN?

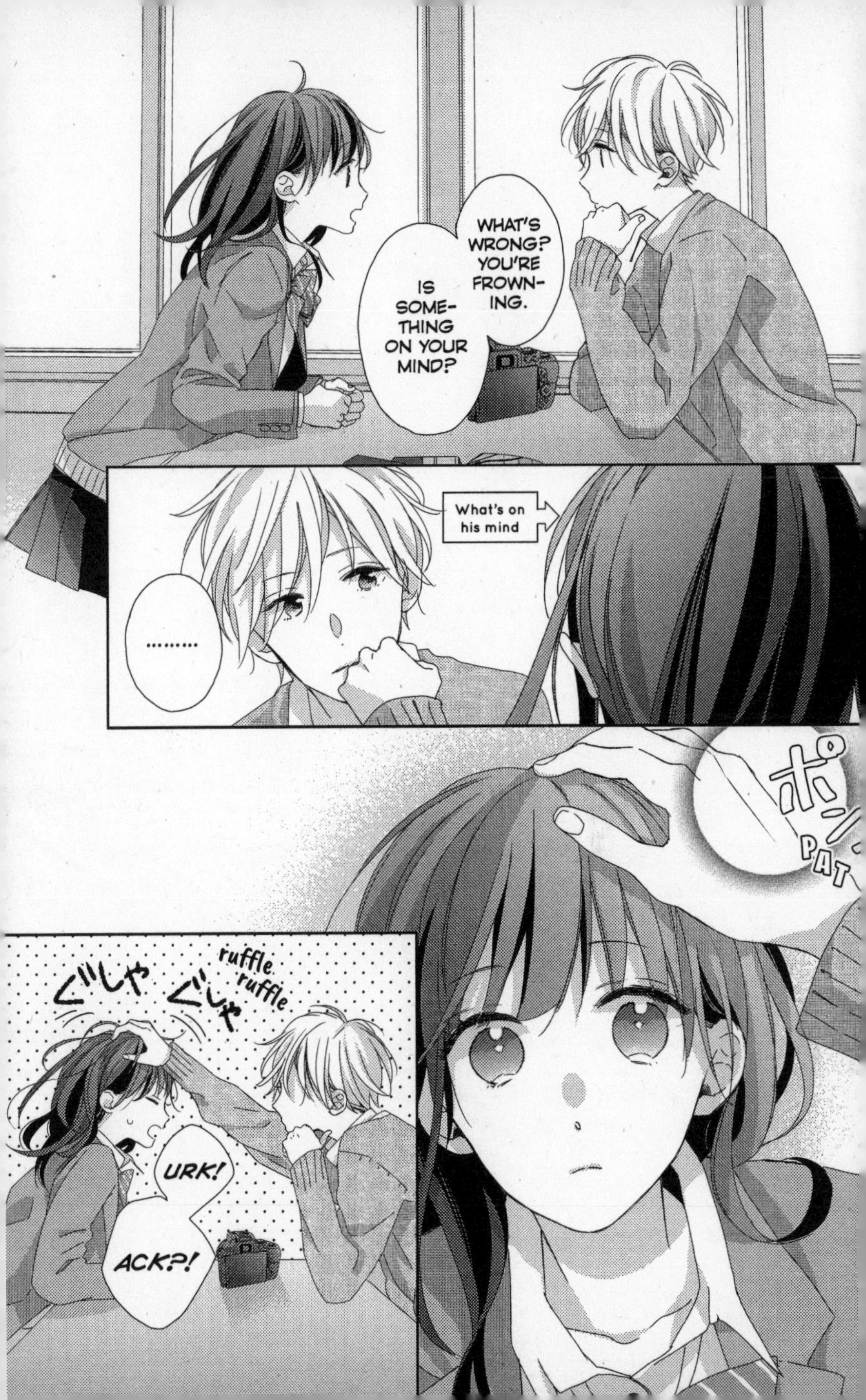
WHAT'S WRONG? YOU'RE FROWNING.
IS SOMETHING ON YOUR MIND?
What's on his mind
....
ポン
PAT
ぐしゃ ぐしゃ
ruffle ruffle
URK!
ACK?!

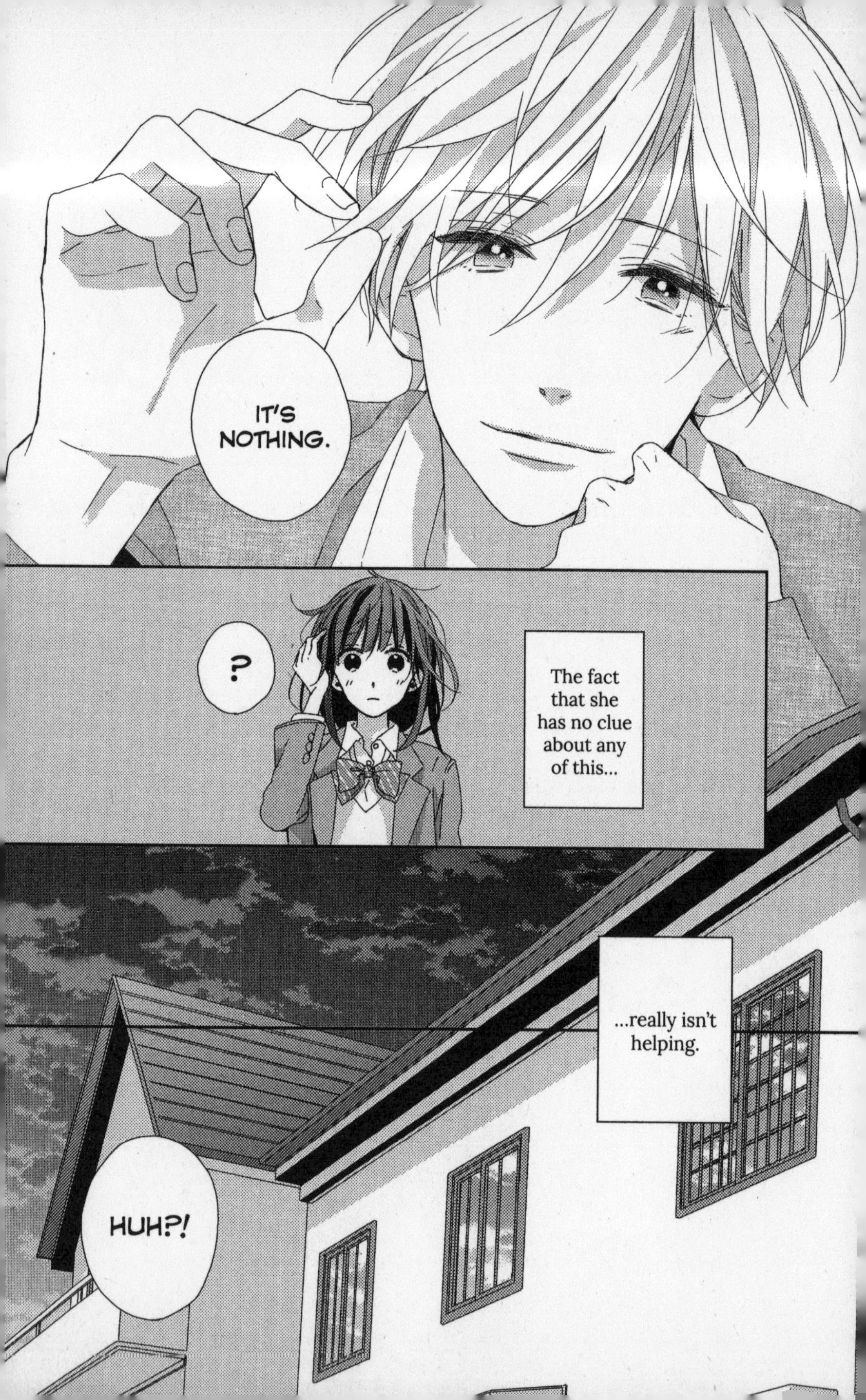
IT'S NOTHING.
The fact that she has no clue about any of this...
?
...really isn't helping.
HUH?!

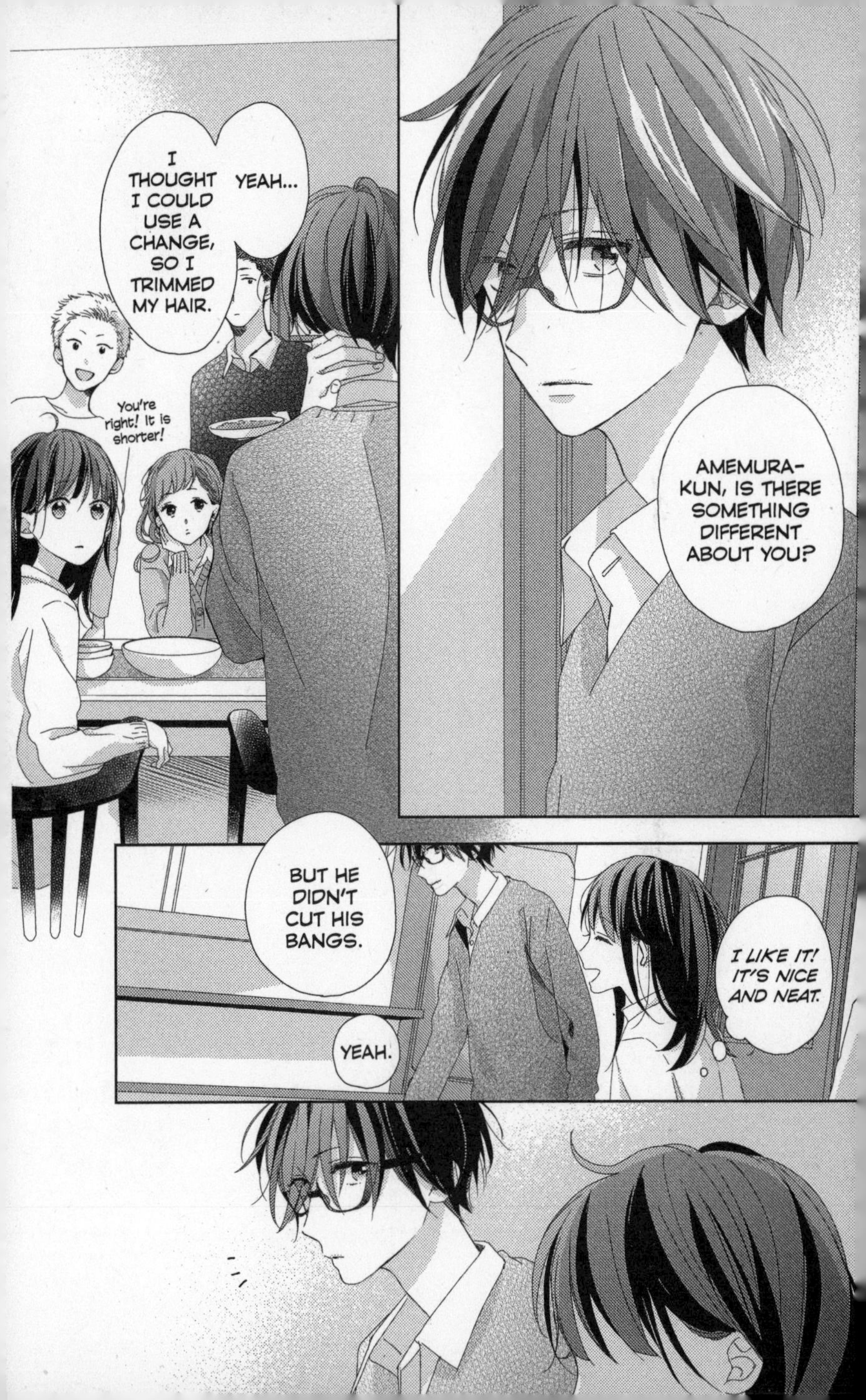
AMEMURA-KUN, IS THERE SOMETHING DIFFERENT ABOUT YOU?
YEAH...
I THOUGHT I COULD USE A CHANGE, SO I TRIMMED MY HAIR.
You're right! It is shorter!
I LIKE IT! IT'S NICE AND NEAT.
BUT HE DIDN'T CUT HIS BANGS.
YEAH.

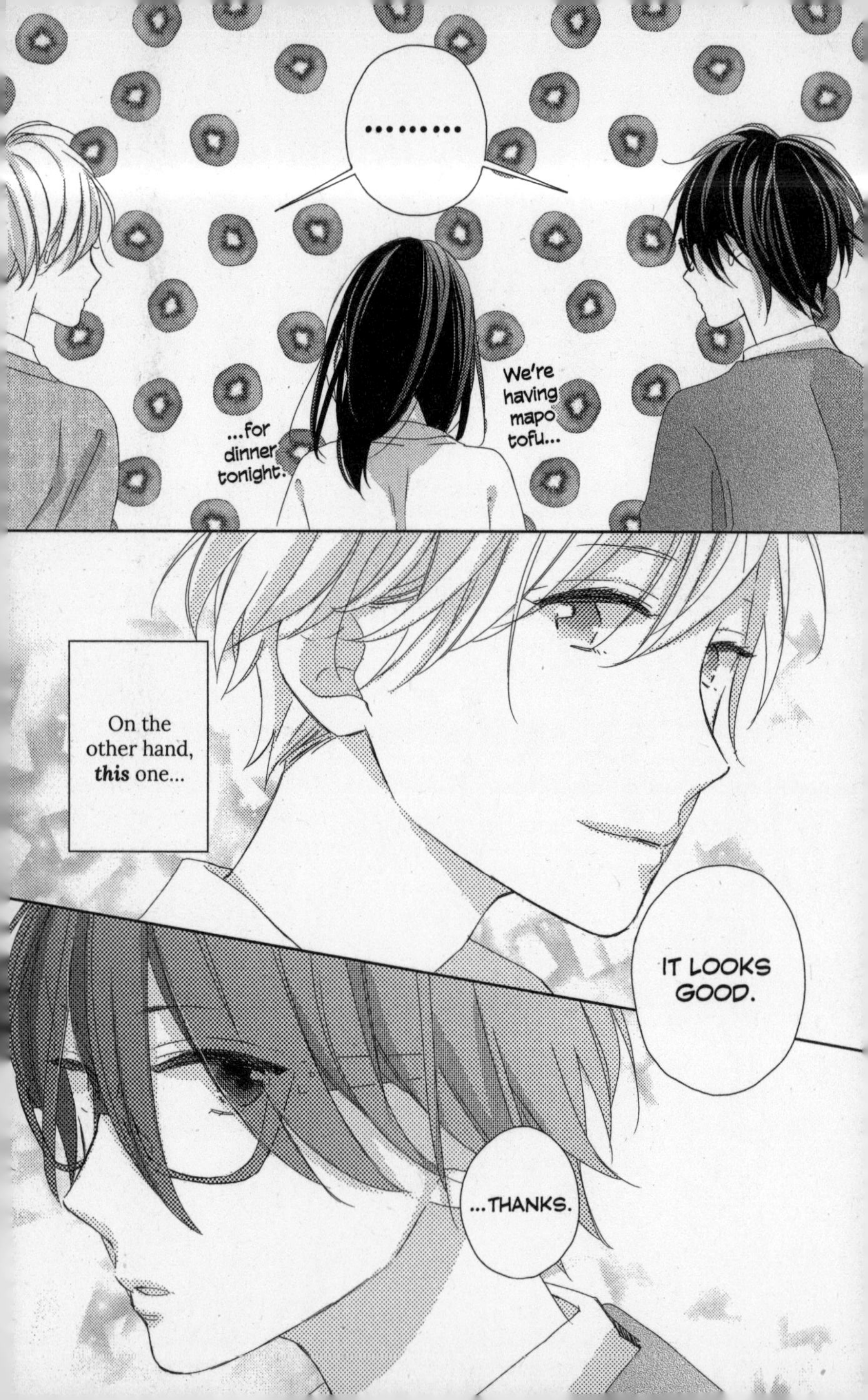
....
We're having mapo tofu...
...for dinner tonight.
On the other hand, *this* one...
IT LOOKS GOOD.
...THANKS.

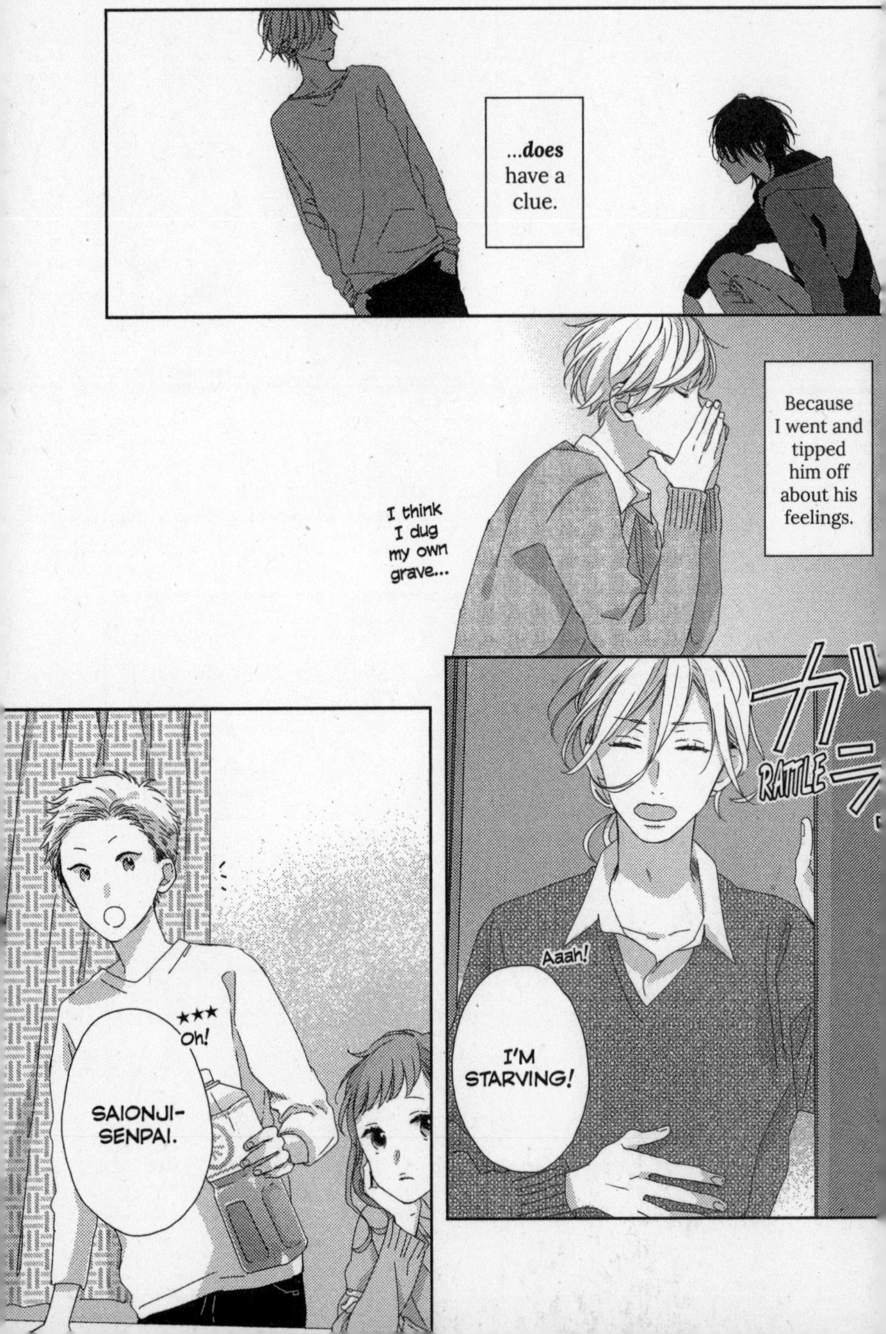
...**does** have a clue.
Because I went and tipped him off about his feelings.
I think I dug my own grave...
RATTLE
Aaah!
I'M STARVING!
Oh!
SAIONJI-SENPAI.

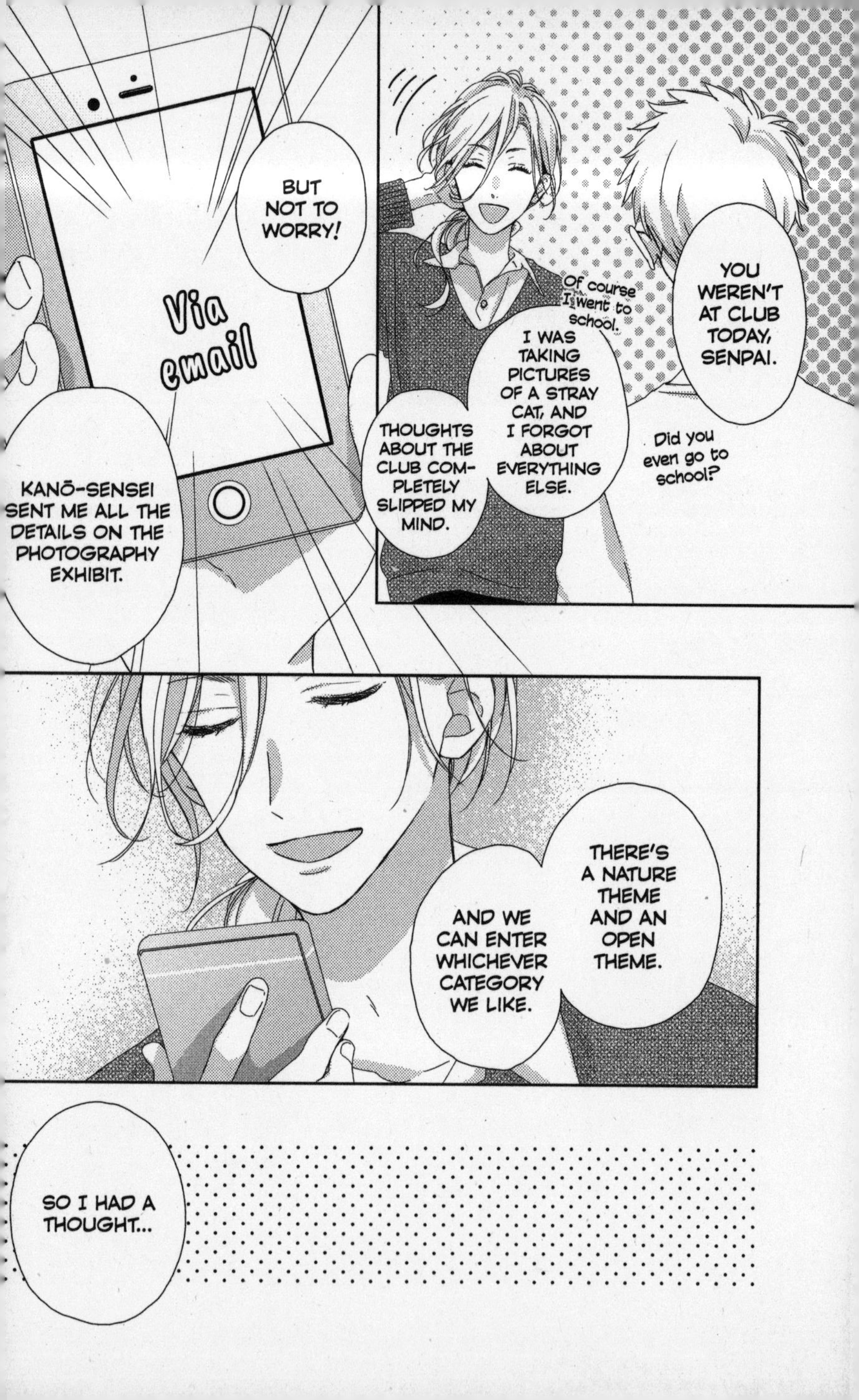
YOU WEREN'T AT CLUB TODAY, SENPAI.
Did you even go to school?
Of course I went to school.
I WAS TAKING PICTURES OF A STRAY CAT, AND I FORGOT ABOUT EVERYTHING ELSE.
THOUGHTS ABOUT THE CLUB COM-PLETELY SLIPPED MY MIND.
BUT NOT TO WORRY!
Via email
KANŌ-SENSEI SENT ME ALL THE DETAILS ON THE PHOTOGRAPHY EXHIBIT.
THERE'S A NATURE THEME AND AN OPEN THEME.
AND WE CAN ENTER WHICHEVER CATEGORY WE LIKE.
SO I HAD A THOUGHT...

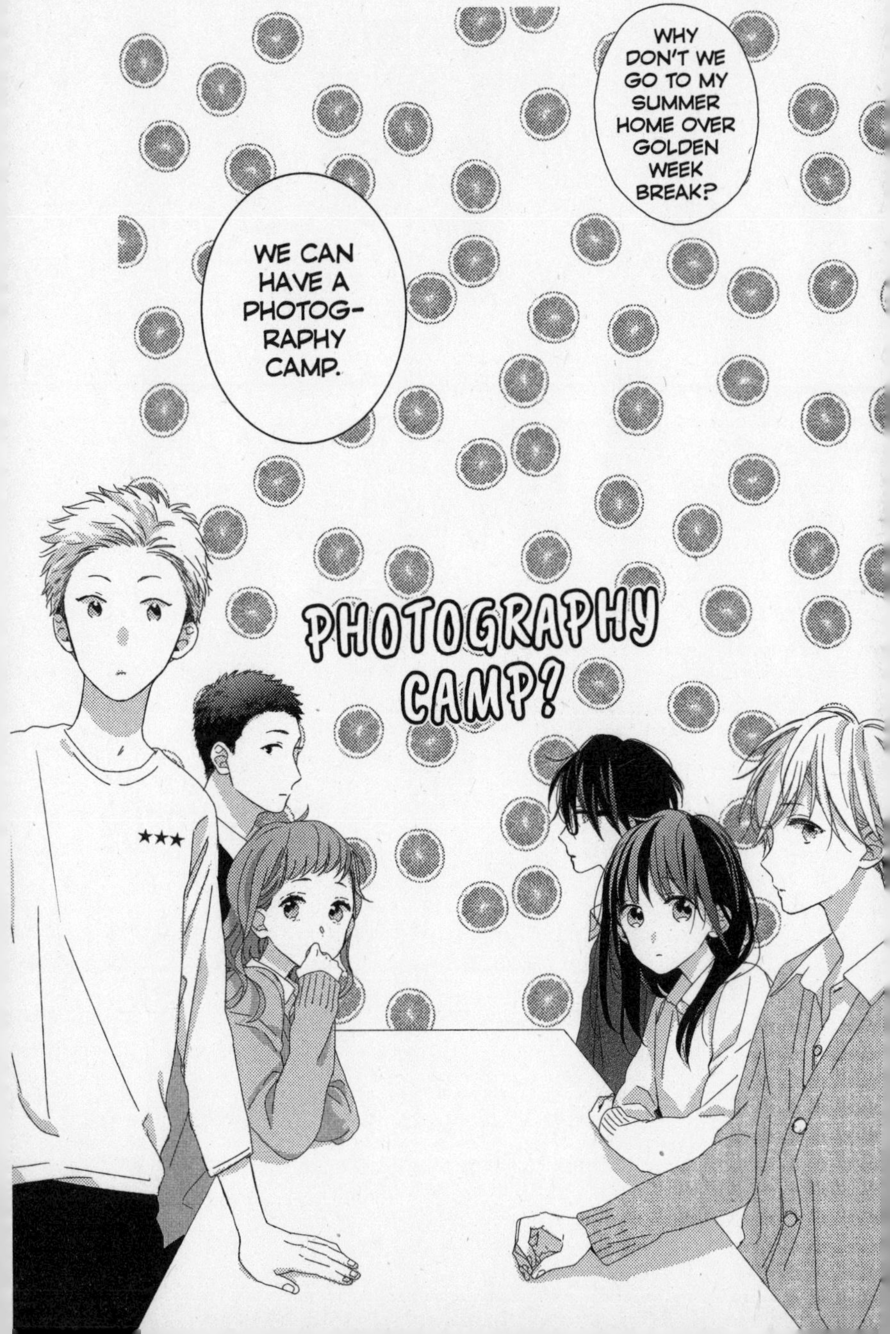
WHY DON'T WE GO TO MY SUMMER HOME OVER GOLDEN WEEK BREAK?
WE CAN HAVE A PHOTOG-RAPHY CAMP.
PHOTOGRAPHY CAMP?

LOVE IN FOCUS

FILM 7

The Pain in the Neck and the Cocky Little Brat

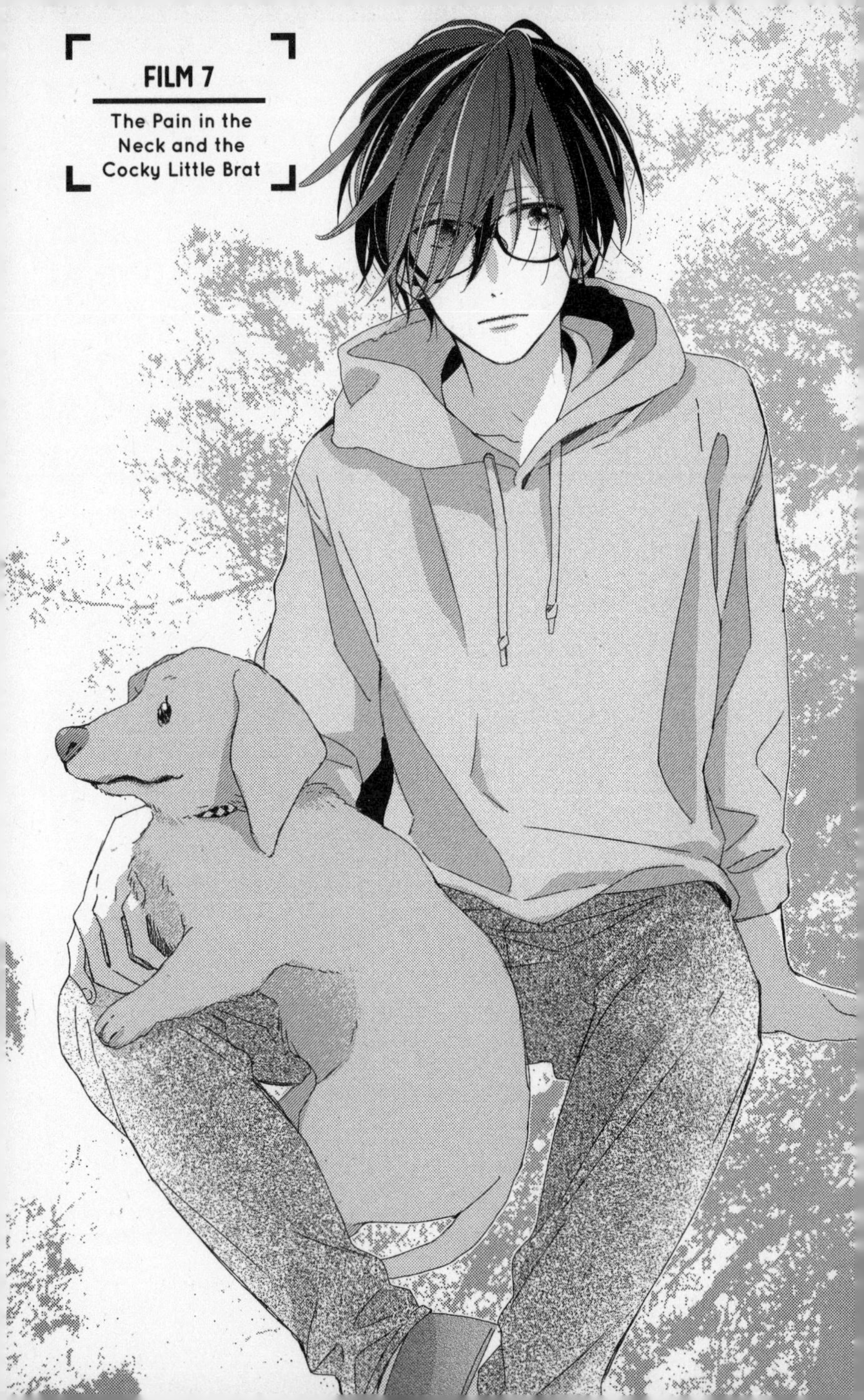

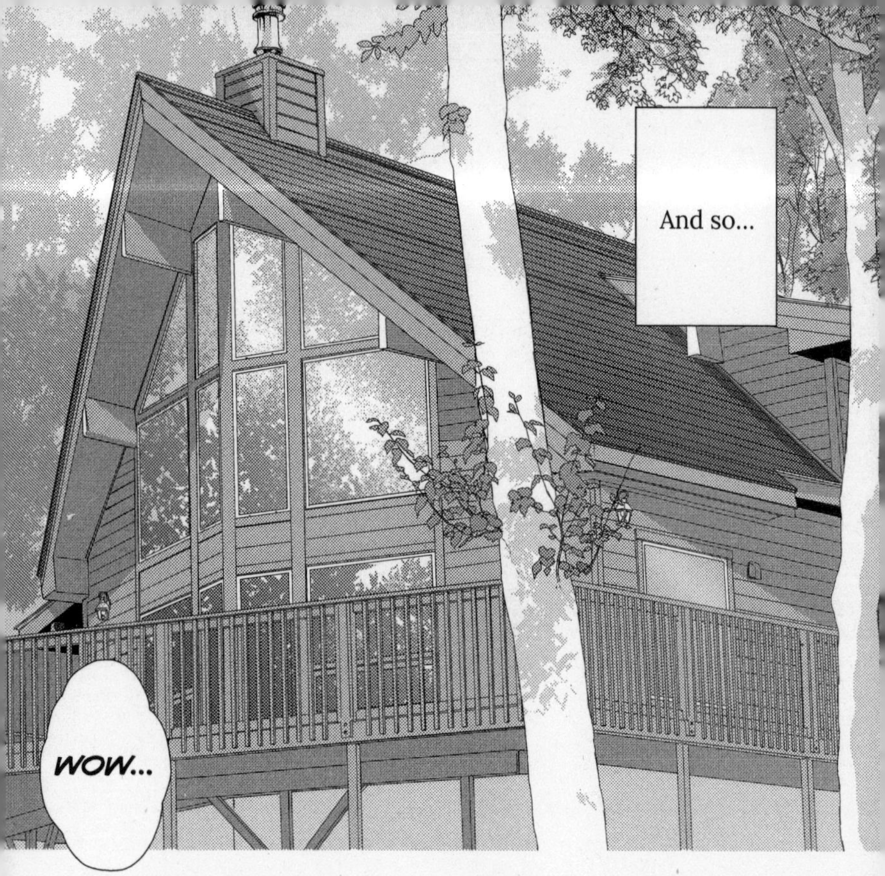
And so...
WOW...

LOVE IN FOCUS

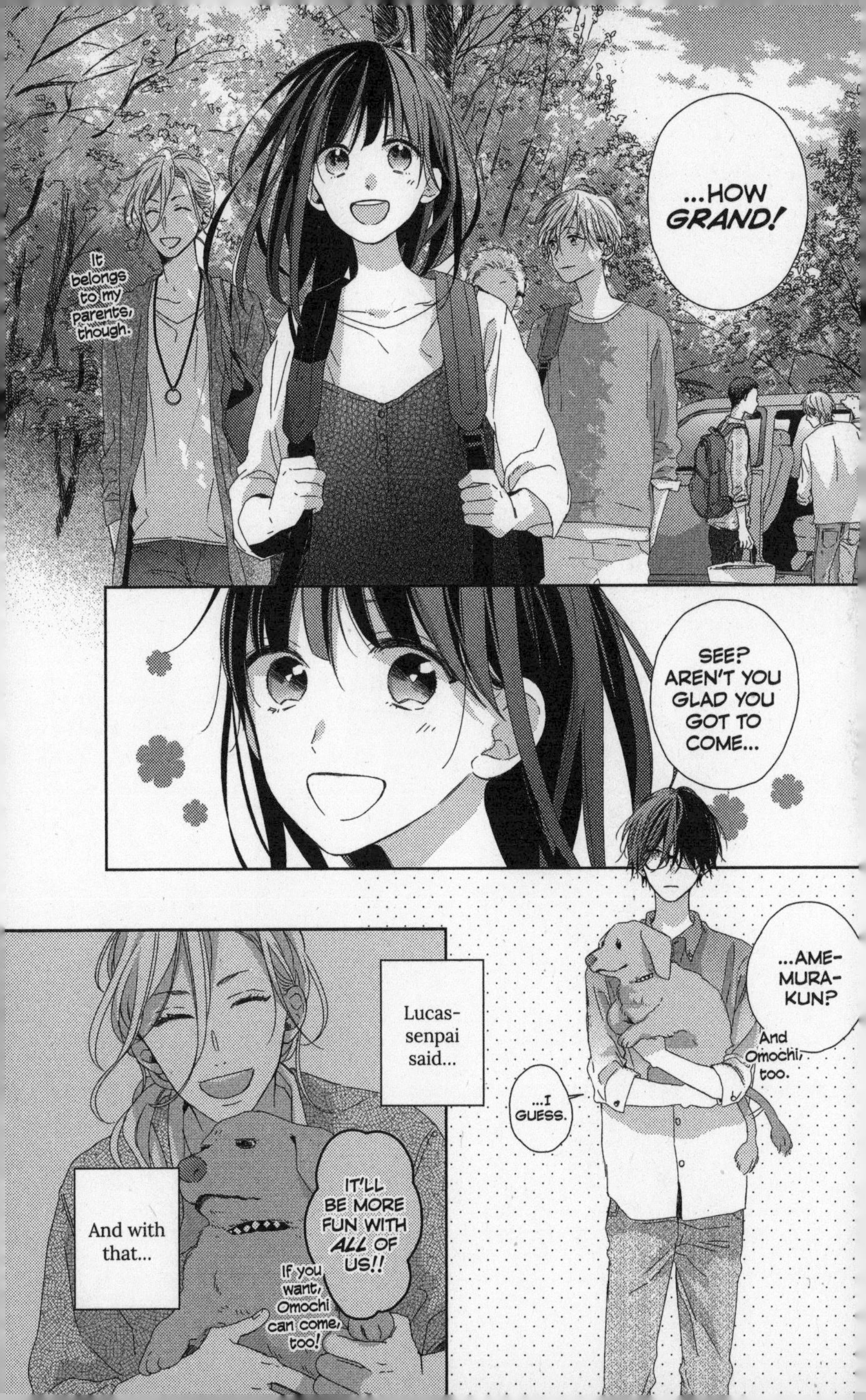
...HOW GRAND!
It belongs to my parents, though.
SEE? AREN'T YOU GLAD YOU GOT TO COME...
...AME-MURA-KUN?
And Omochi, too.
...I GUESS.
Lucas-senpai said...
IT'LL BE MORE FUN WITH ALL OF US!!
If you want, Omochi can come, too!
And with that...

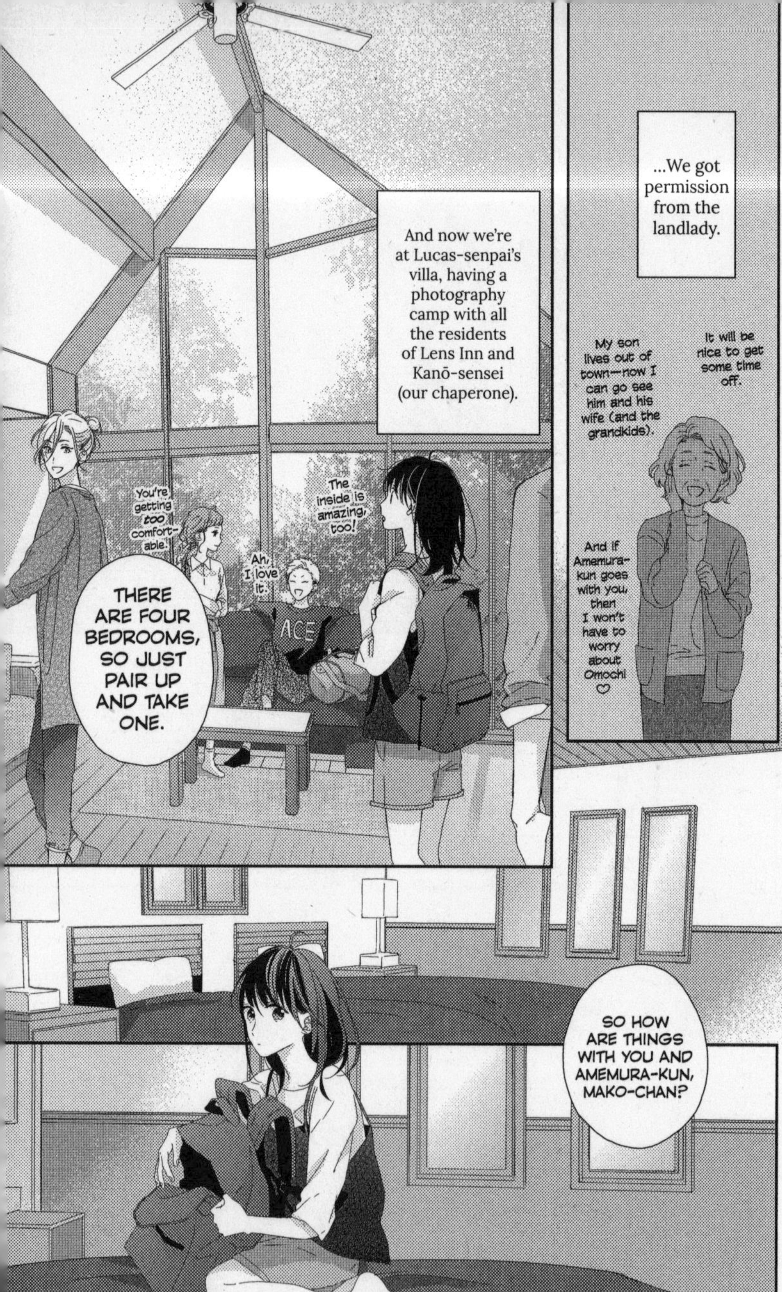
...We got permission from the landlady.
It will be nice to get some time off.
My son lives out of town—now I can go see him and his wife (and the grandkids).
And if Amemura-kun goes with you, then I won't have to worry about Omochi ♡
And now we're at Lucas-senpai's villa, having a photography camp with all the residents of Lens Inn and Kanō-sensei (our chaperone).
The inside is amazing, too!
Ah, I love it.
You're getting *too* comfortable.
THERE ARE FOUR BEDROOMS, SO JUST PAIR UP AND TAKE ONE.
SO HOW ARE THINGS WITH YOU AND AMEMURA-KUN, MAKO-CHAN?

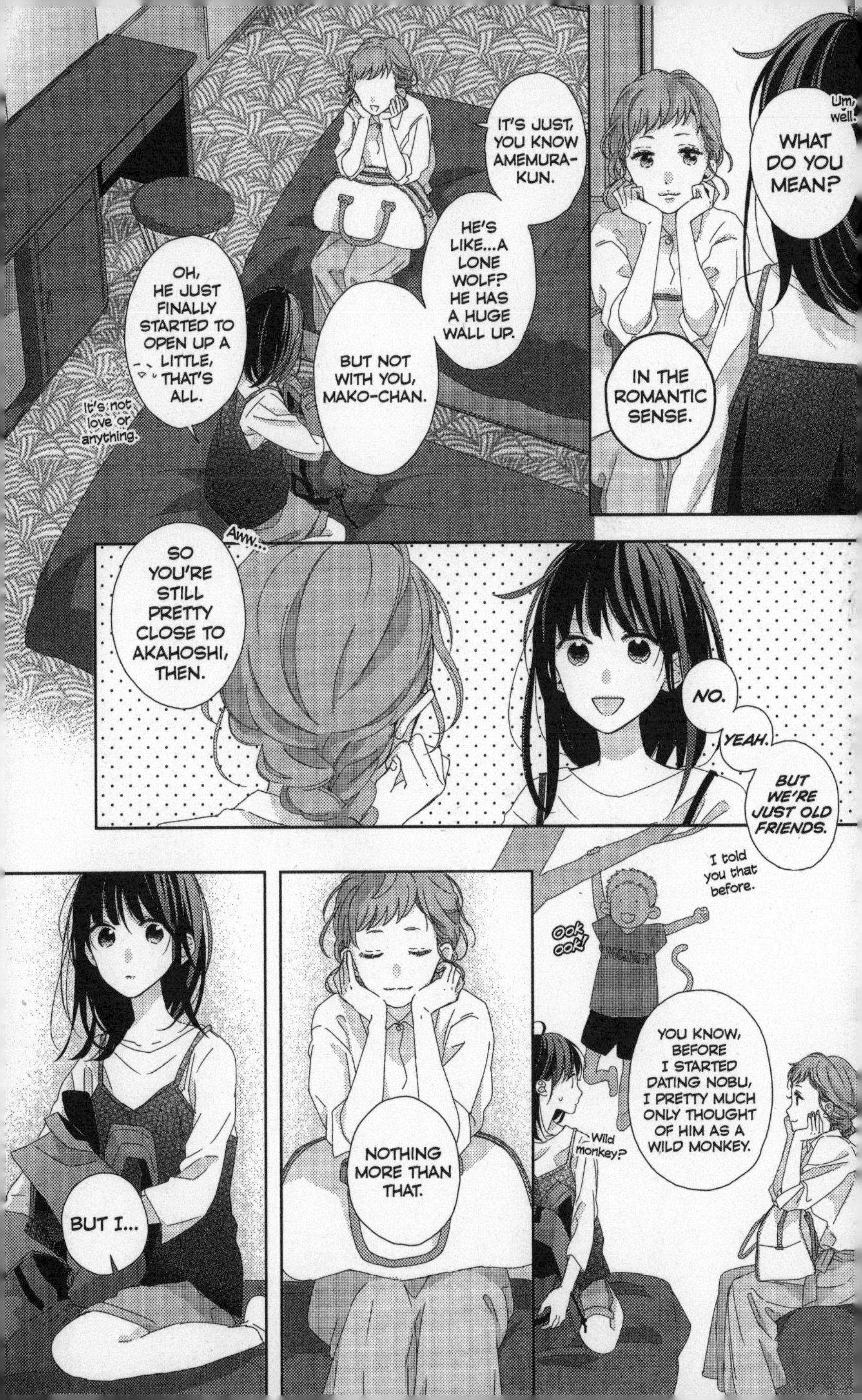
Um, well.
WHAT DO YOU MEAN?
IN THE ROMANTIC SENSE.
IT'S JUST, YOU KNOW AMEMURA-KUN.
HE'S LIKE...A LONE WOLF? HE HAS A HUGE WALL UP.
BUT NOT WITH YOU, MAKO-CHAN.
OH, HE JUST FINALLY STARTED TO OPEN UP A LITTLE, THAT'S ALL.
It's not love or anything.
Aww...
SO YOU'RE STILL PRETTY CLOSE TO AKAHOSHI, THEN.
NO.
YEAH.
BUT WE'RE JUST OLD FRIENDS.
I told you that before.
Ook ook!
YOU KNOW, BEFORE I STARTED DATING NOBU, I PRETTY MUCH ONLY THOUGHT OF HIM AS A WILD MONKEY.
Wild monkey?
NOTHING MORE THAN THAT.
BUT I...

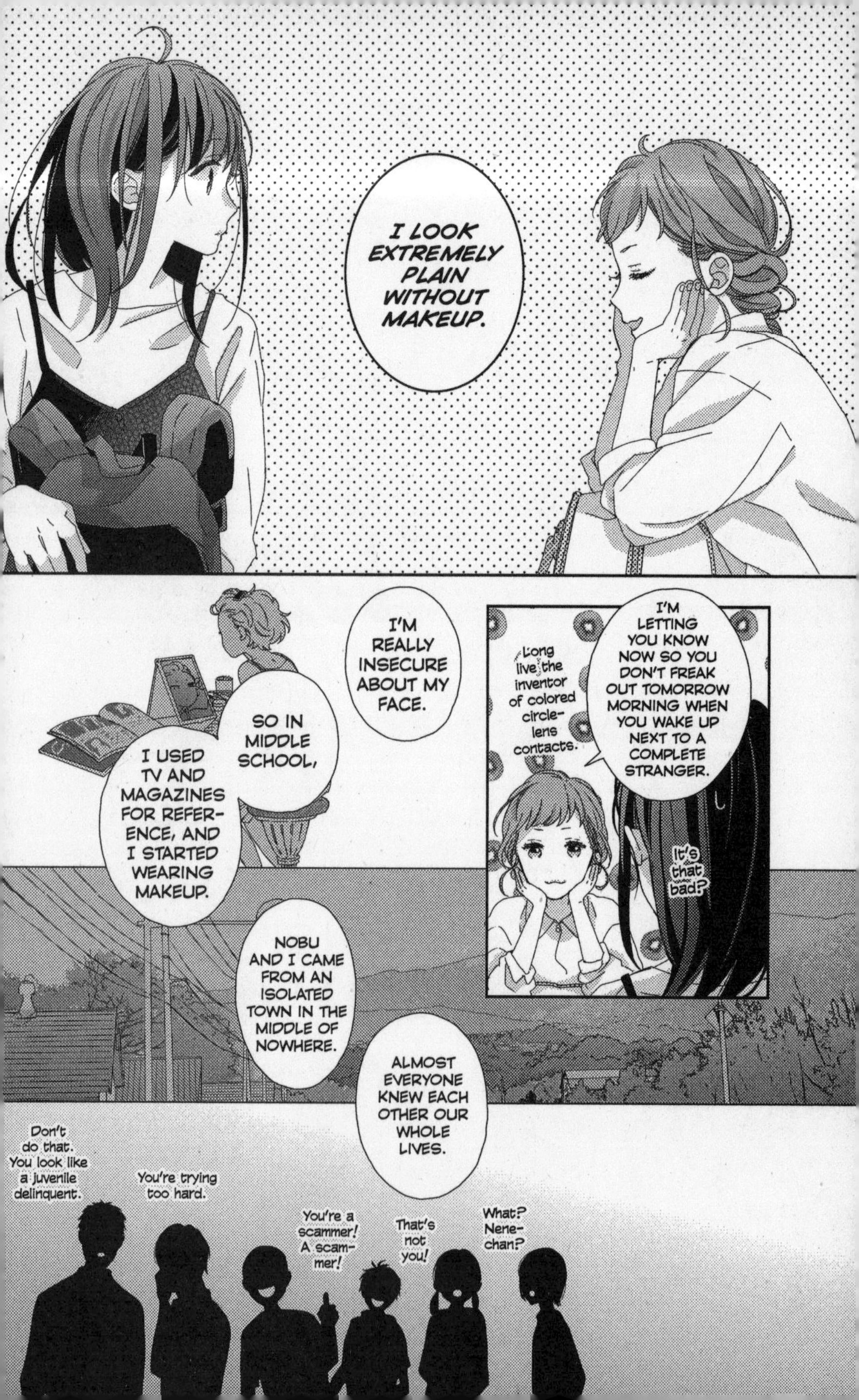

I LOOK EXTREMELY PLAIN WITHOUT MAKEUP.
I'M LETTING YOU KNOW NOW SO YOU DON'T FREAK OUT TOMORROW MORNING WHEN YOU WAKE UP NEXT TO A COMPLETE STRANGER.
Long live the inventor of colored circle-lens contacts.
It's that bad?
I'M REALLY INSECURE ABOUT MY FACE.
SO IN MIDDLE SCHOOL,
I USED TV AND MAGAZINES FOR REFERENCE, AND I STARTED WEARING MAKEUP.
NOBU AND I CAME FROM AN ISOLATED TOWN IN THE MIDDLE OF NOWHERE.
ALMOST EVERYONE KNEW EACH OTHER OUR WHOLE LIVES.
What? Nene-chan?
That's not you!
You're a scammer! A scammer!
You're trying too hard.
Don't do that. You look like a juvenile delinquent.

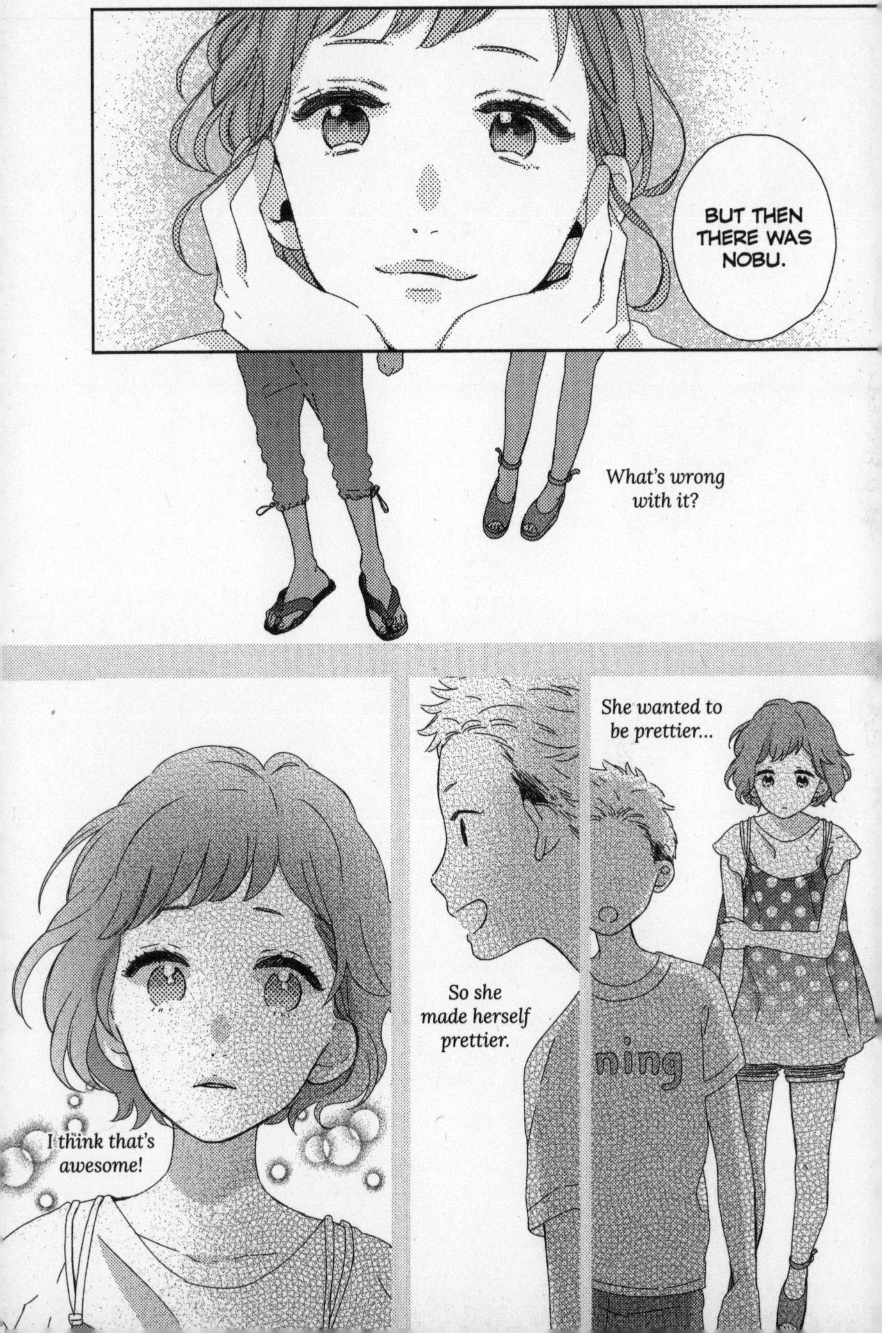
BUT THEN THERE WAS NOBU.
What's wrong with it?
She wanted to be prettier...
So she made herself prettier.
I think that's awesome!

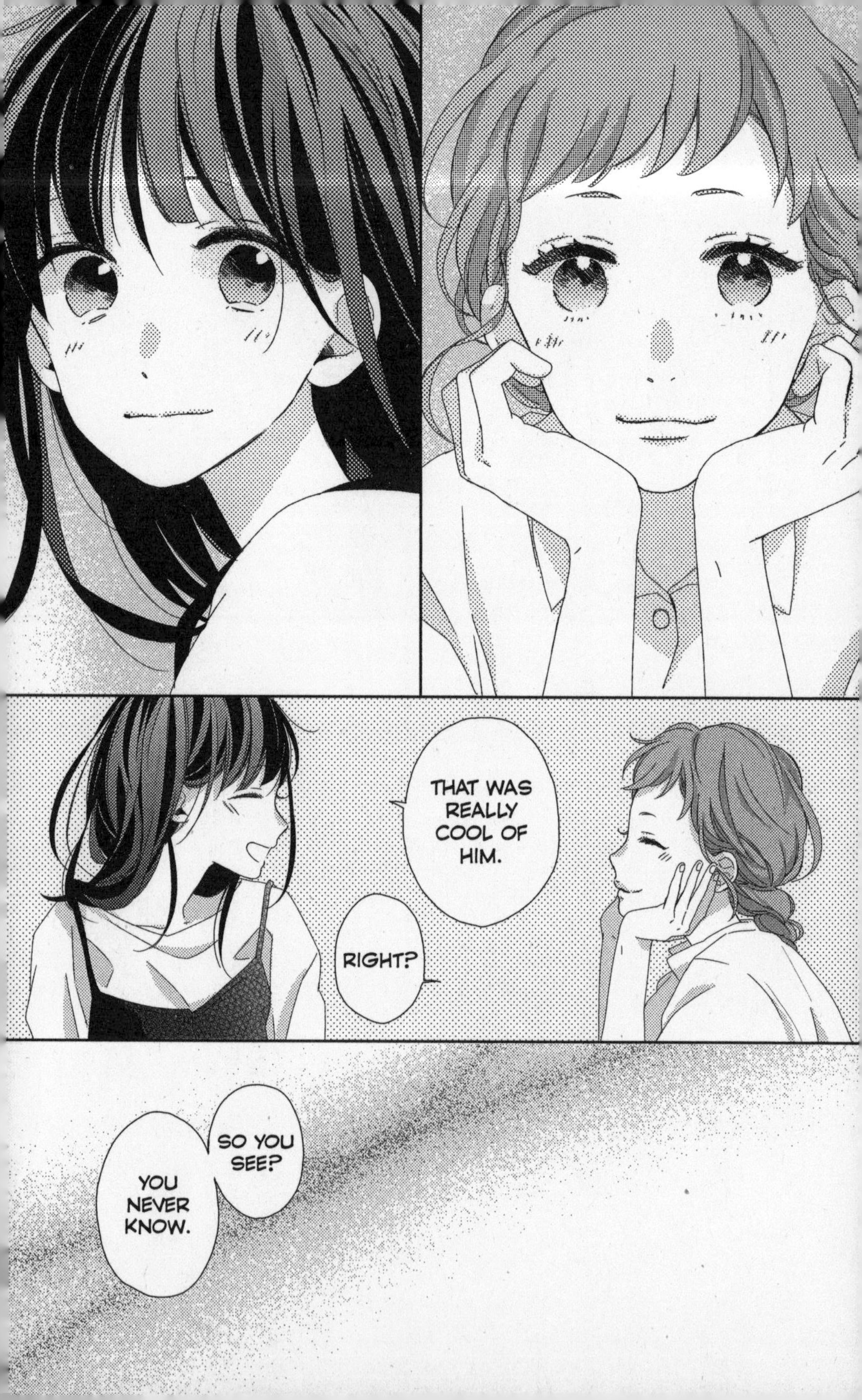
THAT WAS REALLY COOL OF HIM.
RIGHT?
SO YOU SEE?
YOU NEVER KNOW.

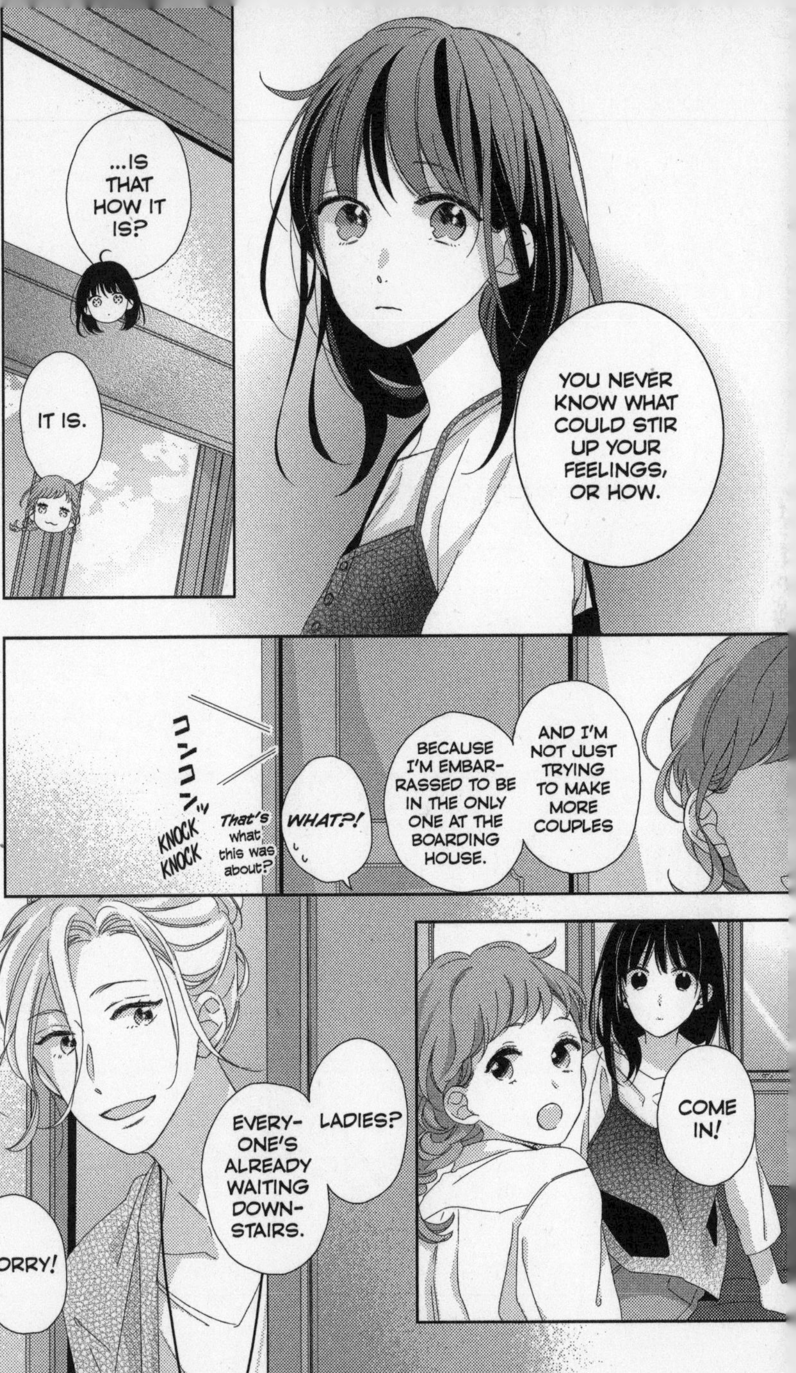
YOU NEVER KNOW WHAT COULD STIR UP YOUR FEELINGS, OR HOW.
...IS THAT HOW IT IS?
IT IS.
AND I'M NOT JUST TRYING TO MAKE MORE COUPLES
BECAUSE I'M EMBAR-RASSED TO BE IN THE ONLY ONE AT THE BOARDING HOUSE.
WHAT?!
That's what this was about?
KNOCK KNOCK
COME IN!
LADIES?
EVERY-ONE'S ALREADY WAITING DOWN-STAIRS.
SORRY!

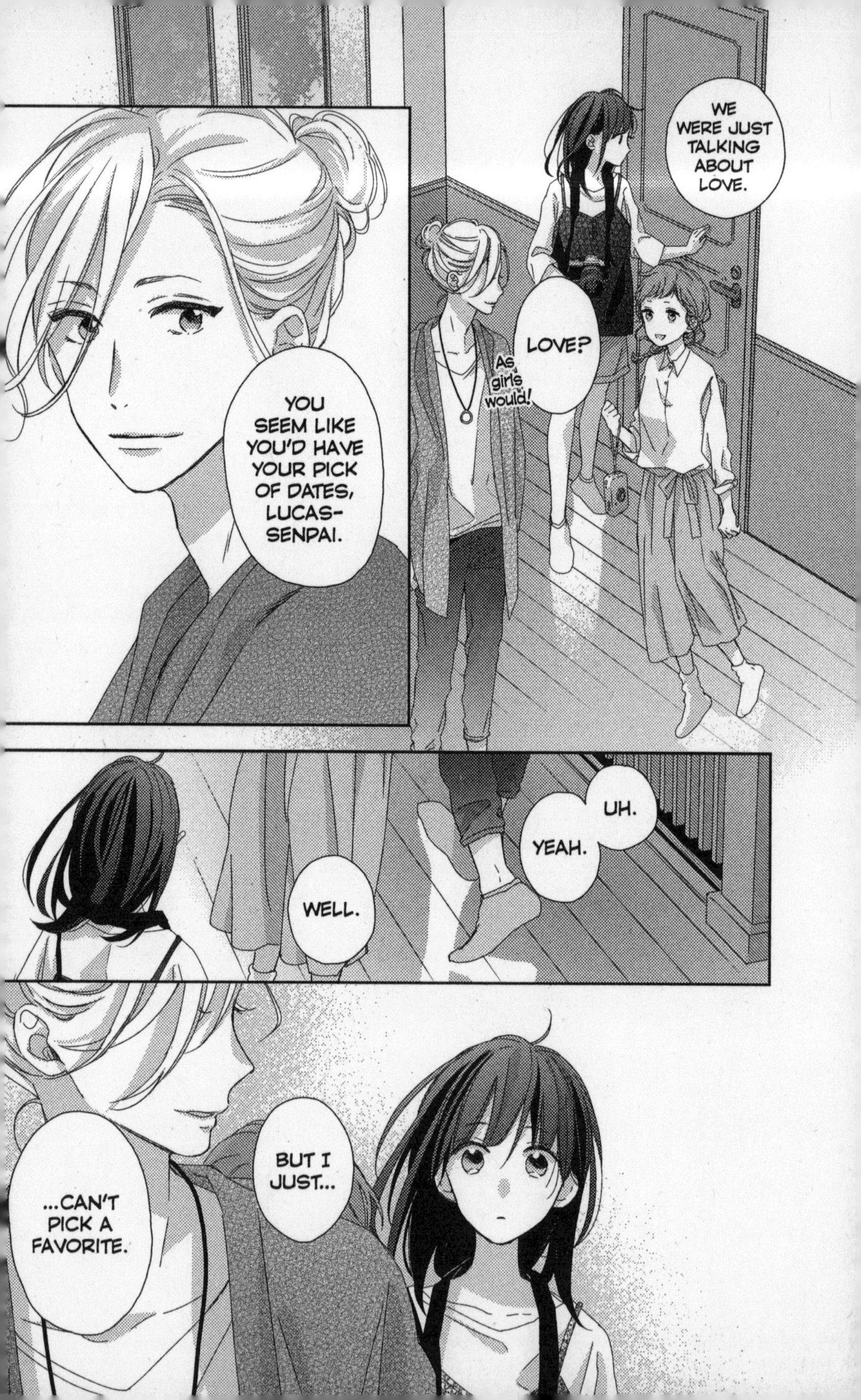
WE WERE JUST TALKING ABOUT LOVE.
LOVE?
As girls would!
YOU SEEM LIKE YOU'D HAVE YOUR PICK OF DATES, LUCAS-SENPAI.
UH.
YEAH.
WELL.
BUT I JUST...
...CAN'T PICK A FAVORITE.

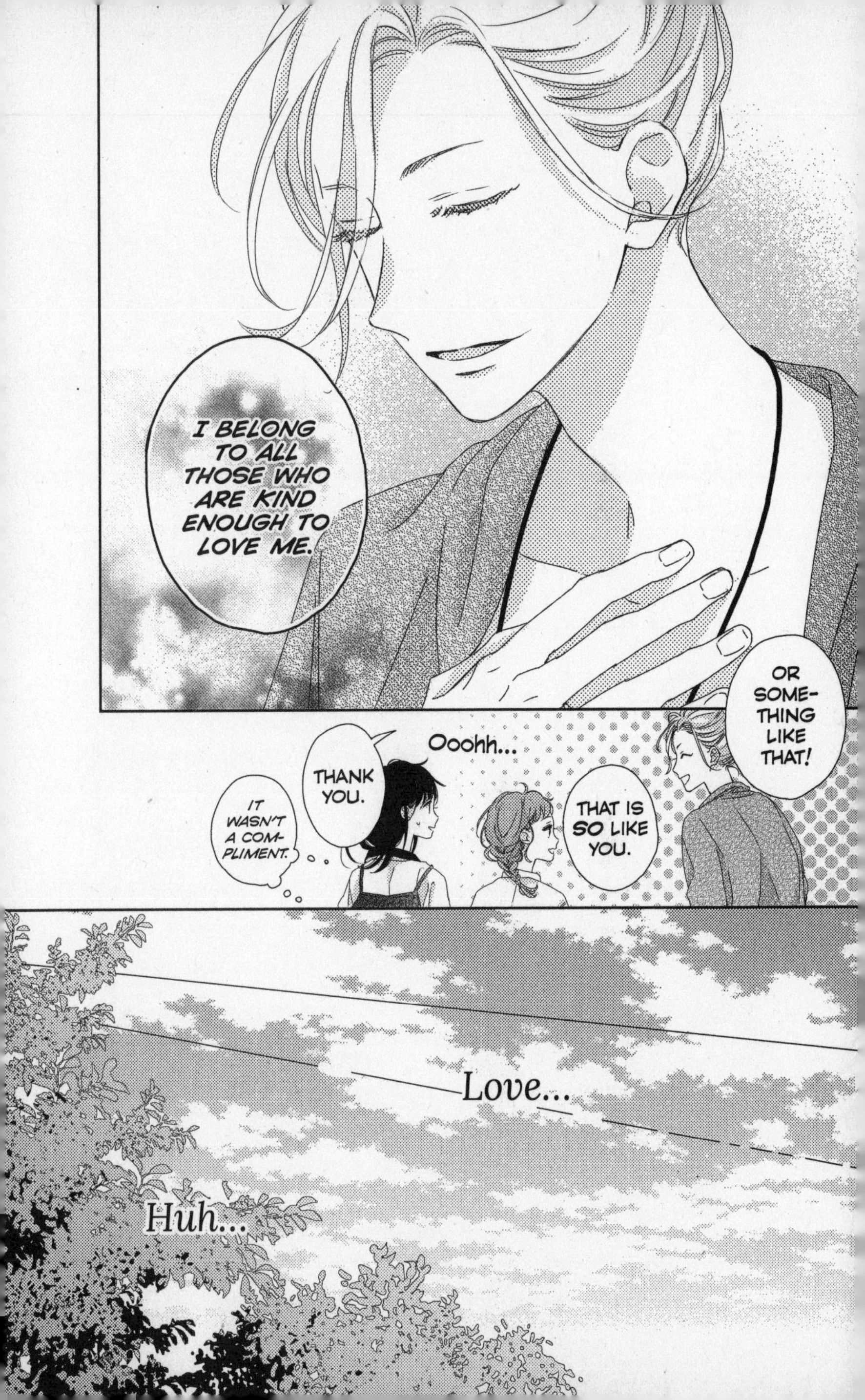
I BELONG TO ALL THOSE WHO ARE KIND ENOUGH TO LOVE ME.
OR SOMETHING LIKE THAT!
THAT IS SO LIKE YOU.
Ooohh...
THANK YOU.
IT WASN'T A COMPLIMENT.
Love...
Huh...

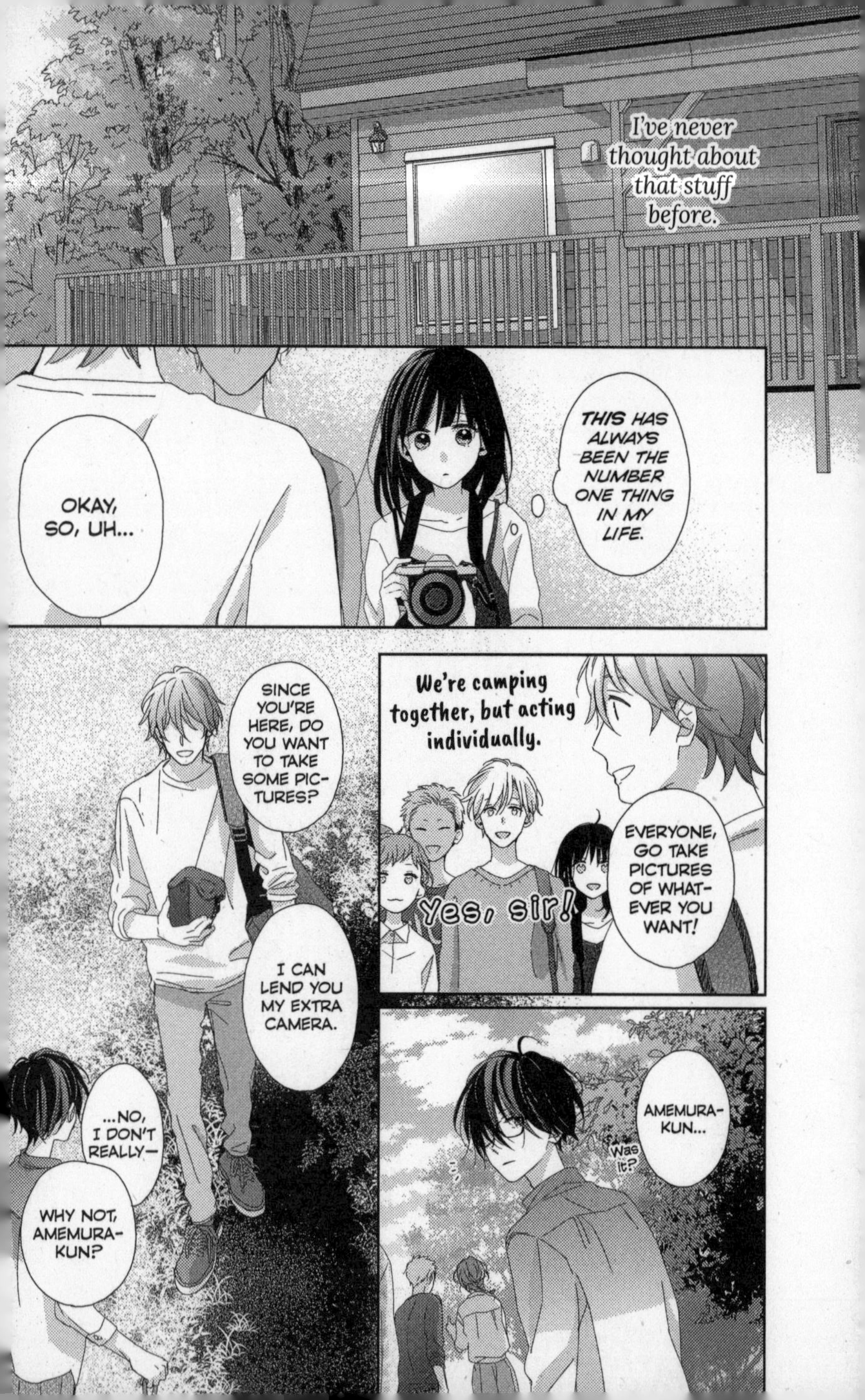
I've never thought about that stuff before.
THIS HAS ALWAYS BEEN THE NUMBER ONE THING IN MY LIFE.
OKAY, SO, UH...
We're camping together, but acting individually.
EVERYONE, GO TAKE PICTURES OF WHAT-EVER YOU WANT!
Yes, sir!
AMEMURA-KUN...
Was it?
SINCE YOU'RE HERE, DO YOU WANT TO TAKE SOME PIC-TURES?
I CAN LEND YOU MY EXTRA CAMERA.
...NO, I DON'T REALLY—
WHY NOT, AMEMURA-KUN?

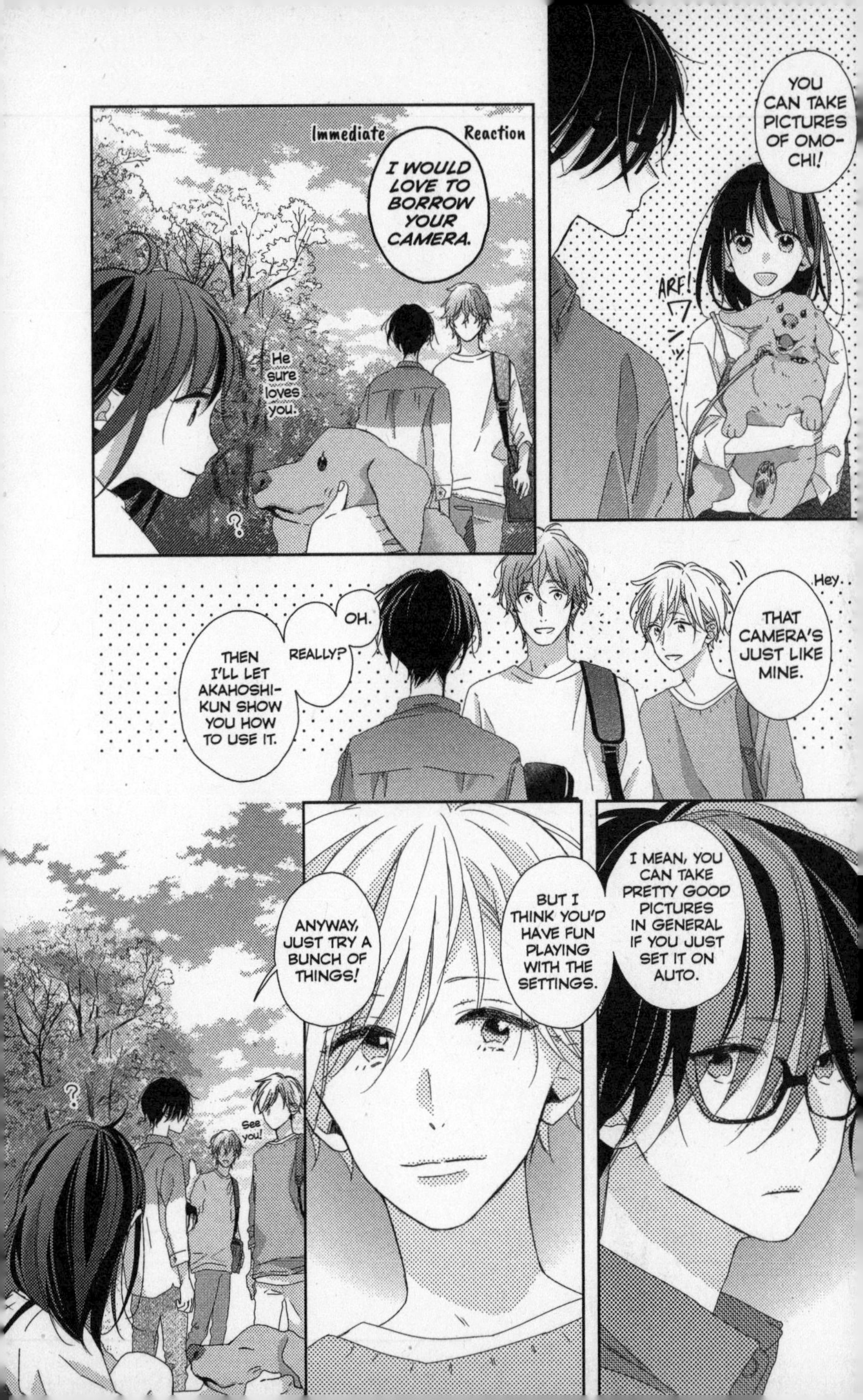
YOU CAN TAKE PICTURES OF OMO-CHI!
ARF!
Immediate Reaction
I WOULD LOVE TO BORROW YOUR CAMERA.
He sure loves you.
?
Hey.
THAT CAMERA'S JUST LIKE MINE.
OH.
REALLY?
THEN I'LL LET AKAHOSHI-KUN SHOW YOU HOW TO USE IT.
I MEAN, YOU CAN TAKE PRETTY GOOD PICTURES IN GENERAL IF YOU JUST SET IT ON AUTO.
BUT I THINK YOU'D HAVE FUN PLAYING WITH THE SETTINGS.
ANYWAY, JUST TRY A BUNCH OF THINGS!
See you!
?

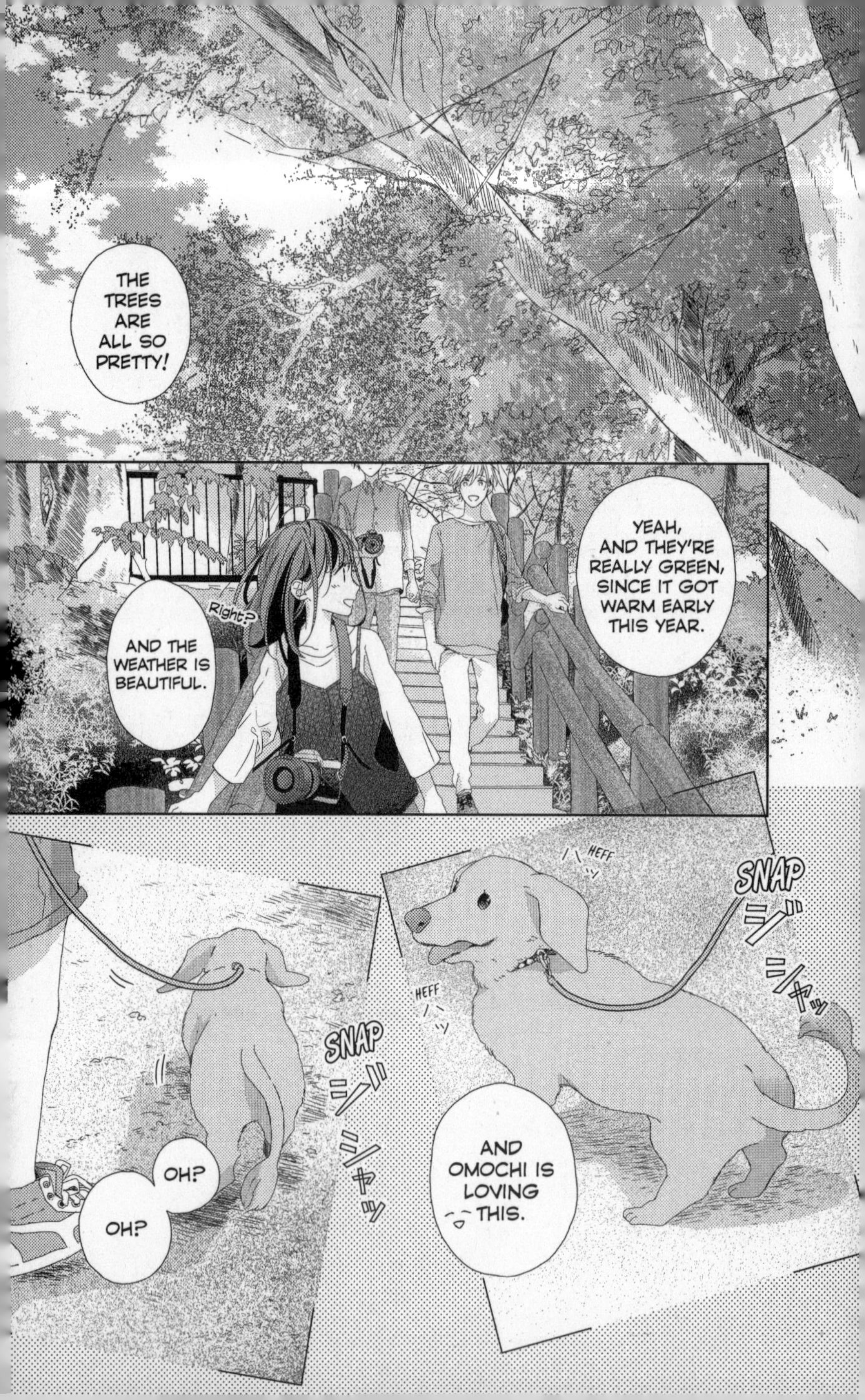

THE TREES ARE ALL SO PRETTY!
YEAH, AND THEY'RE REALLY GREEN, SINCE IT GOT WARM EARLY THIS YEAR.
Right?
AND THE WEATHER IS BEAUTIFUL.
HEFF
SNAP
HEFF
AND OMOCHI IS LOVING THIS.
SNAP
OH?
OH?

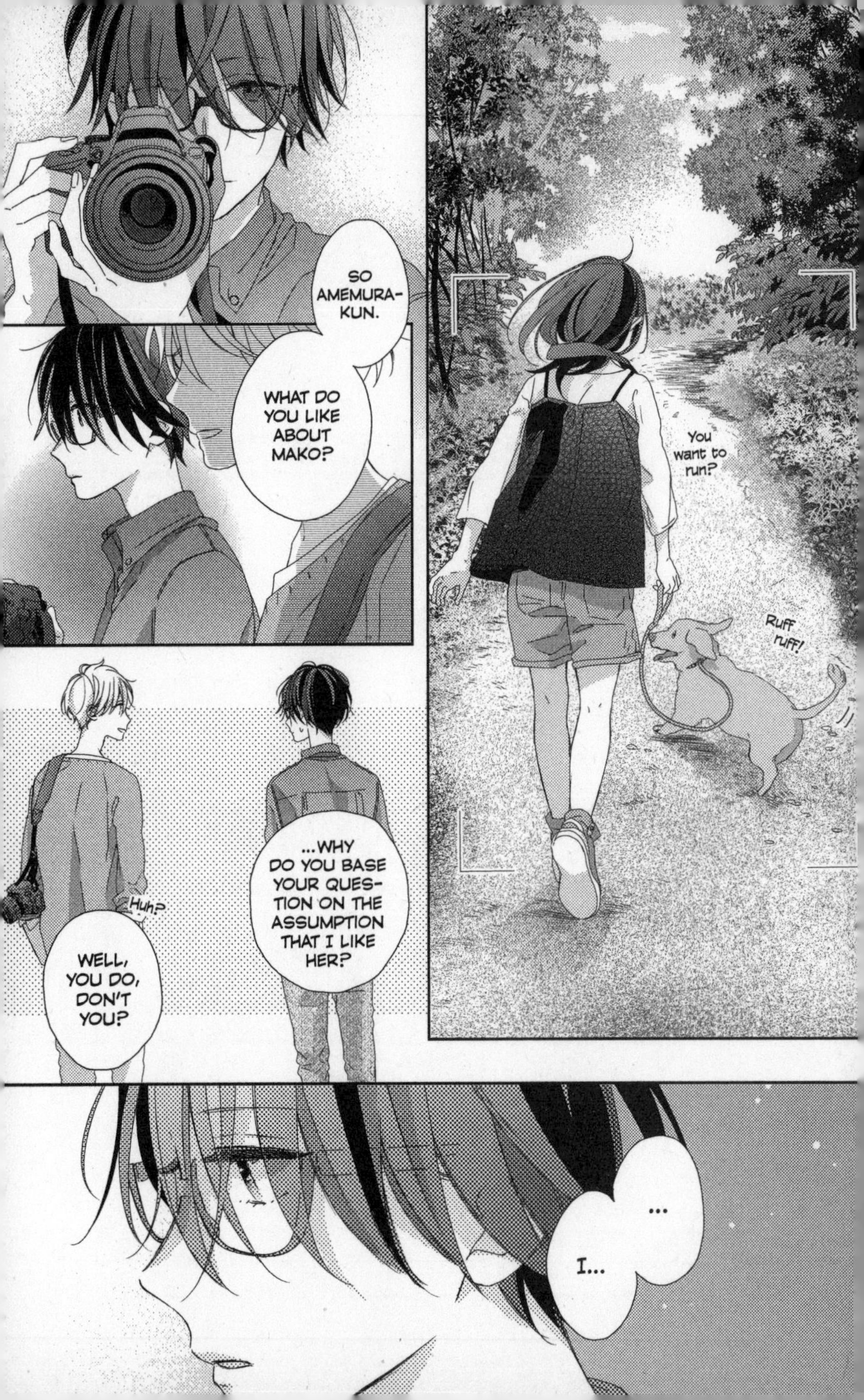
You want to run?
Ruff ruff!
SO AMEMURA-KUN.
WHAT DO YOU LIKE ABOUT MAKO?
...WHY DO YOU BASE YOUR QUESTION ON THE ASSUMPTION THAT I LIKE HER?
Huh?
WELL, YOU DO, DON'T YOU?
...
I...

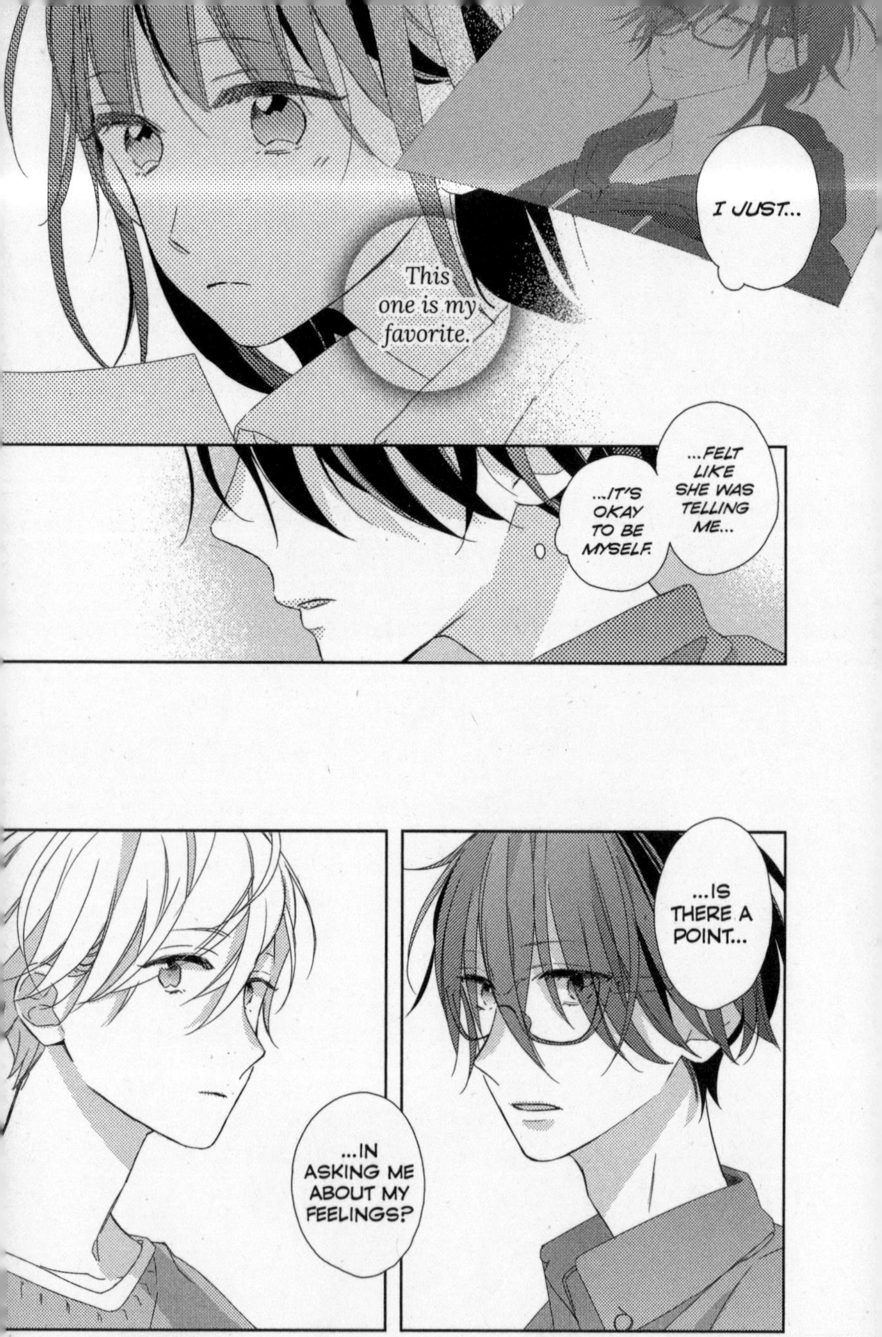
I JUST...
This one is my favorite.
...FELT LIKE SHE WAS TELLING ME...
...IT'S OKAY TO BE MYSELF.
...IS THERE A POINT...
...IN ASKING ME ABOUT MY FEELINGS?

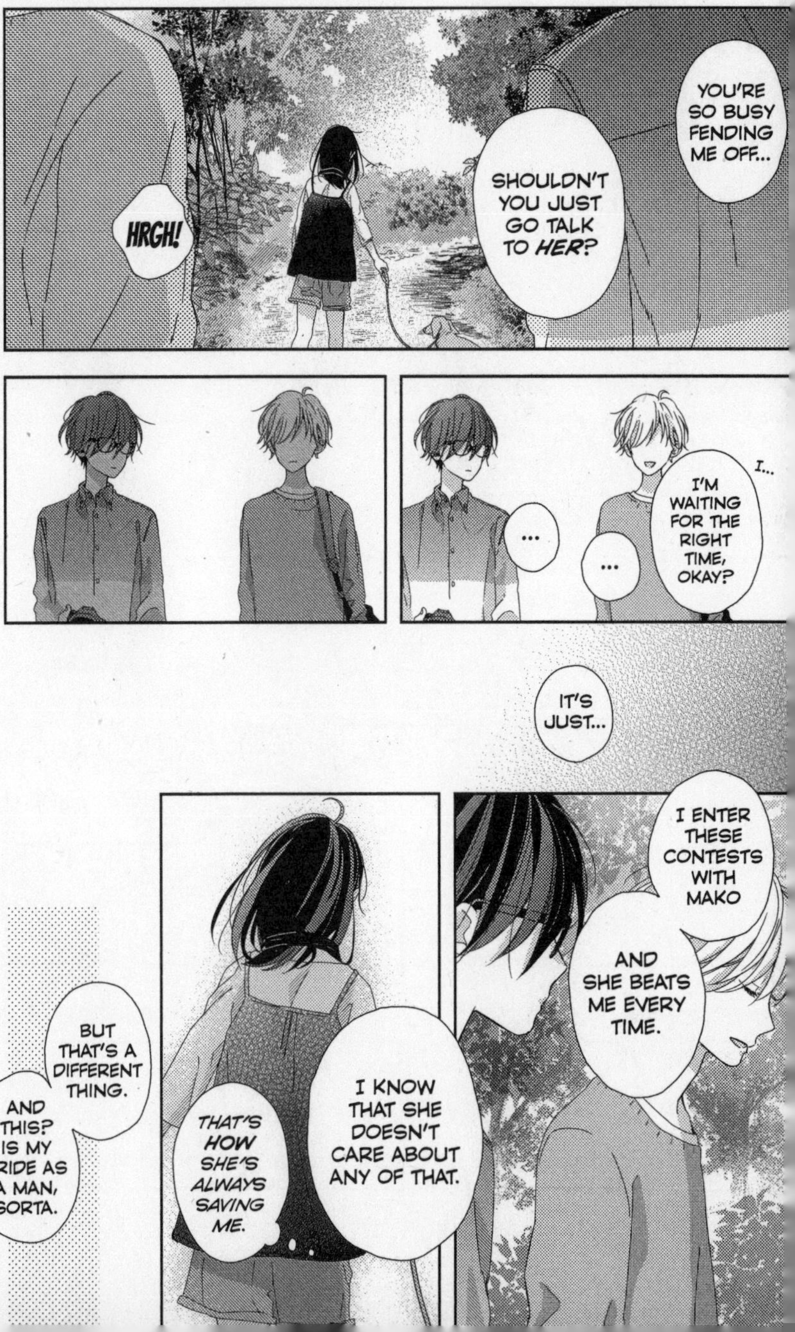
YOU'RE SO BUSY FENDING ME OFF...
SHOULDN'T YOU JUST GO TALK TO *HER*?
HRGH!
I...
I'M WAITING FOR THE RIGHT TIME, OKAY?
...
...
IT'S JUST...
I ENTER THESE CONTESTS WITH MAKO
AND SHE BEATS ME EVERY TIME.
I KNOW THAT SHE DOESN'T CARE ABOUT ANY OF THAT.
THAT'S *HOW* SHE'S ALWAYS SAVING ME.
BUT THAT'S A DIFFERENT THING.
AND THIS? IS MY PRIDE AS A MAN, SORTA.

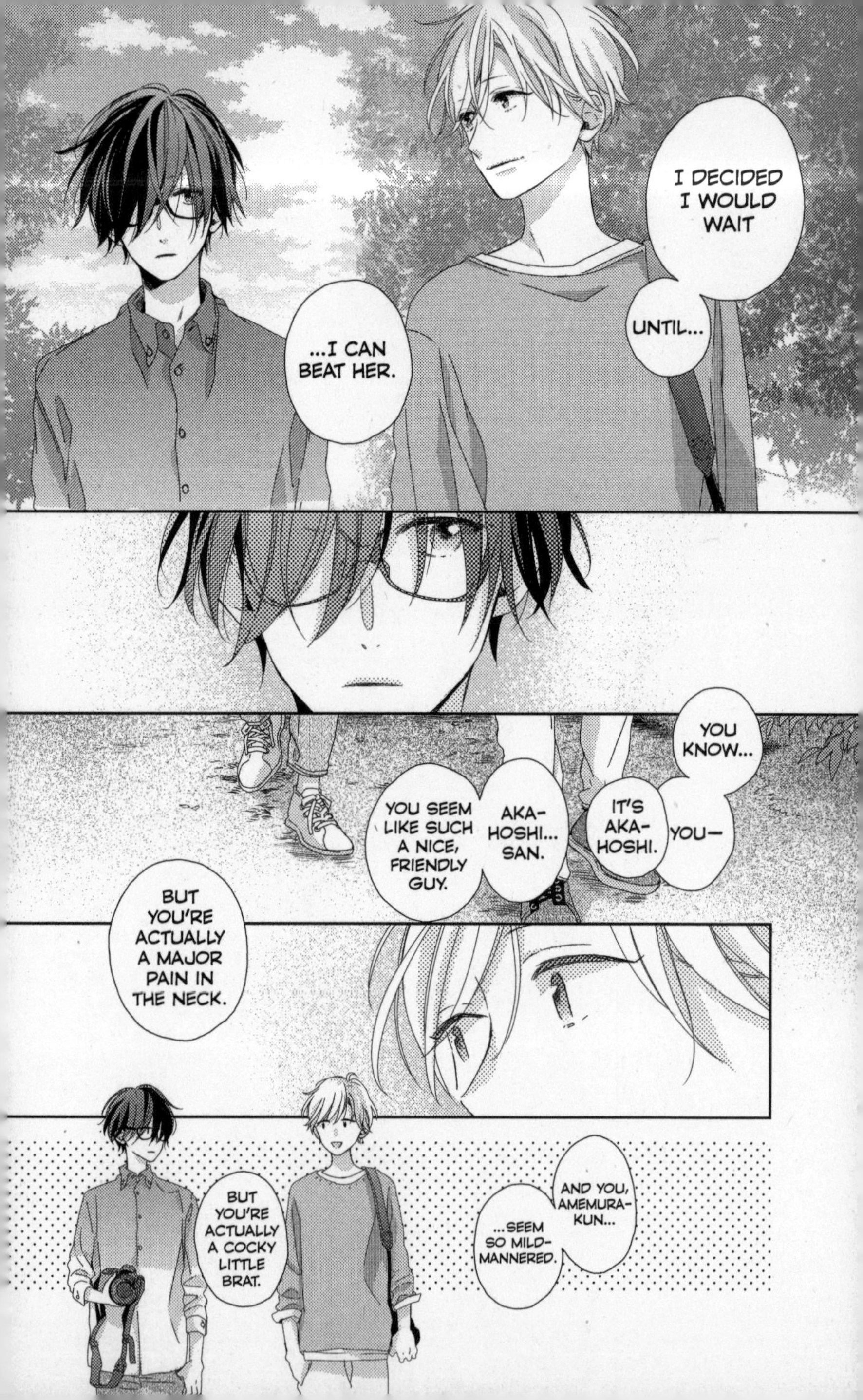
I DECIDED I WOULD WAIT
UNTIL...
...I CAN BEAT HER.
YOU KNOW...
YOU—
IT'S AKA-HOSHI.
AKA-HOSHI... SAN.
YOU SEEM LIKE SUCH A NICE, FRIENDLY GUY.
BUT YOU'RE ACTUALLY A MAJOR PAIN IN THE NECK.
AND YOU, AMEMURA-KUN...
...SEEM SO MILD-MANNERED.
BUT YOU'RE ACTUALLY A COCKY LITTLE BRAT.

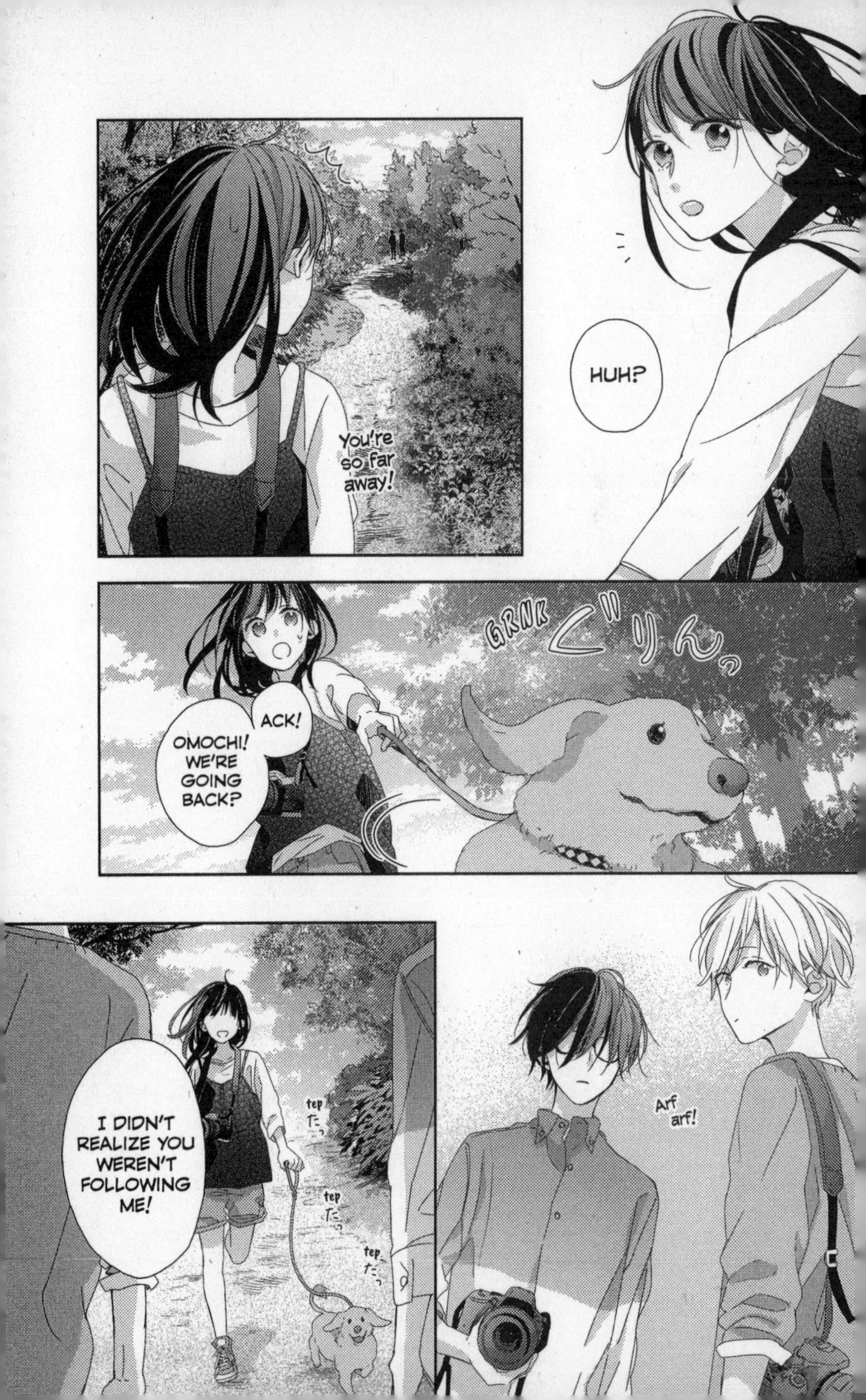
HUH?
You're so far away!
GRNK
ぐりんっ
ACK!
OMOCHI! WE'RE GOING BACK?
Arf arf!
I DIDN'T REALIZE YOU WEREN'T FOLLOWING ME!
tep たっ
tep たっ
tep たっ

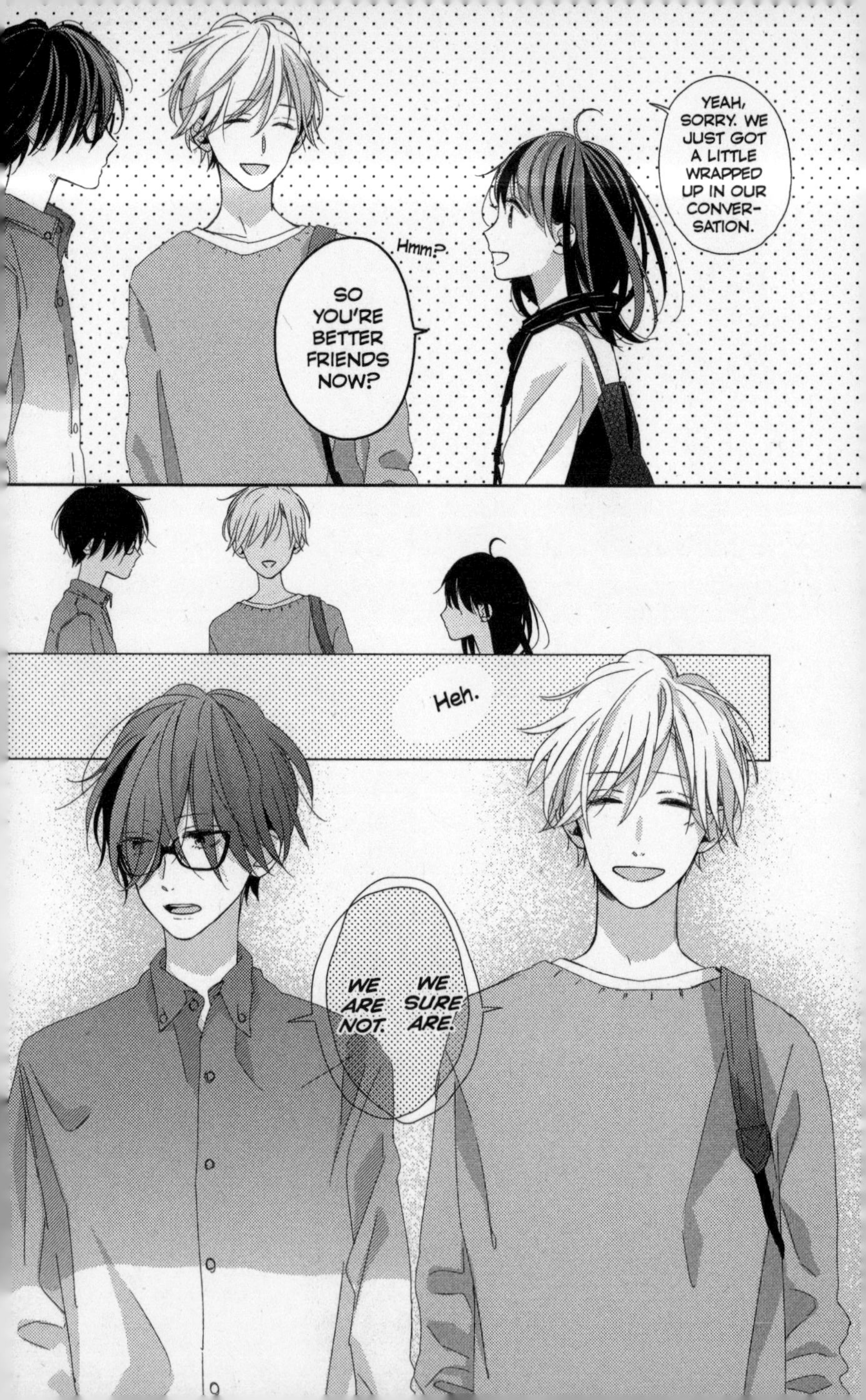
YEAH, SORRY. WE JUST GOT A LITTLE WRAPPED UP IN OUR CONVER-SATION.
Hmm?
SO YOU'RE BETTER FRIENDS NOW?
Heh.
WE SURE ARE.
WE ARE NOT.

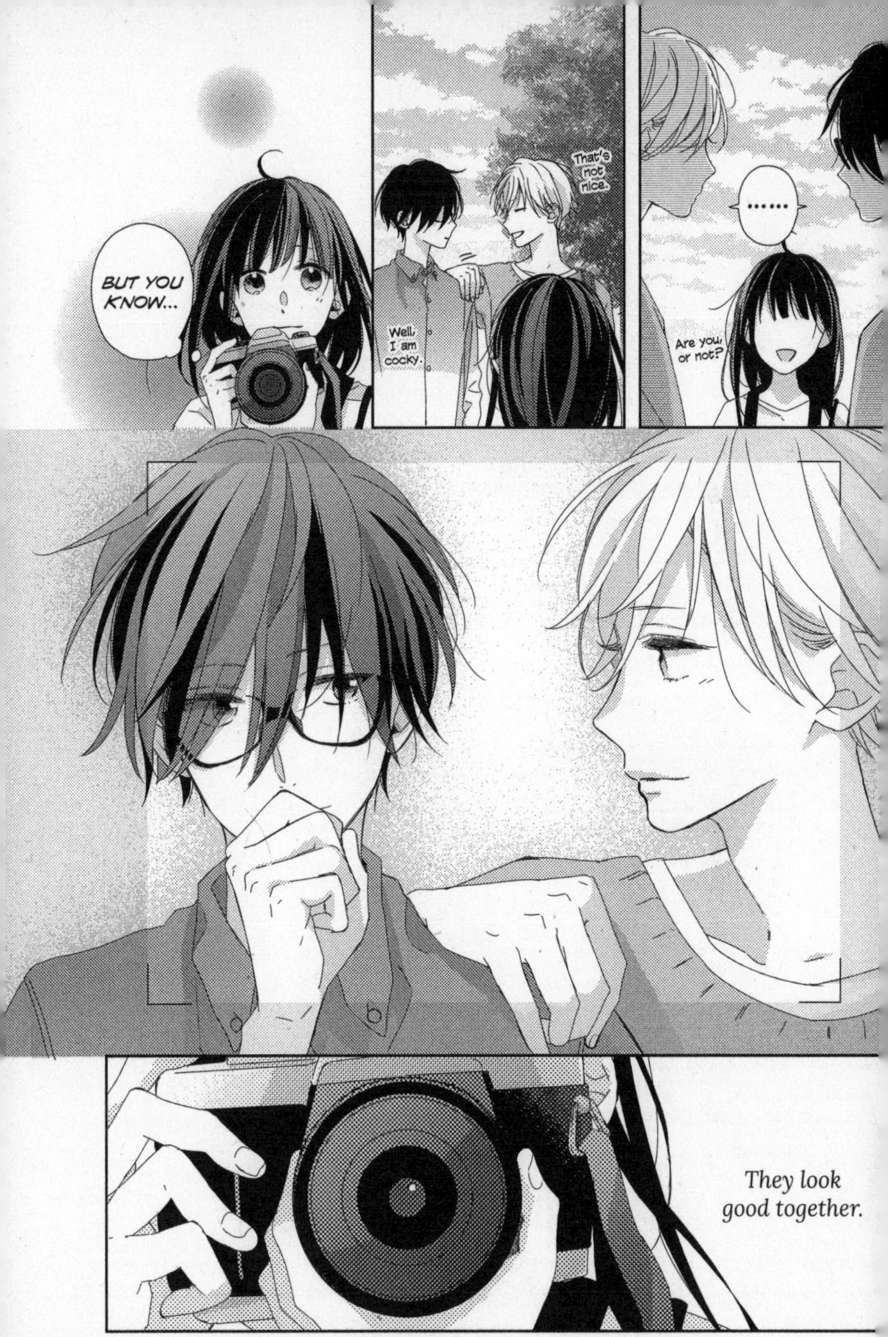
......
Are you, or not?
That's not nice.
Well, I am cocky.
BUT YOU KNOW...
They look good together.

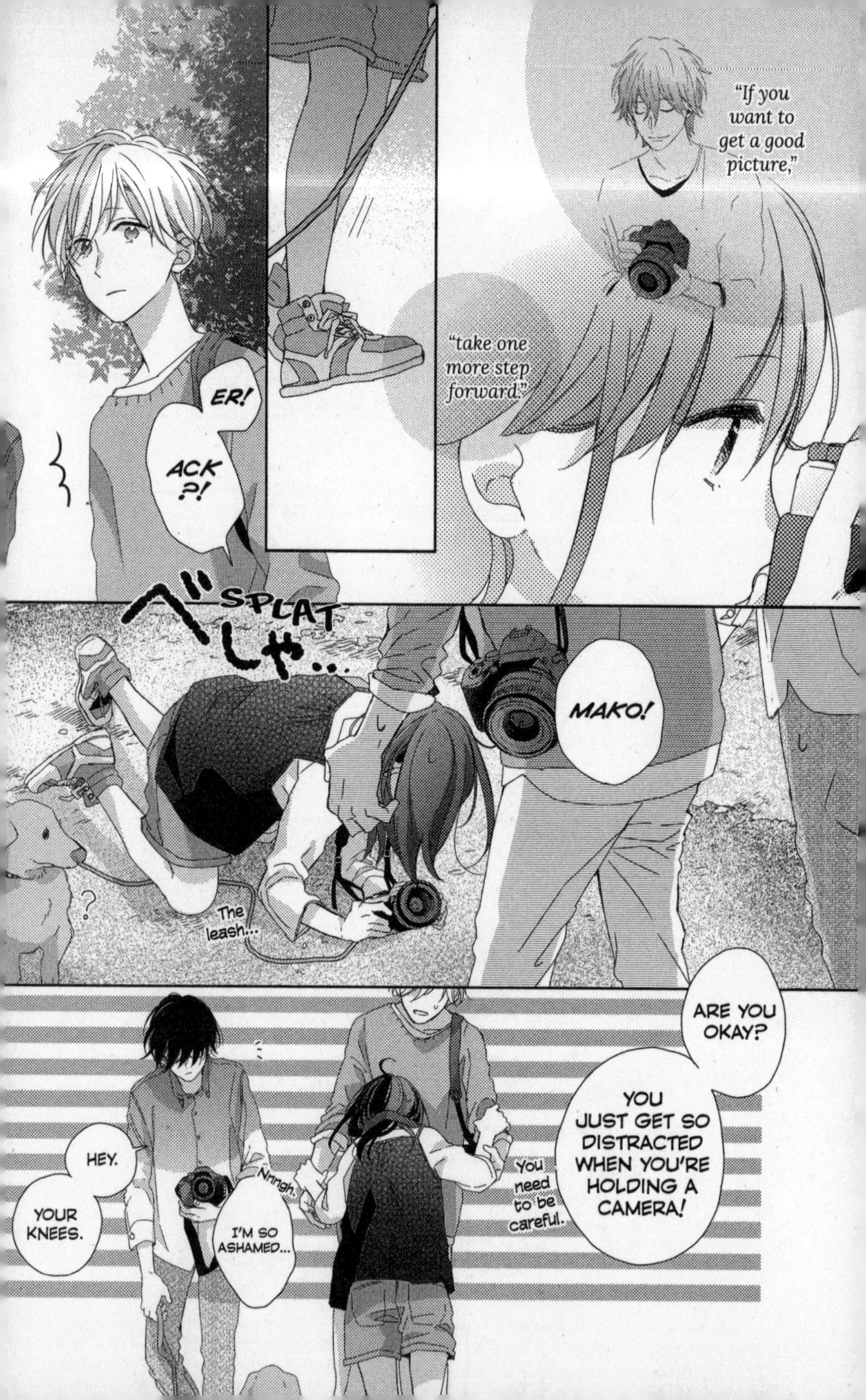
"If you want to get a good picture,"
"take one more step forward."
ER!
ACK ?!
MAKO!
べしゃ...
SPLAT
The leash...
ARE YOU OKAY?
YOU JUST GET SO DISTRACTED WHEN YOU'RE HOLDING A CAMERA!
You need to be careful.
Nnngh.
I'M SO ASHAMED...
HEY.
YOUR KNEES.

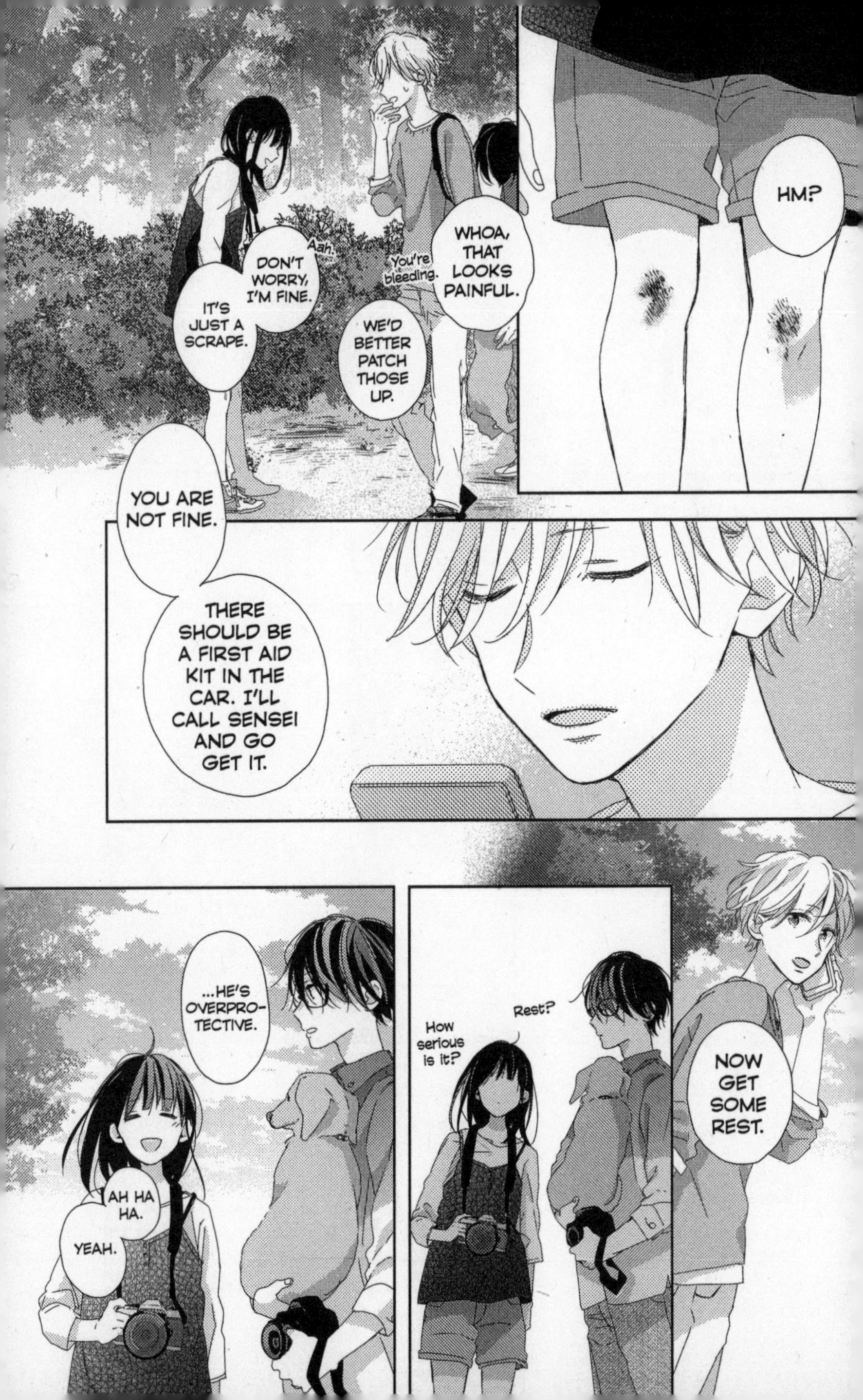
HM?
WHOA, THAT LOOKS PAINFUL.
You're bleeding.
Aah.
DON'T WORRY, I'M FINE.
IT'S JUST A SCRAPE.
WE'D BETTER PATCH THOSE UP.
YOU ARE NOT FINE.
THERE SHOULD BE A FIRST AID KIT IN THE CAR. I'LL CALL SENSEI AND GO GET IT.
NOW GET SOME REST.
Rest?
How serious is it?
...HE'S OVERPROTECTIVE.
AH HA HA.
YEAH.

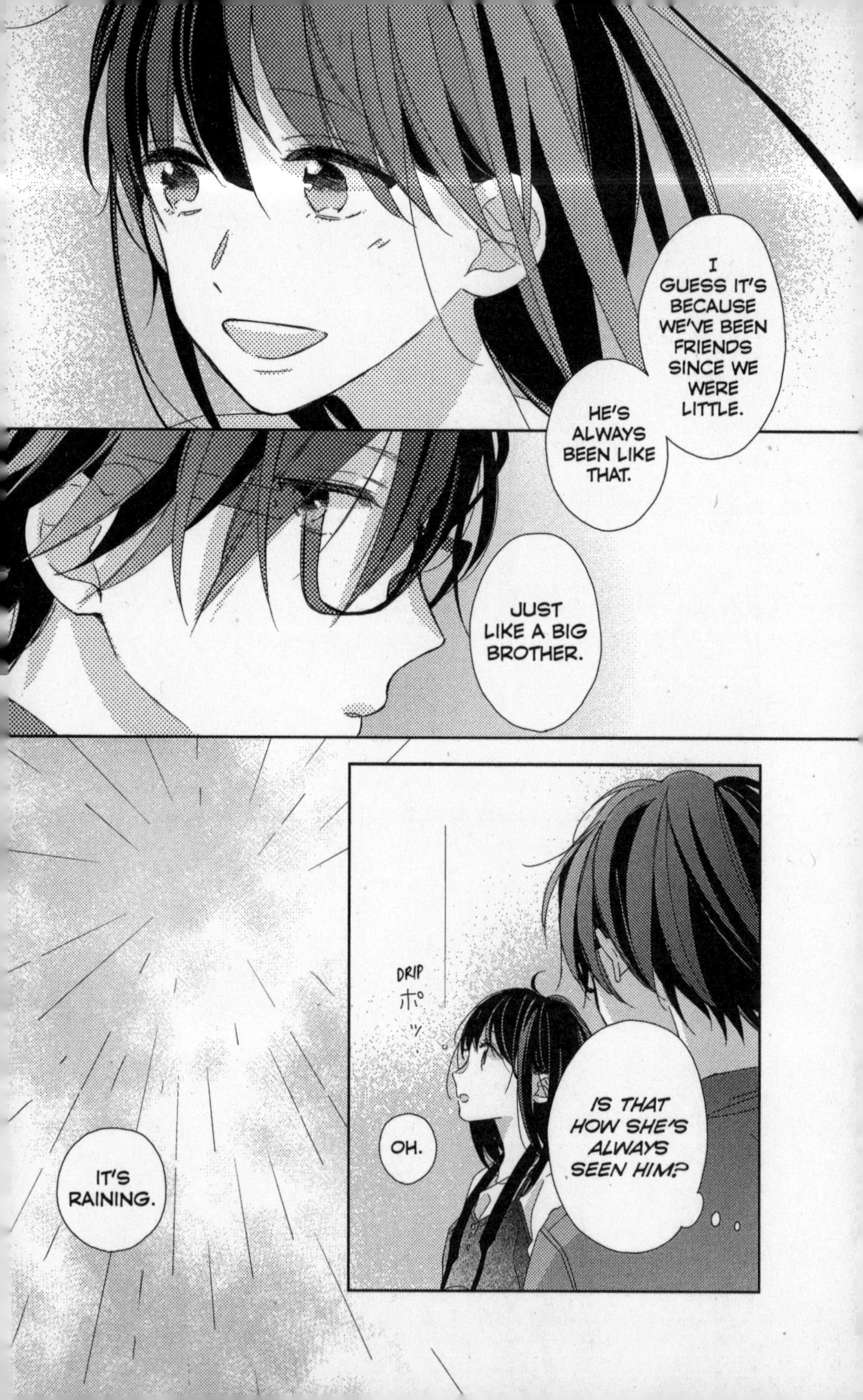
I GUESS IT'S BECAUSE WE'VE BEEN FRIENDS SINCE WE WERE LITTLE.
HE'S ALWAYS BEEN LIKE THAT.
JUST LIKE A BIG BROTHER.
DRIP
ポッ
IS THAT HOW SHE'S ALWAYS SEEN HIM?
OH.
IT'S RAINING.

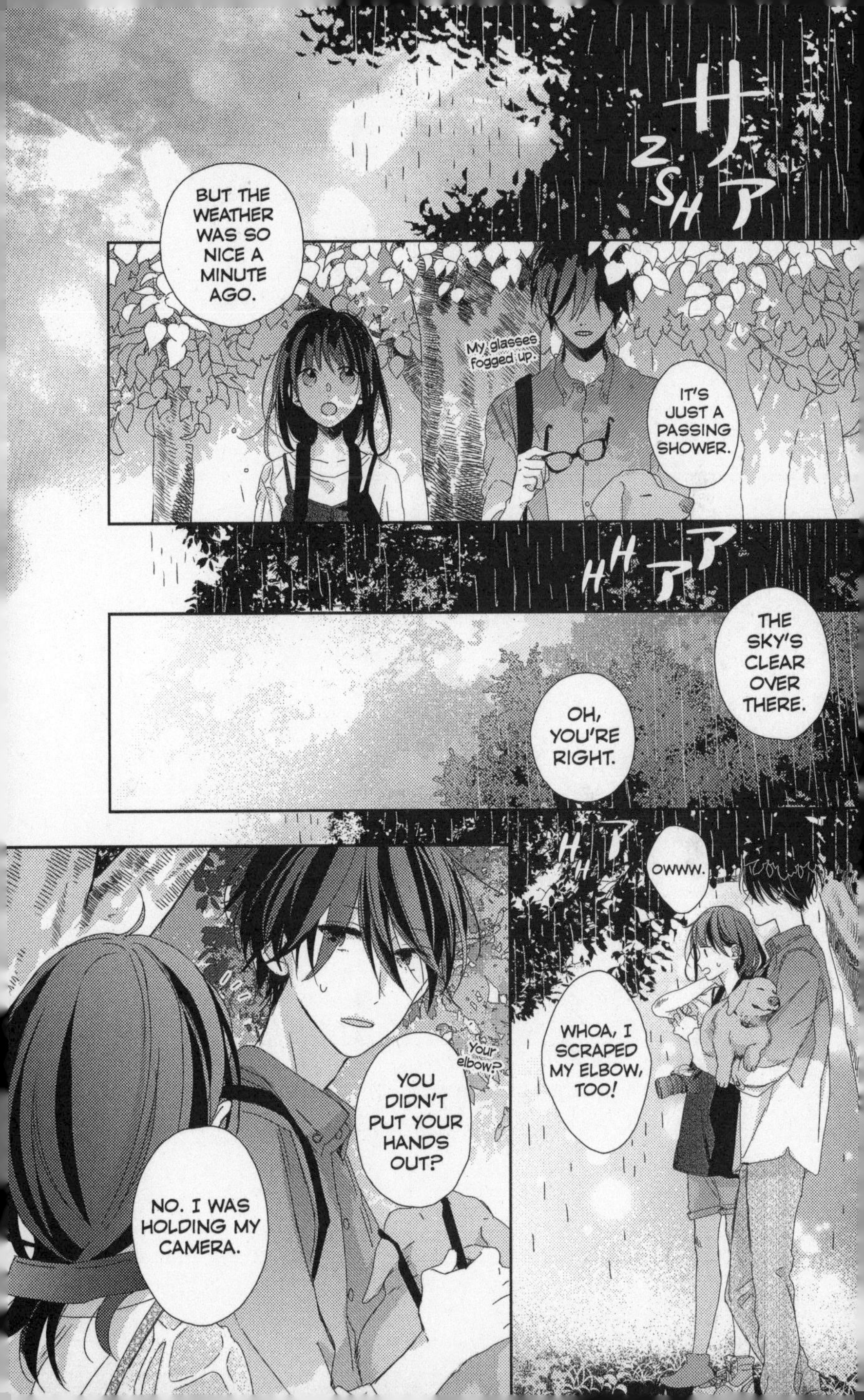

ZSHH
サア
BUT THE WEATHER WAS SO NICE A MINUTE AGO.
My glasses fogged up.
IT'S JUST A PASSING SHOWER.
HHH
アア
THE SKY'S CLEAR OVER THERE.
OH, YOU'RE RIGHT.
HHH
ア
OWWW.
WHOA, I SCRAPED MY ELBOW, TOO!
Your elbow?
YOU DIDN'T PUT YOUR HANDS OUT?
NO. I WAS HOLDING MY CAMERA.

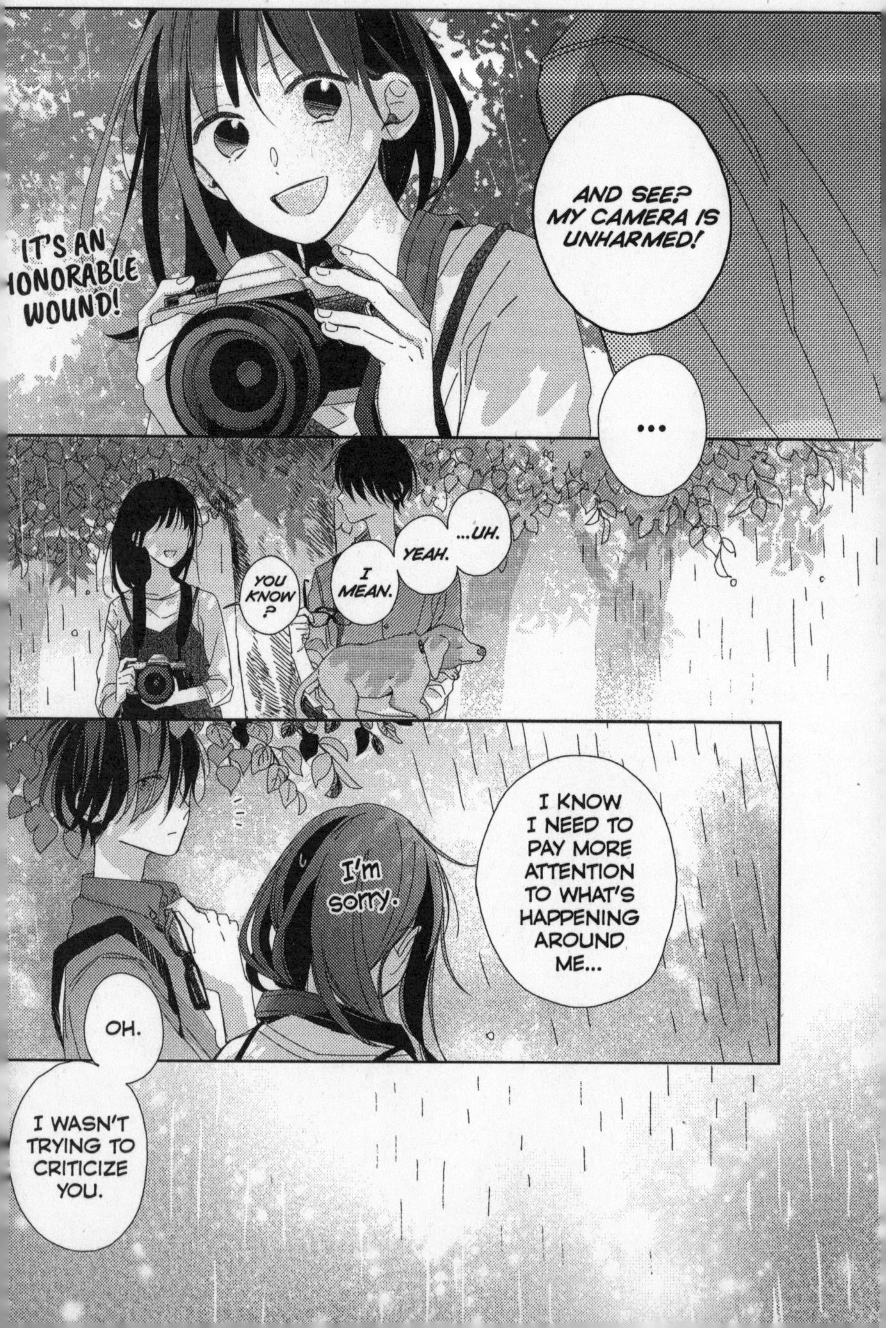
AND SEE? MY CAMERA IS UNHARMED!
IT'S AN HONORABLE WOUND!
...
...UH.
YEAH.
I MEAN.
YOU KNOW?
I KNOW I NEED TO PAY MORE ATTENTION TO WHAT'S HAPPENING AROUND ME...
I'm sorry.
OH.
I WASN'T TRYING TO CRITICIZE YOU.

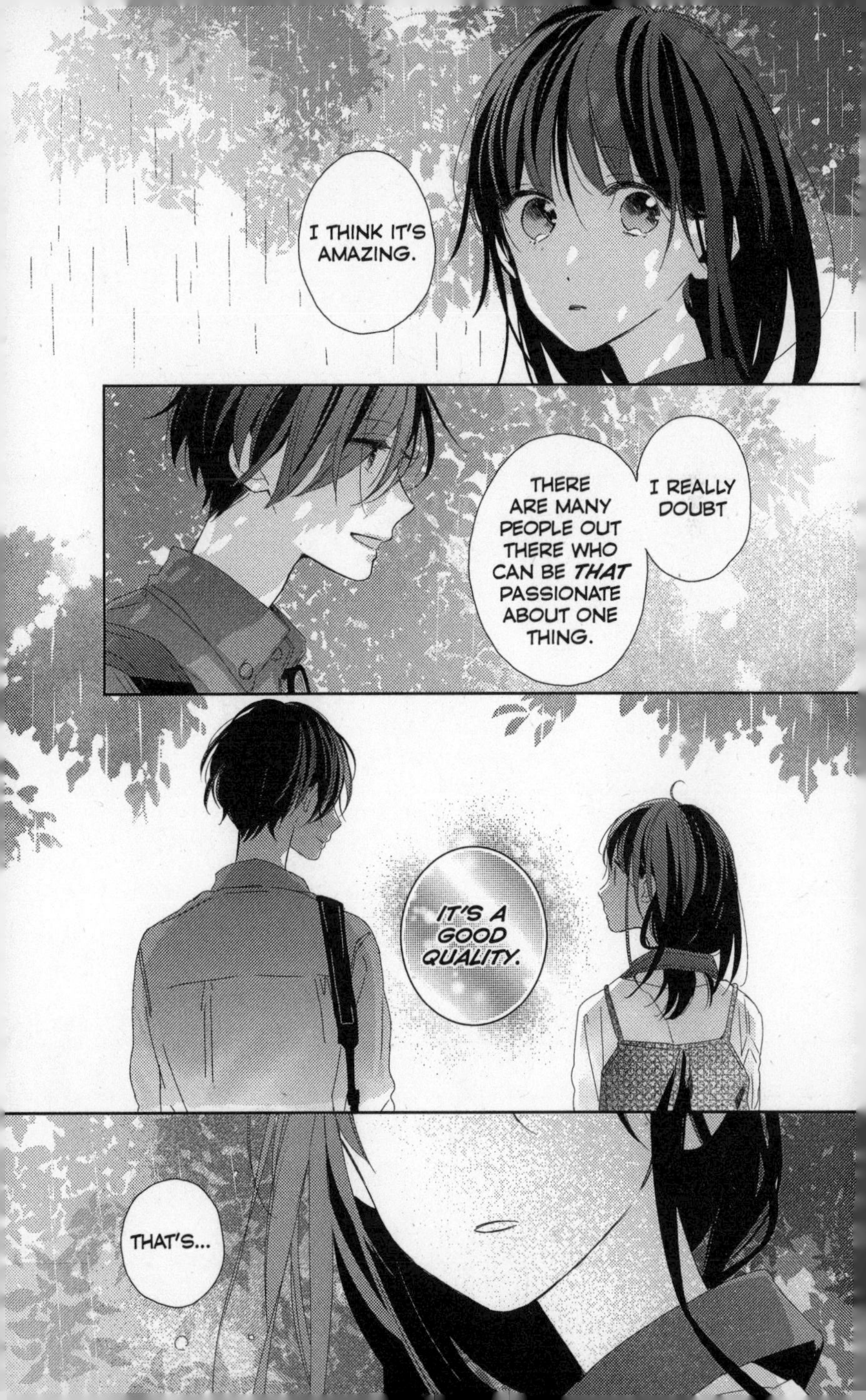
I THINK IT'S AMAZING.
I REALLY DOUBT
THERE ARE MANY PEOPLE OUT THERE WHO CAN BE *THAT* PASSIONATE ABOUT ONE THING.
IT'S A GOOD QUALITY.
THAT'S...

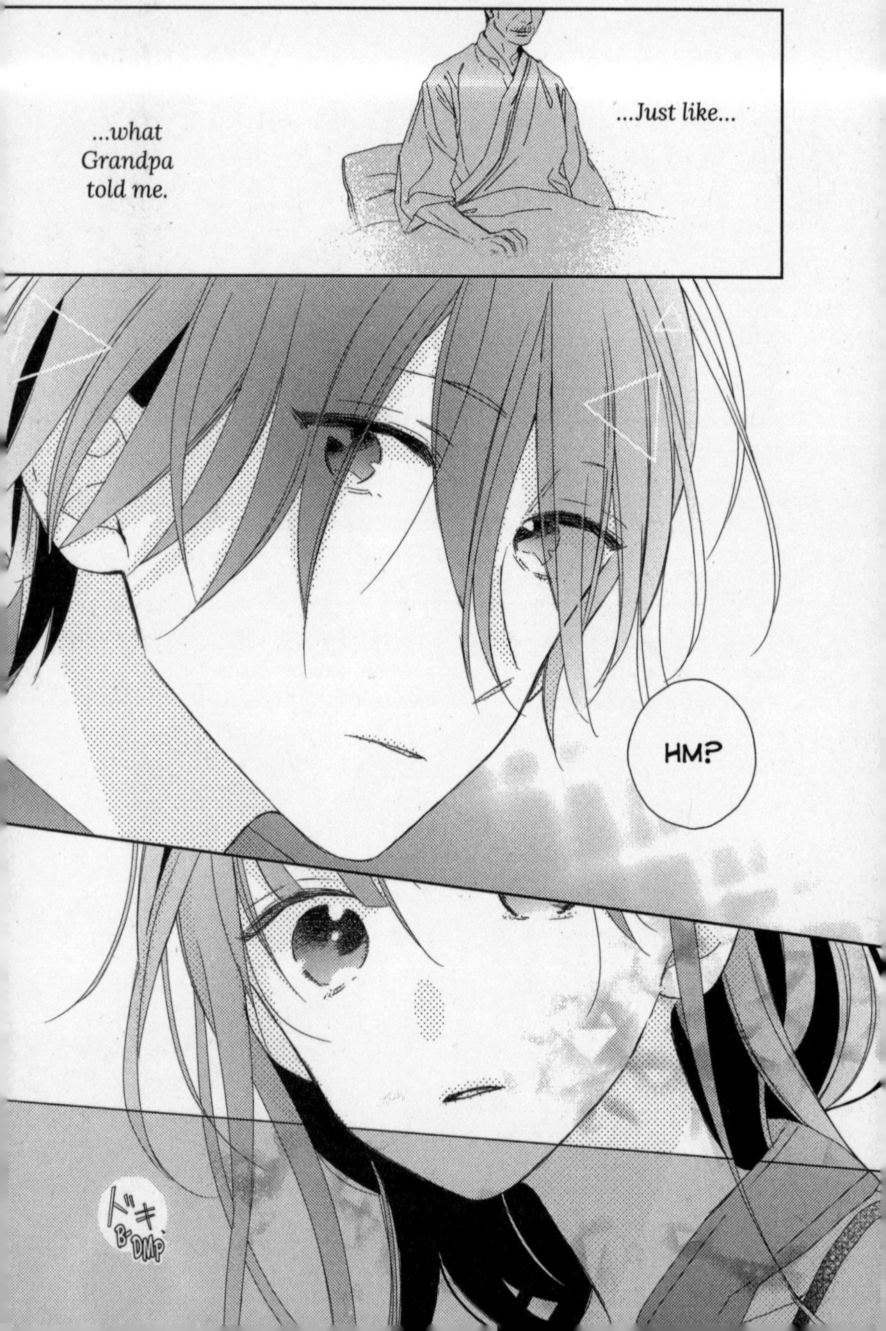
...Just like...
...what Grandpa told me.
HM?
ドキ
B-DMP

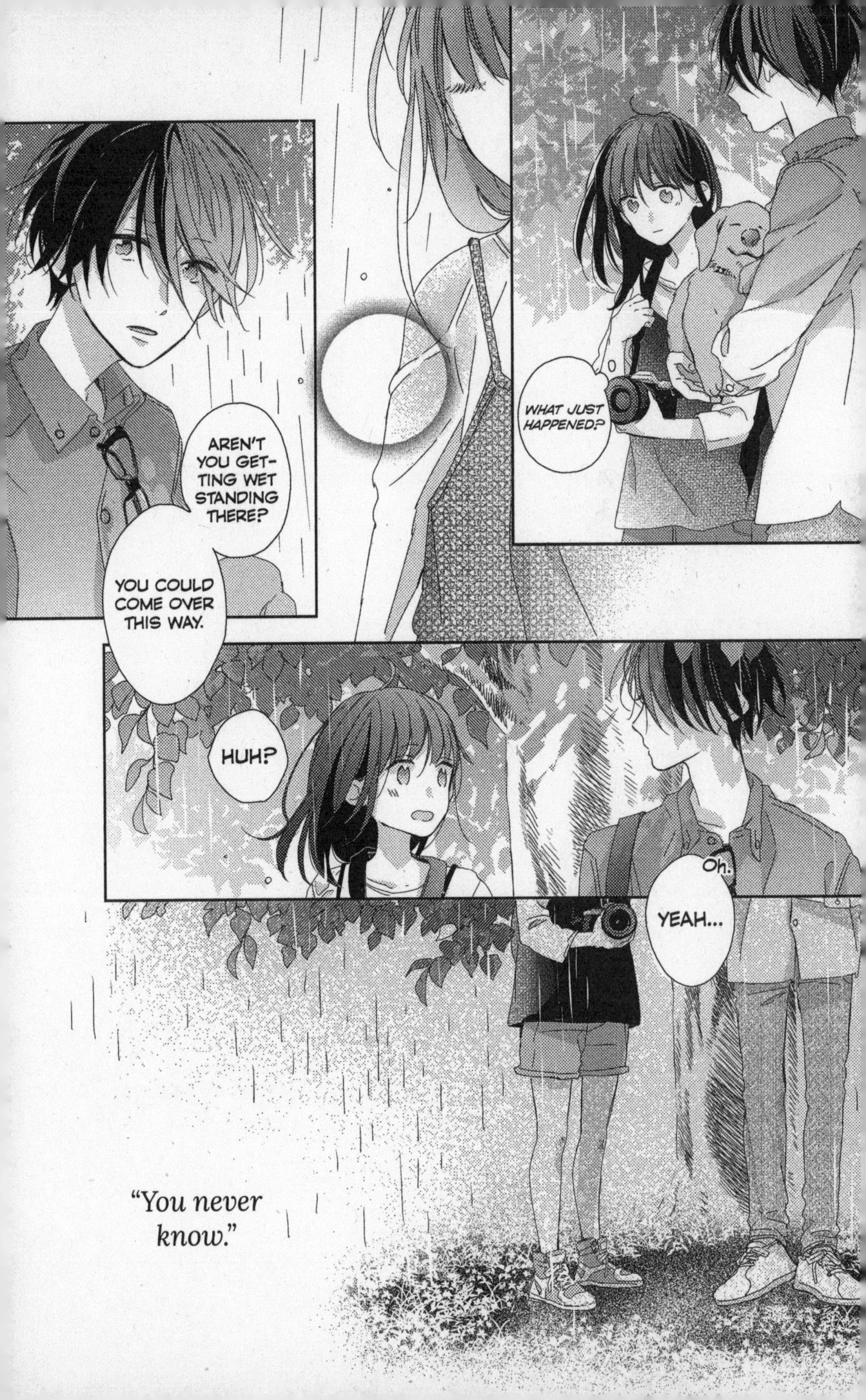
WHAT JUST HAPPENED?
AREN'T YOU GET-TING WET STANDING THERE?
YOU COULD COME OVER THIS WAY.
HUH?
Oh.
YEAH...
"You never know."

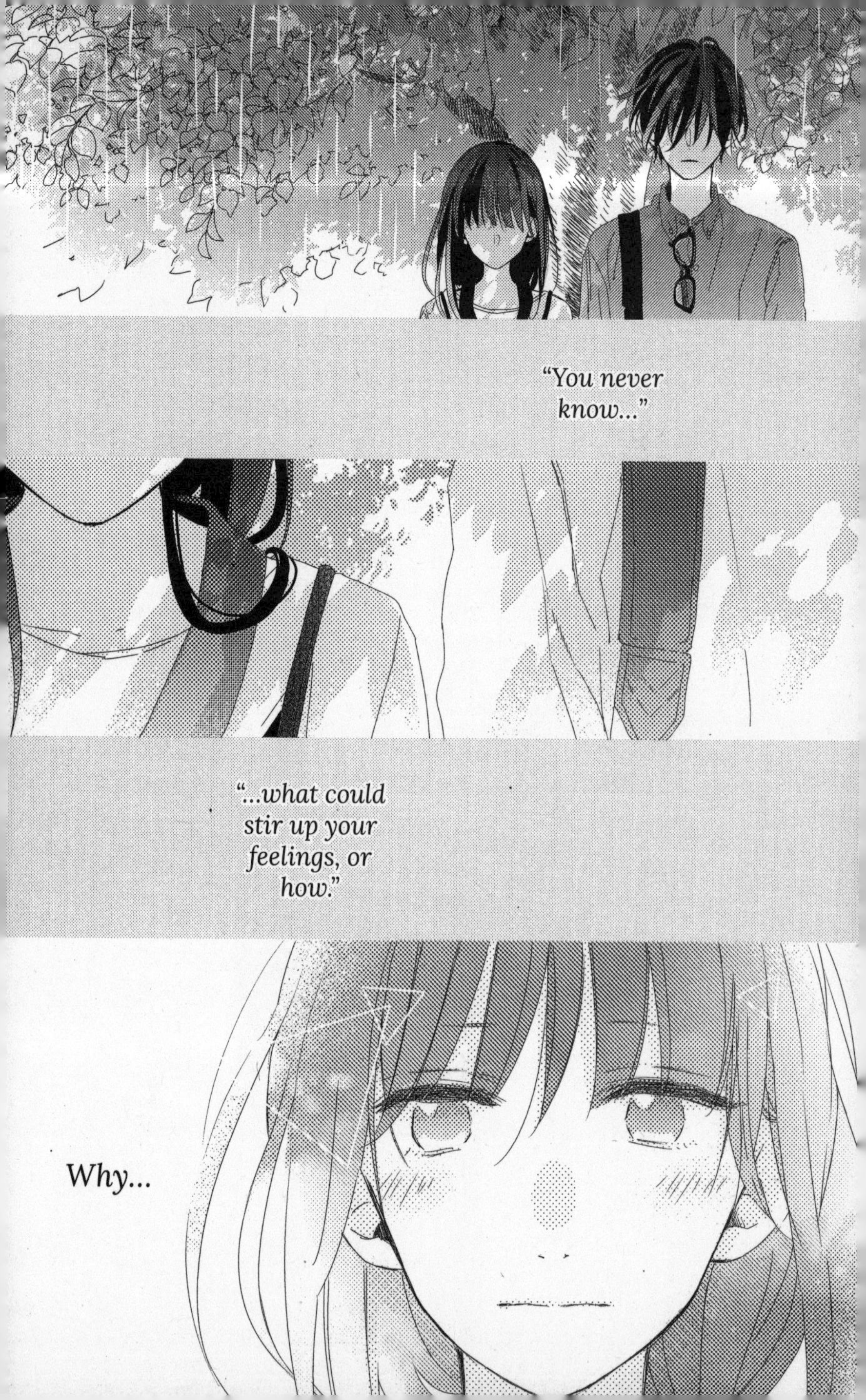
"You never know..."
"...what could stir up your feelings, or how."
Why...

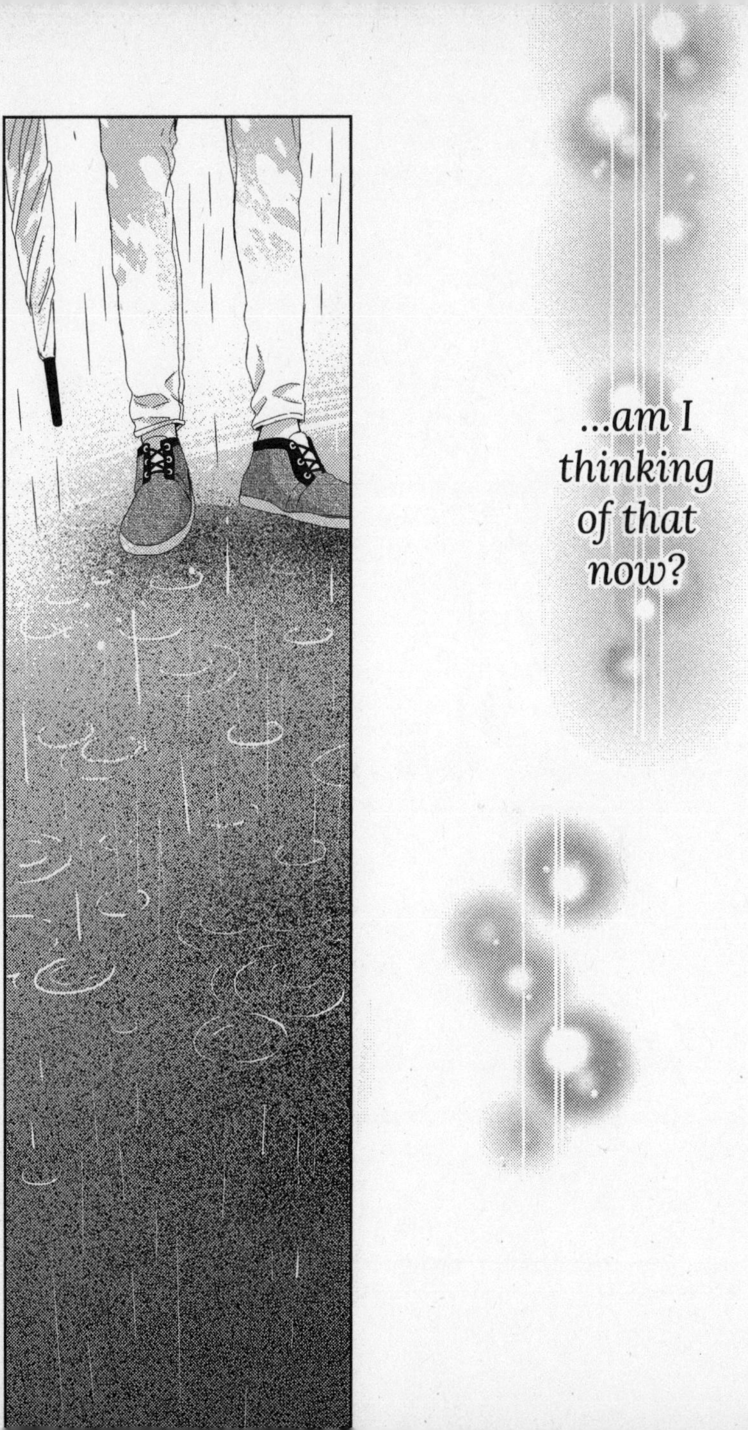
...am I thinking of that now?

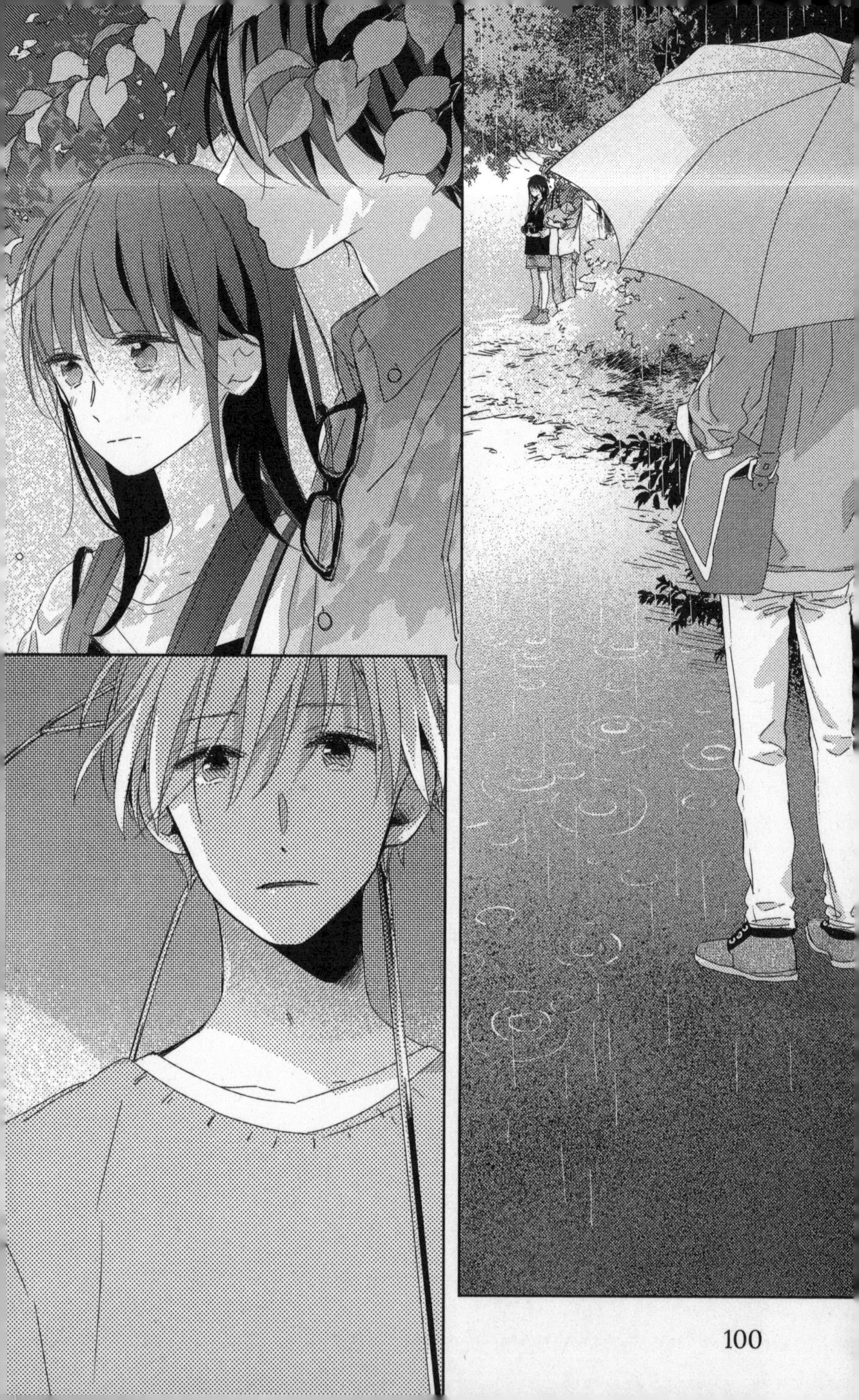

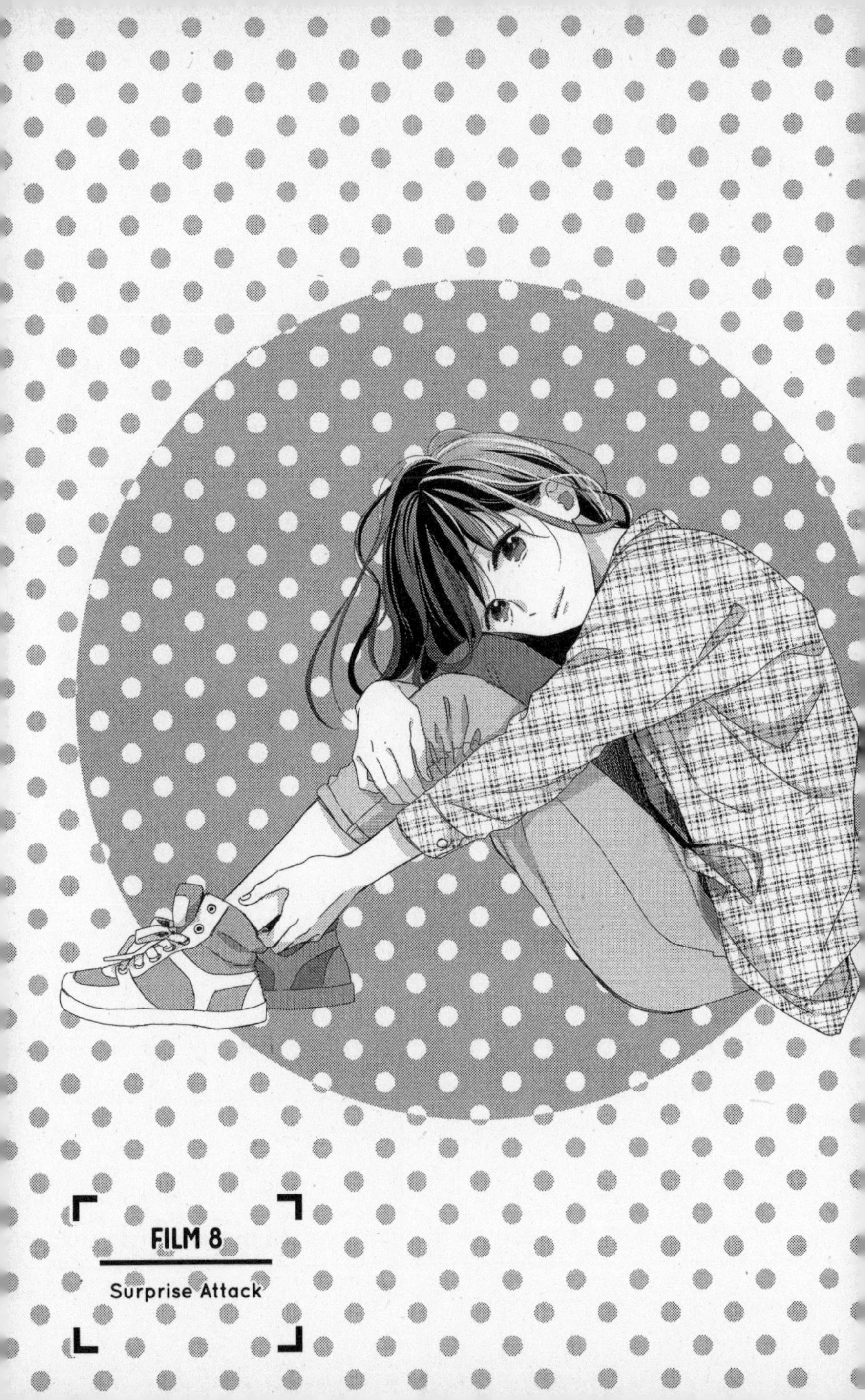

FILM 8

Surprise Attack

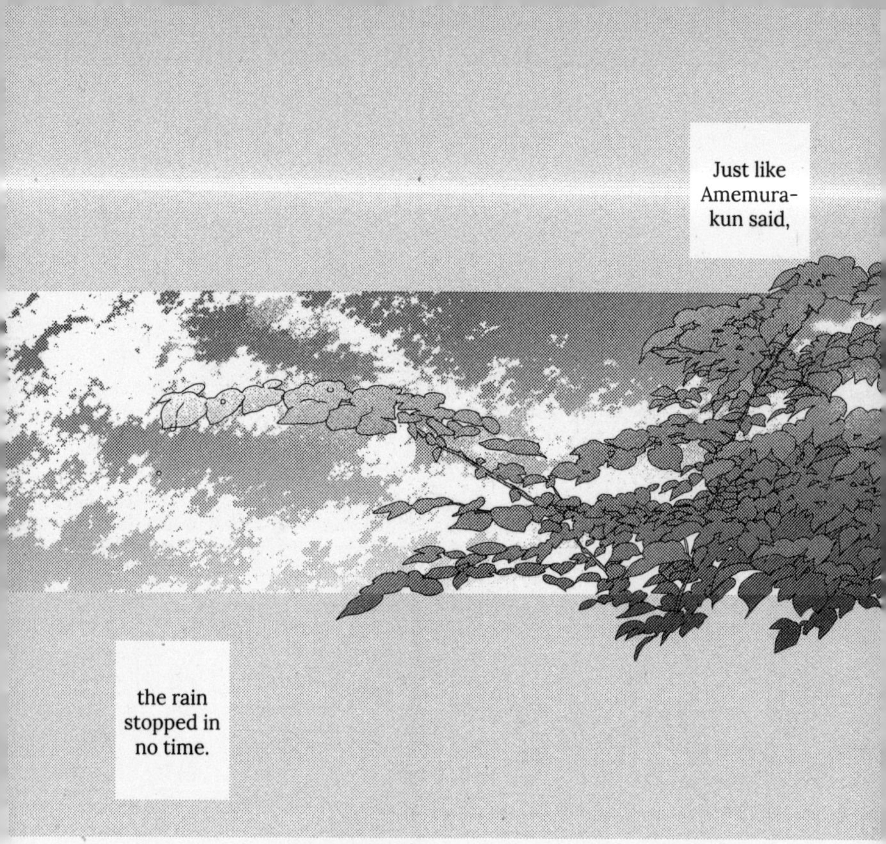
Just like Amemura-kun said,
the rain stopped in no time.

LOVE IN FOCUS

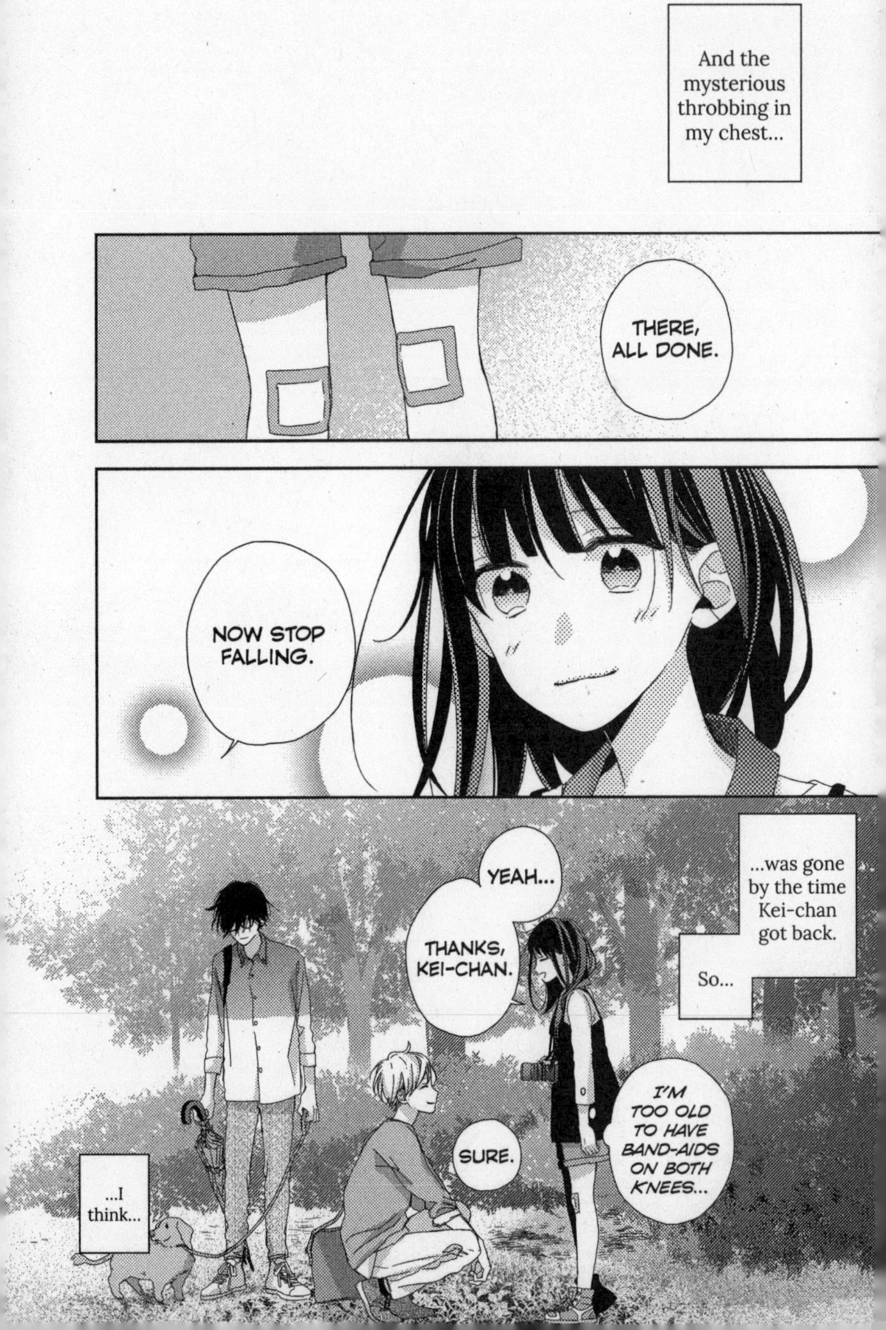
And the mysterious throbbing in my chest...
THERE, ALL DONE.
NOW STOP FALLING.
...was gone by the time Kei-chan got back.
So...
YEAH...
THANKS, KEI-CHAN.
I'M TOO OLD TO HAVE BAND-AIDS ON BOTH KNEES...
SURE.
...I think...

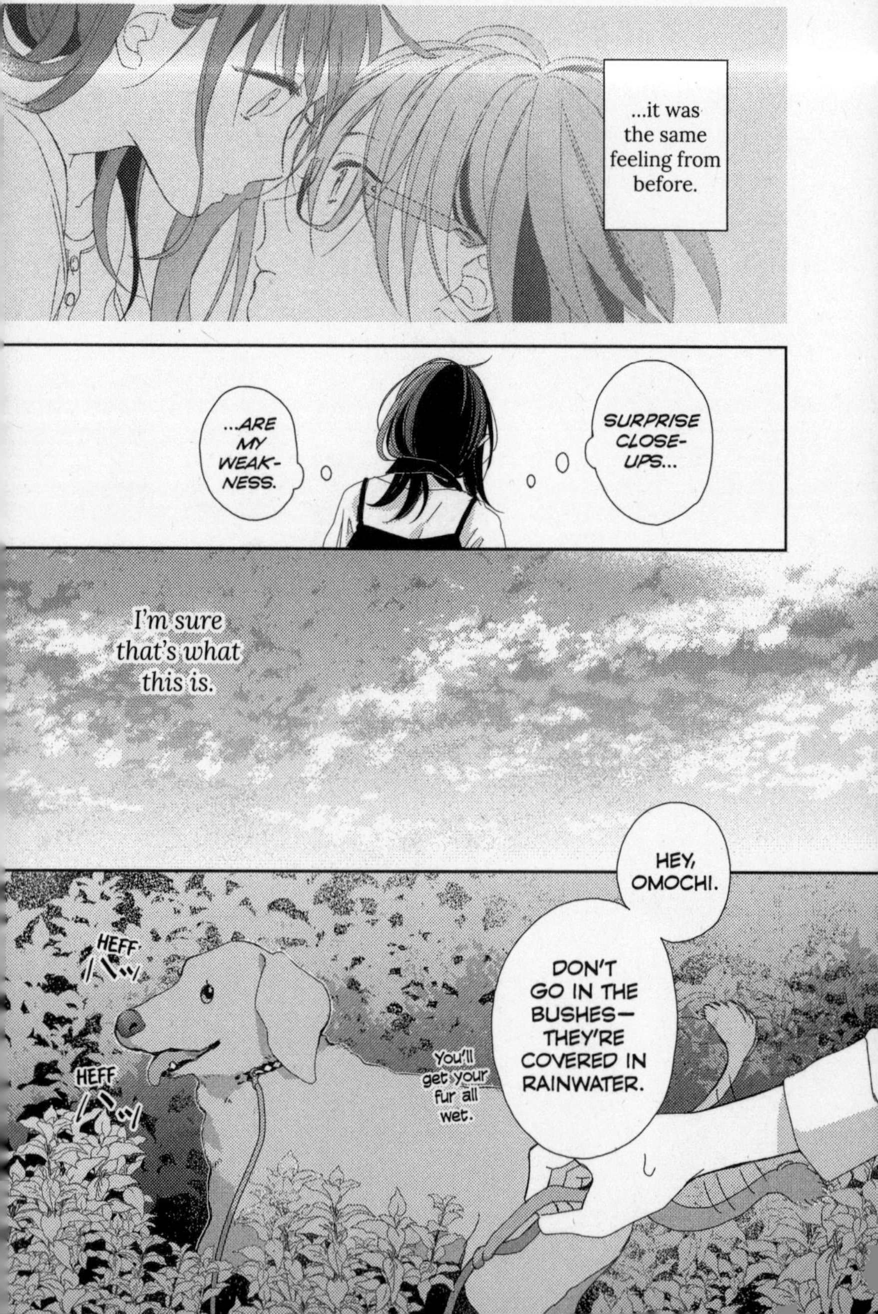

...it was the same feeling from before.
SURPRISE CLOSE-UPS...
...ARE MY WEAK-NESS.
I'm sure that's what this is.
HEY, OMOCHI.
DON'T GO IN THE BUSHES—THEY'RE COVERED IN RAINWATER.
You'll get your fur all wet.
HEFF
HEFF

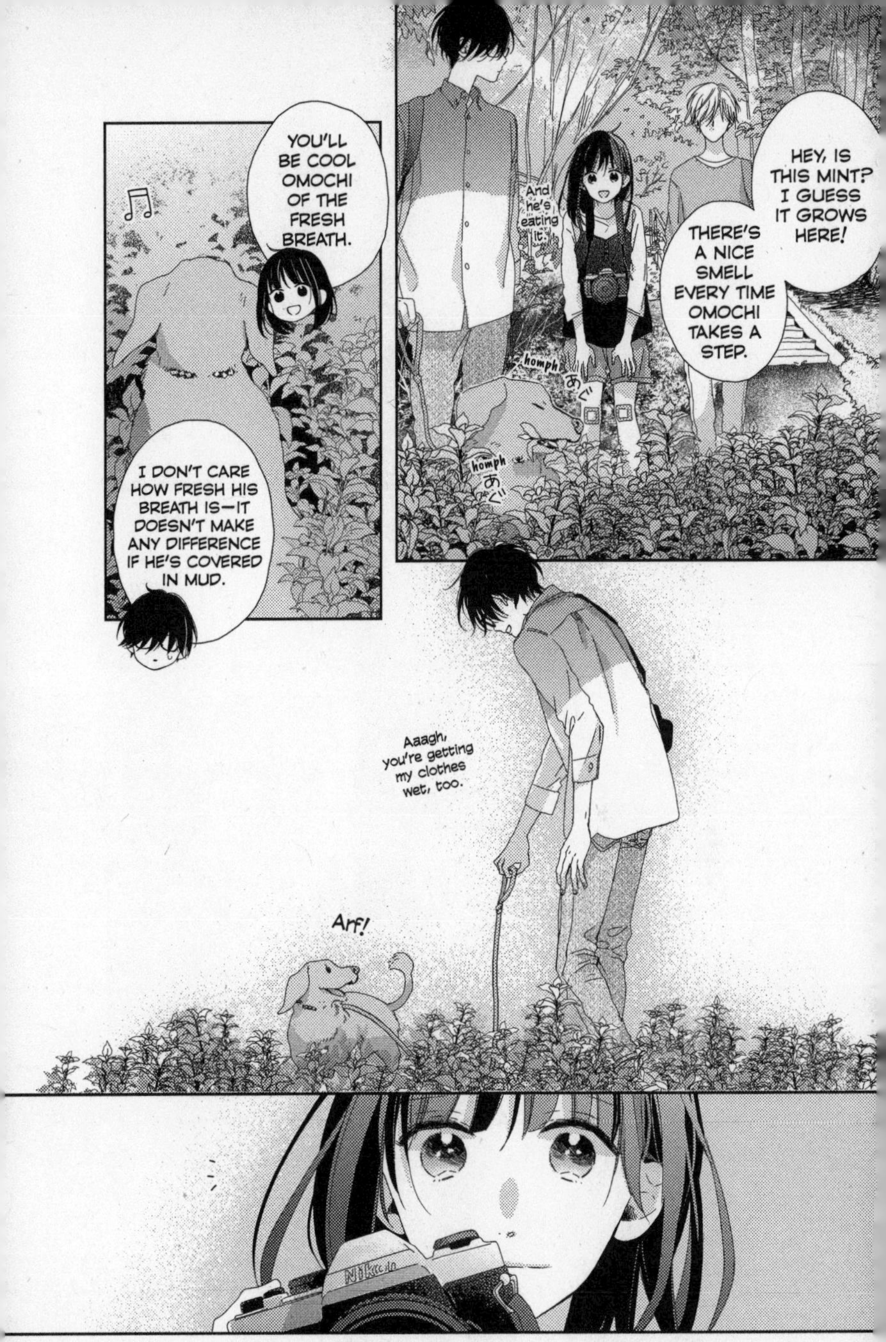
HEY, IS THIS MINT? I GUESS IT GROWS HERE!
THERE'S A NICE SMELL EVERY TIME OMOCHI TAKES A STEP.
And he's eating it.
homph あぐ
homph あぐ
YOU'LL BE COOL OMOCHI OF THE FRESH BREATH.
I DON'T CARE HOW FRESH HIS BREATH IS—IT DOESN'T MAKE ANY DIFFERENCE IF HE'S COVERED IN MUD.
Aaagh, you're getting my clothes wet, too.
Arf!

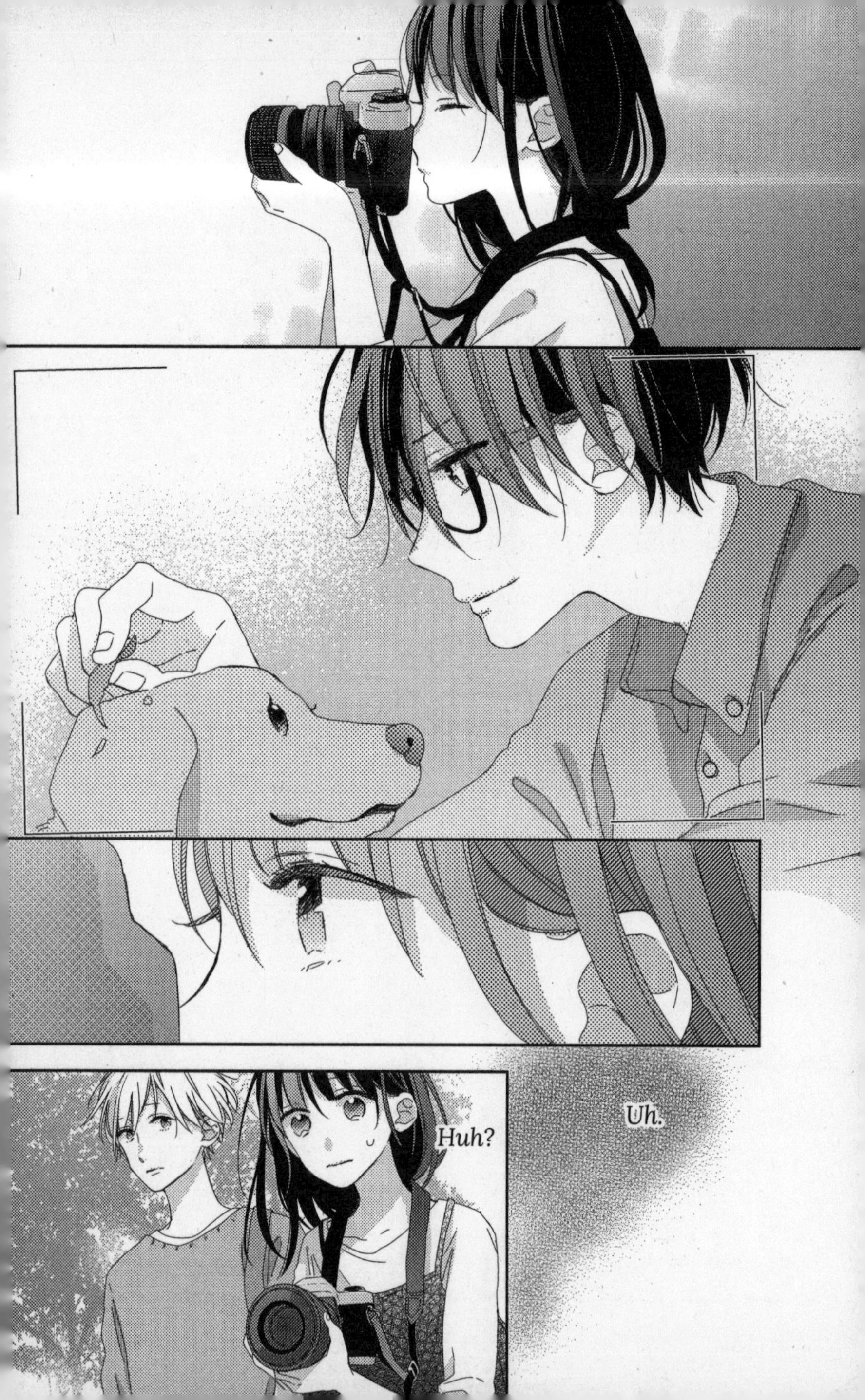
Uh.
Huh?

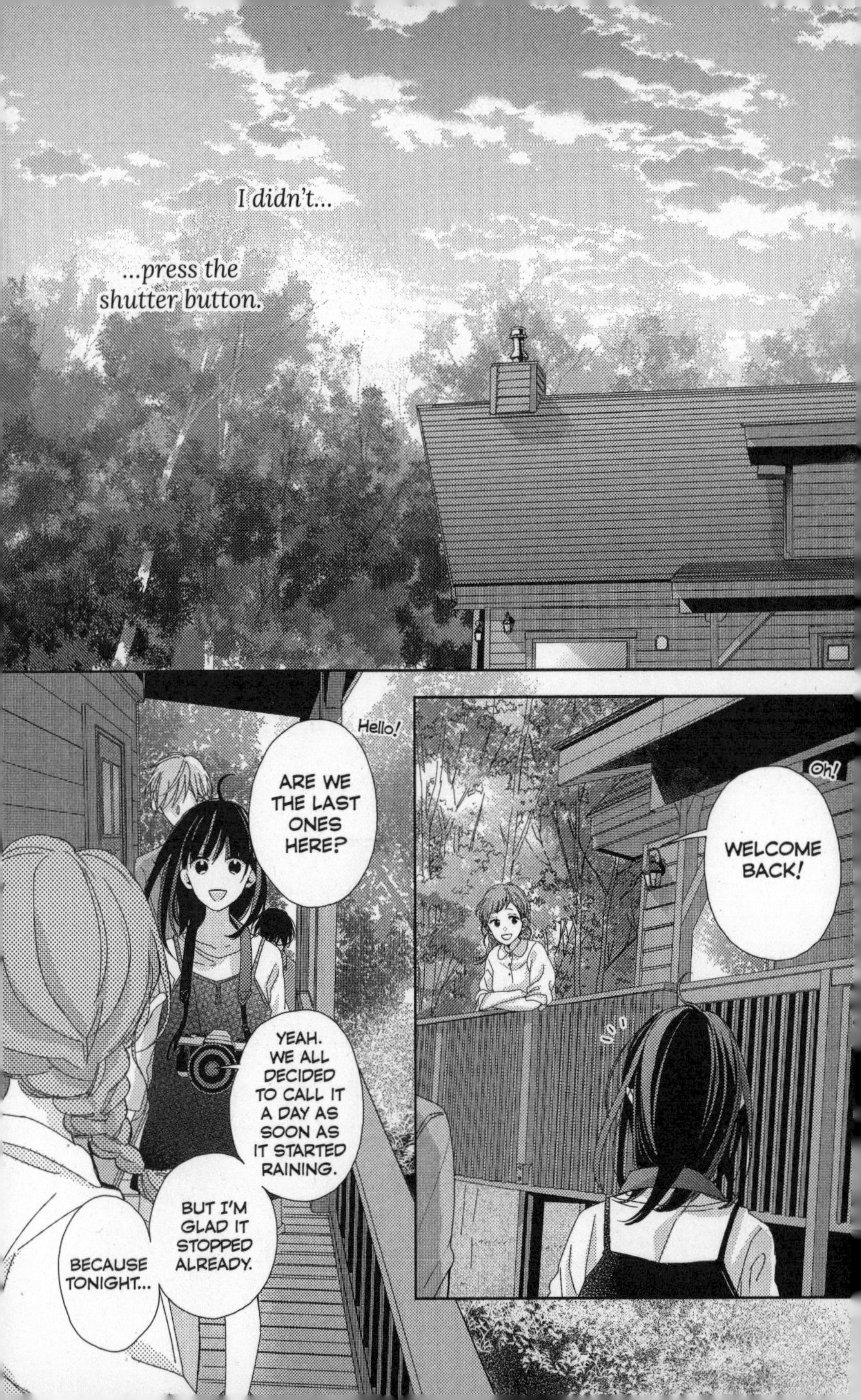
I didn't...
...press the shutter button.
Oh!
WELCOME BACK!
Hello!
ARE WE THE LAST ONES HERE?
YEAH. WE ALL DECIDED TO CALL IT A DAY AS SOON AS IT STARTED RAINING.
BUT I'M GLAD IT STOPPED ALREADY.
BECAUSE TONIGHT...

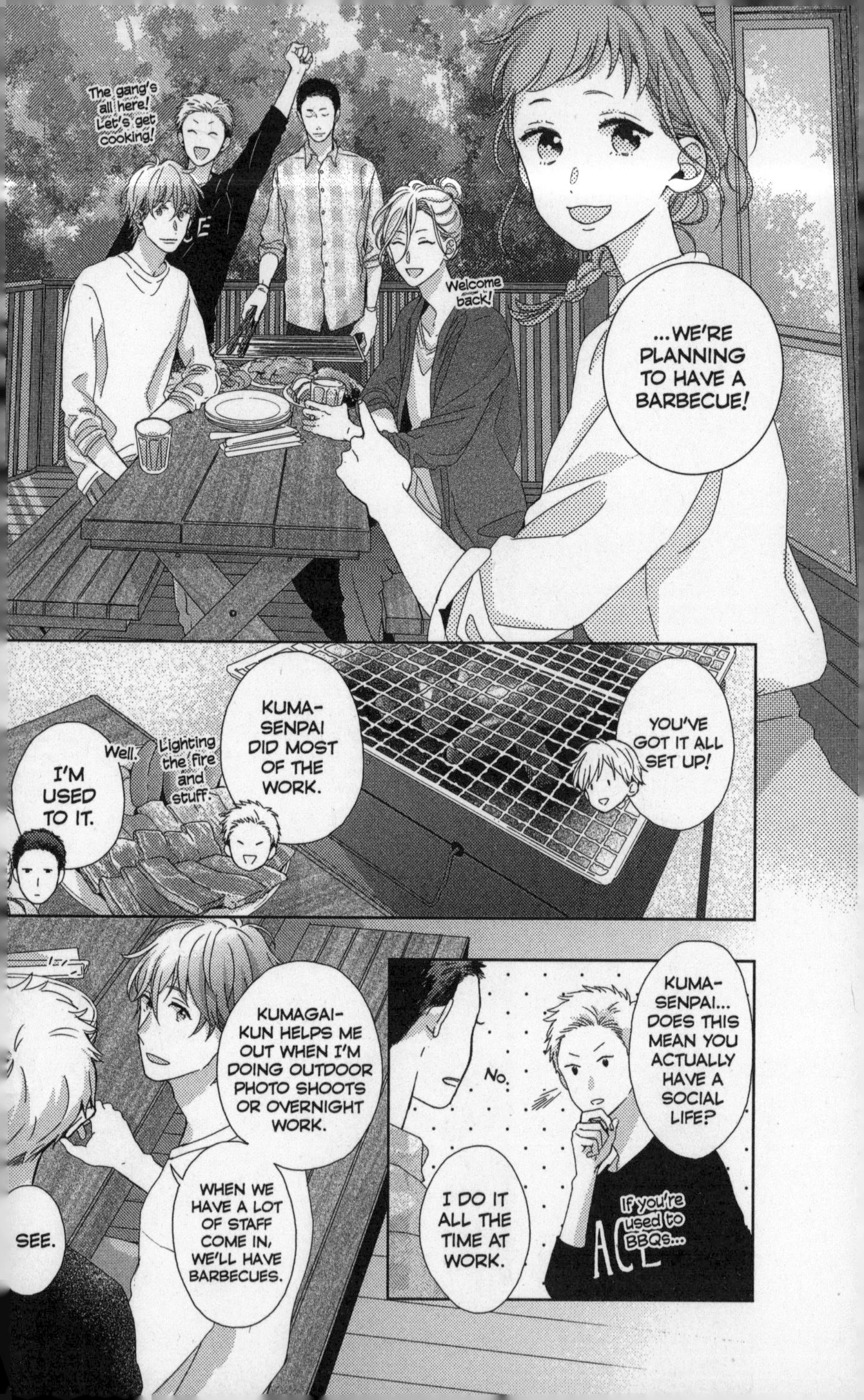
...WE'RE PLANNING TO HAVE A BARBECUE!
Welcome back!
The gang's all here! Let's get cooking!
YOU'VE GOT IT ALL SET UP!
KUMA-SENPAI DID MOST OF THE WORK.
Lighting the fire and stuff.
Well.
I'M USED TO IT.
KUMA-SENPAI... DOES THIS MEAN YOU ACTUALLY HAVE A SOCIAL LIFE?
No.
I DO IT ALL THE TIME AT WORK.
If you're used to BBQs...
KUMAGAI-KUN HELPS ME OUT WHEN I'M DOING OUTDOOR PHOTO SHOOTS OR OVERNIGHT WORK.
WHEN WE HAVE A LOT OF STAFF COME IN, WE'LL HAVE BARBECUES.
SEE.

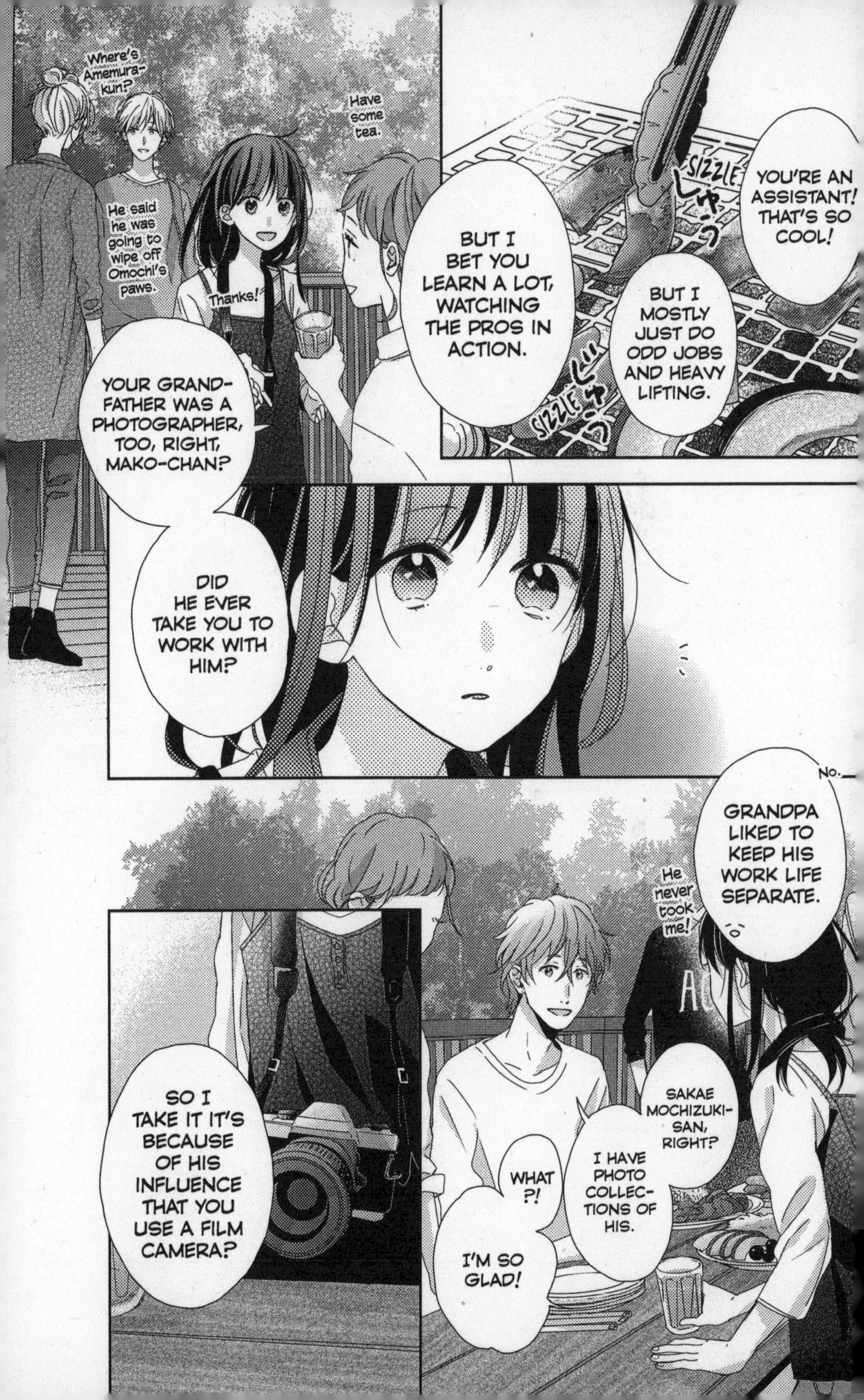
YOU'RE AN ASSISTANT! THAT'S SO COOL!
SIZZLE
BUT I MOSTLY JUST DO ODD JOBS AND HEAVY LIFTING.
SIZZLE
BUT I BET YOU LEARN A LOT, WATCHING THE PROS IN ACTION.
Have some tea.
Thanks!
Where's Amemura-kun?
He said he was going to wipe off Omochi's paws.
YOUR GRANDFATHER WAS A PHOTOGRAPHER, TOO, RIGHT, MAKO-CHAN?
DID HE EVER TAKE YOU TO WORK WITH HIM?
No.
GRANDPA LIKED TO KEEP HIS WORK LIFE SEPARATE.
He never took me!
SAKAE MOCHIZUKI-SAN, RIGHT?
I HAVE PHOTO COLLECTIONS OF HIS.
WHAT?!
I'M SO GLAD!
SO I TAKE IT IT'S BECAUSE OF HIS INFLUENCE THAT YOU USE A FILM CAMERA?

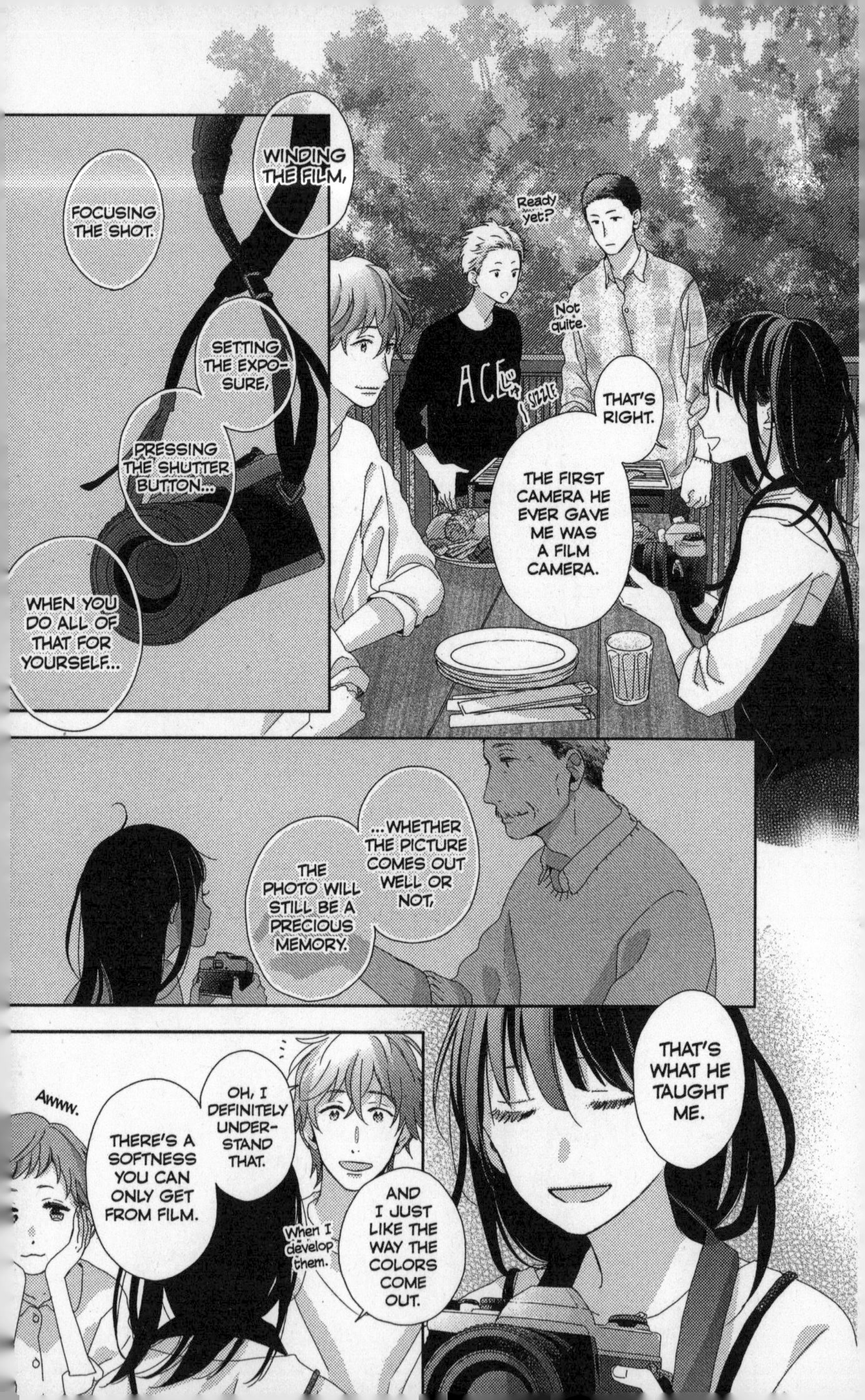
Ready yet?
Not quite.
SIZZLE
THAT'S RIGHT.
THE FIRST CAMERA HE EVER GAVE ME WAS A FILM CAMERA.
WINDING THE FILM,
FOCUSING THE SHOT.
SETTING THE EXPO-SURE,
PRESSING THE SHUTTER BUTTON...
WHEN YOU DO ALL OF THAT FOR YOURSELF...
...WHETHER THE PICTURE COMES OUT WELL OR NOT,
THE PHOTO WILL STILL BE A PRECIOUS MEMORY.
THAT'S WHAT HE TAUGHT ME.
AND I JUST LIKE THE WAY THE COLORS COME OUT.
When I develop them.
OH, I DEFINITELY UNDER-STAND THAT.
THERE'S A SOFTNESS YOU CAN ONLY GET FROM FILM.
Awww.

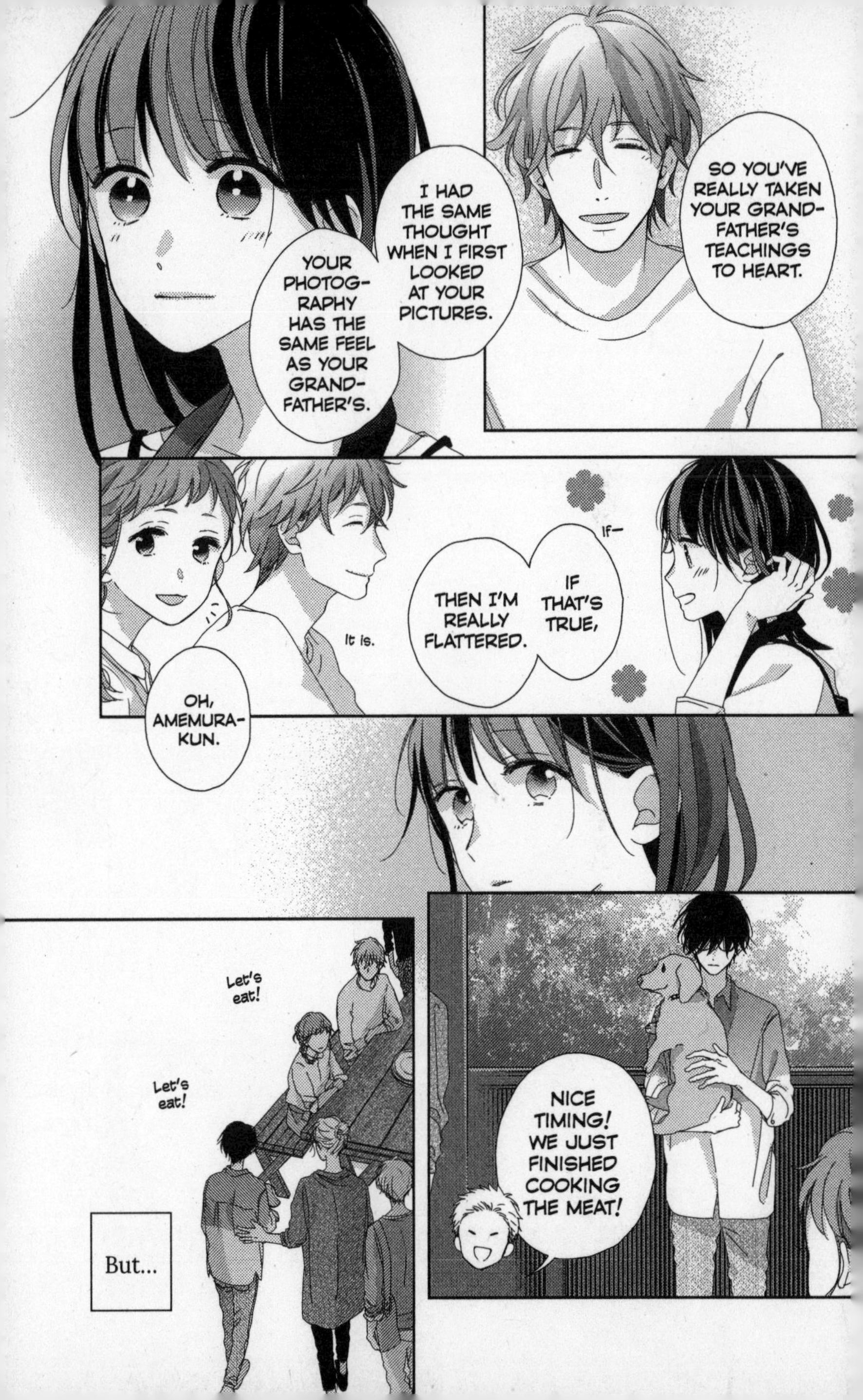
SO YOU'VE REALLY TAKEN YOUR GRAND-FATHER'S TEACHINGS TO HEART.
I HAD THE SAME THOUGHT WHEN I FIRST LOOKED AT YOUR PICTURES.
YOUR PHOTOG-RAPHY HAS THE SAME FEEL AS YOUR GRAND-FATHER'S.
If—
IF THAT'S TRUE,
THEN I'M REALLY FLATTERED.
It is.
OH, AMEMURA-KUN.
NICE TIMING! WE JUST FINISHED COOKING THE MEAT!
Let's eat!
Let's eat!
But...

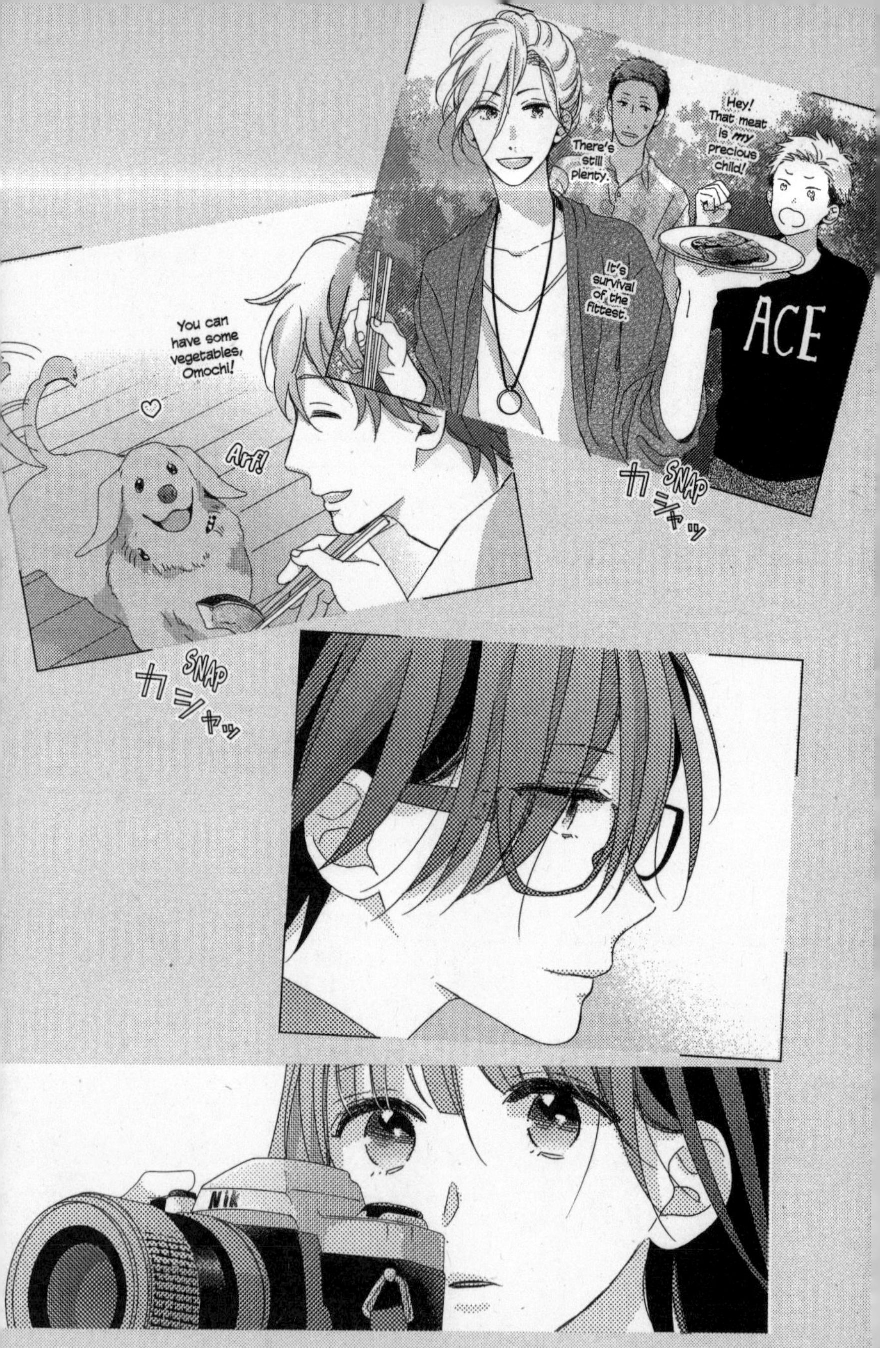
Hey! That meat is *my* precious child!
There's still plenty.
It's survival of the fittest.
SNAP
カシャッ
You can have some vegetables, Omochi!
Arf!
SNAP
カシャッ

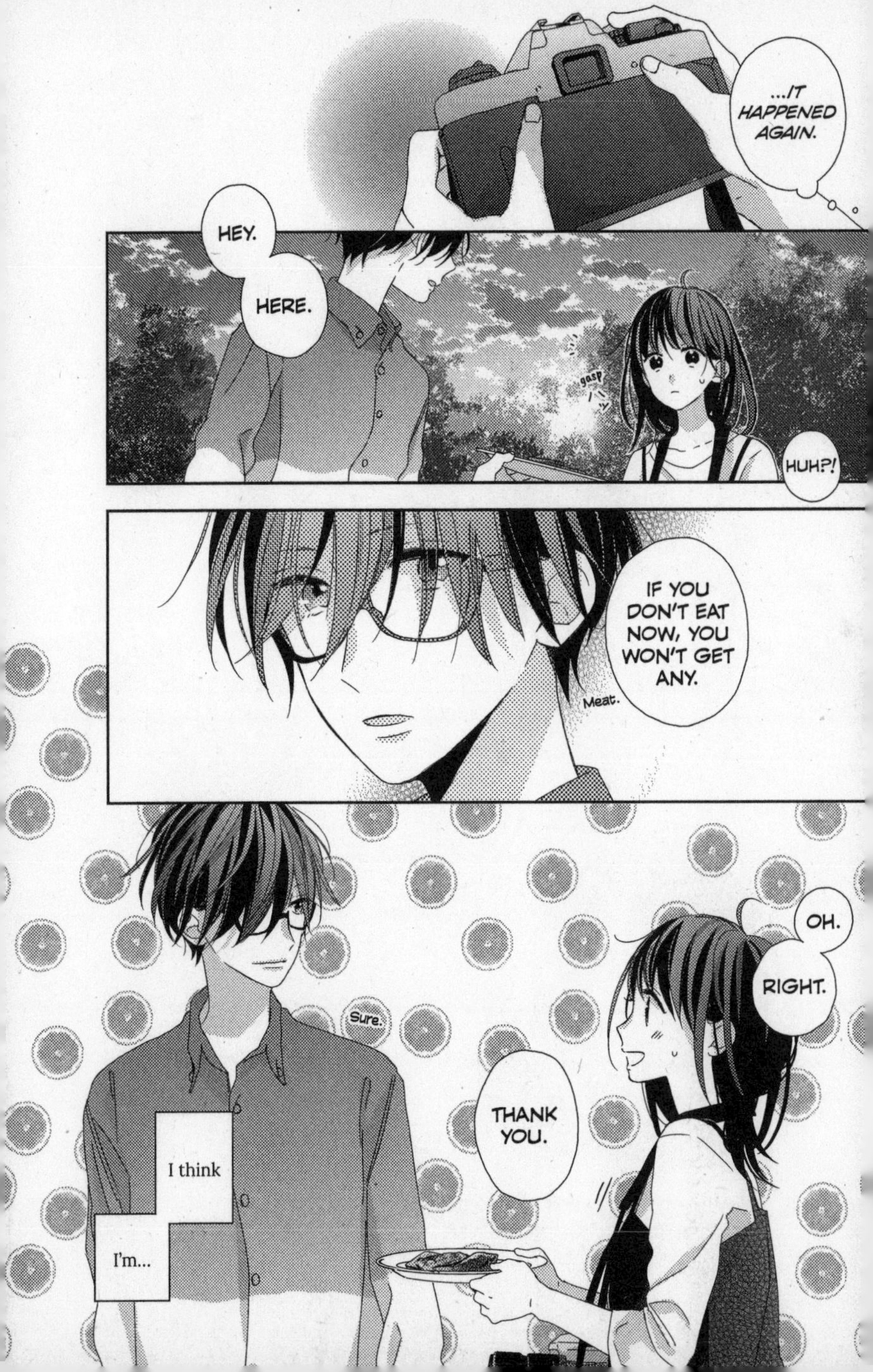
...IT HAPPENED AGAIN.
HEY.
HERE.
gasp
HUH?!
IF YOU DON'T EAT NOW, YOU WON'T GET ANY.
Meat.
OH.
RIGHT.
THANK YOU.
Sure.
I think
I'm...

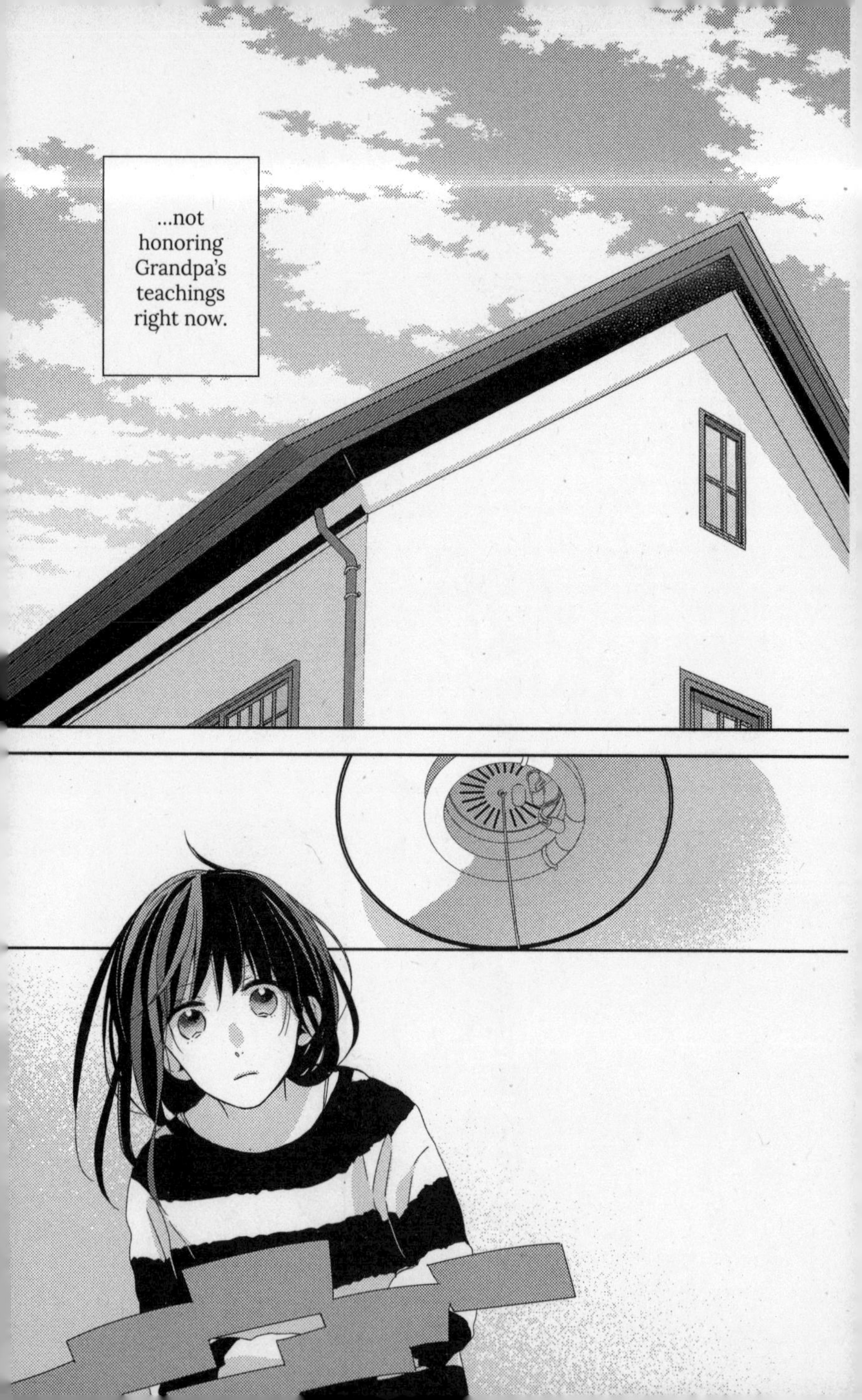
...not honoring Grandpa's teachings right now.

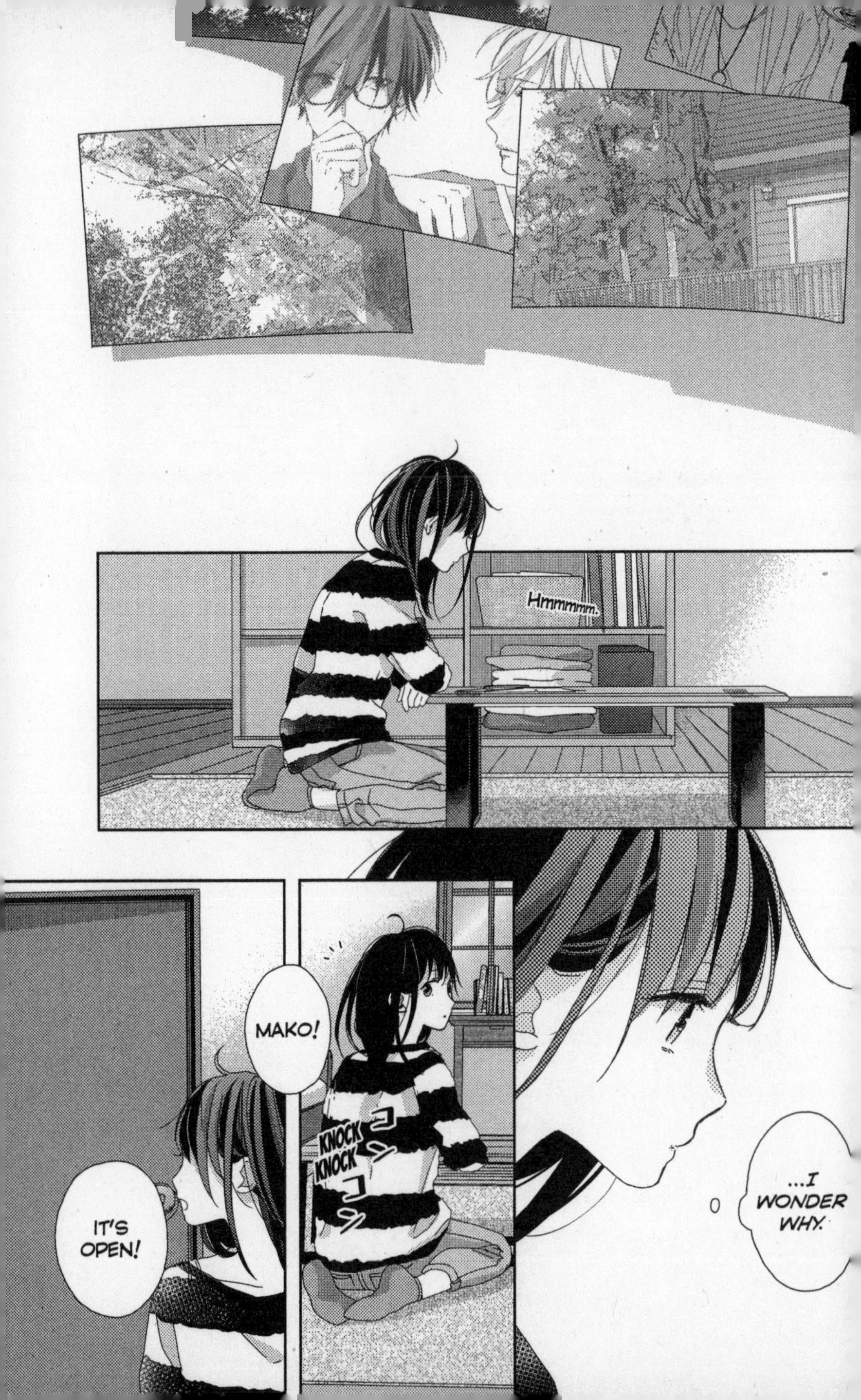
Hmmmmm.
...I WONDER WHY.
MAKO!
KNOCK KNOCK
IT'S OPEN!

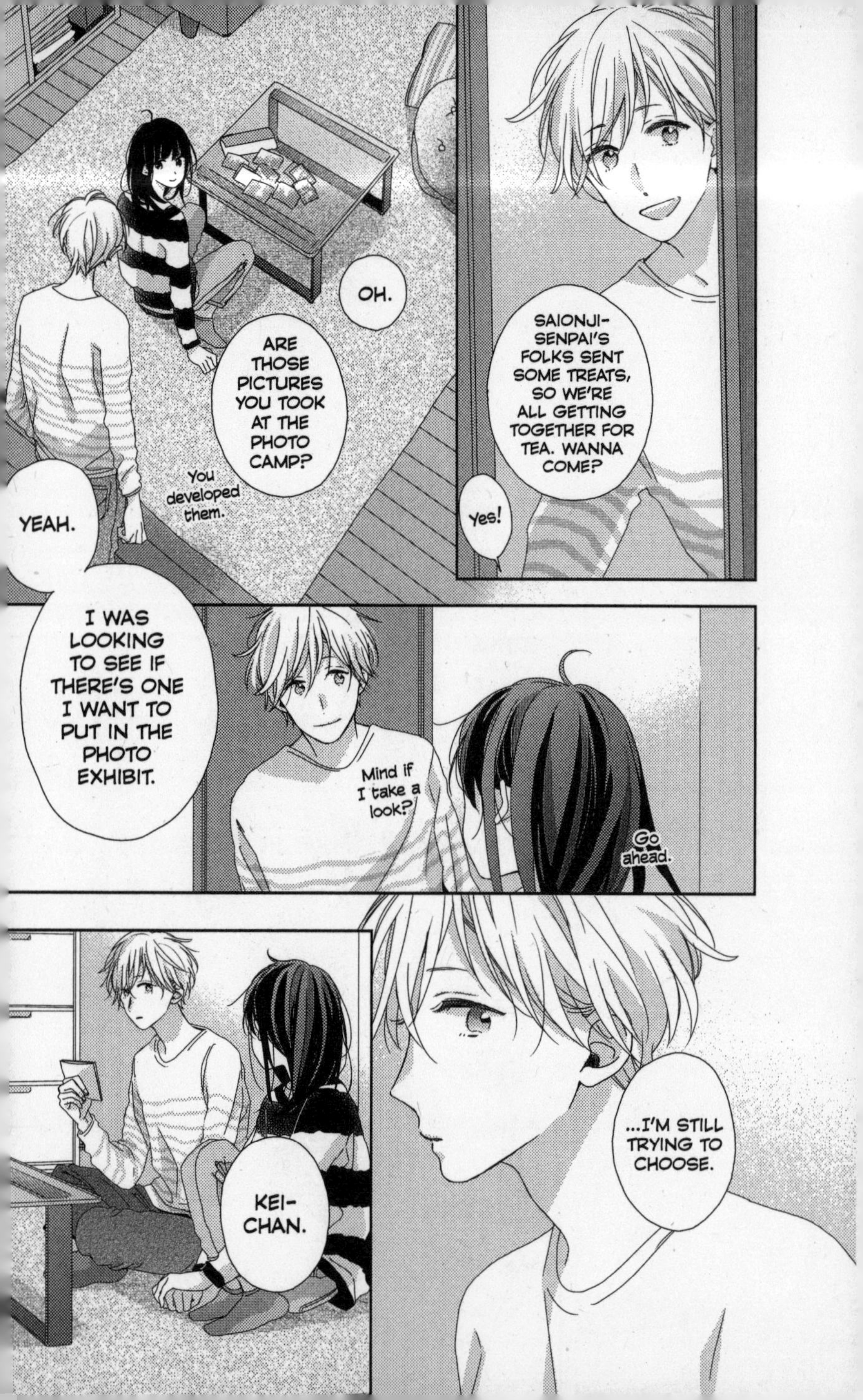
SAIONJI-SENPAI'S FOLKS SENT SOME TREATS, SO WE'RE ALL GETTING TOGETHER FOR TEA. WANNA COME?
Yes!
OH.
ARE THOSE PICTURES YOU TOOK AT THE PHOTO CAMP?
You developed them.
YEAH.
I WAS LOOKING TO SEE IF THERE'S ONE I WANT TO PUT IN THE PHOTO EXHIBIT.
Mind if I take a look?
Go ahead.
...I'M STILL TRYING TO CHOOSE.
KEI-CHAN.

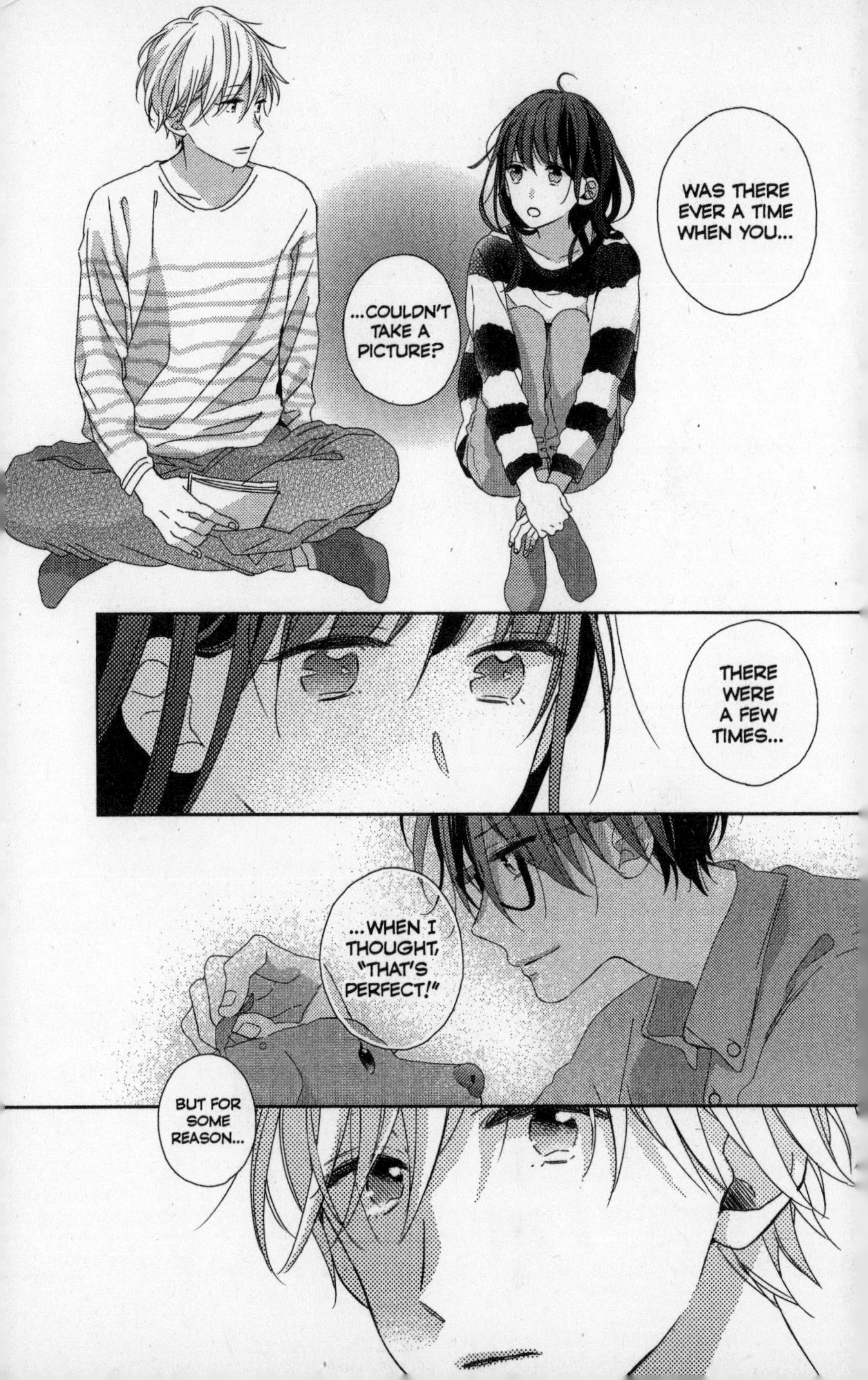
WAS THERE EVER A TIME WHEN YOU...
...COULDN'T TAKE A PICTURE?
THERE WERE A FEW TIMES...
...WHEN I THOUGHT, "THAT'S PERFECT!"
BUT FOR SOME REASON...

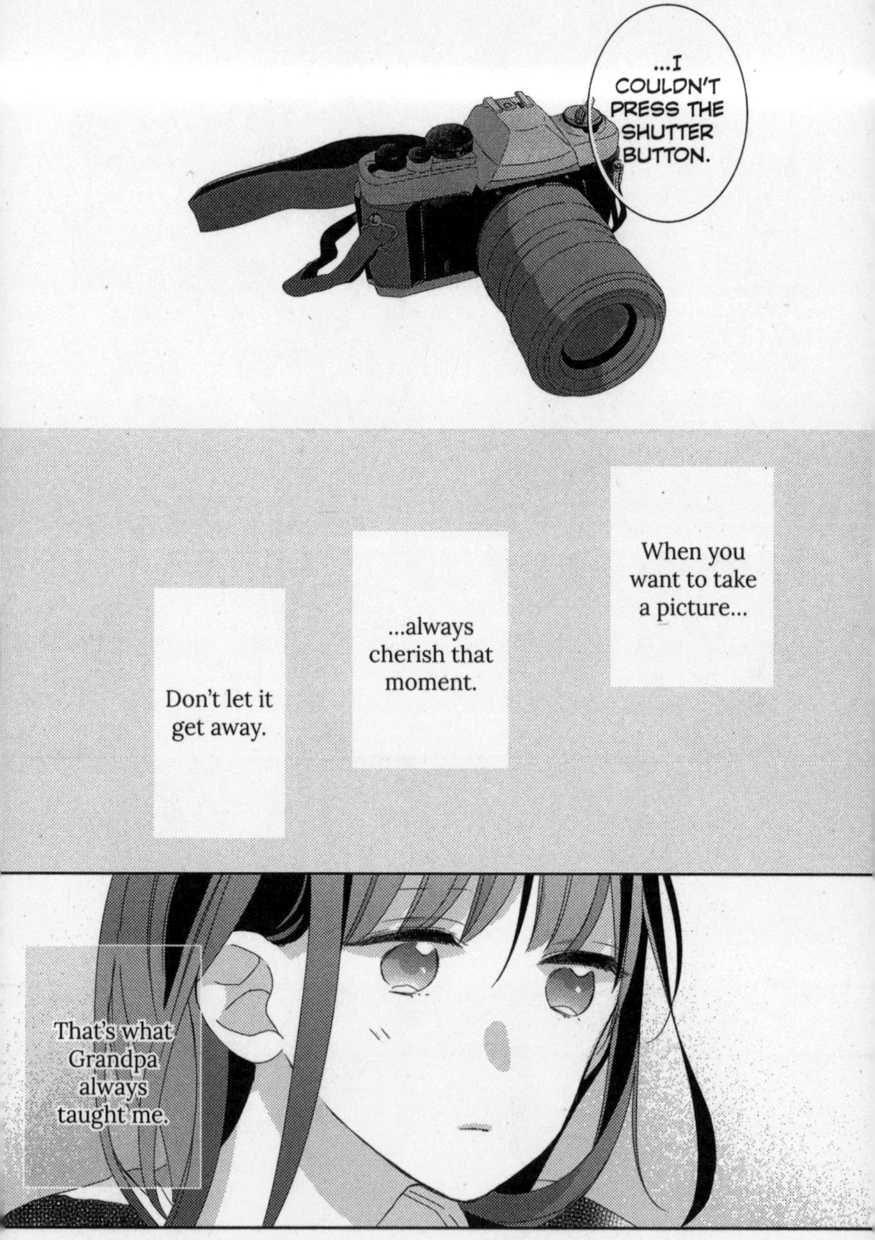
...I COULDN'T PRESS THE SHUTTER BUTTON.
When you want to take a picture...
...always cherish that moment.
Don't let it get away.
That's what Grandpa always taught me.

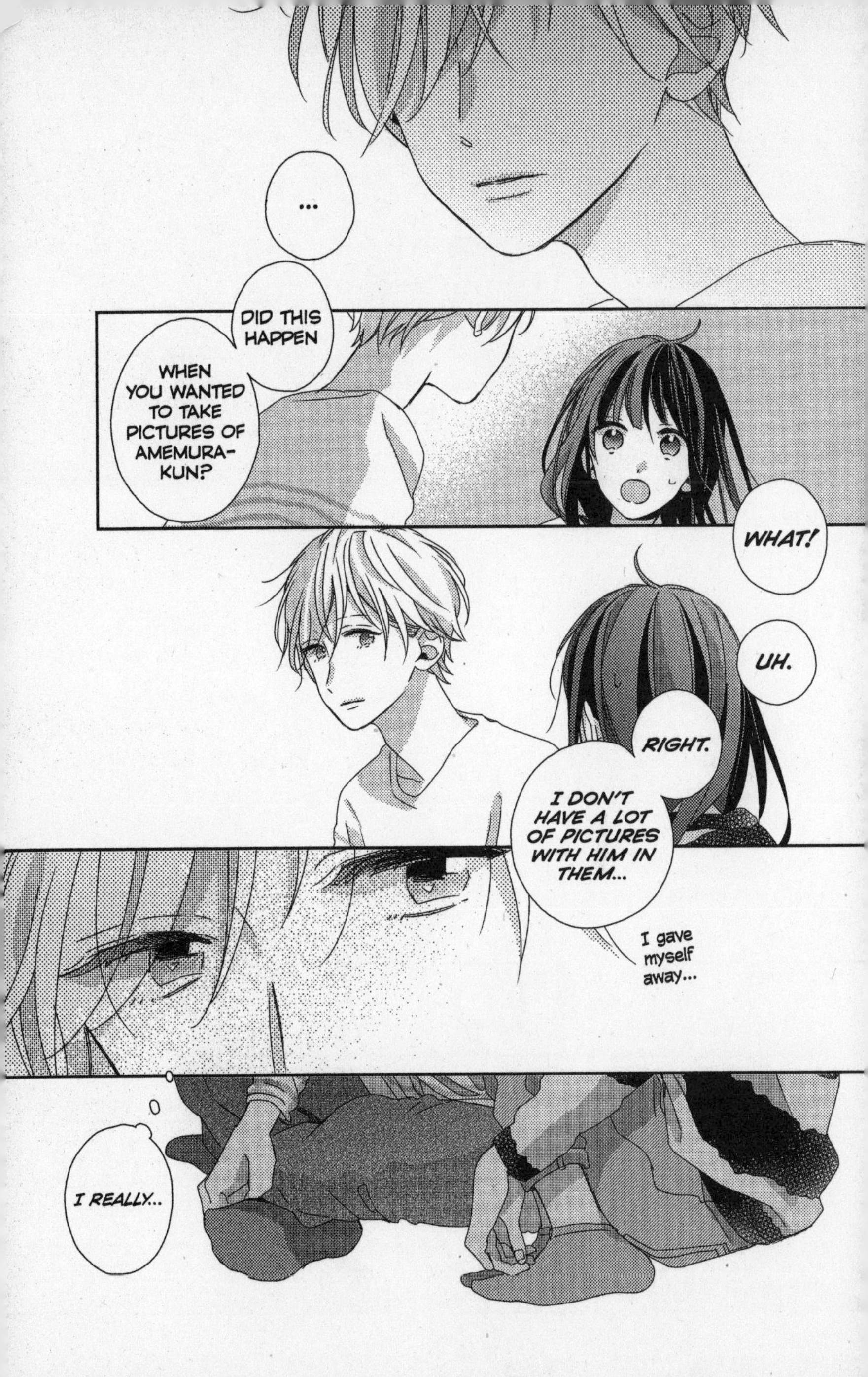
...
DID THIS HAPPEN
WHEN YOU WANTED TO TAKE PICTURES OF AMEMURA-KUN?
WHAT!
UH.
RIGHT.
I DON'T HAVE A LOT OF PICTURES WITH HIM IN THEM...
I gave myself away...
I REALLY...

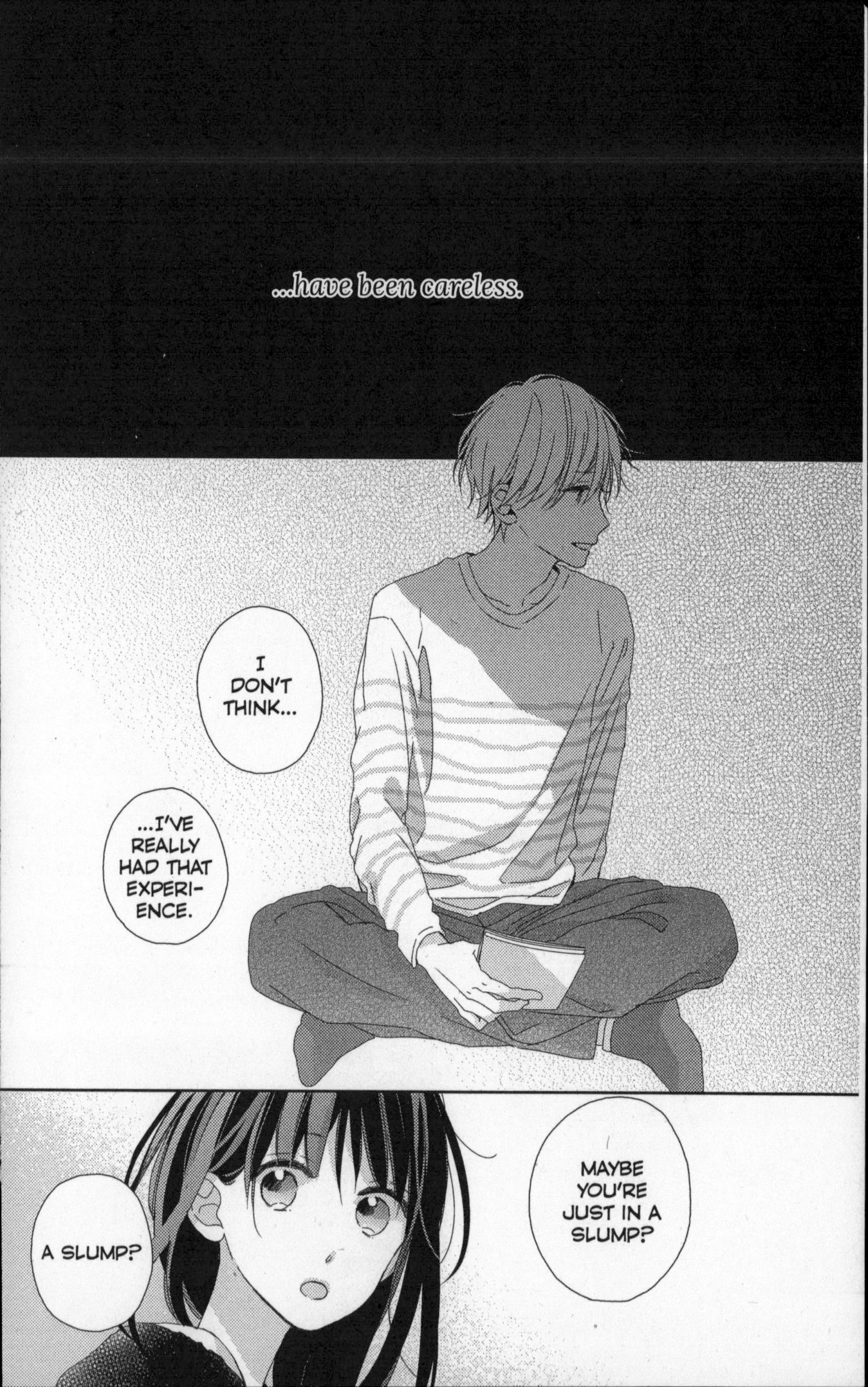
...have been careless.
I DON'T THINK...
...I'VE REALLY HAD THAT EXPERIENCE.
MAYBE YOU'RE JUST IN A SLUMP?
A SLUMP?

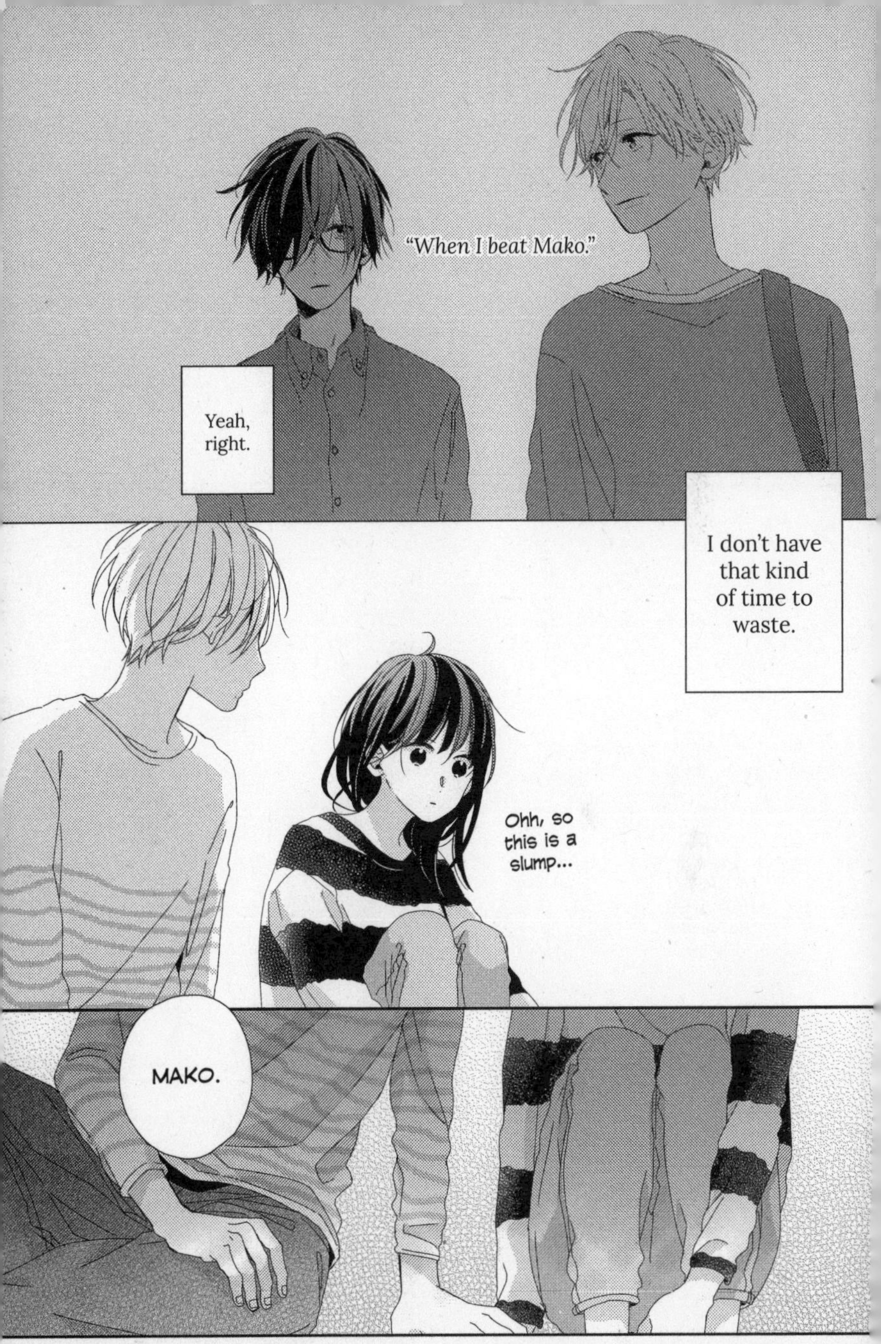
"When I beat Mako."
Yeah, right.
I don't have that kind of time to waste.
Ohh, so this is a slump...
MAKO.

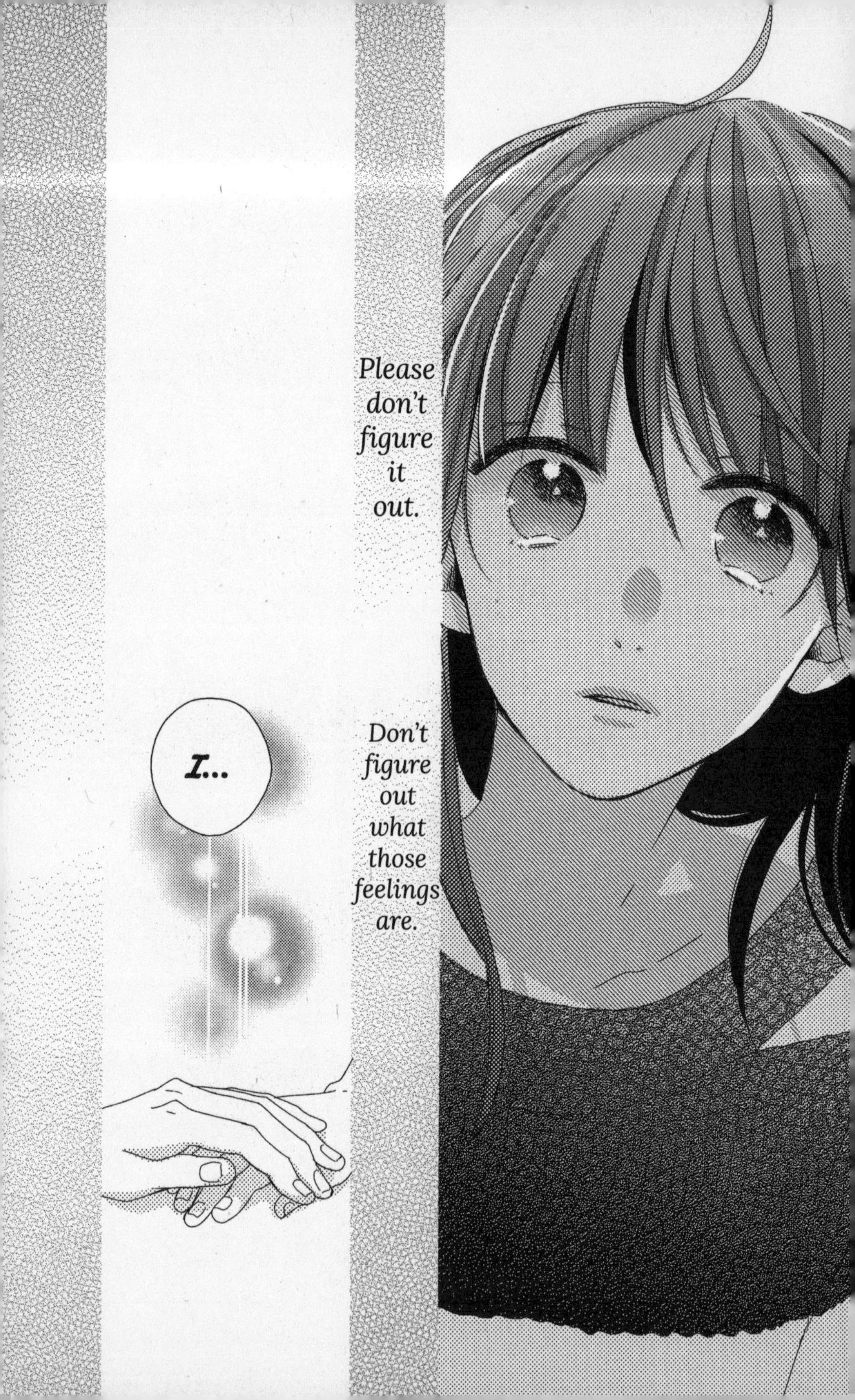
Please don't figure it out.
Don't figure out what those feelings are.
I...

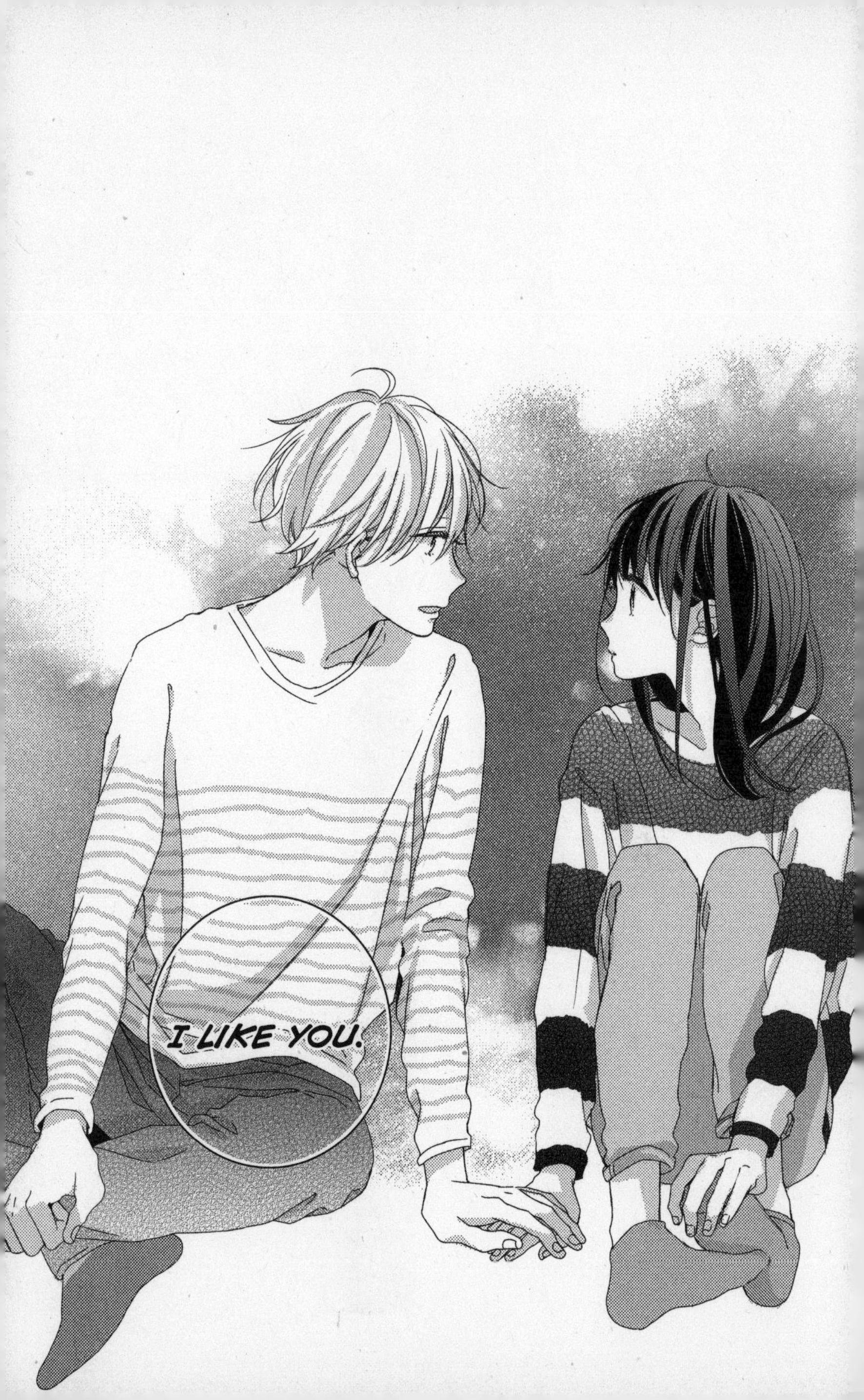
I LIKE YOU.

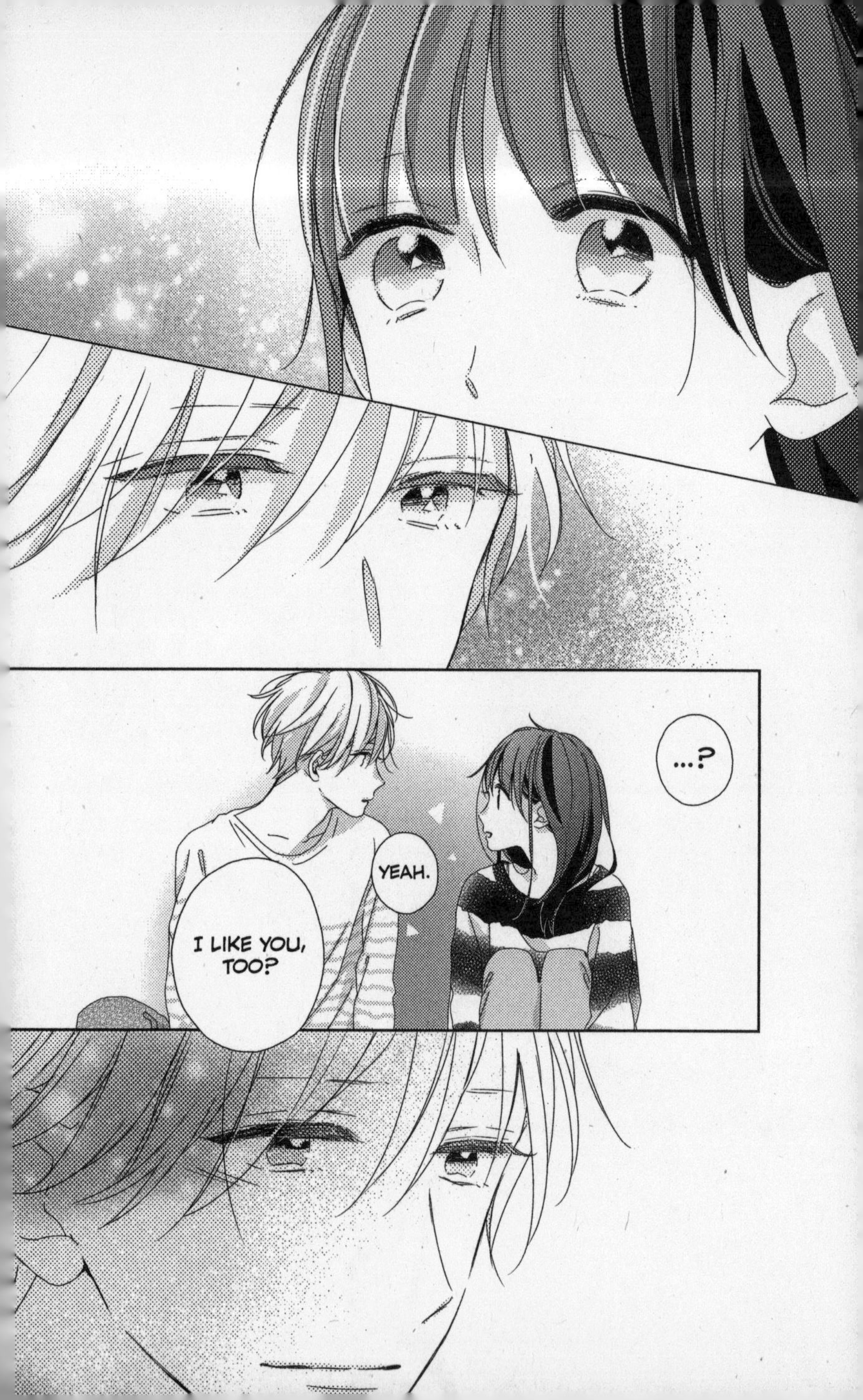
...?
YEAH.
I LIKE YOU, TOO?

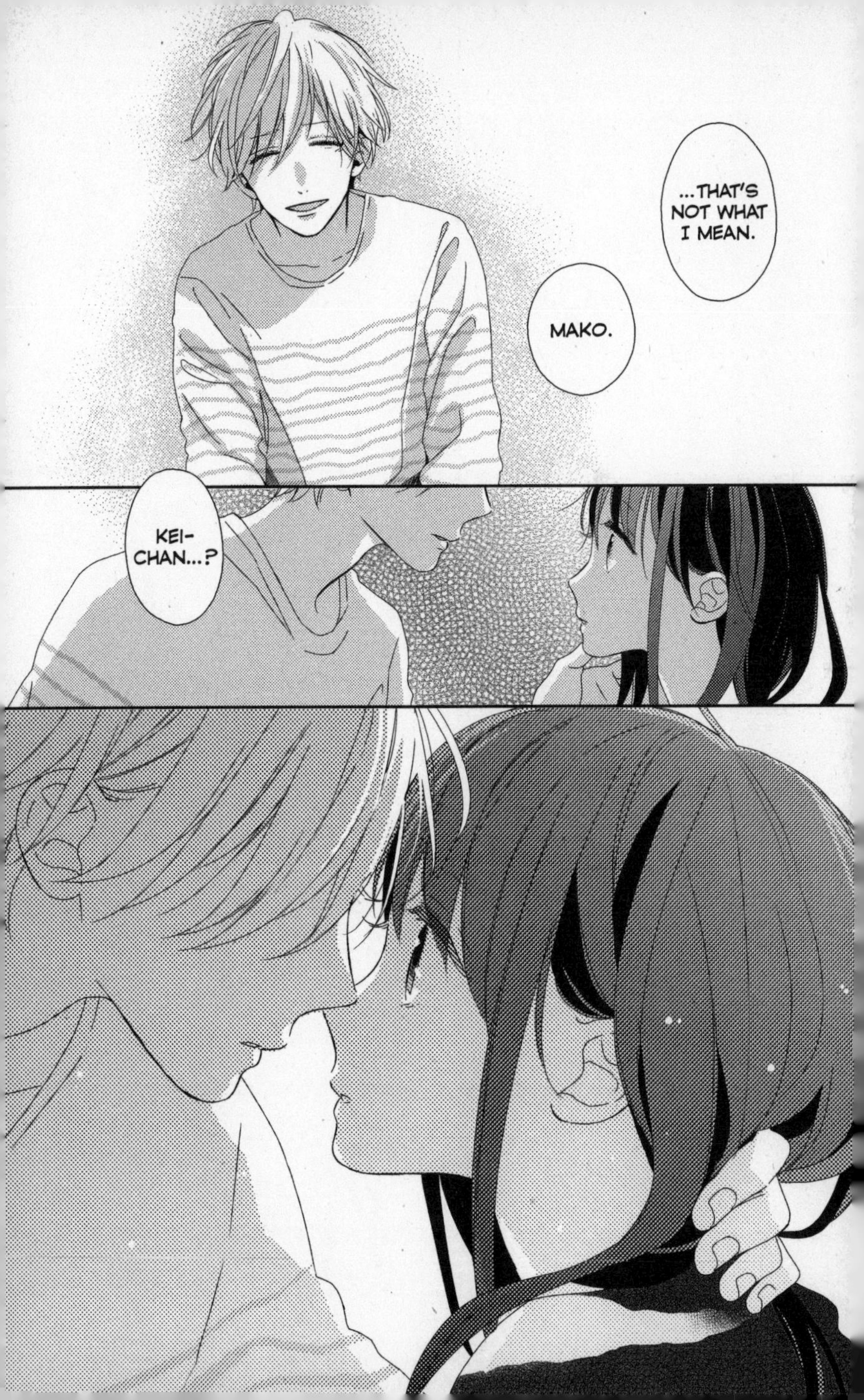
...THAT'S NOT WHAT I MEAN.
MAKO.
KEI-CHAN...?

A surprise close-up.

126

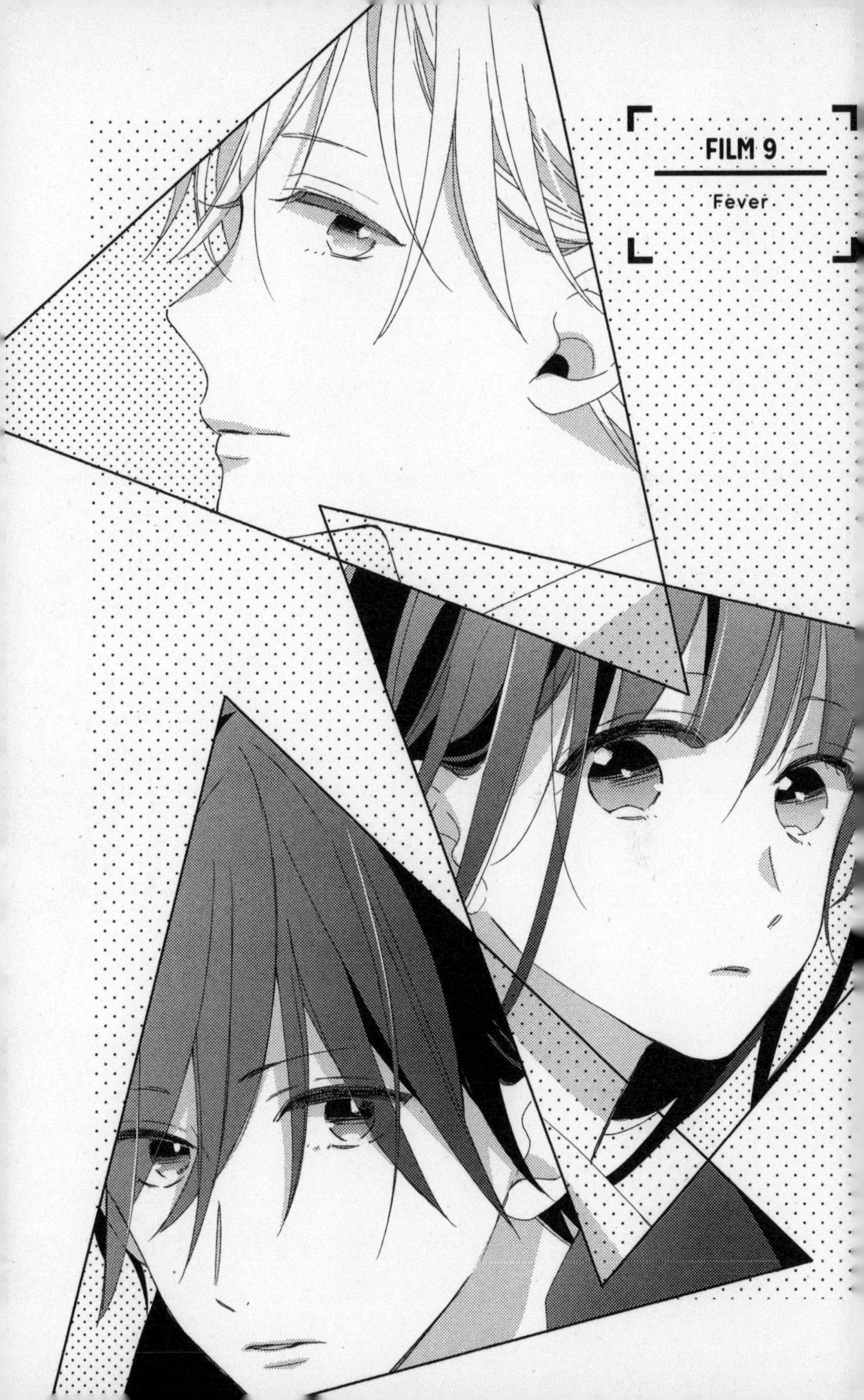
FILM 9
Fever

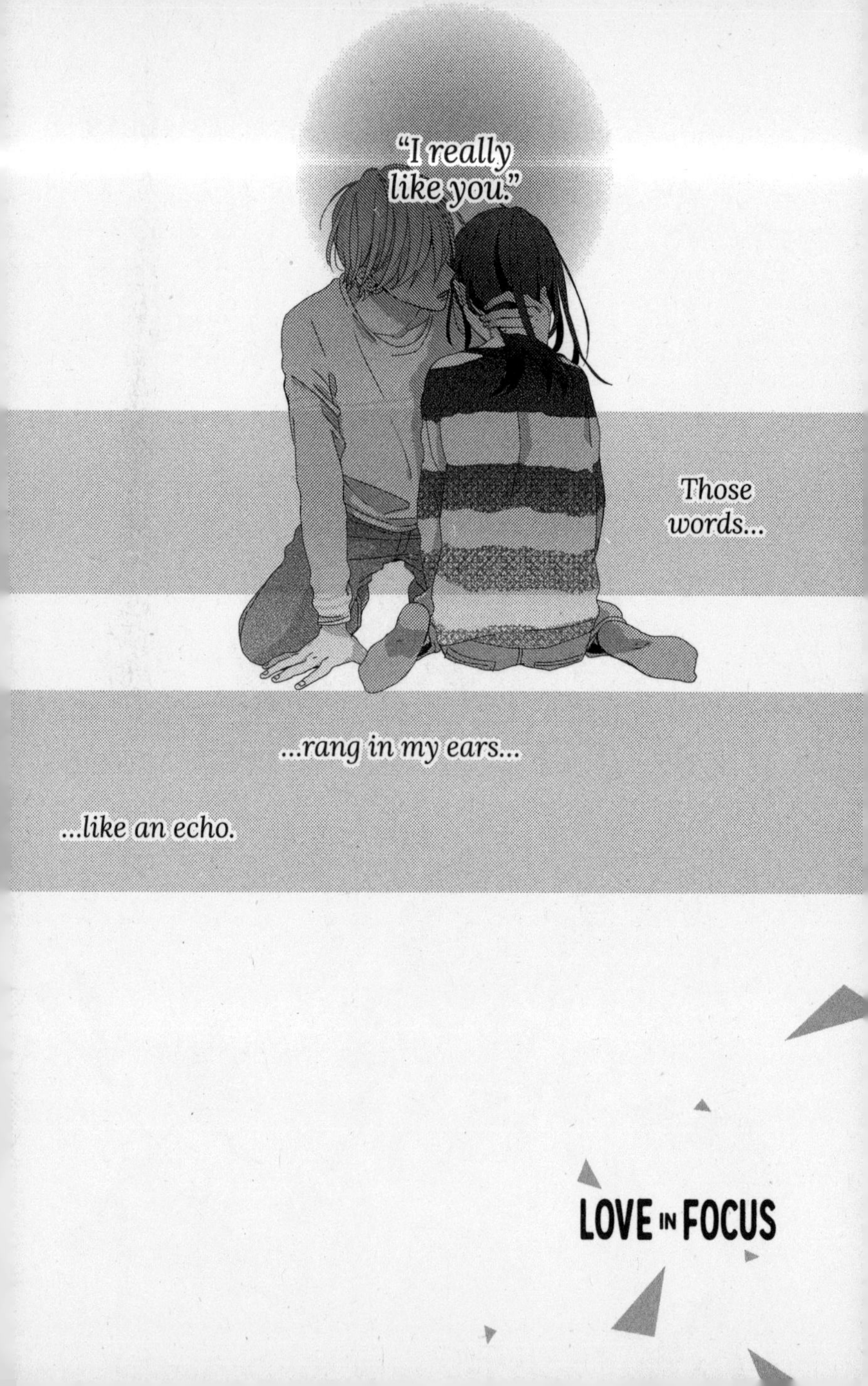
"I really like you."
Those words...
...rang in my ears...
...like an echo.
LOVE IN FOCUS

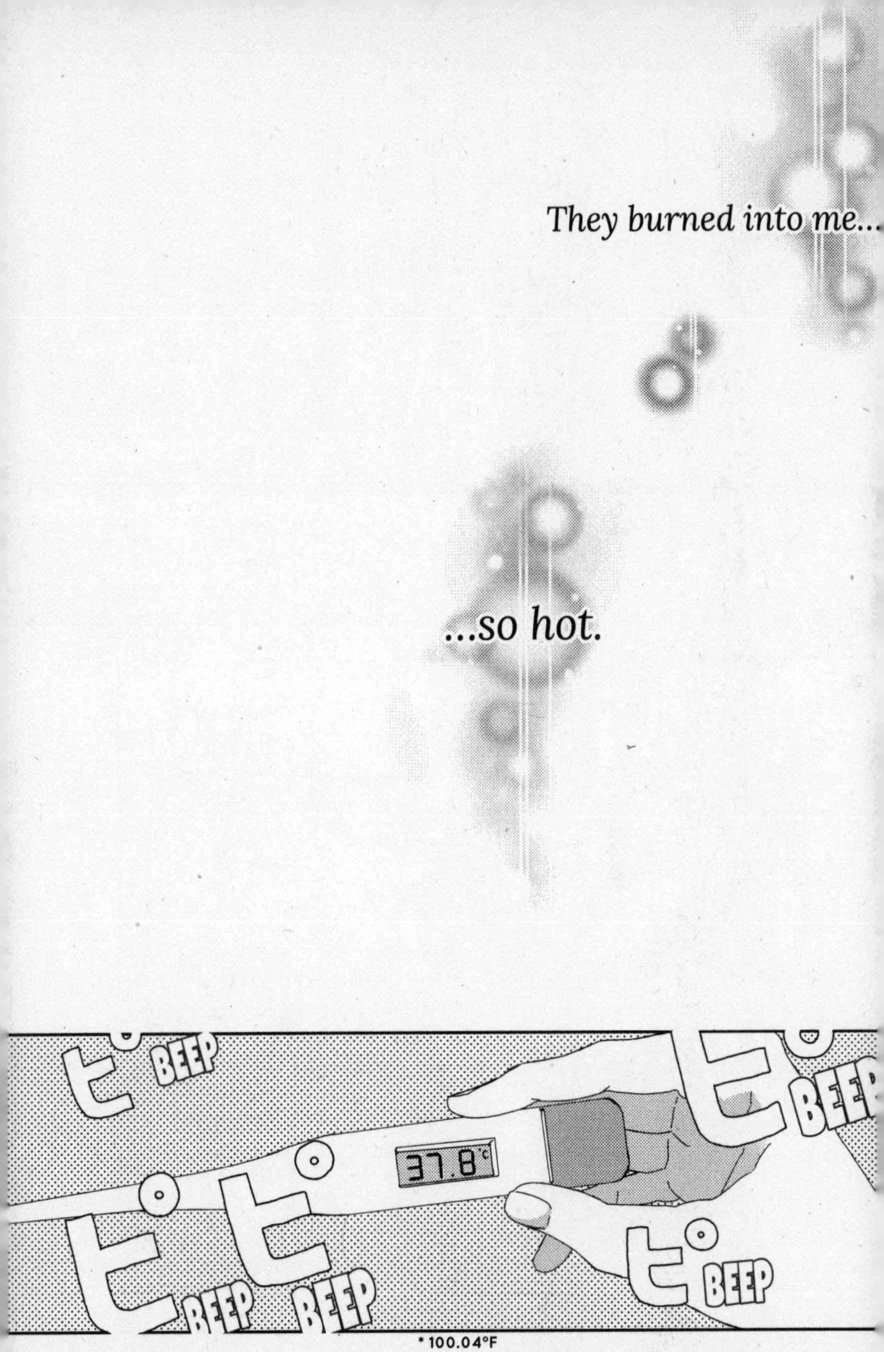

They burned into me...

...so hot.

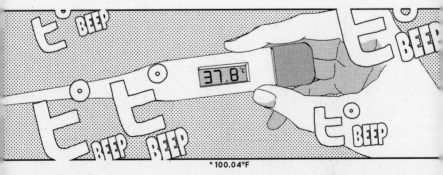

BEEP

BEEP

37.8℃

BEEP

BEEP

BEEP

* 100.04°F

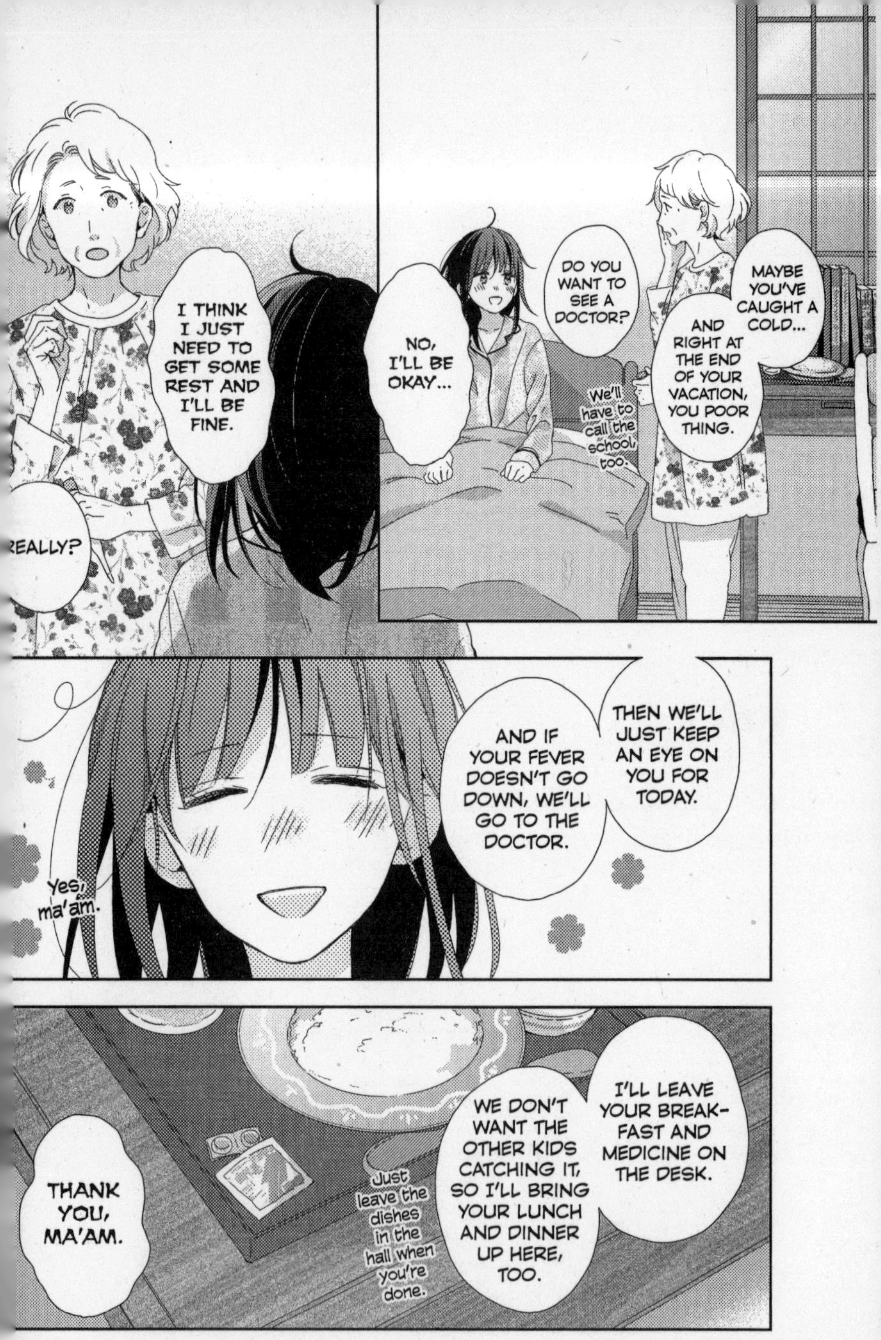

MAYBE YOU'VE CAUGHT A COLD...
AND RIGHT AT THE END OF YOUR VACATION, YOU POOR THING.
DO YOU WANT TO SEE A DOCTOR?
We'll have to call the school, too.
NO, I'LL BE OKAY...
I THINK I JUST NEED TO GET SOME REST AND I'LL BE FINE.
REALLY?
THEN WE'LL JUST KEEP AN EYE ON YOU FOR TODAY.
AND IF YOUR FEVER DOESN'T GO DOWN, WE'LL GO TO THE DOCTOR.
Yes, ma'am.
I'LL LEAVE YOUR BREAK-FAST AND MEDICINE ON THE DESK.
WE DON'T WANT THE OTHER KIDS CATCHING IT, SO I'LL BRING YOUR LUNCH AND DINNER UP HERE, TOO.
Just leave the dishes in the hall when you're done.
THANK YOU, MA'AM.

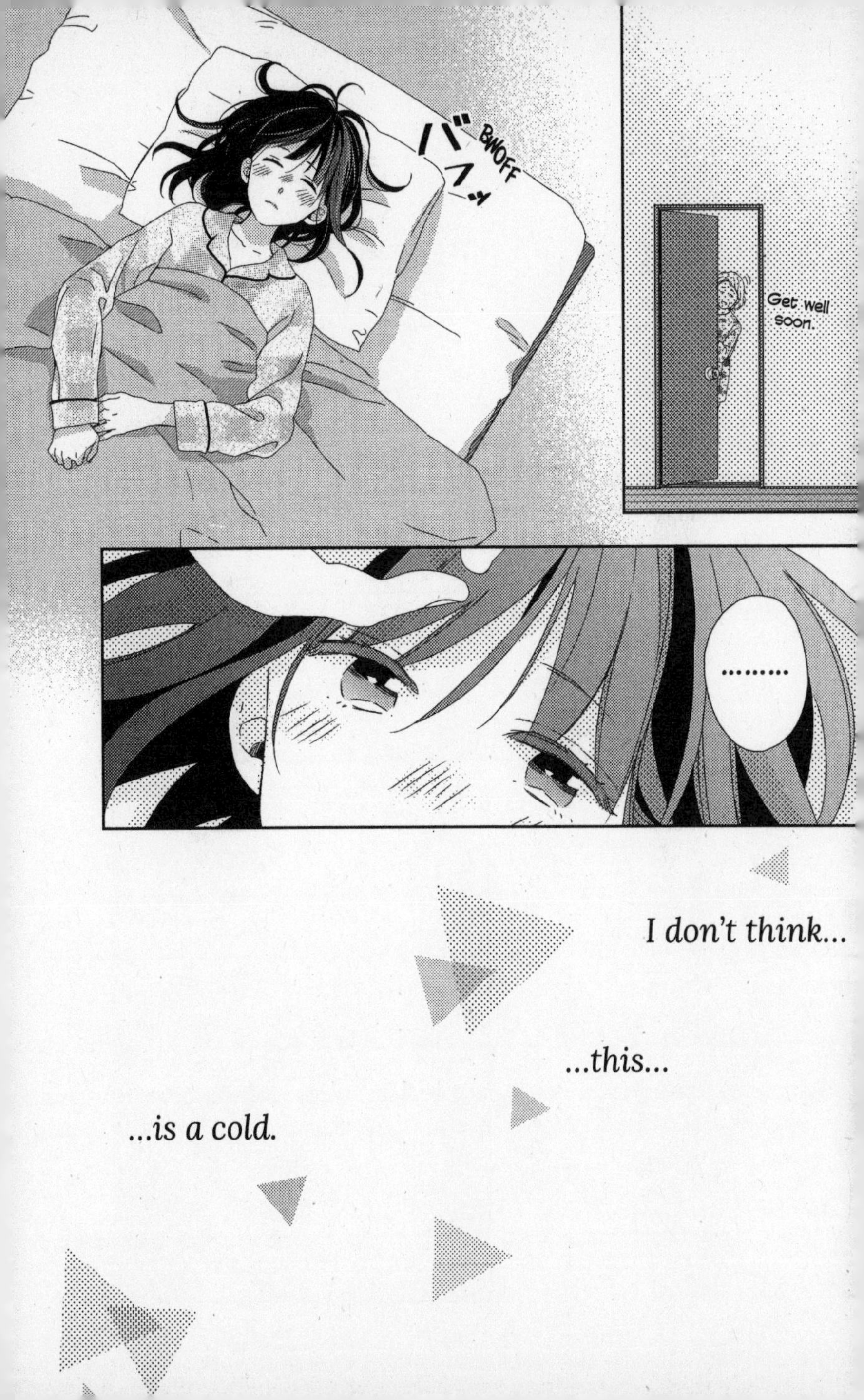
Get well soon.
BWOFF
バフッ
....
I don't think...
...this...
...is a cold.

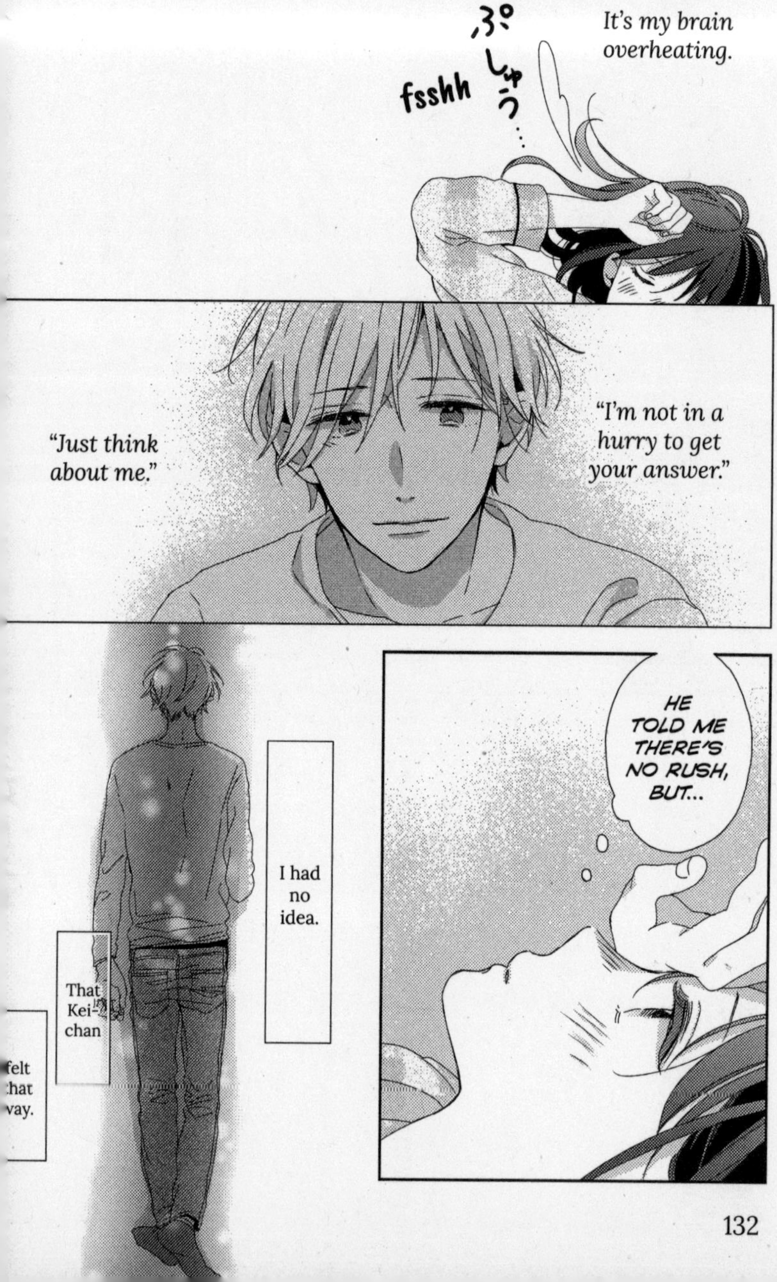
It's my brain overheating.
ぷしゅう…
fsshh
"I'm not in a hurry to get your answer."
"Just think about me."
HE TOLD ME THERE'S NO RUSH, BUT...
I had no idea.
That Kei-chan
felt

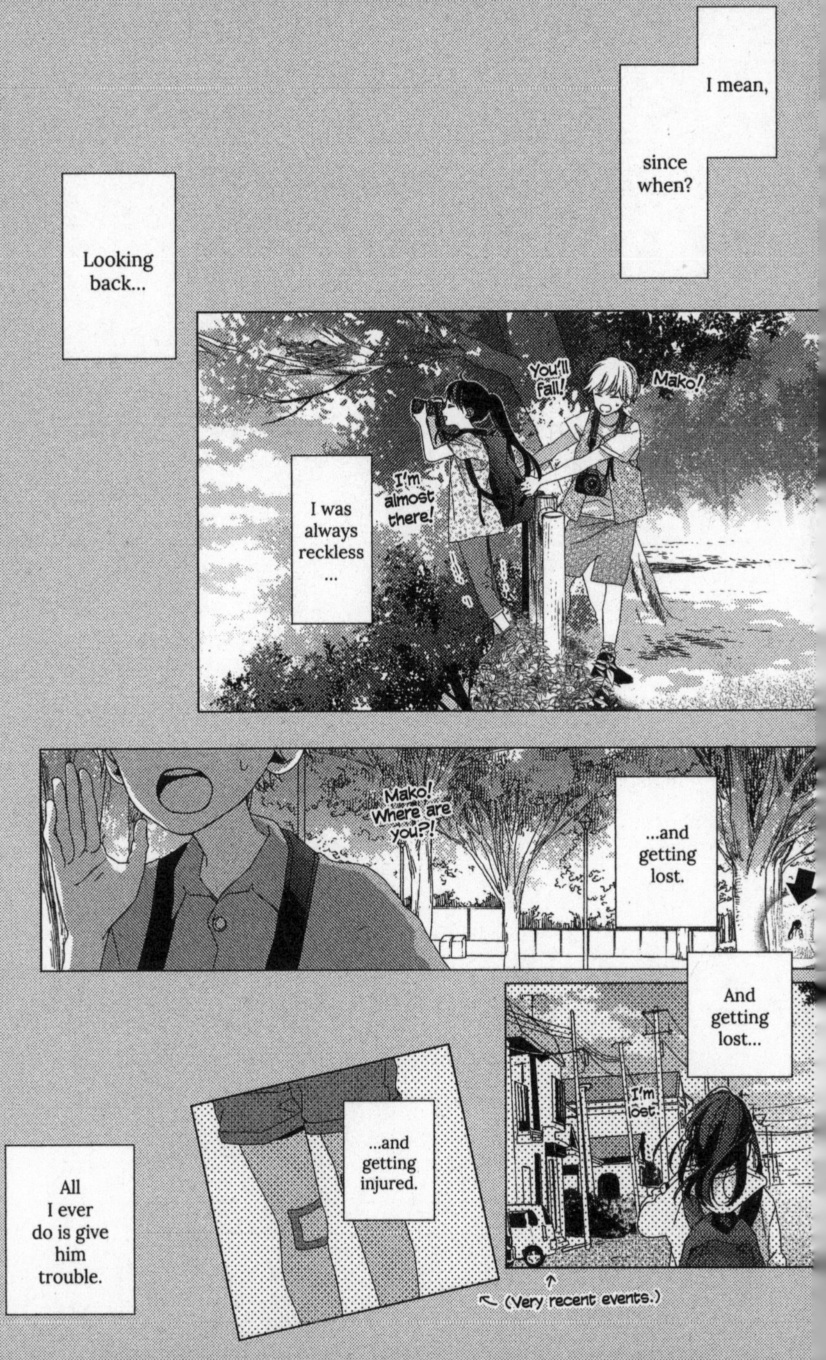
I mean,
since when?
Looking back...
Mako!
You'll fall!
I'm almost there!
I was always reckless ...
...and getting lost.
Mako! Where are you?!
And getting lost...
I'm lost.
(Very recent events.)
...and getting injured.
All I ever do is give him trouble.

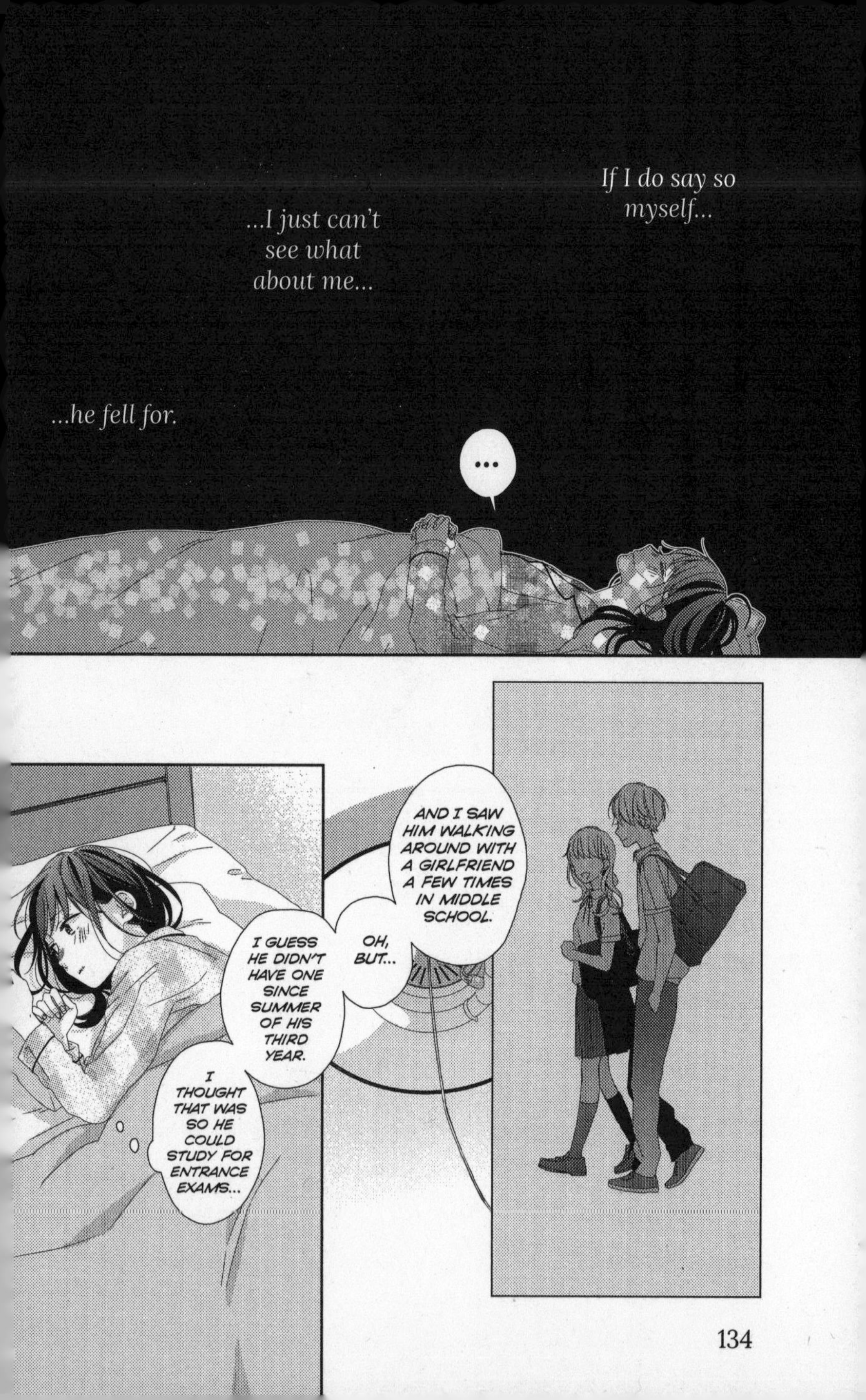
If I do say so myself...
...I just can't see what about me...
...he fell for.
...
AND I SAW HIM WALKING AROUND WITH A GIRLFRIEND A FEW TIMES IN MIDDLE SCHOOL.
OH, BUT...
I GUESS HE DIDN'T HAVE ONE SINCE SUMMER OF HIS THIRD YEAR.
I THOUGHT THAT WAS SO HE COULD STUDY FOR ENTRANCE EXAMS...

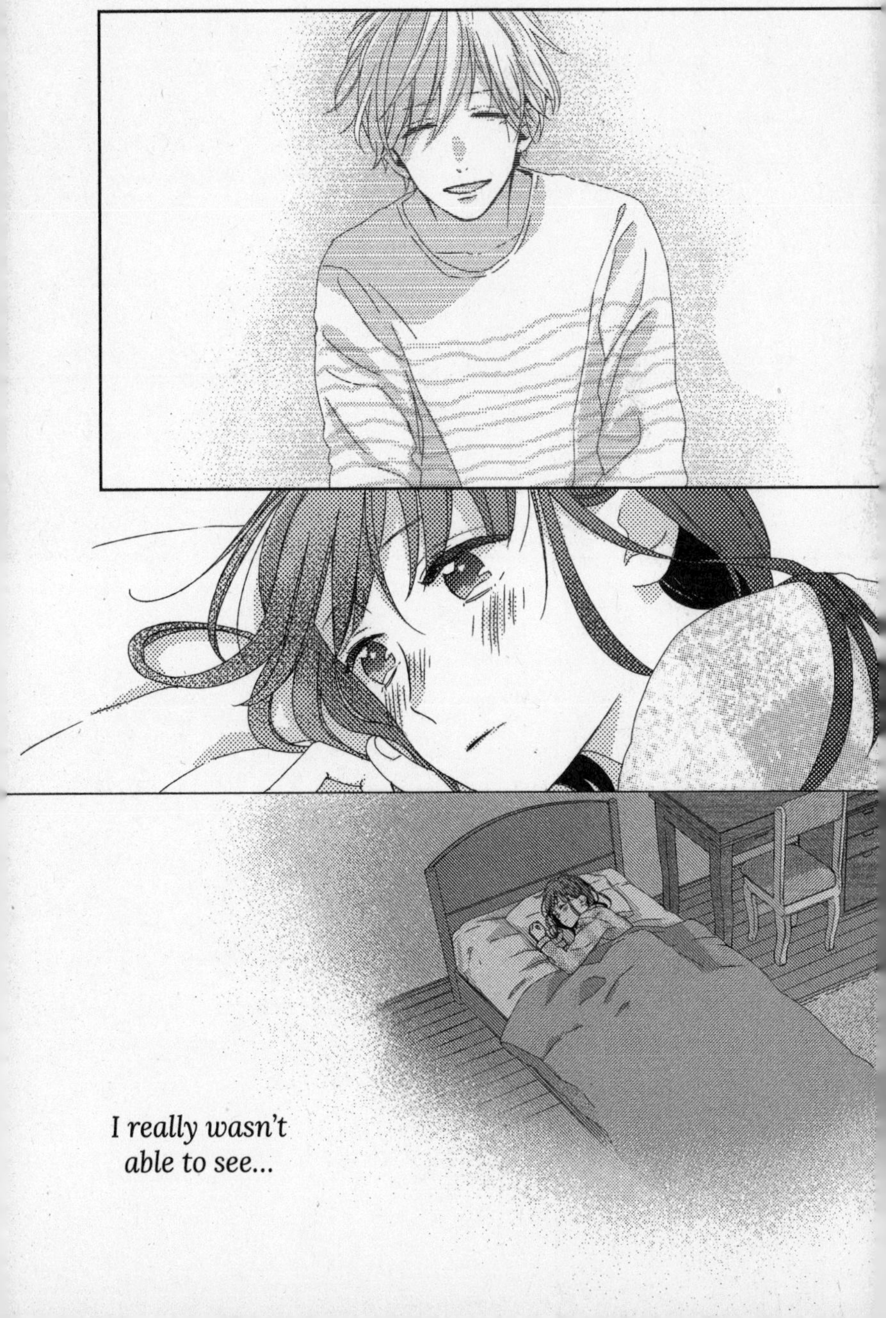
I really wasn't
able to see...

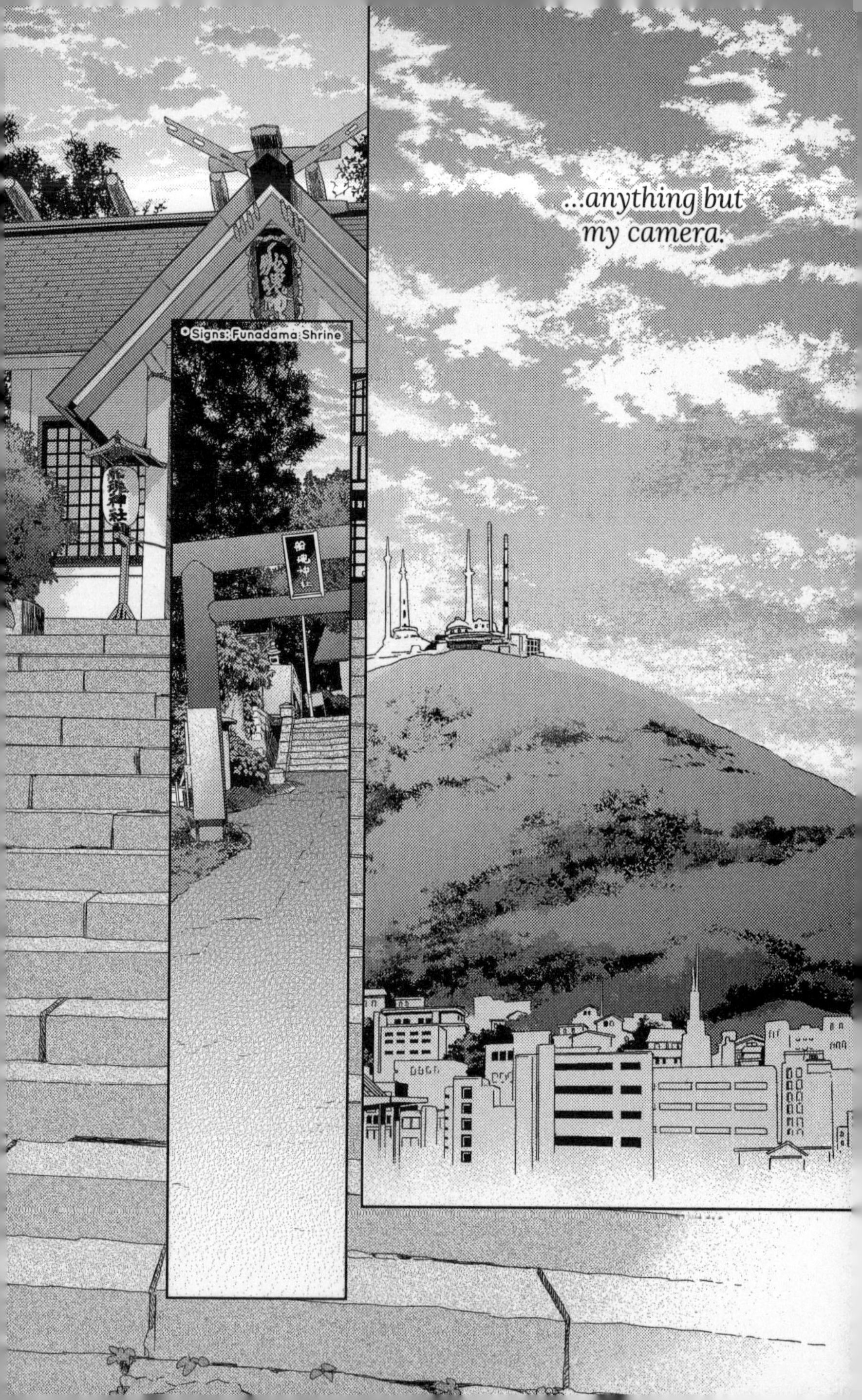
...anything but my camera.
* Signs: Funadama Shrine

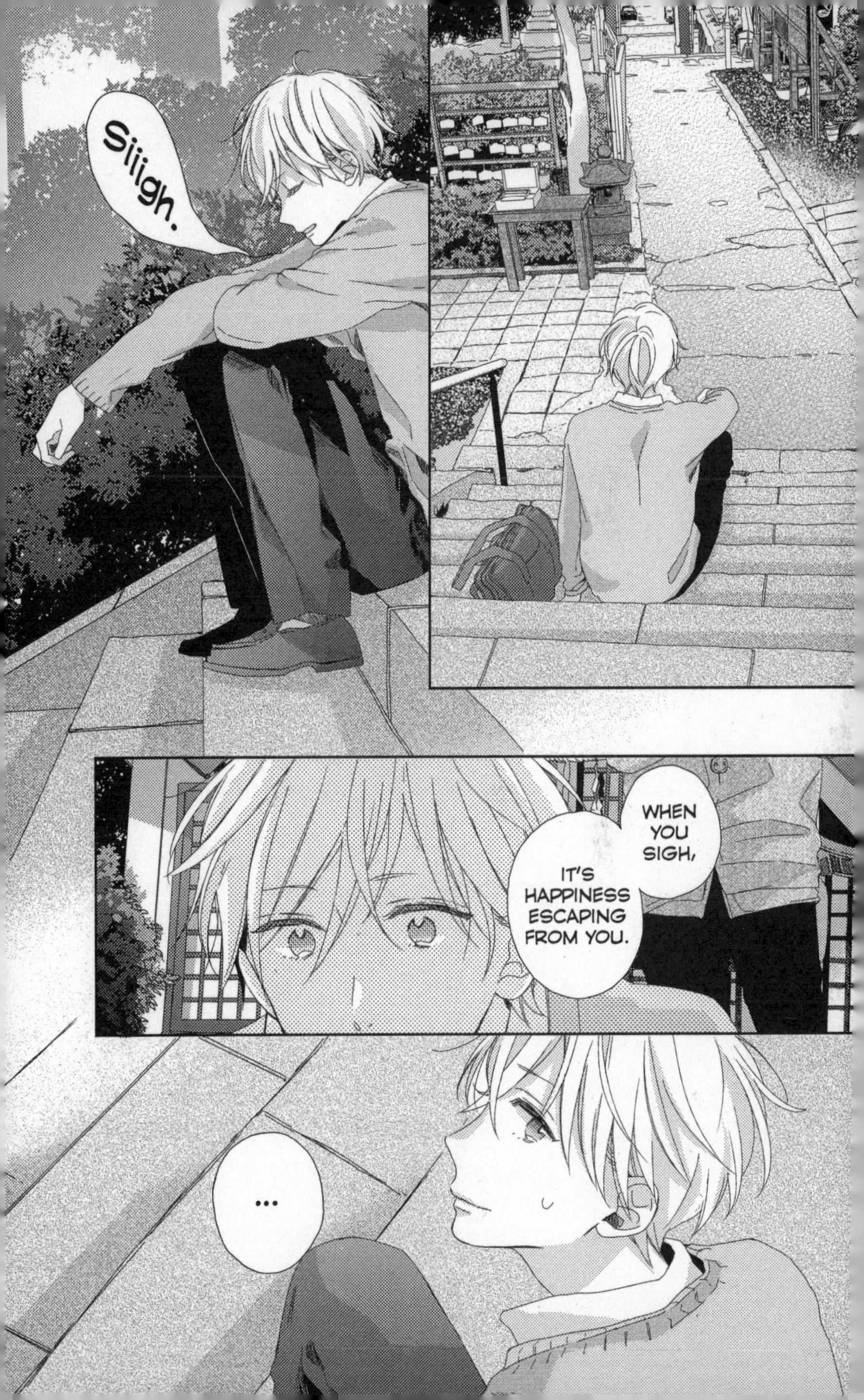
Siiigh.
WHEN YOU SIGH,
IT'S HAPPINESS ESCAPING FROM YOU.
...

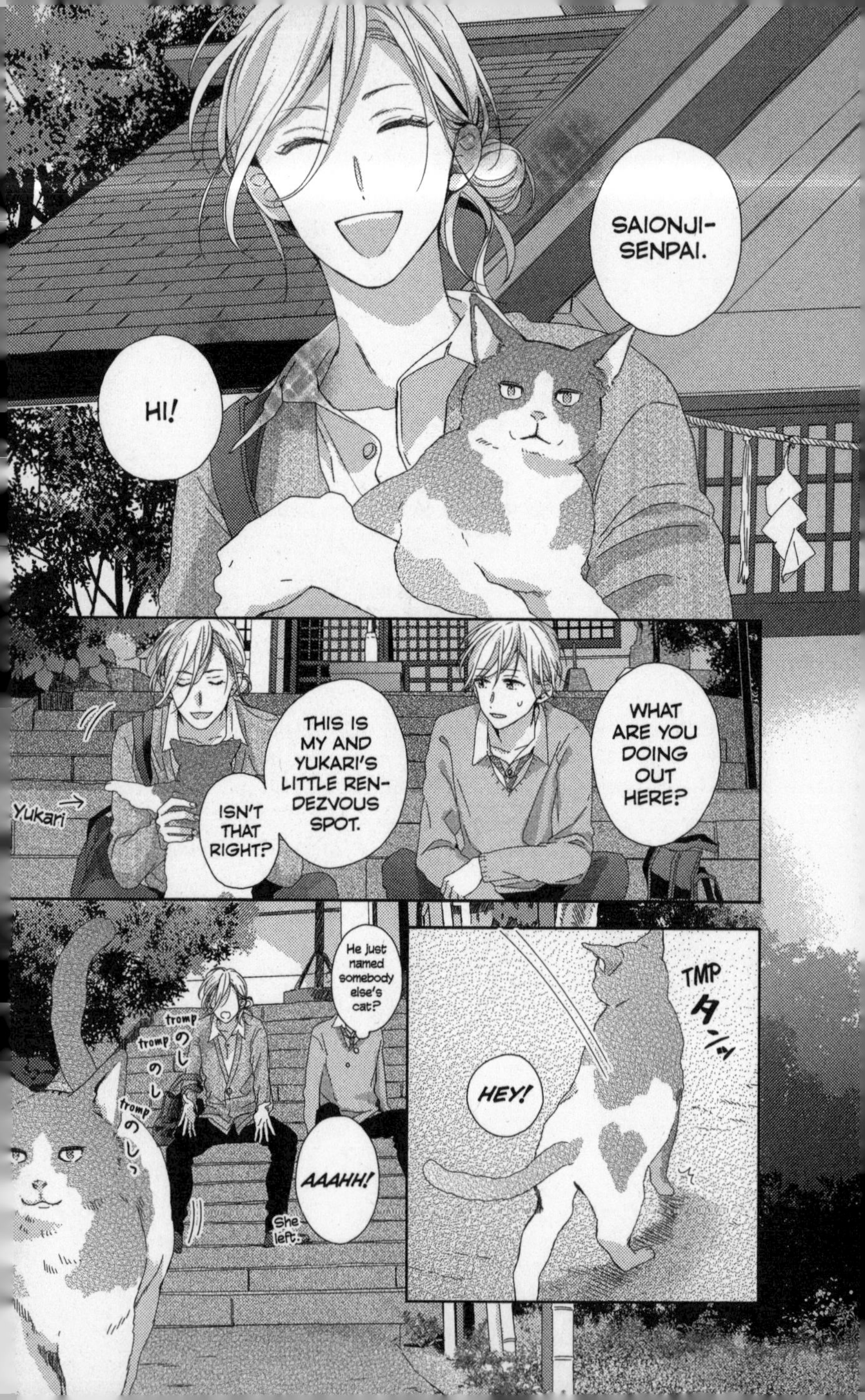
SAIONJI-SENPAI.
HI!
WHAT ARE YOU DOING OUT HERE?
THIS IS MY AND YUKARI'S LITTLE REN-DEZVOUS SPOT.
ISN'T THAT RIGHT?
Yukari
TMP タンッ
HEY!
He just named somebody else's cat?
tromp のし
tromp のし
tromp のしっ
AAAHH!
She left.

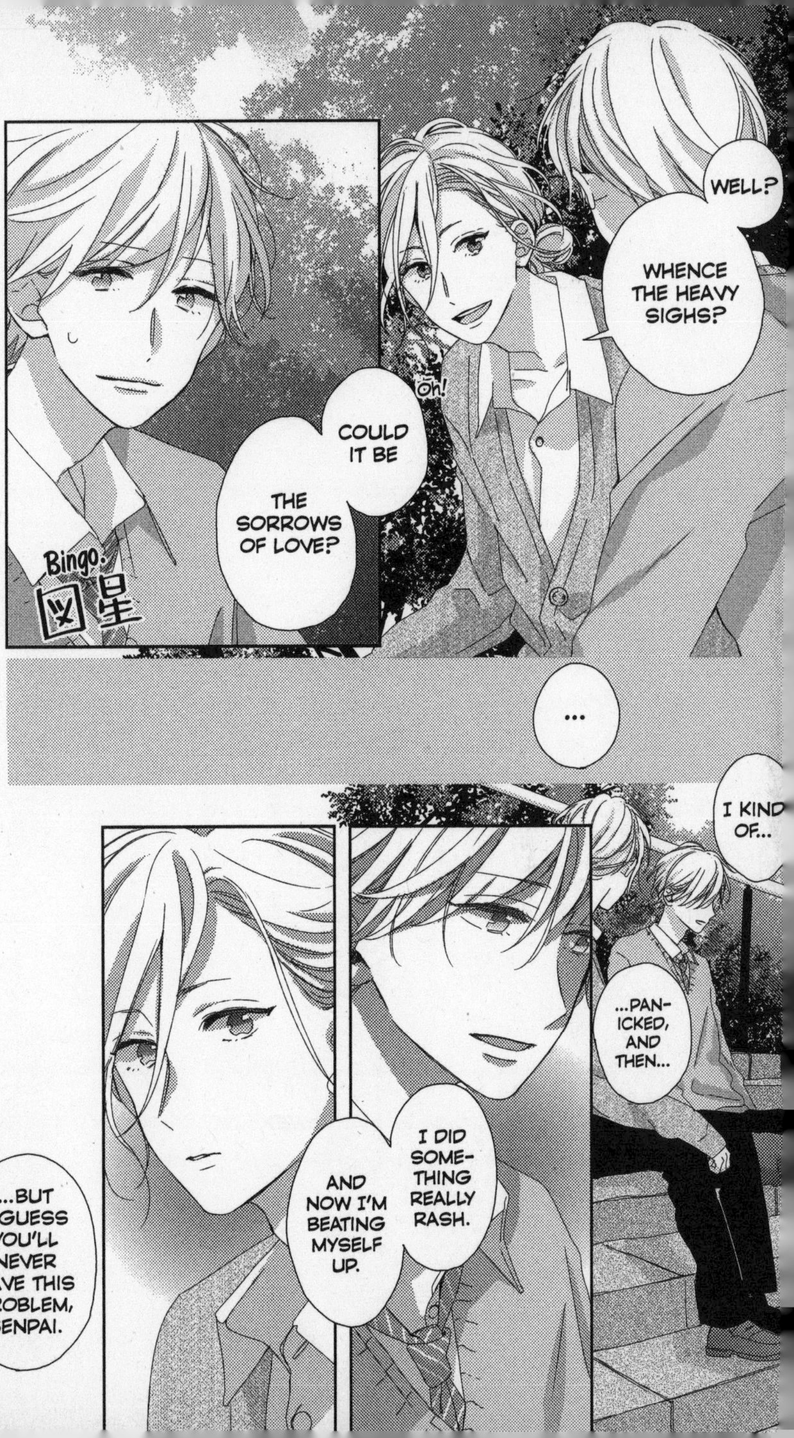
WELL?
WHENCE THE HEAVY SIGHS?
Oh!
COULD IT BE THE SORROWS OF LOVE?
Bingo.
図星
...
I KIND OF...
...PAN-ICKED, AND THEN...
I DID SOME-THING REALLY RASH.
AND NOW I'M BEATING MYSELF UP.
...BUT I GUESS YOU'LL NEVER HAVE THIS PROBLEM, SENPAI.

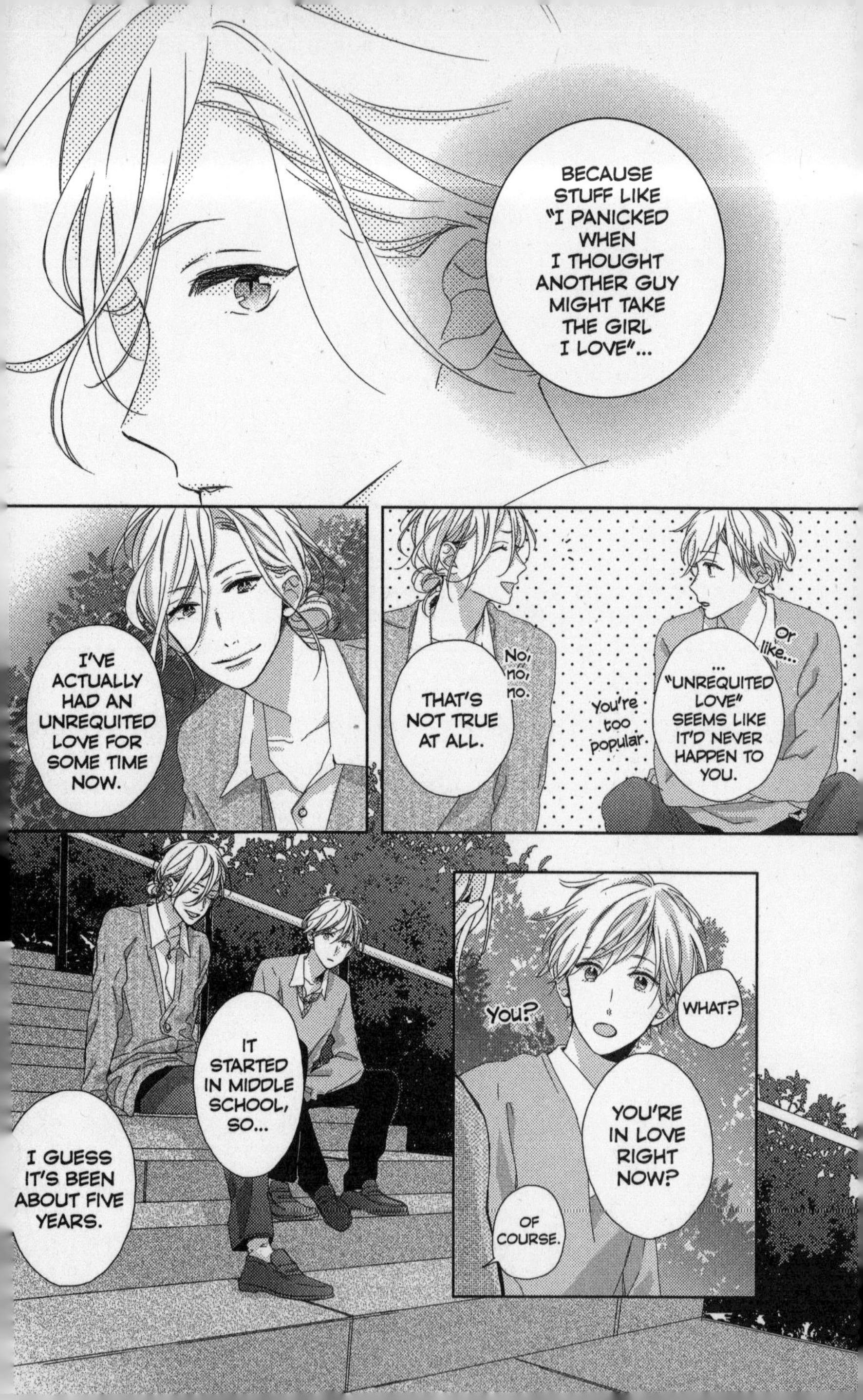
BECAUSE STUFF LIKE "I PANICKED WHEN I THOUGHT ANOTHER GUY MIGHT TAKE THE GIRL I LOVE"...
Or like...
... "UNREQUITED LOVE" SEEMS LIKE IT'D NEVER HAPPEN TO YOU.
You're too popular.
No, no, no.
THAT'S NOT TRUE AT ALL.
I'VE ACTUALLY HAD AN UNREQUITED LOVE FOR SOME TIME NOW.
WHAT?
You?
YOU'RE IN LOVE RIGHT NOW?
OF COURSE.
IT STARTED IN MIDDLE SCHOOL, SO...
I GUESS IT'S BEEN ABOUT FIVE YEARS.

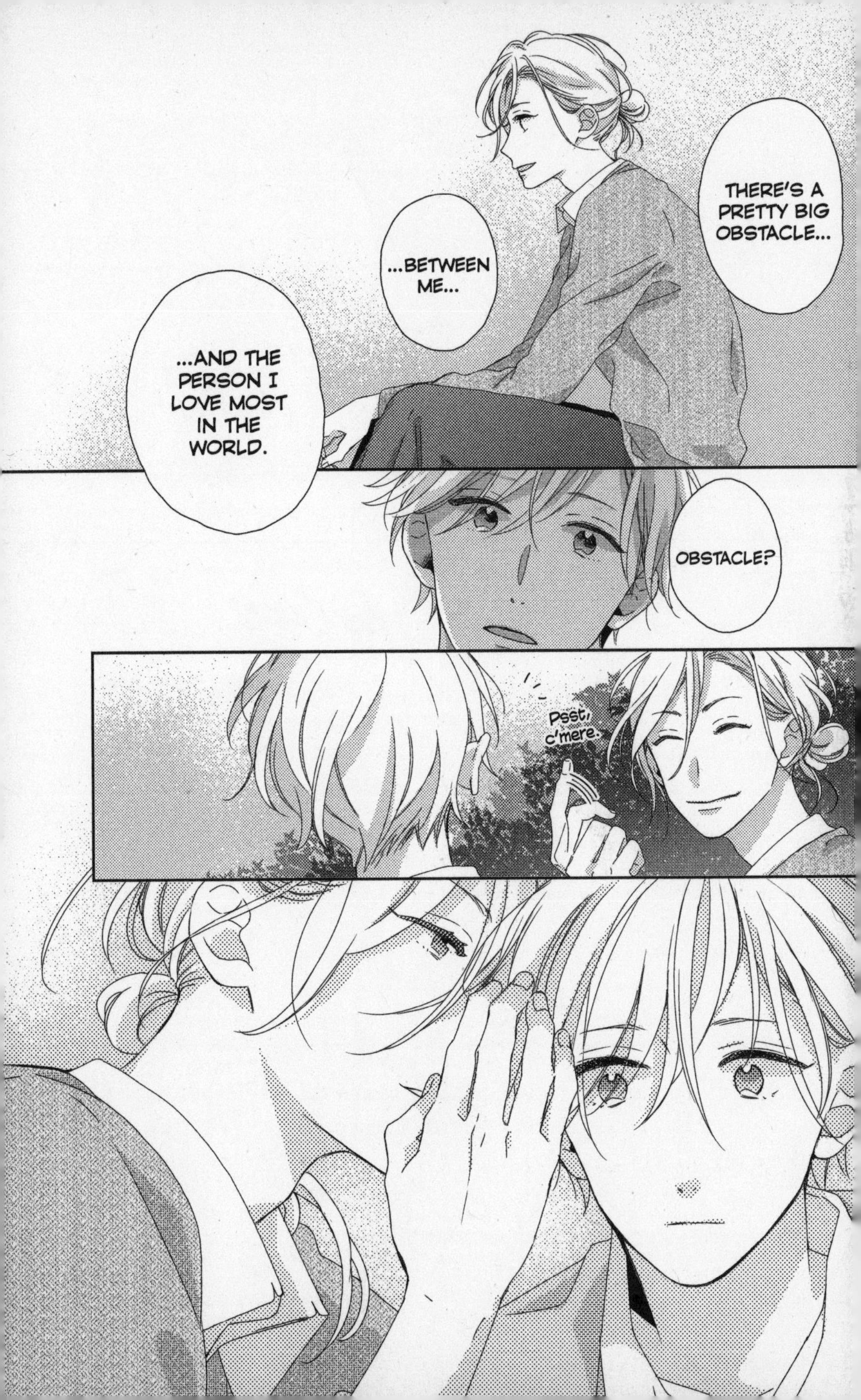
THERE'S A PRETTY BIG OBSTACLE...
...BETWEEN ME...
...AND THE PERSON I LOVE MOST IN THE WORLD.
OBSTACLE?
Psst, c'mere.

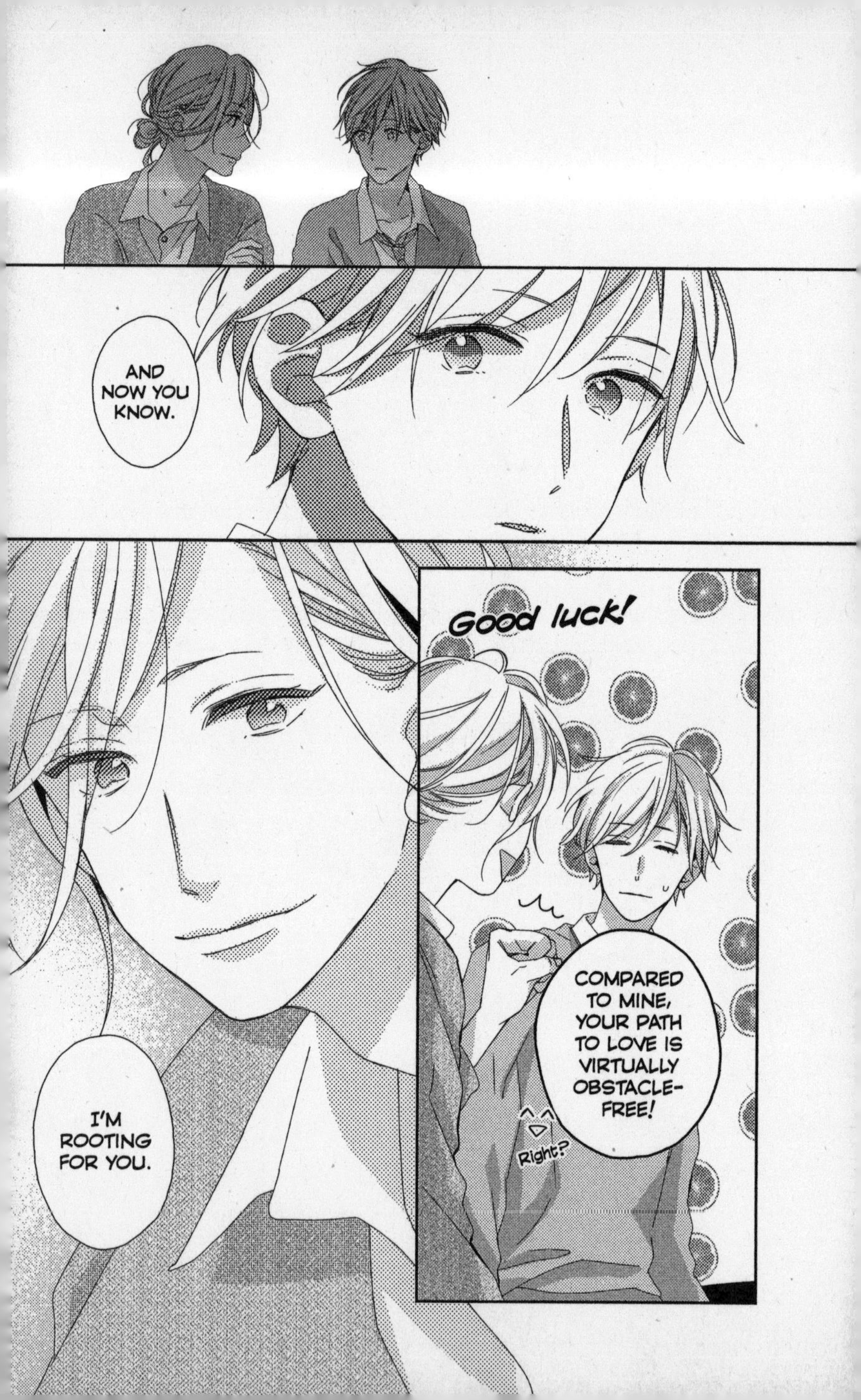
AND NOW YOU KNOW.
Good luck!
COMPARED TO MINE, YOUR PATH TO LOVE IS VIRTUALLY OBSTACLE-FREE!
Right?
I'M ROOTING FOR YOU.

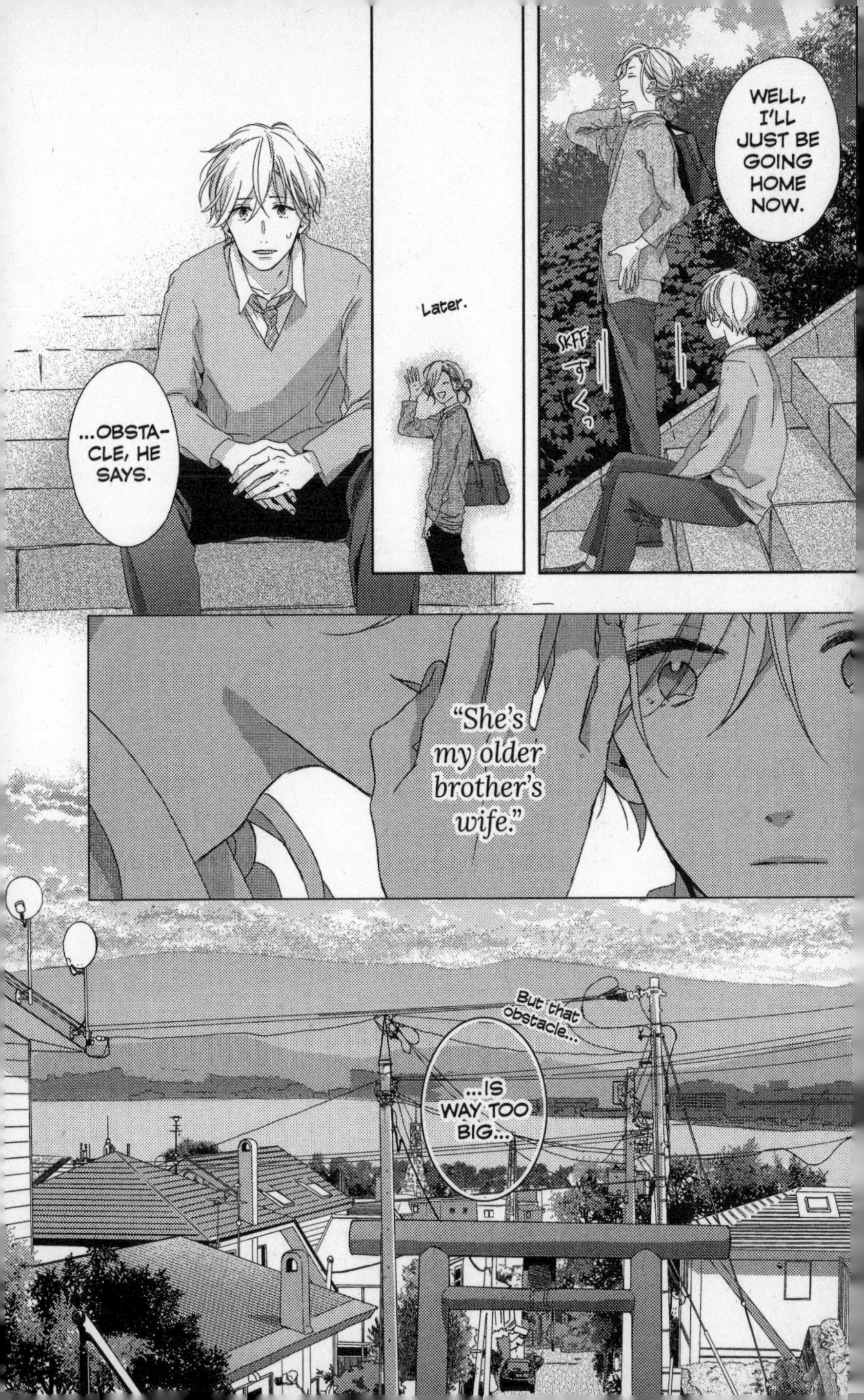
WELL, I'LL JUST BE GOING HOME NOW.
SKFF
すくっ
Later.
...OBSTA-CLE, HE SAYS.
"She's my older brother's wife."
But that obstacle...
...IS WAY TOO BIG...

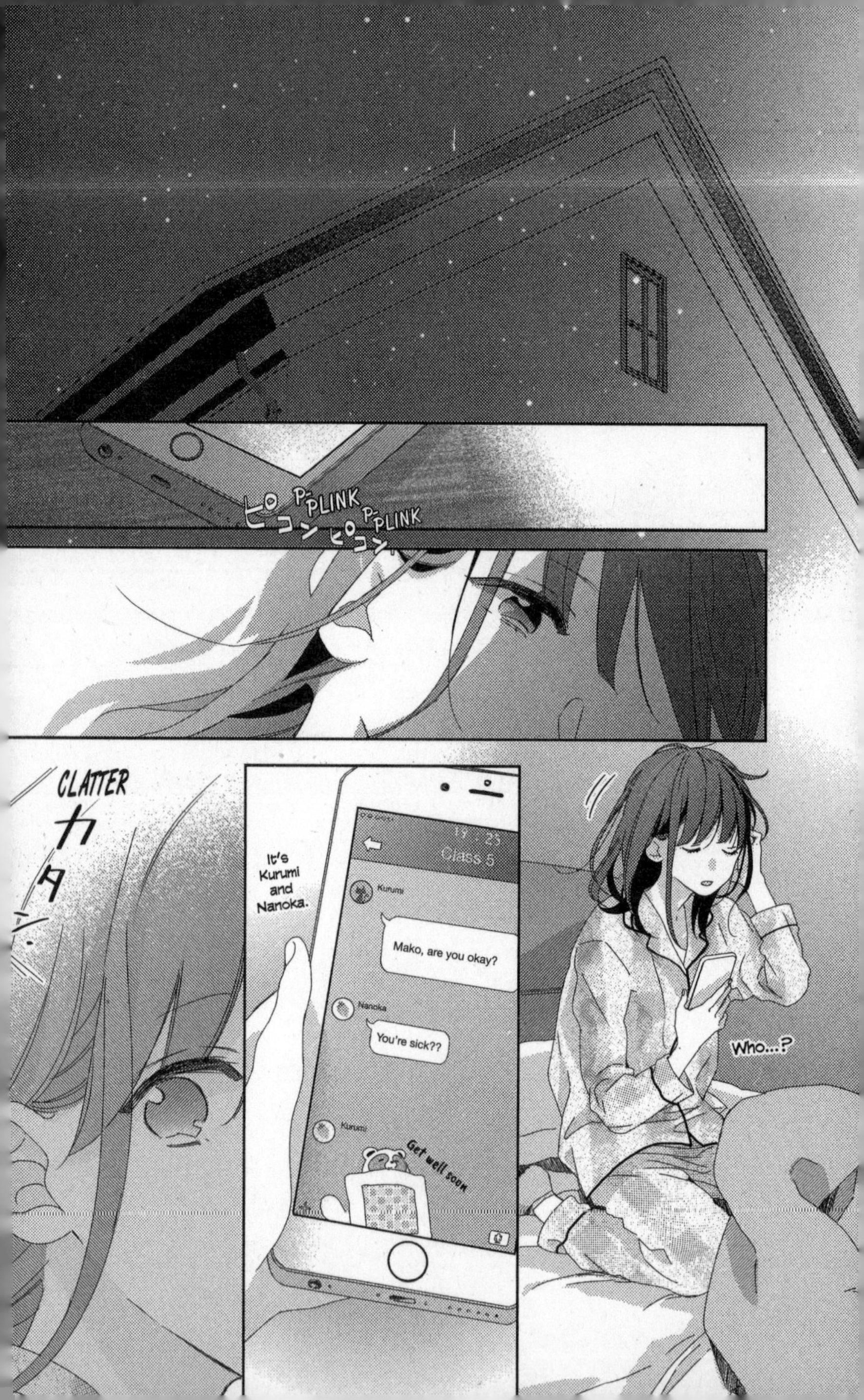

ピコン P-PLINK
ピコン P-PLINK
Who...?
It's Kurumi and Nanoka.
Class 5
Kurumi
Mako, are you okay?
Nanoka
You're sick??
Kurumi
Get well soon
CLATTER
カタン

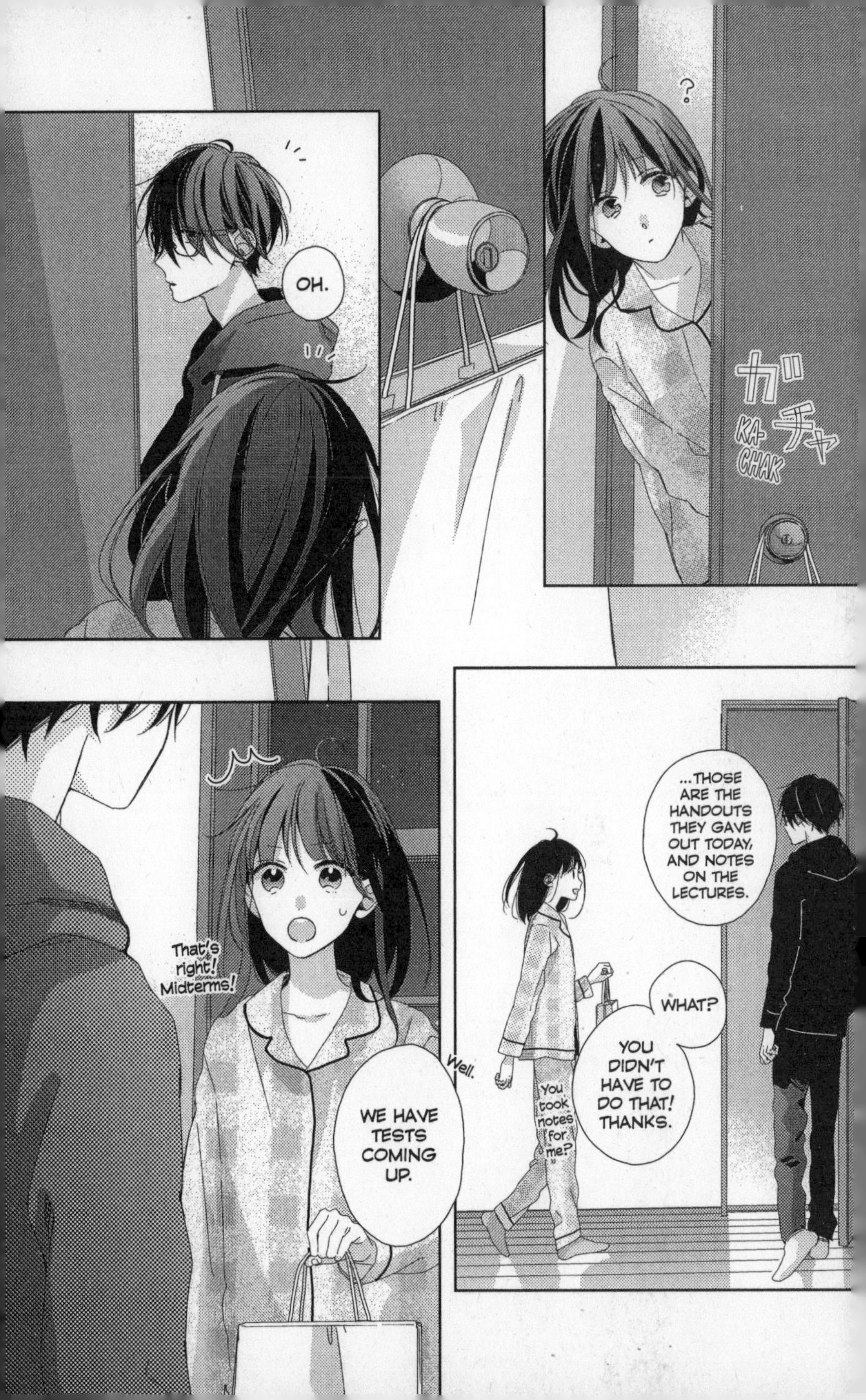
?
ガチャ
KA-CHAK
OH.
...THOSE ARE THE HANDOUTS THEY GAVE OUT TODAY, AND NOTES ON THE LECTURES.
WHAT?
YOU DIDN'T HAVE TO DO THAT! THANKS.
You took notes for me?
Well.
WE HAVE TESTS COMING UP.
That's right! Midterms!

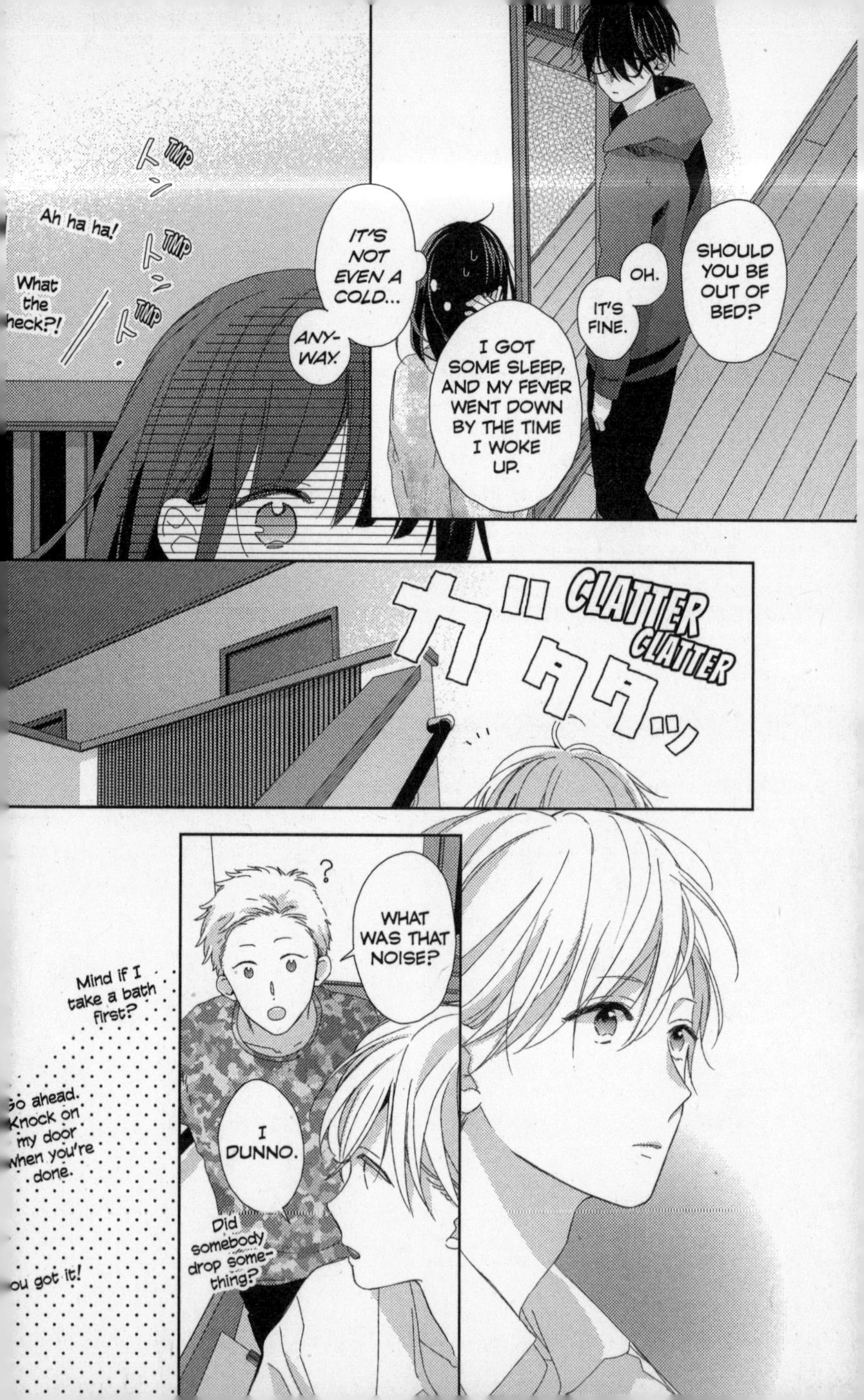
SHOULD YOU BE OUT OF BED?
OH.
IT'S FINE.
I GOT SOME SLEEP, AND MY FEVER WENT DOWN BY THE TIME I WOKE UP.
IT'S NOT EVEN A COLD...
ANY-WAY.
TMP
TMP
TMP
Ah ha ha!
What the heck?!
CLATTER
CLATTER
WHAT WAS THAT NOISE?
I DUNNO.
Did somebody drop some-thing?
Mind if I take a bath first?
Go ahead. Knock on my door when you're done.
ou got it!

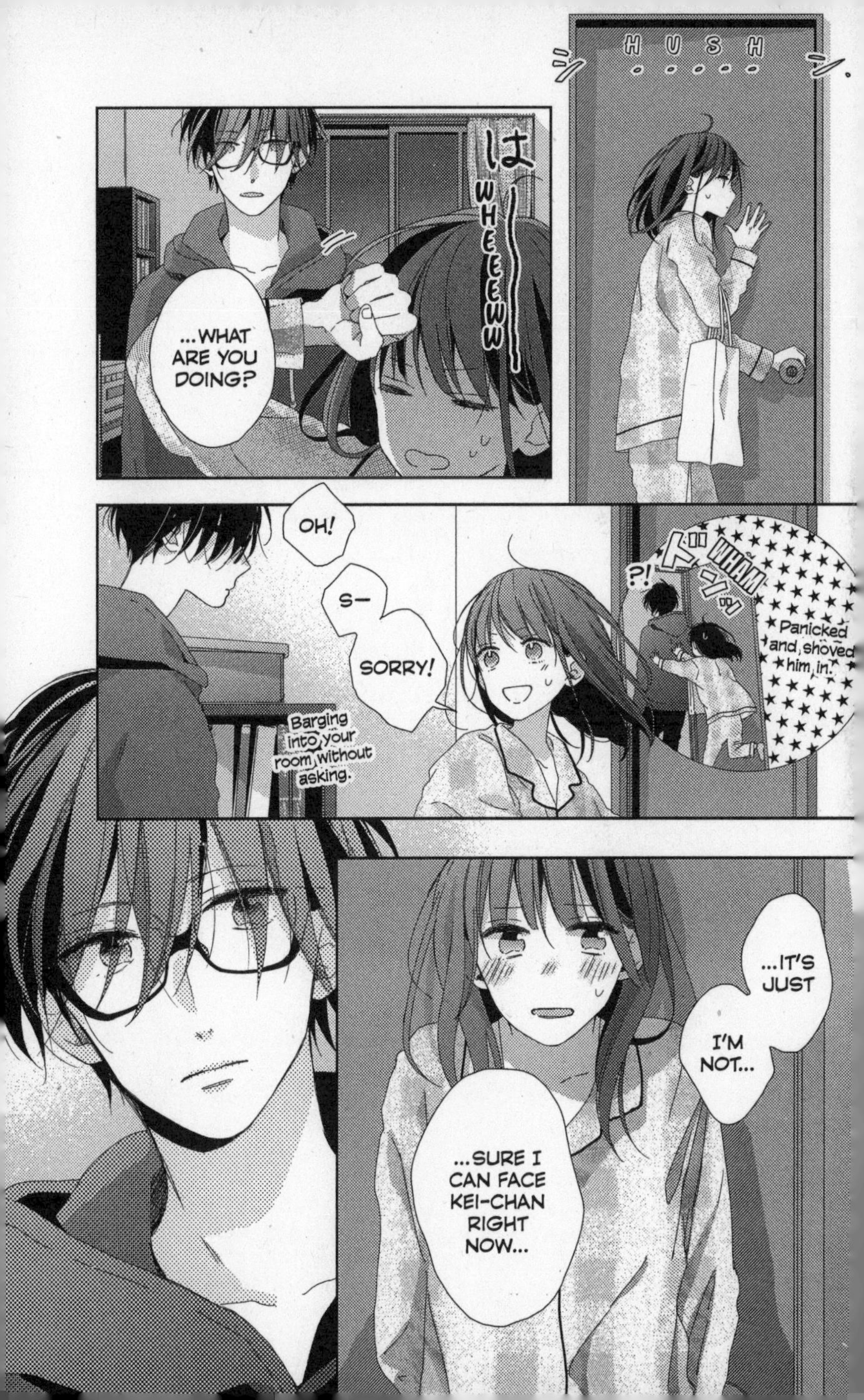
HUSH....
はー
WHEEEEWW
...WHAT ARE YOU DOING?
ド
WHAM
ン
?!
Panicked and shoved him in.
OH!
S—
SORRY!
Barging into your room without asking.
...IT'S JUST
I'M NOT...
...SURE I CAN FACE KEI-CHAN RIGHT NOW...

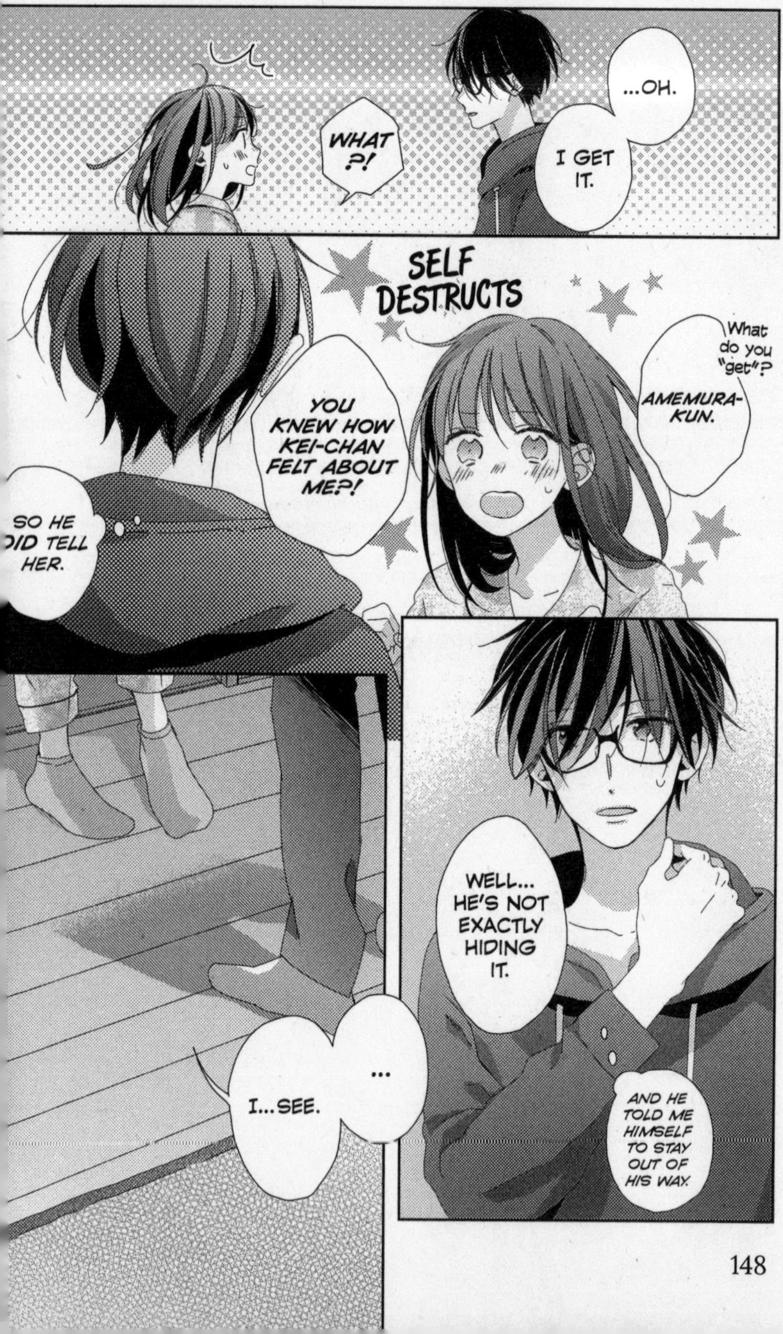
...OH.
I GET IT.
WHAT?!
What do you "get"?
AMEMURA-KUN.
SELF DESTRUCTS
YOU KNEW HOW KEI-CHAN FELT ABOUT ME?!
SO HE DID TELL HER.
WELL... HE'S NOT EXACTLY HIDING IT.
AND HE TOLD ME HIMSELF TO STAY OUT OF HIS WAY.
...
I...SEE.

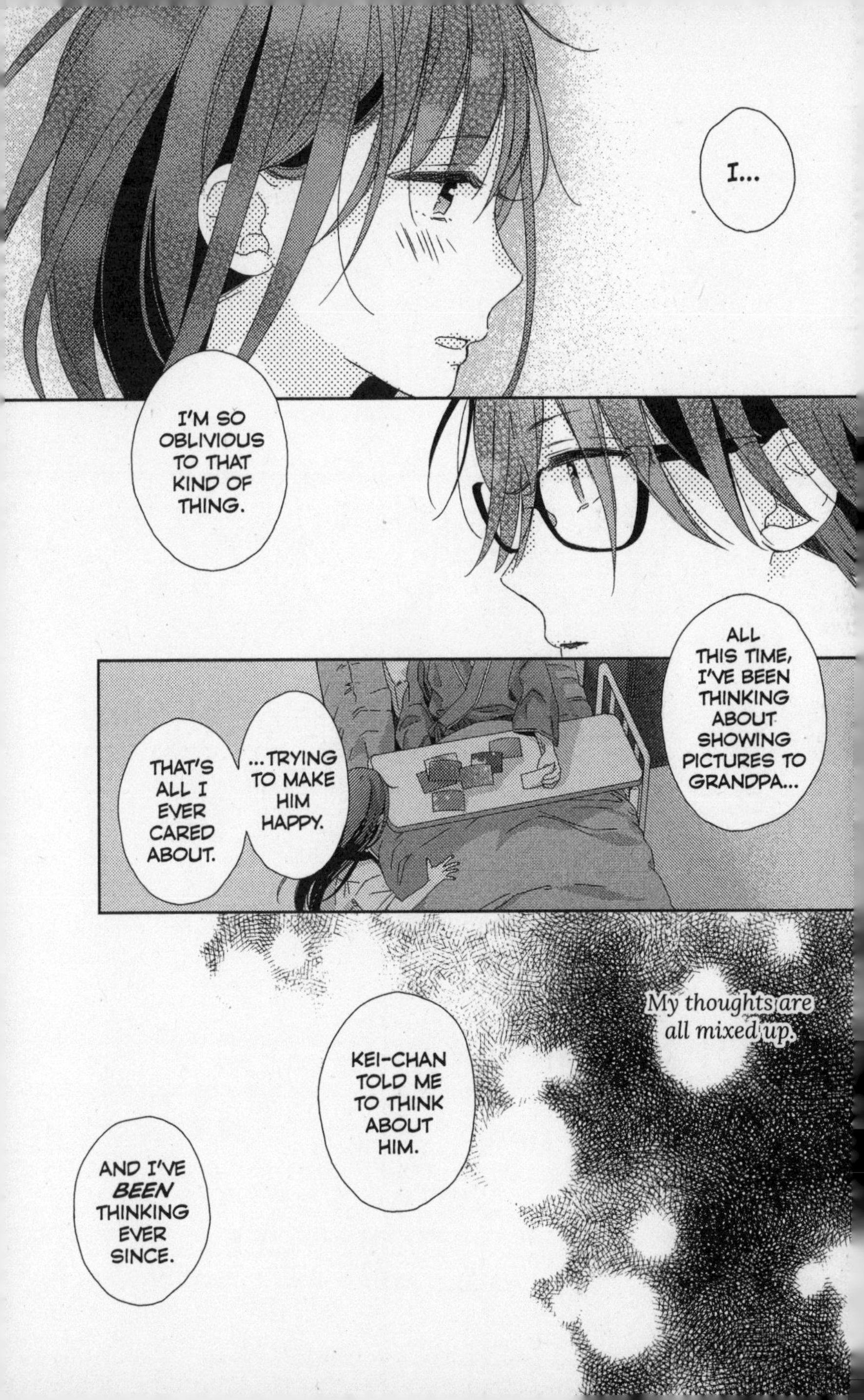
I...
I'M SO OBLIVIOUS TO THAT KIND OF THING.
ALL THIS TIME, I'VE BEEN THINKING ABOUT SHOWING PICTURES TO GRANDPA...
...TRYING TO MAKE HIM HAPPY.
THAT'S ALL I EVER CARED ABOUT.
My thoughts are all mixed up.
KEI-CHAN TOLD ME TO THINK ABOUT HIM.
AND I'VE *BEEN* THINKING EVER SINCE.

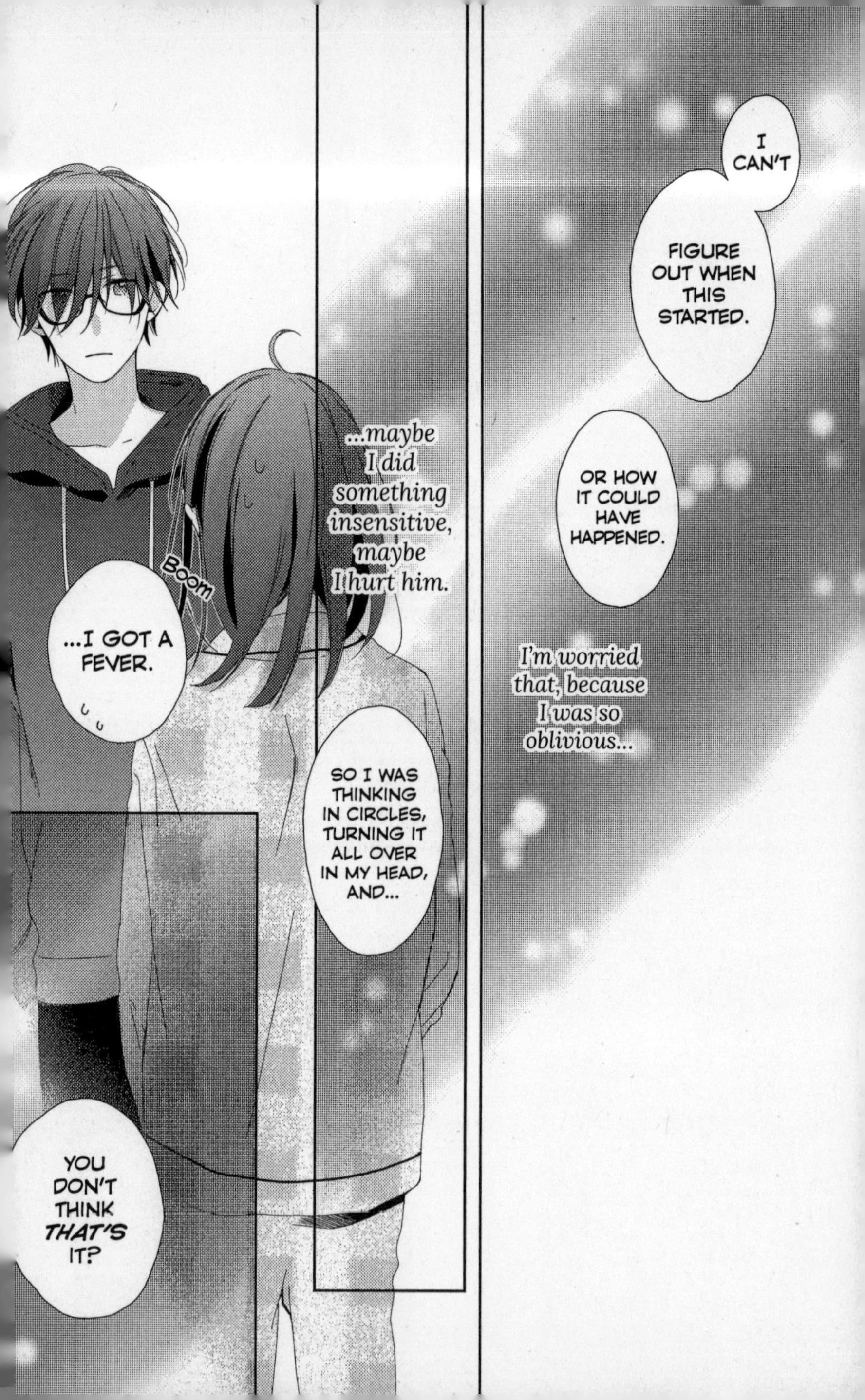
I CAN'T
FIGURE OUT WHEN THIS STARTED.
OR HOW IT COULD HAVE HAPPENED.
I'm worried that, because I was so oblivious...
...maybe I did something insensitive, maybe I hurt him.
SO I WAS THINKING IN CIRCLES, TURNING IT ALL OVER IN MY HEAD, AND...
Boom
...I GOT A FEVER.
YOU DON'T THINK *THAT'S* IT?

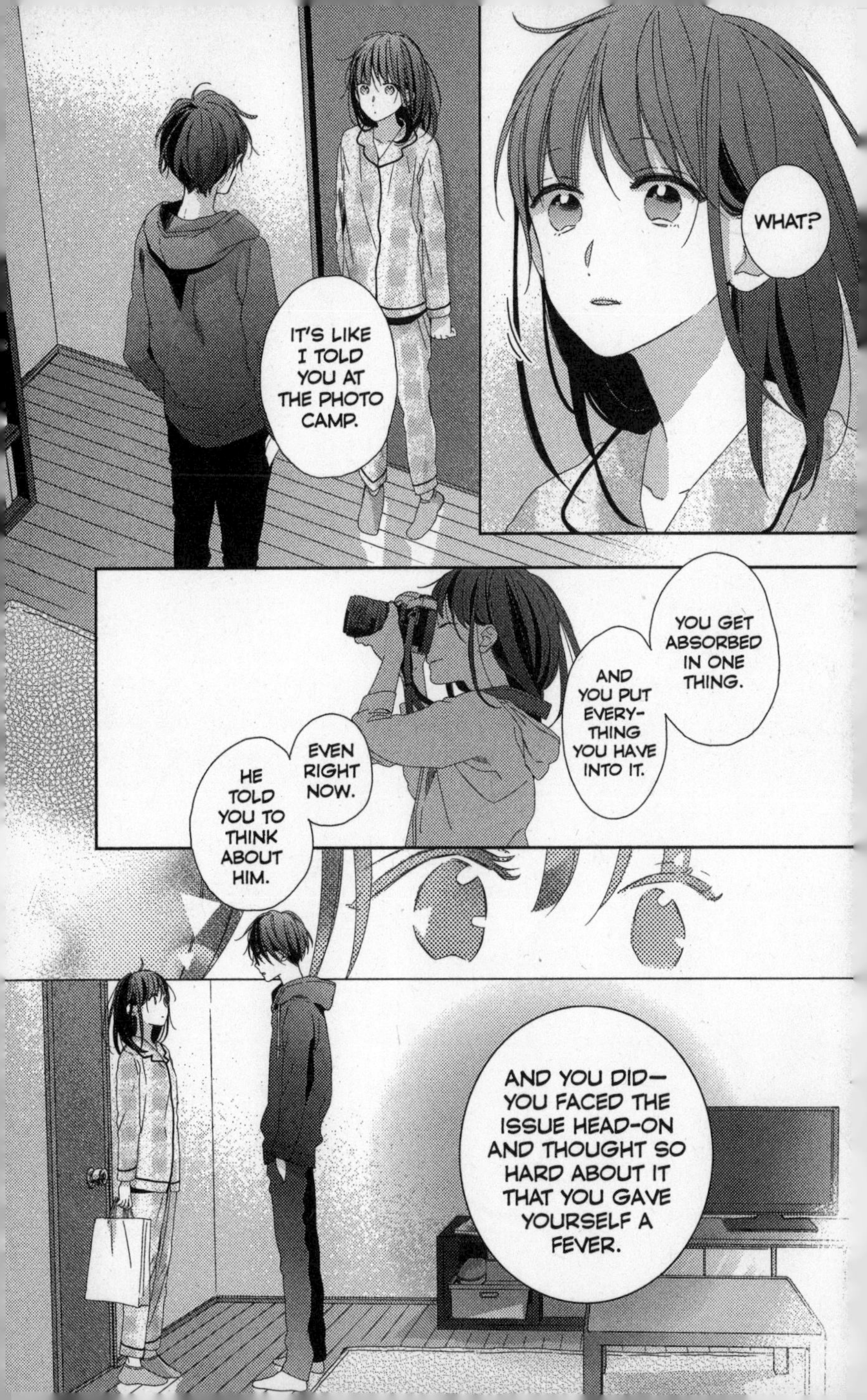
WHAT?
IT'S LIKE I TOLD YOU AT THE PHOTO CAMP.
YOU GET ABSORBED IN ONE THING.
AND YOU PUT EVERY-THING YOU HAVE INTO IT.
EVEN RIGHT NOW.
HE TOLD YOU TO THINK ABOUT HIM.
AND YOU DID—YOU FACED THE ISSUE HEAD-ON AND THOUGHT SO HARD ABOUT IT THAT YOU GAVE YOURSELF A FEVER.

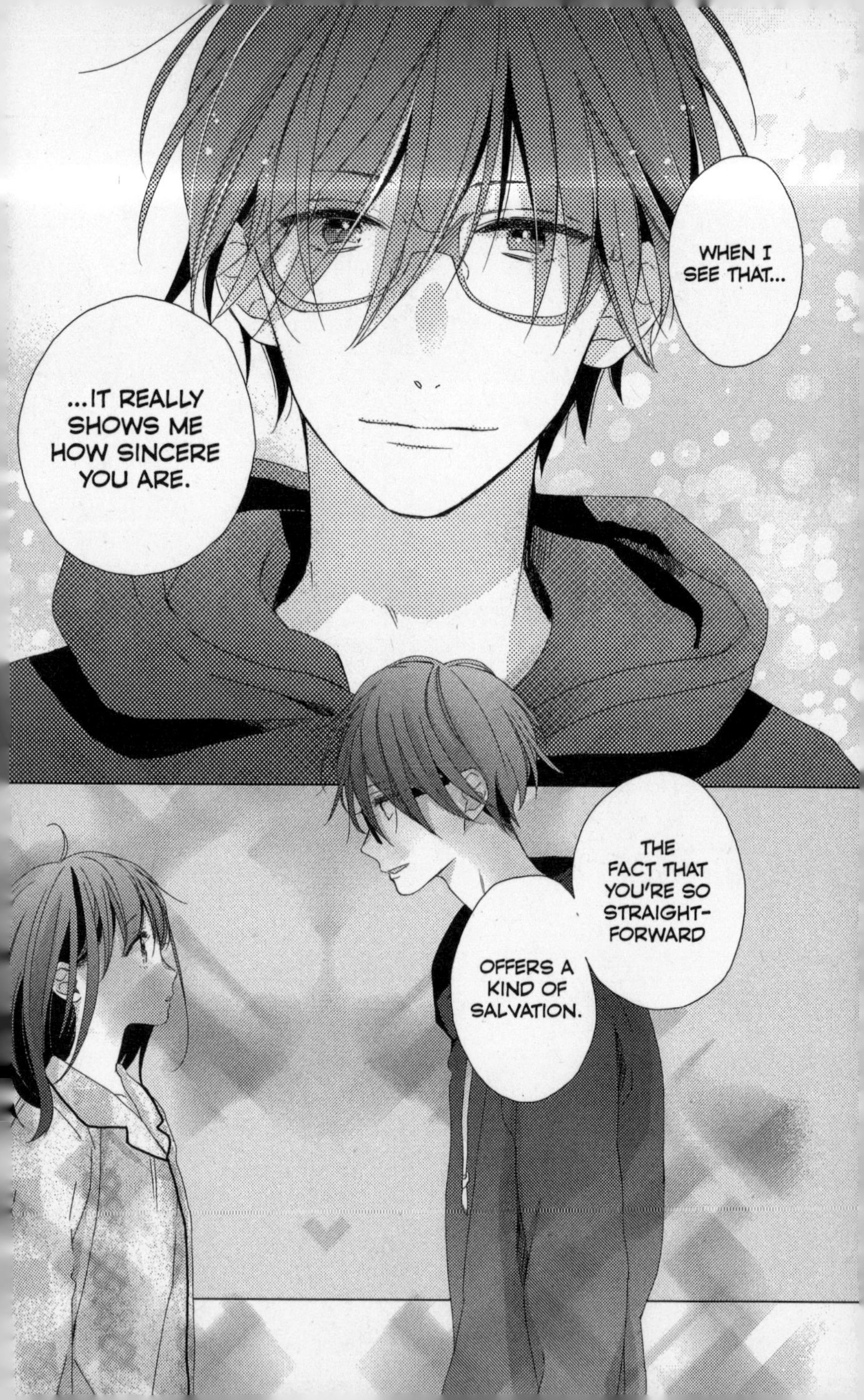
WHEN I SEE THAT...
...IT REALLY SHOWS ME HOW SINCERE YOU ARE.
THE FACT THAT YOU'RE SO STRAIGHT-FORWARD
OFFERS A KIND OF SALVATION.

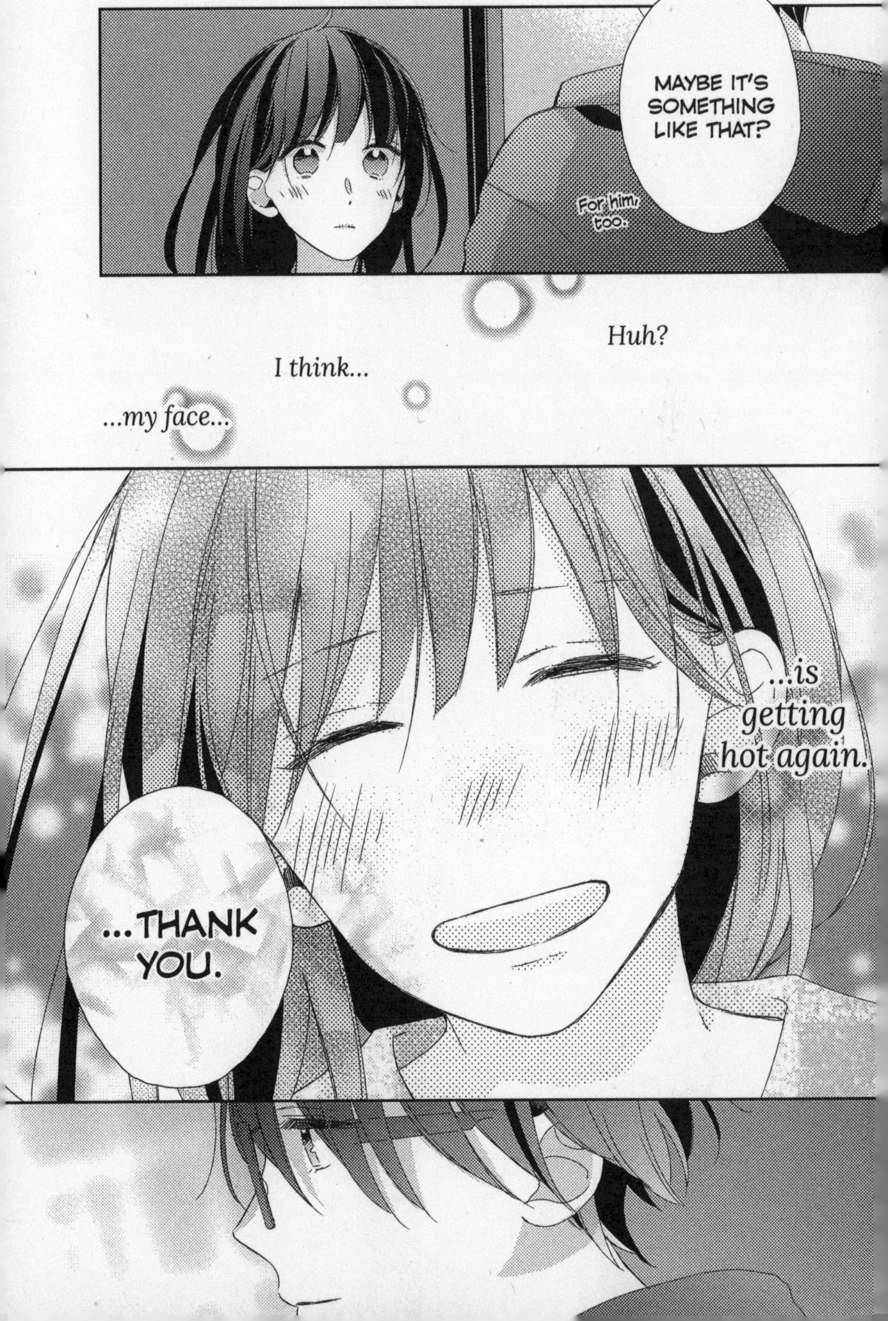
MAYBE IT'S SOMETHING LIKE THAT?
For him, too.
Huh?
I think...
...my face...
...is getting hot again.
...THANK YOU.

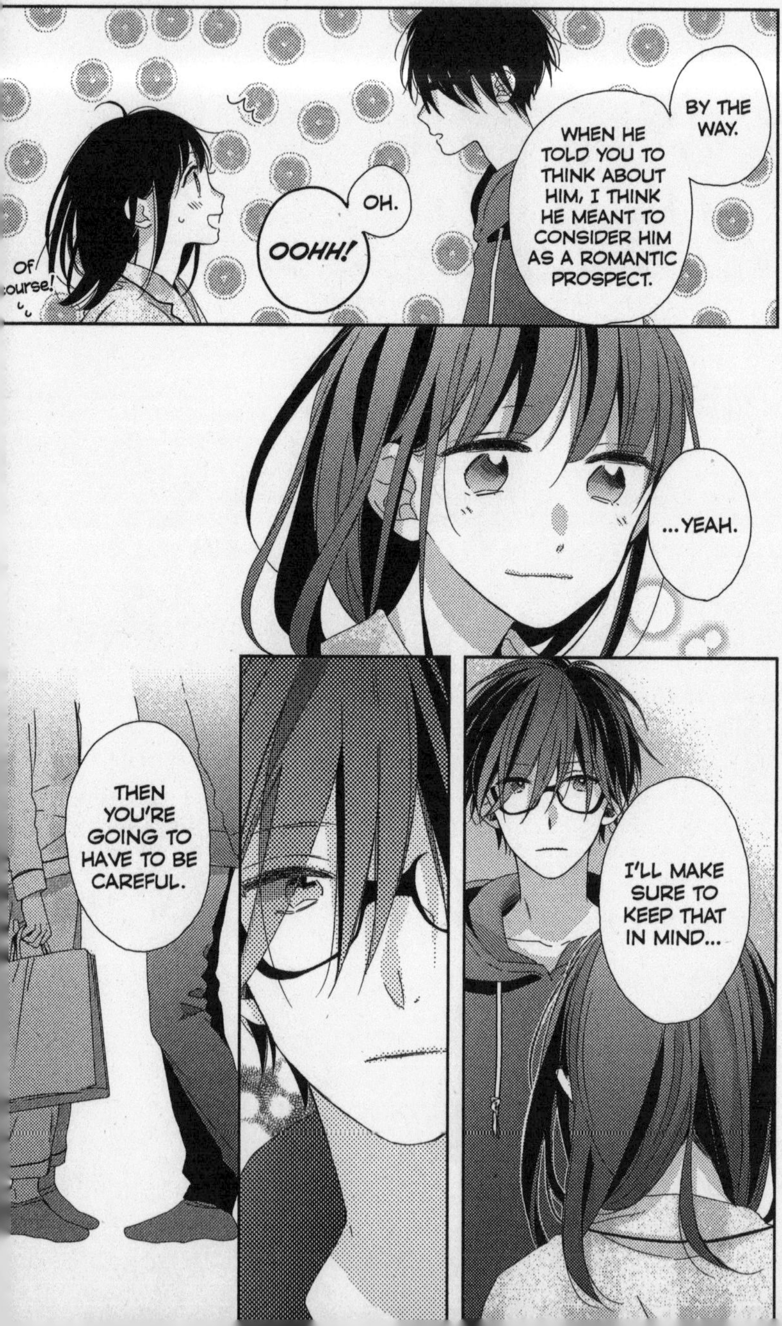

BY THE WAY.
WHEN HE TOLD YOU TO THINK ABOUT HIM, I THINK HE MEANT TO CONSIDER HIM AS A ROMANTIC PROSPECT.
OH.
OOHH!
Of course!
...YEAH.
I'LL MAKE SURE TO KEEP THAT IN MIND...
THEN YOU'RE GOING TO HAVE TO BE CAREFUL.

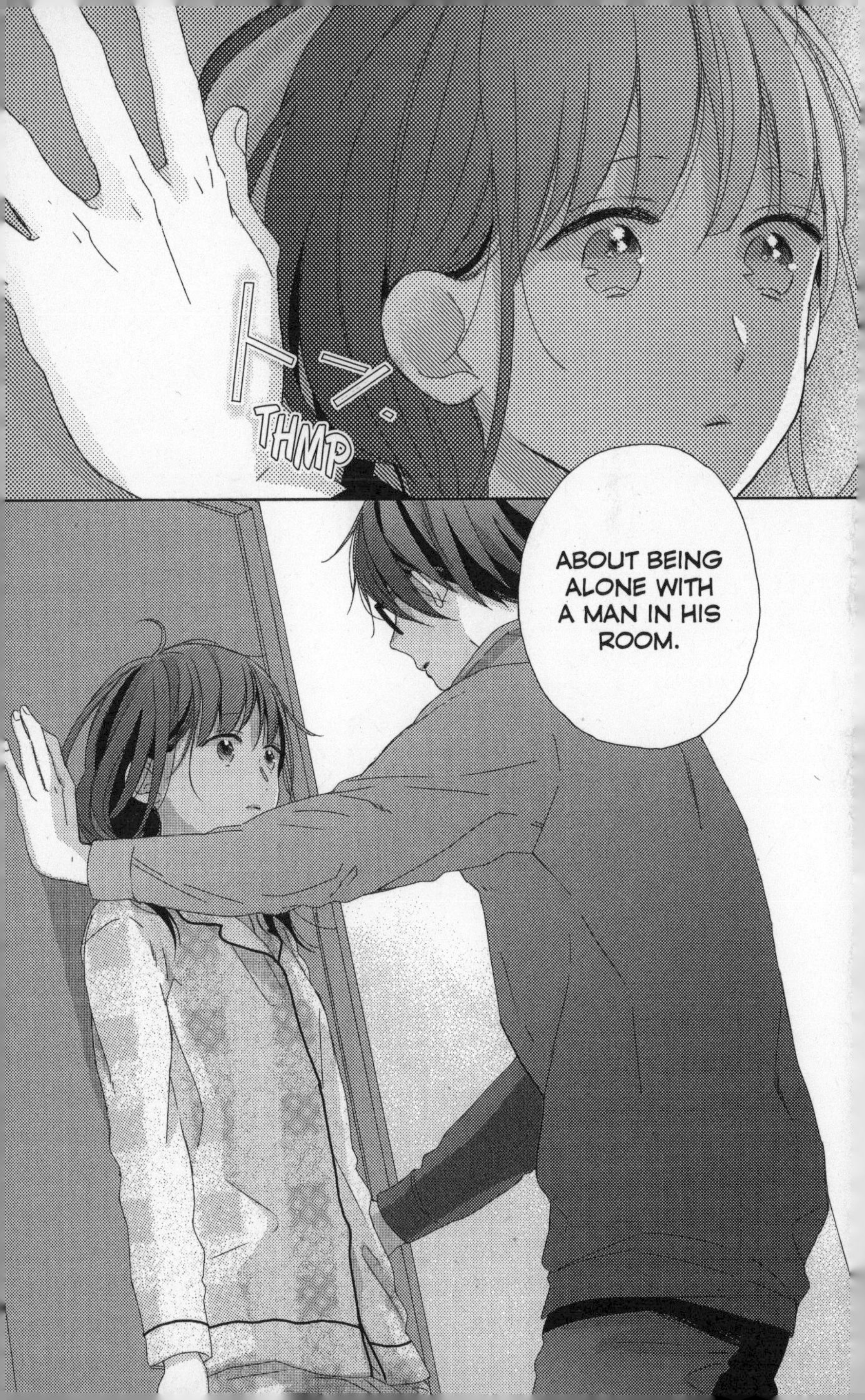
トン
THMP
ABOUT BEING ALONE WITH A MAN IN HIS ROOM.

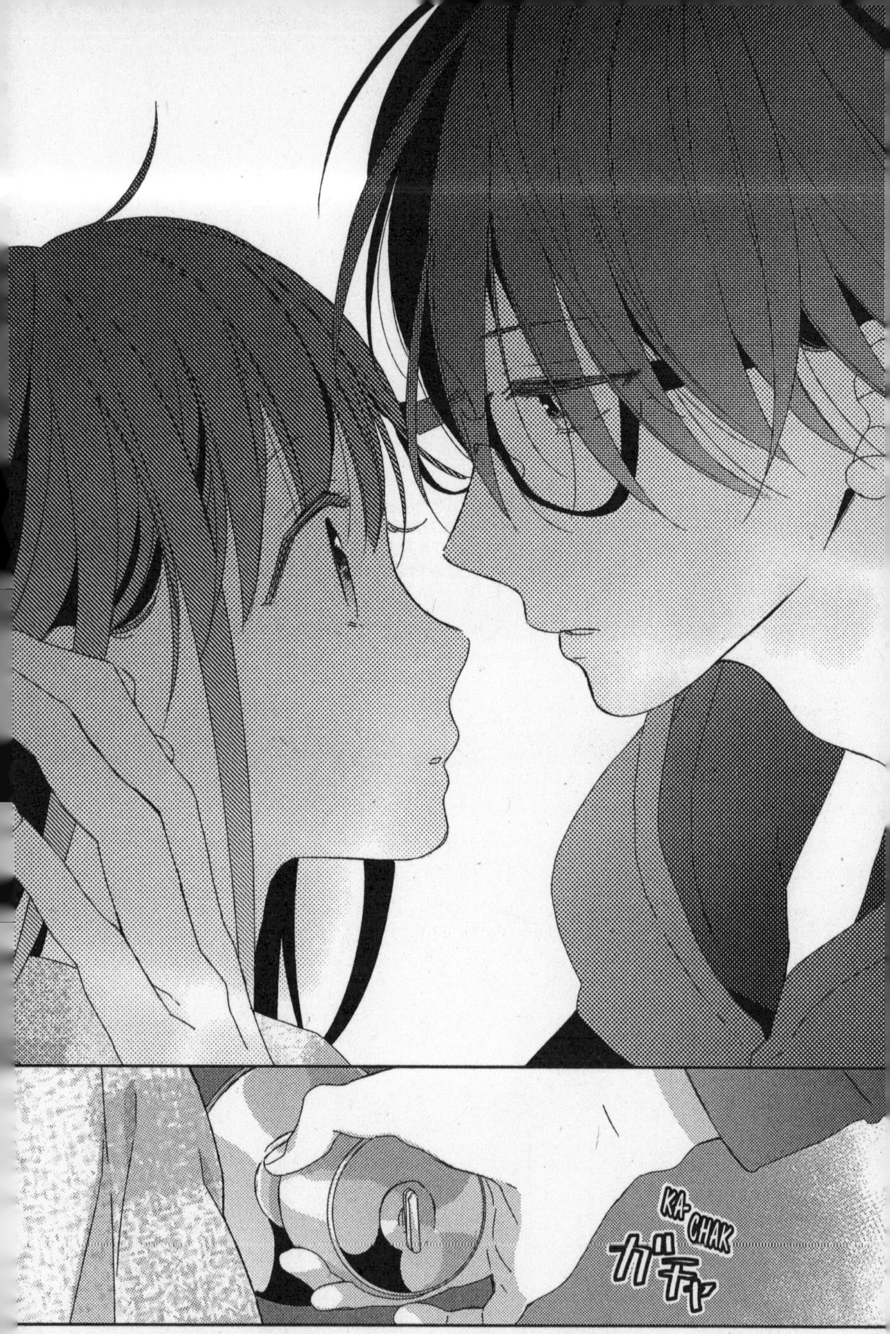
KA-CHAK
ガチャ

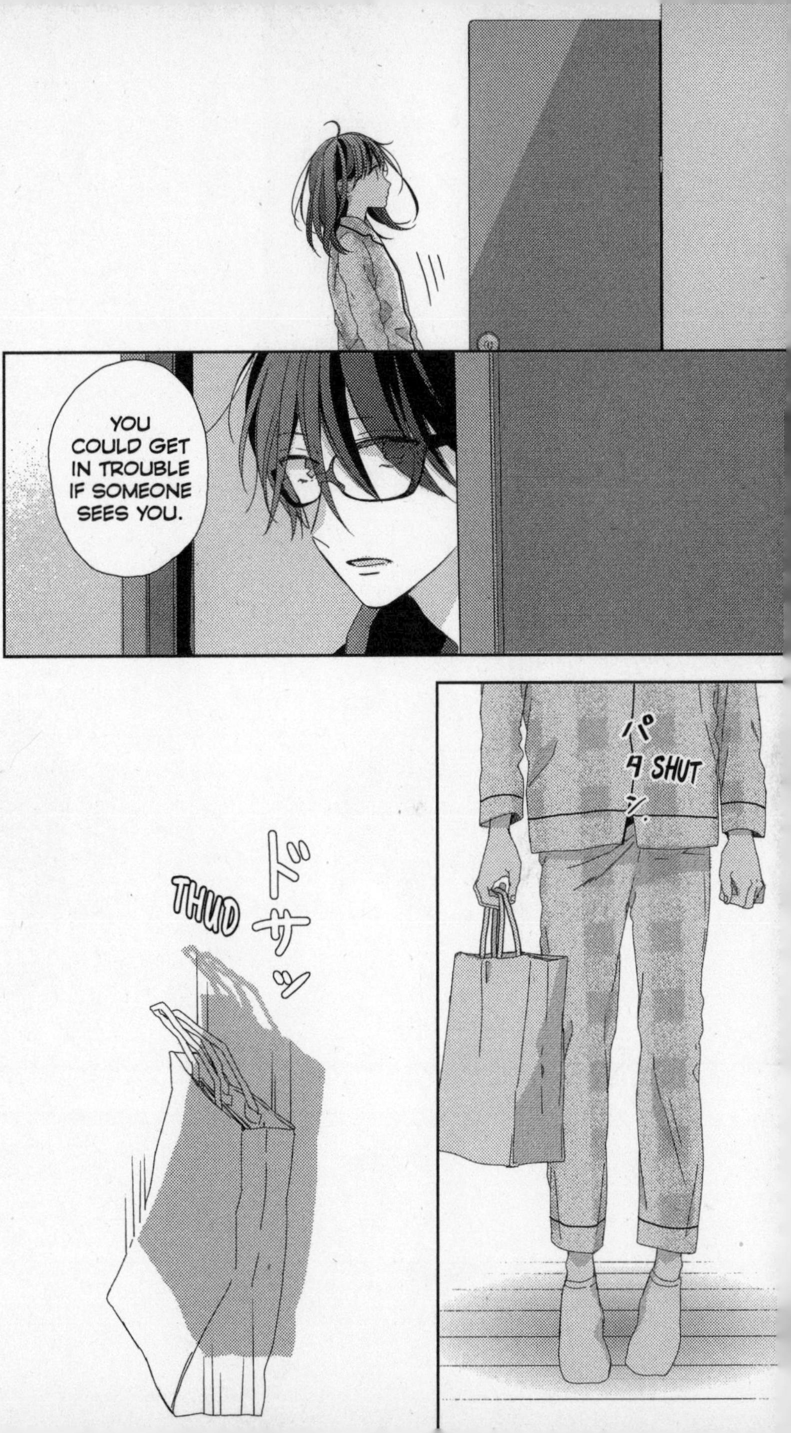
YOU COULD GET IN TROUBLE IF SOMEONE SEES YOU.
パタン
SHUT
ドサッ
THUD

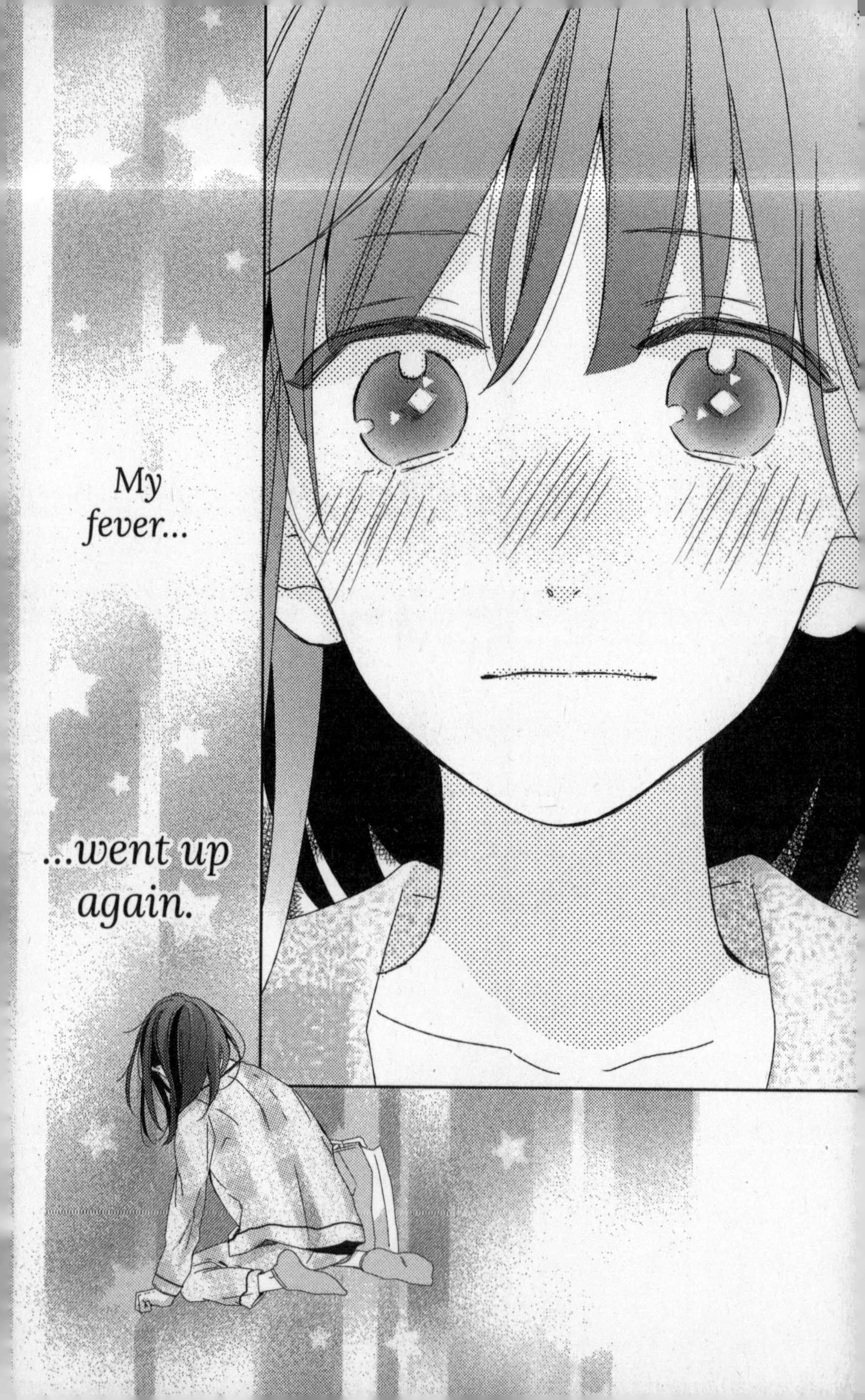

My fever...
...went up again.

to be continued

Chapter 6 Side Story

BONUS SHORT

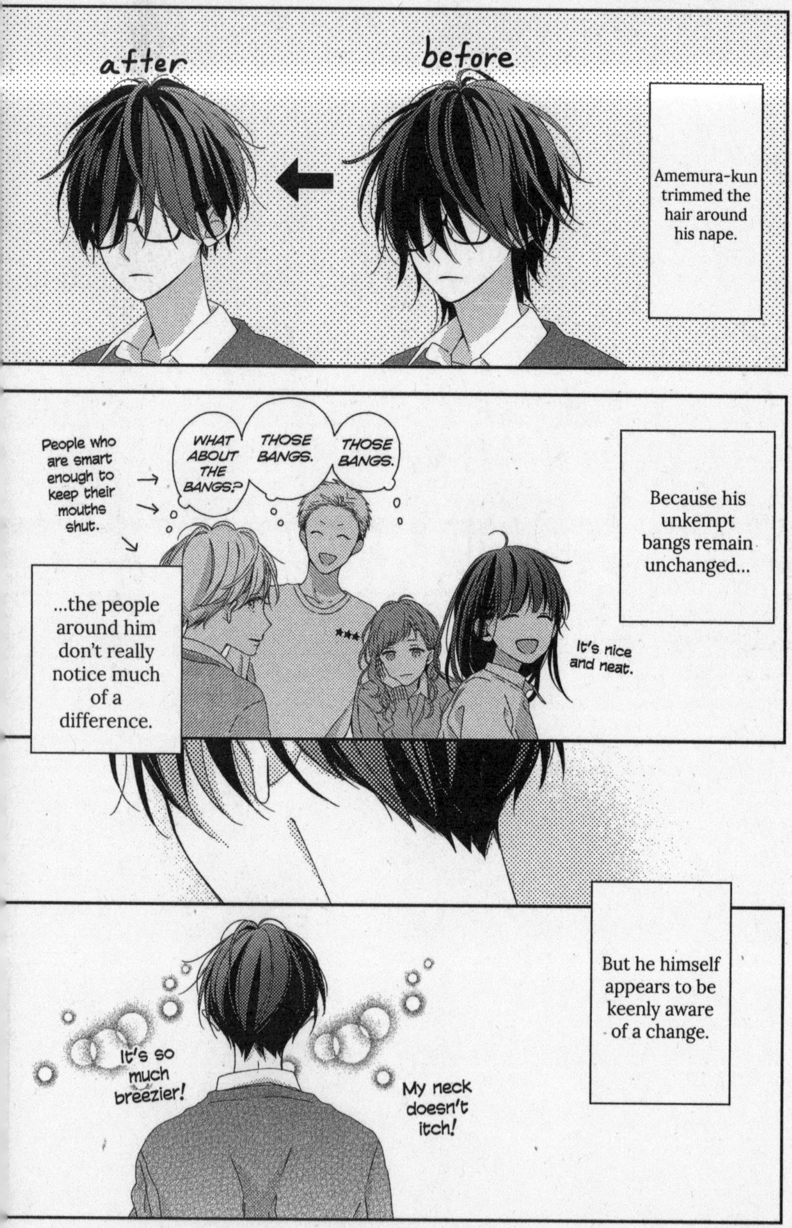
Amemura-kun trimmed the hair around his nape.
before
after
Because his unkempt bangs remain unchanged...
It's nice and neat.
THOSE BANGS.
THOSE BANGS.
WHAT ABOUT THE BANGS?
People who are smart enough to keep their mouths shut.
...the people around him don't really notice much of a difference.
But he himself appears to be keenly aware of a change.
My neck doesn't itch!
It's so much breezier!

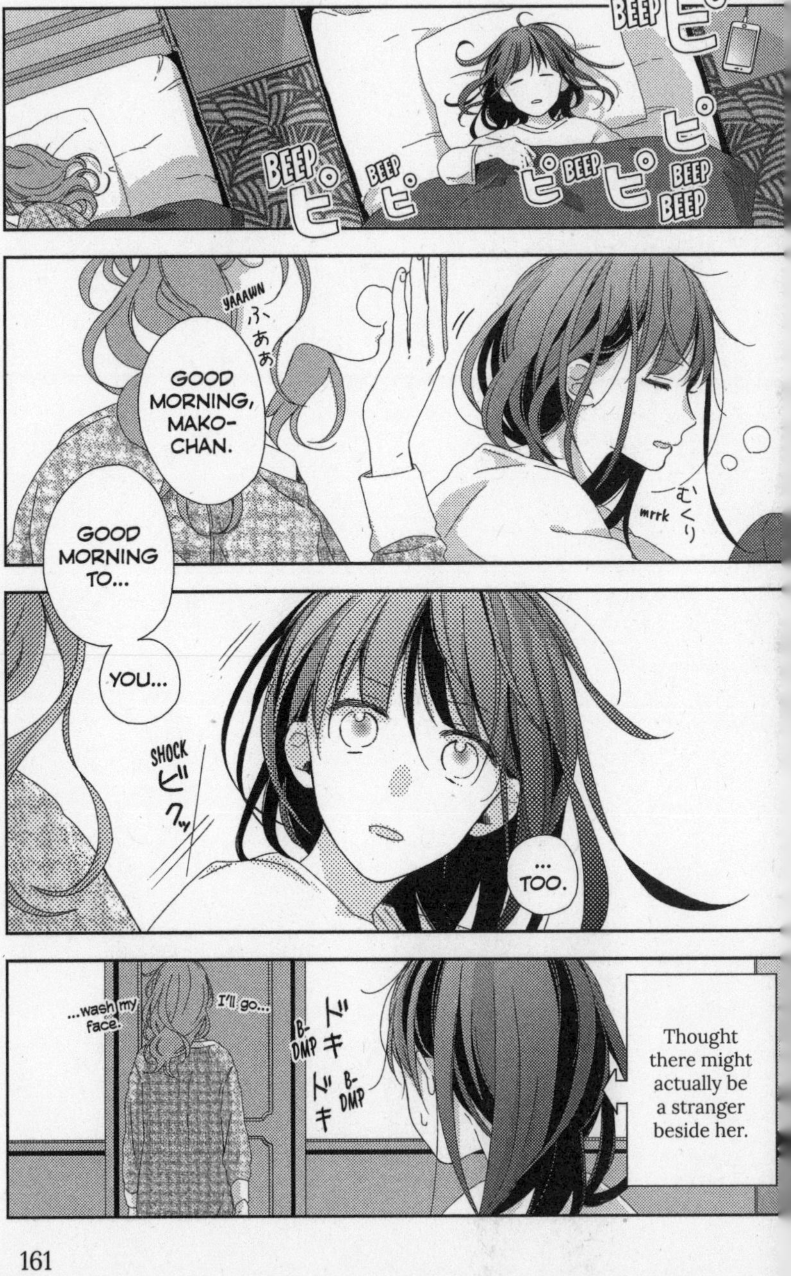
BEEP ピ
BEEP ピ
ピ
BEEP BEEP
ピ BEEP
ピ BEEP
BEEP ピ
BEEP ピ
mrrk むくり
GOOD MORNING, MAKO-CHAN.
YAAAWN ふあぁ
GOOD MORNING TO...
YOU...
... TOO.
SHOCK ビクッ
Thought there might actually be a stranger beside her.
B-DMP ドキ
B-DMP ドキ
I'll go...
...wash my face.

Afterword

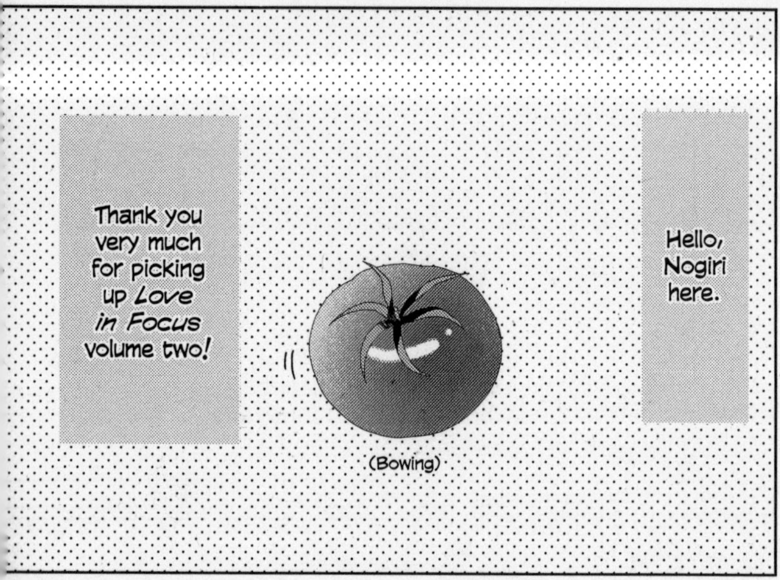
Hello, Nogiri here.
Thank you very much for picking up *Love in Focus* volume two!
(Bowing)

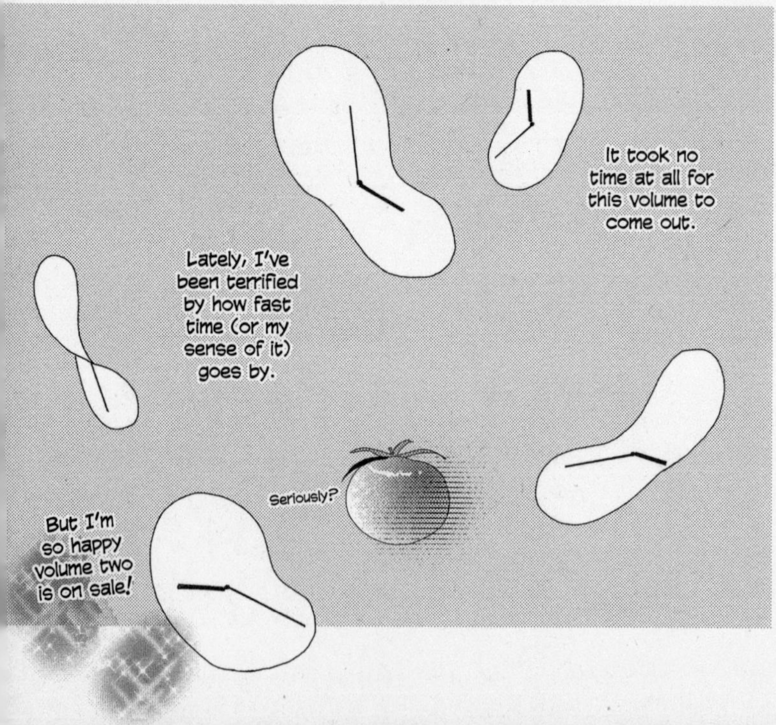
It took no time at all for this volume to come out.
Lately, I've been terrified by how fast time (or my sense of it) goes by.
Seriously?
But I'm so happy volume two is on sale!

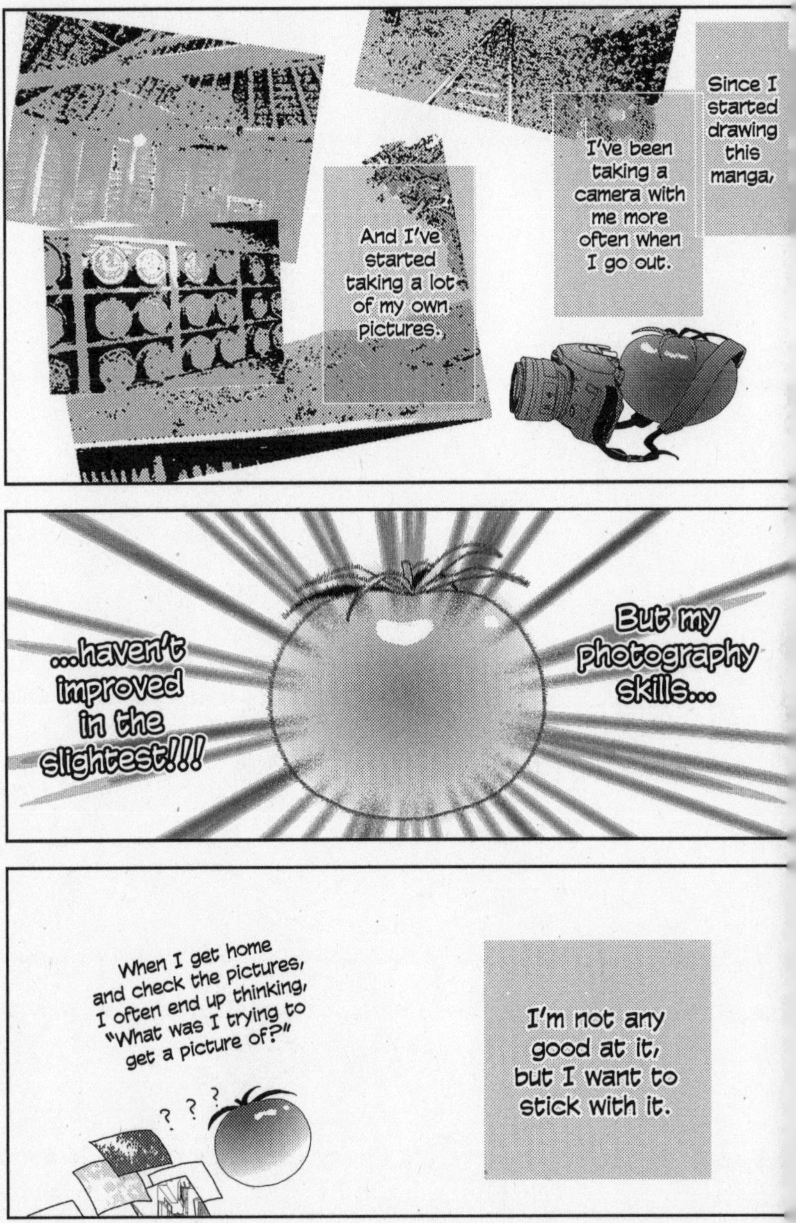
Since I started drawing this manga,
I've been taking a camera with me more often when I go out.
And I've started taking a lot of my own pictures.
But my photography skills...
...haven't improved in the slightest!!!
I'm not any good at it, but I want to stick with it.
When I get home and check the pictures, I often end up thinking, "What was I trying to get a picture of?"
? ? ?

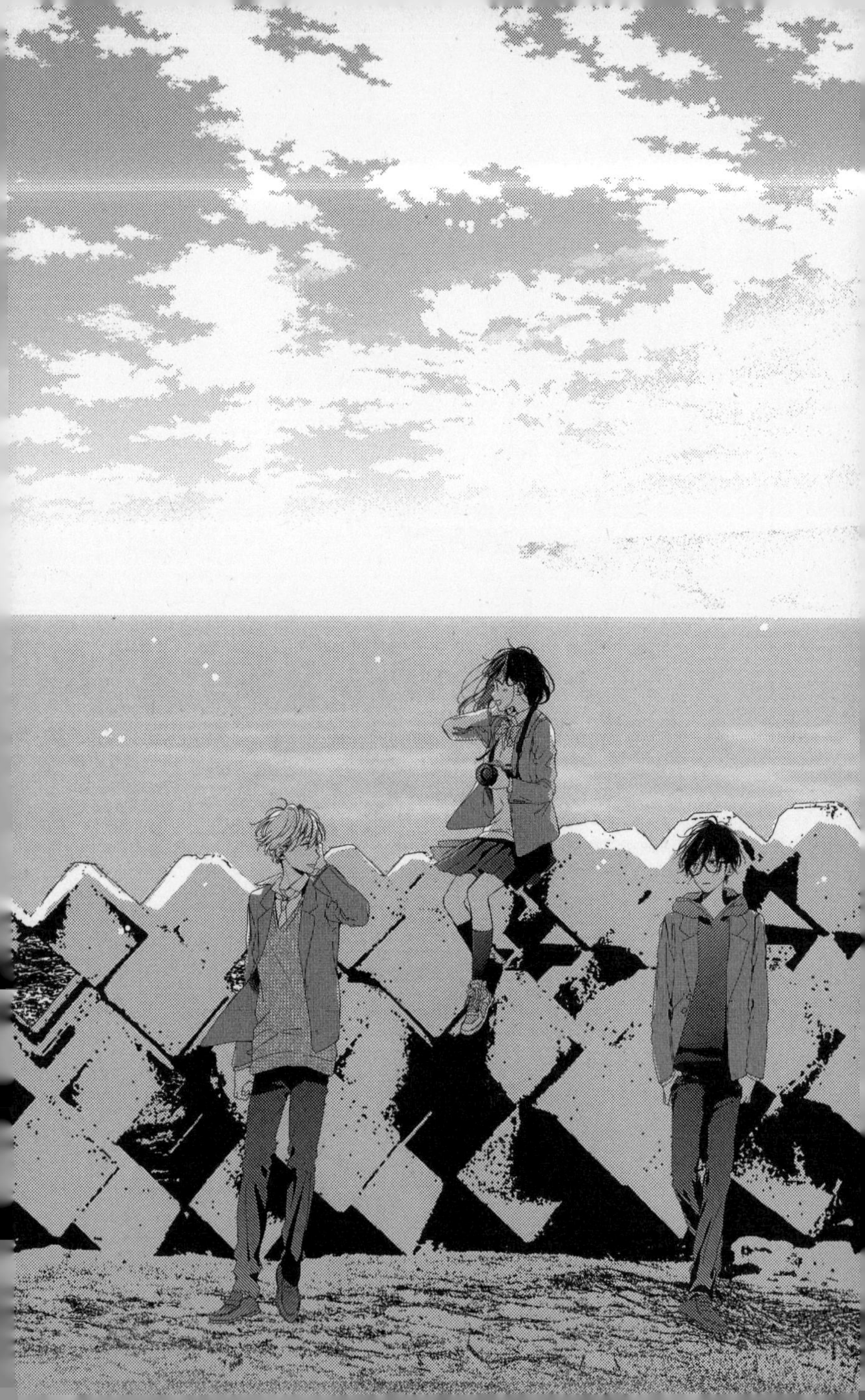

Special Thanks.

Aki Nishihiro-chan.
My friends and family.
My editor-sama.

Everyone in the Aria editorial
department.
Everyone who was involved in
the production of this book.

Everyone who read this book...

...Thank you very much!

See you again in volume three!

I'd love to
hear what
you think!

Attn: Love In Focus
Kodansha Comics
451 Park Ave. South, 7th Floor
New York, NY 10016

✿ Omochi History ✿

Omochi
first came to
the boarding
house...

...when
a tenant
brought him
six years ago.

Young
Omochi

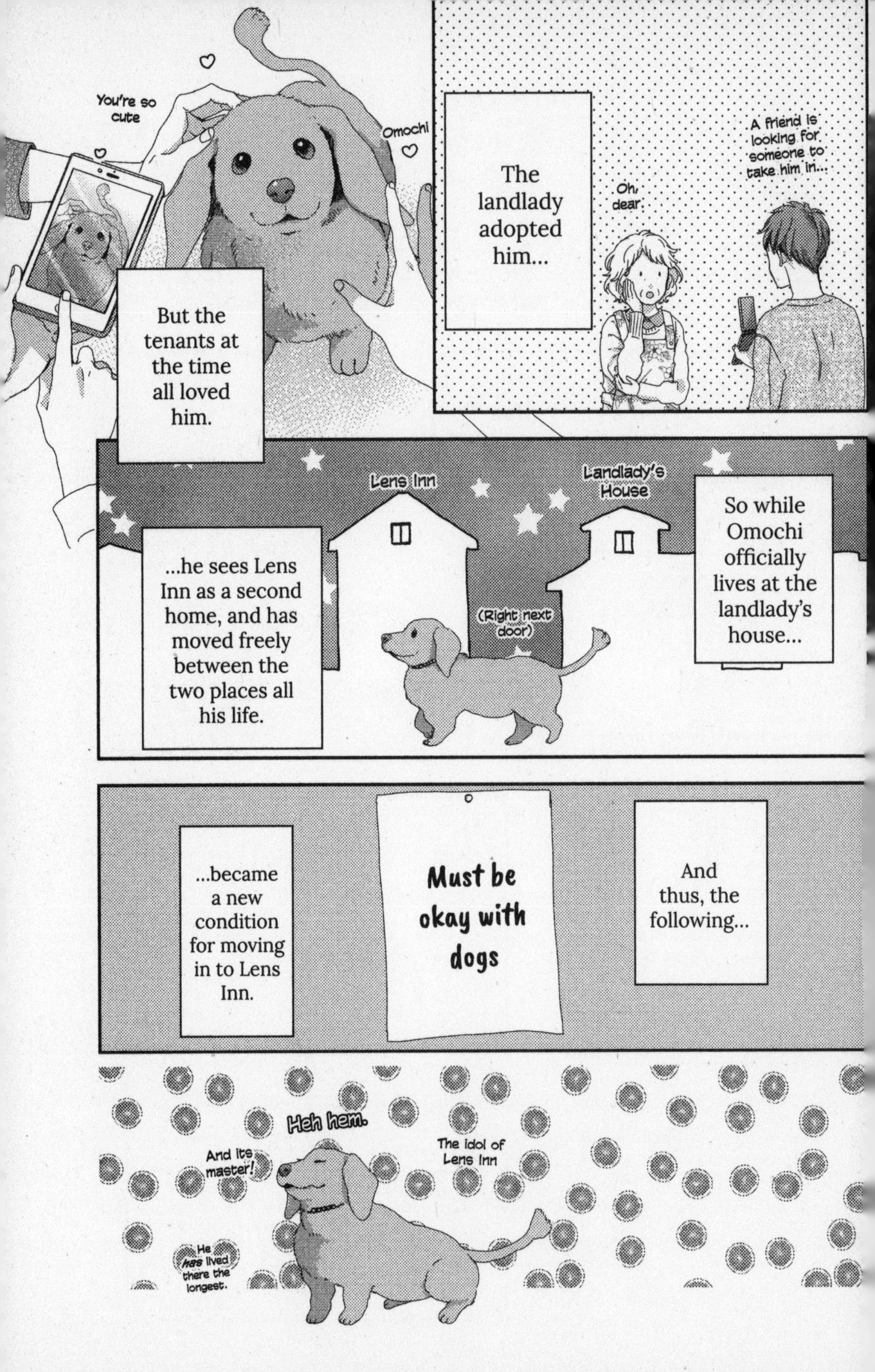
A friend is looking for someone to take him in...
Oh, dear.
The landlady adopted him...
Omochi
You're so cute
But the tenants at the time all loved him.
So while Omochi officially lives at the landlady's house...
Landlady's House
Lens Inn
(Right next door)
...he sees Lens Inn as a second home, and has moved freely between the two places all his life.
And thus, the following...
Must be okay with dogs
...became a new condition for moving in to Lens Inn.
The idol of Lens Inn
Heh hem.
And its master!
He *has* lived there the longest.

TRANSLATION NOTES

Day duty, page 8

In Japanese schools, the students in each class take turns with certain clerical responsibilities, such as keeping the class diary and preparing materials for certain classes. Some of these responsibilities, such as making sure the classroom is presentable, require the students to arrive early.

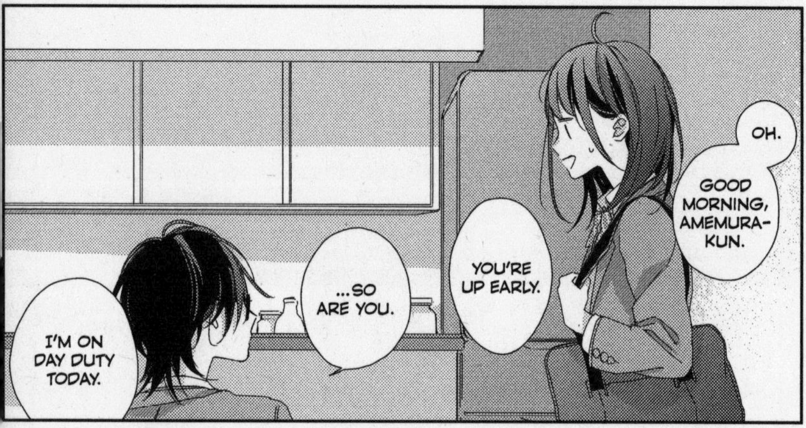
OH.
GOOD MORNING, AMEMURA-KUN.
YOU'RE UP EARLY.
...SO ARE YOU.
I'M ON DAY DUTY TODAY.

Get an A, page 46

While these grades are somewhat similar to standard grading system in the United States, they mean a little bit more in this circumstance. Kei is taking a mock exam to prepare for the entrance exam for M High. The letter grades given represent a rough estimate of his chances of passing the real test. If he gets an A, that will indicate a very high likelihood of getting in.

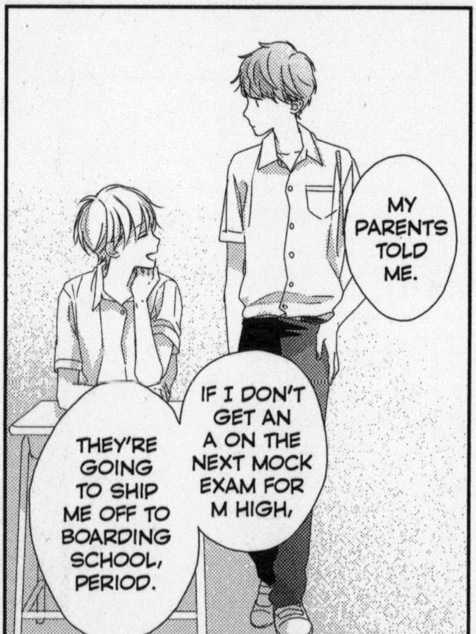
MY PARENTS TOLD ME.
IF I DON'T GET AN A ON THE NEXT MOCK EXAM FOR M HIGH,
THEY'RE GOING TO SHIP ME OFF TO BOARDING SCHOOL, PERIOD.

TRANSLATION NOTES

My extra camera, page 80
More specifically, Kanō-sensei is offering to lend Amemura-kun his "hobby use" camera—in other words, it's the one he uses just for fun, and not to take professional pictures.

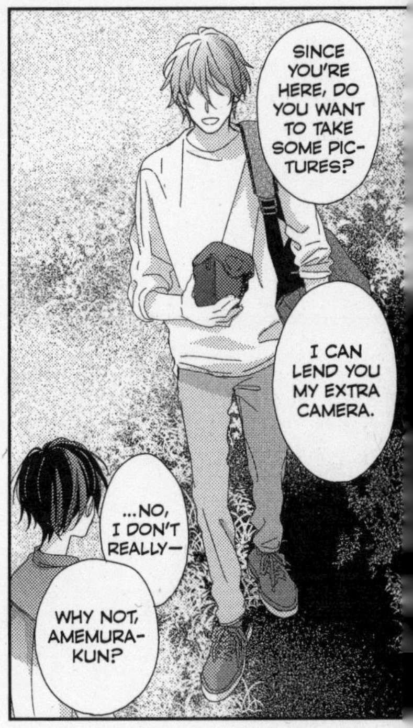
SINCE YOU'RE HERE, DO YOU WANT TO TAKE SOME PIC-TURES?
I CAN LEND YOU MY EXTRA CAMERA.
...NO, I DON'T REALLY—
WHY NOT, AMEMURA-KUN?

Akahoshi, page 86
In Japanese, when speaking to someone, it is often more formal to use that person's name as a second-person pronoun, instead of any of the many words available meaning "you." Here, Amemura-kun has called Kei "you," and Kei corrects him by giving him the name he would like Amemura-kun to use for him. He offers his surname, likely because they're not close enough to be on a first-name basis.

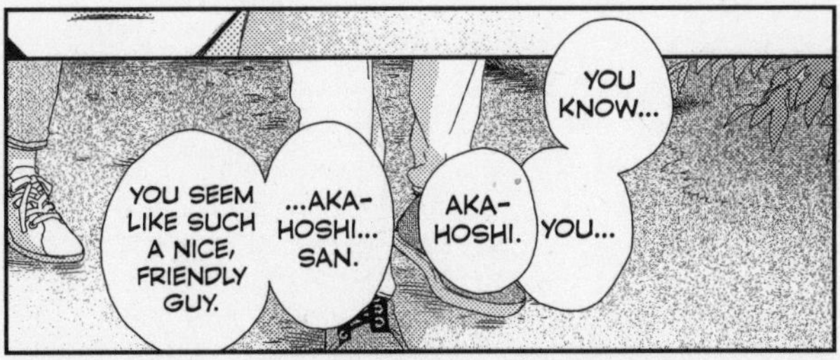
YOU KNOW...
YOU...
AKA-HOSHI.
...AKA-HOSHI... SAN.
YOU SEEM LIKE SUCH A NICE, FRIENDLY GUY.

LOVE IN FOCUS

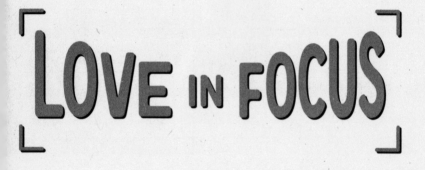

THE MAGICAL GIRL CLASSIC THAT BROUGHT A GENERATION OF READERS TO MANGA, NOW BACK IN A DEFINITIVE, HARDCOVER COLLECTOR'S EDITION!

CARDCAPTOR SAKURA
COLLECTOR'S EDITION
CLAMP

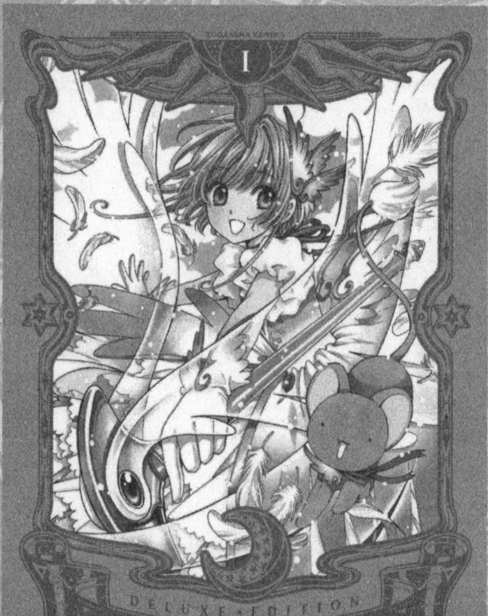
I
DELUXE EDITION
Cardcaptor Sakura
CLAMP

Ten-year-old Sakura Kinomoto lives a pretty normal life with her older brother, Tōya, and widowed father, Fujitaka—until the day she discovers a strange book in her father's library, and her life takes a magical turn...

- A deluxe large-format hardcover edition of CLAMP's shojo manga classic
- All-new foil-stamped cover art on each volume
- Comes with exclusive collectible art card

KC KODANSHA COMICS